VICTORIA OCAMPO

VICTORIA OCAMPO

Against the Wind and the Tide

by

Doris Meyer

With a Selection of Essays
by Victoria Ocampo
Translated by Doris Meyer

GEORGE BRAZILLER
New York

For information address the publisher:
George Braziller, Inc.
One Park Avenue, New York 10016

Library of Congress Cataloging in Publication Data
Meyer, Doris.
Victoria Ocampo
1. Ocampo, Victoria, 1890–   — Biography.
2. Authors, Argentine — 20th century — Biography.
I. Ocampo, Victoria, 1890–
PQ7797.0295Z78   868[B]   78-56302
ISBN: 0–8076–0900–5

Printed in the United States of America
First Printing
Designed by Allan Mogel

ACKNOWLEDGMENTS

Excerpts from the unpublished letters and from the copyrighted works of Victoria Ocampo are used by permission of Victoria Ocampo and Editorial Sur, S. A., the Revista de Occidente press, and Editorial Sudamericana, S. A. The translations of Victoria Ocampo's essays are published with the permission of Victoria Ocampo, Editorial Sur, S. A., and Editorial Sudamericana, S. A.

The excerpt from Act IV of *Phaedra* by Jean Racine, translated by Bernard Grebanier, is reprinted by permission of Barron's Educational Series, Inc. © 1958 by Barron's Educational Series, Inc., Woodbury, New York.

The excerpts from the published letters of Virginia Woolf to Victoria Ocampo are used by permission of Quentin Bell.

The excerpt from Canto XVII from *Paradiso* of *The Divine Comedy* of Dante Alighieri, translated by John D. Sinclair, is reprinted by permission of The Bodley Head. Copyright by The Bodley Head, Ltd.

The excerpts from the unpublished letters of Gabriela Mistral to Victoria Ocampo are used by permission of Doris Dana.

The excerpt from "Ahora canta el Danubio" is from *Las uvas y el viento* by Pablo Neruda. Copyright 1954 by Pablo Neruda, Editorial Nascimiento, Santiago de Chile. English translation by Doris Meyer. Translation Copyright © 1979 by Farrar, Straus & Giroux, Inc. Used by permission of Farrar, Straus & Giroux, Inc.

The excerpts from the unpublished letters of Waldo Frank to Victoria Ocampo are used by permission of Jean K. Frank.

The excerpts from *Tagore, A Biography* by Krishna Kripalani are reprinted with the permission of Krishna Kripalani. © 1962 by Krishna Kripalani.

The excerpt from "Gitanjali" is reprinted from *Collected Poems and Plays* by Rabindranath Tagore. Copyright 1941, 1942 by Rabindranath Tagore. Copyright 1944, 1945, 1946, 1949 by Rabindranath Tagore. Copyright 1913, 1914, 1916, 1917, 1918, 1921, 1937 by The Macmillan Company. Used by permission of Macmillan Publishing Co., Inc.

The photograph of Victoria Ocampo by Man Ray is reproduced with the permission of Juliet Man Ray, la Société Civile Man Ray and the A.D.A.G.P., Paris.

The excerpts from the unpublished letters of Vita Sackville-West to Victoria Ocampo are used with the permission of Nigel Nicolson.

The excerpts from the letters and works of José Ortega y Gasset are used by permission of Soledad Ortega and the Revista de Occidente press.

The excerpts from *Letters*, Vol. 1: 1906–1950, by C. G. Jung, edited by Gerhard Adler and Aniela Jaffe, translated by R.F.C. Hull, Boilingen Series XCV, are reprinted by permission of Princeton University Press. © 1971, 1973 by Princeton University Press.

"Message to Victoria Ocampo in Argentina" from *Tala* by Gabriela Mistral is reprinted by permission of Editorial Sur, S.A. © 1938 by Editorial Sur, S.A. Translation rights were granted by Doris Dana.

The translation of "Virginia Woolf in My Memory" is reprinted with the permission of the editors of *Nimrod*. © 1976 by the University of Tulsa.

The excerpts from "Puravi," "Sesh Lekha," and another prose poem by Rabindranath Tagore and from two letters from Rabindranath Tagore to Victoria Ocampo are reprinted by permission of Visva-Bharati Publishing Department, Calcutta, India.

*For my mother, María,
born in Buenos Aires,
this symbolic recognition*

TABLE OF CONTENTS

VICTORIA
OCAMPO

As this book was about to go to press, I received the sad news from Buenos Aires that Victoria Ocampo died at her home in San Isidro in the early hours of January 27, 1979. Though she did not often talk of death itself, one of her last letters to me closed with the following: "The effect of spring is visible everywhere and the garden is very green and blooming. What a pity we can't renew ourselves in the same way. But there must be a reason why."

D.M.

PREFACE

Thinking back on her struggle for intellectual existence during the first half of this century, Victoria Ocampo has said that it often seemed a futile and exhausting enterprise, like sailing against the wind and the tide — *contra viento y marea*. The winds and tides she confronted were those of the southern latitudes where she was born, the daughter of a wealthy and aristocratic Argentine family whose forebears had settled and governed the region since the days of the Spanish conquistadors.

At the turn of the twentieth century, women of the upper classes in Latin America were, despite appearances to the contrary, an oppressed minority. They lived in large homes with servants, had wardrobes purchased in Europe, and spent all their time on domestic, social, and religious activities. However, the reality of their life, viewed from today's perspective, was far from appealing; they had virtually no freedom, not even in their own homes. Everything they did was subject to a strict code of conduct that required unquestioning submission.

The Catholic Church and proper society had dictated the way in which a woman of aristocratic position should be raised, educated, chaperoned, and married. An endless litany of moral precepts guided her movements from childhood to old age. At every stage of life, she was subject to a paternalistic rule that dominated Hispanic life long before news of the New World first reached King Ferdinand and Queen Isabel. The honor of a *caballero* and his family depended upon the irreproachable virtue and obedience of his wife, mother, or daughter.

It was a rule Victoria Ocampo could not resign herself to accept. Drawn to literature and the arts as a child, she dreamed of a more stimulating, independent, and expressive existence. Risking the censure of those around her, she set out as an adult to find it, defying conventions and provoking scandals. Sailing against the wind and the tide, Victoria accomplished more in the area of culture than any other woman in her country's history — perhaps in the history of Latin America. Even today, however, the mention of her name raises eyebrows in Argentina because Victoria Ocampo, at the age of eighty-eight, is still a rebel.

Author of more than ten volumes of essays and a dozen shorter works, founder and director of a literary review (often called the finest in Latin America) which has endured more than four decades; publisher, translator, lecturer, benefactor of the arts, friend of famous men and women the world over—Victoria Ocampo is all of this and more. She has been compared to other twentieth-century women of letters—Adrienne Monnier, Harriet Munroe, Nancy Cunard, Ottoline Morrell, Vita Sackville-West—who were authors, patronesses, publishers, or a combination thereof. Yet her name is not as well known as theirs outside Latin America.

In her own country, she is a legend. Argentines know her not only as a woman of cultural accomplishment, but as a famous beauty, admired and sought after by men of distinction, a woman who broke many rules and paid for her opposition to dictatorship with imprisonment. Yet even in Argentina, her legend carries an aura of mystery; few people know the real Victoria Ocampo. Precisely because she led such an unorthodox life, apocryphal anecdotes and misconceptions about her have been as abundant as the criticisms she faced.

The struggle that once seemed futile and exhausting has become an inspiration to others, both in the Americas and abroad, who have recognized and honored her in recent years. Not only is she the first woman to be elected to the Argentine Academy of Letters, she is also, among other tributes, an Official of the French Legion of Honor, Commander of the French Order of Arts and Letters, a Commander of the Most Excellent Order of the British Empire, a recipient of the Italian Order of Merit, and an Honorary Doctor of Letters both at the University of Visva-Bharati in India and at Harvard University in the United States. The words that accompanied the degree conferred upon her by Harvard in June 1967 (the tenth woman so honored in the University's history) express the admiration shared by many who know her determination and integrity: "Dauntless lady; bright burning spirit; exemplar and defender of the unfettered mind."

In a long lifetime of devotion to literature and the arts, Victoria Ocampo's name has become synonymous with two objectives: the pursuit of creative excellence and the nurturing of cultural dialogues between nations of all continents. Through her review and publishing house, both of which are named *Sur*, she has led what began as a personal crusade to export the finest examples of Argentine culture and, at the same time, import the highest quality of literary and artistic expression from abroad. Seeking out authors and works that represent the best aspects of contemporary culture, whatever their country or political affiliation, has been both her business and her pleasure.

If there is one quality that characterizes Victoria Ocampo today just as it did in her youth, it is her intellectual generosity, her eagerness to share her enthusiasms with others. Those who have known her personally, as well as those who know her only by the publications that carry her name, can testify to the bountiful nature of the woman whom her friend André Malraux once called "la superbe Argentine."[1]

I am one of those who has been enriched by knowing Victoria Ocampo. In the autumn of her years and the spring of mine, she responded generously to the request of a college student who wanted to write an honors thesis about her. A fellowship from a Harvard–Radcliffe program for research abroad made possible a trip to Argentina, where I spent the summer of 1962 gathering information for my project. Victoria was in Europe during those months, but her sister Angélica, her colleagues at *Sur*, and her friends—among them the authors Eduardo Mallea and Jorge Luis Borges—welcomed me warmly and provided me with the information I sought. Fortunately, Victoria stopped in New York on her way home that fall, so my work culminated with our meeting there. Having heard and read so much about her, I felt rather apprehensive as I knocked on her door at the Waldorf Astoria. Then the door swept open and a tall, extremely handsome, silver-haired woman with a flower pinned on her jacket greeted me with a smile and queries about my stay in Buenos Aires, lamenting that she had not been there herself to show me around. We spoke for several hours, mostly in English (hers flawless and British-accented). I remember thinking then, and the next time that we met during her stay in New York, that Victoria Ocampo was, without question, the most vitally expressive person I had ever met.

Thirteen years later, in 1975, I knocked again on another door at the Waldorf and there was Victoria, still handsome, still energetic at eighty-five, and pleased to learn that I was now teaching Spanish at the same college where her close friend, Valborg Anderson, was a professor of English. (It was Val who told me that Victoria was in town and planned to stay for several months.) Victoria knew that I had come with another project in mind: what would she think about my writing a book that would introduce her to the English-speaking public, to readers in North America who knew little if anything about her and her accomplishments? I particularly wanted to tell the story of her experiences as a Latin American woman who refused to follow the conventions of her society and who became a feminist when the notion of equal rights for women was considered not just scandalous but immoral in her country. I also wanted to include a selection of her essays in translation, virtually inaccessible to non-Spanish readers. Would she be willing to cooperate with me, I wondered, giving me permission to consult private documents and sharing her personal recollections? I was well aware, as I broached the subject, that Victoria was notoriously reluctant to discuss certain aspects of her private life.

The idea appealed to her. Not only was she interested in my project but she was enormously anxious to learn more about the women's movement in the United States (coincidentally that day had been proclaimed Equal Rights Amendment Day: November 4, 1975). She asked me as many questions as I asked her. Tired from a recent bout with the flu, she leaned back against some bed pillows. In her customary tailored slacks, simple blouse, cardigan sweater, and silk scarf, she looked elegantly casual, surprisingly at home in a nondescript hotel room filled with books and magazines. But her frame of mind was anything but complacent. Why were so many women in the States opposed to the Equal Rights Amendment, she wanted to know, incredulous that such "sabotage," as she called it, could exist in such an advanced country. What were women's studies programs like in North American universities? What were the latest books by women writers in the U.S.? What progress had been made by women in government? And what did I think of Susan Brownmiller's book on rape? Many times, our exchange of ideas involved comparisons between her country and mine.

Thereafter, we met several times a week. Over tea and cinnamon toast in Oscar's, the hotel coffee shop, on our way to and from the movies on Third Avenue (did I realize how much Pasqualino in Wertmuller's *Settebelleze* was like an Argentine *compadrito*), with friends or alone, we continued our discussions. In deference to Victoria's dislike for the formality of tape recorders, I took to jotting down notes for the book after we parted each day. Before she left for Argentina in February 1976, three weeks prior to the military coup that brought Isabel Perón's regime to an end, we agreed that I would spend four weeks in Buenos Aires in July and August. Victoria offered me her home and I gratefully accepted. Would I mind the lack of central heating during a chilly Argentine winter, she asked? I assured her that I would not.

Not only did I spend that fascinating month with her, but I also returned in January 1977 to visit her for three weeks at her summer home in the seaside resort of Mar del Plata. Later, during a sabbatical leave, I went twice, in January and August of 1978, to spend five more weeks with her. I am more than qualified to testify to Victoria Ocampo's legendary generosity and hospitality. No words of thanks, however, could adequately express what her friendship has meant to me—far beyond the scope of writing this book.

Her two lovely homes were the principal settings in which I did most of my research. (Both homes were deeded to UNESCO in 1973 with the stipulation that they be used as international centers for literary and cultural activities. In November 1977 the first UNESCO-organized activity was held in her home near Buenos Aires, a "Dialogue of Cultures" over which she presided as honorary president.) Immersed in the ambience and presence of Victoria Ocampo, I devoted several hours each morning and evening to reading her unpublished memoirs and collections of personal letters, her books and articles, and parts of her vast library which fills several rooms and spills over into corridors and hallways. Over meals and tea at five, she and I would discuss whatever I was reading at the time. Naturally, our conversations followed other tangents as well, especially when we were joined by friends or members of her family. I would also spend occasional afternoons researching at the *Sur* offices, or perhaps interviewing people who had known or worked with Victoria. Over the course of my visits, I met many delightful and generous people in Argentina. I truly came to feel that the country my mother had left as a child had welcomed me back in her place.

This book, then, reflects my personal knowledge of Victoria Ocampo. Future biographers may describe her more dispassionately or they may emphasize aspects of her life that I only touch upon. If the reader does not find herein as much depiction of her love life as of the loves of her life, it is because I have purposely focused my attention on the latter in my interpretation of her accomplishments. Hopefully, Victoria's memoirs will be published one day soon, for there the reader will find her intimate stories told with matchless grace and humor. (Albert Camus, who read portions of her memoirs as she was writing them in the 1950s, urged her to publish them and added that, in his opinion, she would have made an admirable novelist.[2])

The following pages are meant to be an introduction to the life and work of an extraordinary woman of our time, not a complete biography. Nor, for that matter, is it "official" in any sense. I have pointed out Victoria's weaknesses as well as her strengths, insofar as I understand them; she never suggested that I do otherwise. For discretion's sake, however, I did agree not to mention one or two names or quote from certain highly personal documents.

At my request, Victoria has read the manuscript in two of its preparatory stages. She has also read the translations that accompany the text and has generously authorized the use of photographs and of quotations from her works as well as from other works published by *Sur*. Her observations and corrections (dates, names, places, and some slight modifications in the phraseology of the essays) have undoubtedly improved my work; but the final result and any flaws it may contain are my responsibility alone. With the hope that it will be of interest to students and specialists as well as to general readers, I have appended chapter notes and a selected bibliography.

The fifteen essays which I have translated were chosen 1) for their representative qualities, 2) in order to illustrate incidents and themes discussed in the preceding text, and 3) because they appealed to the translator. They have been arranged in chronological order by subject— by the date of their impact on Victoria's life—not by the date of composition, indicated at the beginning of each essay. All foreign words and phrases have been left as in the original essays and are explained in notes following the translations. The essays are offered to the reader as an integral and essential part of Victoria Ocampo's self-expression. To omit them would be to deny the non-Spanish speaker a part of her which only she can convey and without which no introduction to her life would be complete.

To all those who helped me in ways large and small in the preparation of this book, I am very grateful.

I would first like to acknowledge the support of three foundations which enabled me to go to Argentina four times in the past two years and also made possible a year's leave from teaching during which time this book was written. My thanks thus go to the Research Foundation of the City University of New York for two consecutive grants, to the Penrose Fund of the American Philosophical Society for another grant, and to the National Endowment for the Humanities for a Fellowship for Independent Study and Research.

Many generous people on several continents provided me with indispensable information and advice. Some knew Victoria Ocampo well and others did not, but all gladly offered me the benefit of their knowledge and experience and thus immeasurably enhanced my work. In Argentina, I would like to express my special appreciation to Victoria's surviving sisters, Angélica and Silvina, who received me so warmly and reminisced on occasion about life with their older sibling. I also feel honored to have known two exceptional women, María Rosa Oliver and Fryda Schultz de Mantovani, who passed away while this book was being written; their kindness to me and their generous contributions to my efforts to portray their friend and colleague at *Sur* were more appreciated than they ever realized. Whenever I went to the offices of *Sur*, three hospitable and capable women, Yvonne Castresana, Lily Iriarte and Nélida Mariperisena de González, helped me find whatever I needed; to them and to others associated with *Sur* and with Victoria's households (especially José Luis Alvarez, Haydée Sirito, and Clara Aunchayna) I am very grateful. My thanks also go to two esteemed friends, Enrique

Pezzoni and María Renée Cura, who read portions of the manuscript in preparation and offered observations and encouragement, and I should also like to thank José Bianco, Alicia Moreau de Justo, Susana Larguía, Cristina de Aparicio, Marieta de González Garaño, and Syria Poletti for being kind enough to share their thoughts and memories with me.

For permission to quote from published and unpublished writings of her father, José Ortega y Gasset, I am indebted to Soledad Ortega. My thanks also to Quentin Bell for allowing me to quote from the unpublished letters of Virginia Woolf to Victoria Ocampo; likewise to Nigel Nicolson for the letters of Vita Sackville-West; to Doris Dana for letters, photos and documents pertaining to Gabriela Mistral; to Jean Frank for letters of her husband, Waldo Frank; to Victoria Kent and Louise Crane for material relating to Victoria's imprisonment, and to Gisèle Freund for supplying photos of Victoria and of Virginia Woolf.

Several colleagues at Brooklyn College gave me advice on specialized topics: Hobart Spalding, Jr., Thomas Mermall, Gerald Storzer, and Ernest Leo. I am indebted to them and to Lola Szladits, the Curator of the Berg Collection at the New York Public Library, where I read parts of the diary of Virginia Woolf, as well as to Neda Westlake, Curator of the Rare Books Collection at the University of Pennsylvania, where the letters of Victoria to Waldo Frank were made available to me.

This book might never have come into being had Juan Marichal and Raimundo Lida, two distinguished professors at Harvard, not told me about Victoria Ocampo many years ago, and had they and another eminent author and educator, Francisco Ayala, a former colleague at Brooklyn College, not encouraged and supported my plans to write it. I wish to thank them and the following friends in New York who know Victoria well and who have helped me in so many ways: María Luisa Bastos, who was very kind to me in 1962 when I first stopped in at *Sur* and who has continued to be equally generous here in New York; Ronald Christ, who graciously read an early draft of the manuscript and gave me the benefit of his knowledge and support; Mildred Adams, with whom I had so many pleasant conversations and who read the translations at my request; and Valborg Anderson, who has been unstinting in her encouragement, devoted in her critical reading of portions of the work in progress, and always eager to talk with me about our beloved mutual friend.

To my editor, Elizabeth Hock, I am grateful for many astute observations.

Finally, to Richard Hertz, whose concern, understanding, and marvelous sense of humor sustained me throughout, a very special thank you.

New York City
September 1978

PART I

CHAPTER ONE

EMBARKING ON A SWEET SEA

Twenty kilometers upstream from the port city of Buenos Aires the broad, flat banks of the River Plate rise sharply into small bluffs carved centuries ago by the flowing waters. These are the *barrancas* of the suburb of San Isidro, where Spanish colonial and modern villas stand side by side commanding a panoramic view of the lowlands and the river beyond. Luxuriant hillside trees and gardens planted by generations of well-to-do *porteños* seeking a refuge from the congested streets of the capital overlook sparsely cultivated riverbanks. Seen from the barrancas, the river seems as wide as the ocean. Porteños call it "the sweet sea." Even on a clear day, the coast of Uruguay lies over the horizon, beyond the line visible to the naked eye. Ships and barges heading upstream on the river's tranquil waters look like toys in the distance.

On the edge of the barrancas of San Isidro, looking out over a sleek, new sailing club and a rapidly expanding residential community, stands the graceful sentinel of another age, a French Victorian mansion surrounded by giant palms, eucalyptus, and araucaria pines. Its three stories crowned by a mansard roof and decorative grillwork make it more imposing and more noticeable than other houses on the bluffs. Appropriately so, for this is Villa Ocampo, the home of Argentina's unique lady of letters, Victoria Ocampo. Like her, it is the product of two worlds, America and Europe.

For all its Old World exterior, Villa Ocampo has an unmistakable New World feel to it. Perhaps it comes from the touch of indigenous colonial architecture on the main facade, where the date of the building's

3

completion, 1891, is carved with ornate flourishes. Or perhaps it's the profusion of native trees (*ombú, palo borracho, tipa, gomero*) and flowering shrubs (*jasmín, Santa Rita, hibisco, laurel rosado*) that surrounds the house and shades its green lawns. Maybe it is a feeling created by the understated elegance of its interior, where quantities of books and photographs of friends who wrote them are more valued than art objects or antiques. Certainly it is a house to be lived in, with its comfortable sitting rooms conducive to hours of relaxed conversation, wide terraces for sunning and strolling, and large, high-ceilinged rooms through which the morning and afternoon breezes carry the calls of doves, *benteveos*, and green parrots. In winter, *quebracho* wood burns in the fireplaces of most of the twenty-odd rooms. In summer, the louvered shutters, upstairs and down, are closed at midday as the temperature outside rises to 29 or 30 degrees C. Whatever the season, Villa Ocampo is an oasis of peace and natural beauty in an increasingly populated and commercialized suburban environment.

Standing on the terrace surveying the broad expanse of the River Plate in the distance, Victoria Ocampo admits to an ongoing love affair: "Just look how the color changes in the late afternoon light," she points out, a tone of wonderment in her voice that more than eighty years of familiarity with the river's moods hasn't dispelled. From the terrace that runs the width of the house, from her corner bedroom, her library, or from downstairs in the dining room at the enormous, oval table, the river is always within view, a faithful companion, ever the same, ever changing.

Like many great rivers of the world, the River Plate has been a symbol of growth and progress, a lifeline for those in Argentina who have depended upon it for trade and transport. Some prefer to think of it as a passageway to freedom, a means of escaping from the remoteness of the southern latitudes. Others, unimpressed by its muddy waters and its monotonous tranquility, ignore it altogether. They forget that the profile of Argentine history is mirrored in the river: the founding of Buenos Aires in 1536 by don Pedro de Mendoza, soldier of the Spanish Empire; its abandonment and later resettlement in 1580; the British invasions of 1806–1807; the deposing of the colonial viceroy in 1810 followed by the proclamation of independence from Spain in 1816; the Unitarian-Federalist controversy in the nineteenth century; and the economic expansion and political turmoil of the twentieth.

For Victoria, the river has been a reminder of both her Argentine heritage and her European cultural ties. One of her distant ancestors sailed up the wide waters of the Plate seeking wealth and adventure with don Pedro de Mendoza. Almost four hundred years later, Victoria set out on another kind of journey from the New World to the Old—and to the

North as well—in search of other kinds of wealth and adventure. Unlike her ancestor, however, she returned from her journeys laden with treasure, a treasure she knew would never diminish by being shared with her countrymen.

The Ocampos and the Aguirres

The history of Victoria's family is closely tied to the story of Argentina's development from a colony of the Spanish Empire to an independent, modern nation. Ancestors on both her father's and her mother's sides belonged to the small number of influential families of what has been called the Argentine aristocracy or oligarchy. This class of landowners, whose holdings included vast regions of the pampas and the Andean foothills from Patagonia to El Chaco, ruled Argentina with its power and wealth from the sixteenth to the early twentieth century. It is no exaggeration to say that some of the most famous names in Argentine history were familiar to Victoria long before she was able to read about them in history books. They were names her parents and relatives would mention with admiration—and sometimes with disdain—each time family anecdotes were told.

On the Ocampo side, her great-great-great grandfather, Sebastián José de Ocampo, who was of Basque descent, had been one of the colonial governors of Cuzco before he moved southeast across the Andes to the Viceroyalty of the River Plate when it was established as a separate entity in the late eighteenth century.[1] His son, Manuel José de Ocampo, was the chief magistrate of Buenos Aires in 1810 when the city fathers wrested control of the government from the viceroy, declaring themselves loyal to the Spanish king who had been imprisoned by Napoleon. The name of Manuel José de Ocampo is recorded among those who first governed the new nation when independence was finally declared.

Following the family tradition of public service, Victoria's great-grandfather, Manuel José de Ocampo y González, was a prominent politician who ran unsuccessfully for the presidency of the republic in 1886. His close friends included a former president, Domingo Faustino Sarmiento, whom he also advised in financial matters, and Vicente Fidel López, a noted historian. Patriotism was taken very seriously in the old colonial house on Florida and Viamonte streets where Victoria used to play as a small child. "Tata Ocampo," as his great-grandchildren called him, and his wife, Clara Lozano de Ocampo, had a typically large family for the time: three sons and six daughters. Four of the daughters never married and continued to live in the family home, which was demolished after their father's death in 1895 to make way for a modern mansion in the *fin de siècle* European style.

Victoria's grandfather, Manuel Anselmo Ocampo, was an *estanciero*, a cattle baron. A photograph taken of him at his estancia in Pergamino with five-year-old Victoria leaning shyly against his knee reveals a patriarchal figure in the standard garb of a seasoned rancher. It is said that he was a man of impressive stature who possessed a volcanic temperament to match his size. Victoria recalls feeling awed as a child by his abundant white beard and his stern disposition, yet she cherishes happy memories of yearly vacations spent at "Papa Manuel's" estancia. There she was free to play in the fields of alfalfa, watch the *gauchos* who rode in to see the *patrón*, and witness the ritual shearing of the sheep. She and her sisters had their own small cart pulled by rams for exploring the less distant parts of the estancia, which extended for hundreds of kilometers in every direction. Contrary to most of the Ocampos, who were partial to refined European fashion and taste, Papa Manuel was a man of the rough outdoors who observed very *criollo*, or native Argentine customs such as sipping *mate* tea from a gourd through a long silver *bombilla*. He was known for his colorful vocabulary, not always fit for young ears, and for his tendency to be imperious and exacting. He also had a melancholy streak which was why, he once said, he planted *casuarinas*, or weeping pines, along the road leading into the estancia. To Victoria, he must have been a rather romantic character whose life, by very contrast with her own, was immensely appealing. He and his wife, Angélica Gabriela Ocampo Regueira, were first cousins, not an unusual occurrence in upper class Argentine society.

On Victoria's mother's side her ancestors were even more illustrious. One of the most famous was Domingo de Irala, companion of Pedro de Mendoza and conquistador of Asunción. Irala eventually became governor and captain-general of the Spanish colonies of the River Plate after Mendoza's death, and, according to the English historian Cunninghame Graham, he governed "wisely and well."[2]

Another ancestor, of Swiss Calvinist and Irish stock, the brother of Victoria's great-great-grandmother, was General Juan Martín de Pueyrredón, the Supreme Commander of the Argentine independence movement and friend of the renowned General José de San Martín, Argentina's foremost hero and the liberator of Chile and Peru. Still another ancestor, a distant third cousin of Victoria's great-great-grandfather, was Argentina's first dictator-*caudillo*, Juan Manuel de Rosas, whose tyranny lasted more than two decades until he was overthrown in 1852. The right to claim both the liberator and dictator, hero and antihero of the last century, as her ancestors is an ironic coincidence of history and biology that Victoria appreciates. She never fails to point out, however, that the honor of being related to Pueyrredón cannot entirely erase the blemish of Rosas's legacy.

In one sense, the coincidence merely confirms the interrelationship of most of the powerful families in Argentina's history; in another, it is a vivid reminder of the moral dichotomy inherent in all men.

In the early 1800s, General Pueyrredón used to meet and discuss military strategy with his friend General San Martín at his farm on the banks of the River Plate, not far from where Victoria's Villa Ocampo stands today. The farm, or *chacra,* is now a national monument and a classic example of early Spanish colonial architecture, comparable in historical importance to George Washington's Mount Vernon on the banks of the Potomac. For many years after the death of General Pueyrredón and his family, the single-story, white villa with its columned arcades stood neglected by all but a few devotees of Argentine history. In the late 1950s, Victoria and a friend had the idea that it would be a perfect backdrop for a Sound and Light performance—a dramatic representation of Argentine history—albeit one of much more modest proportions than those staged in Europe. The charm of the general's farmhouse lies in its unpretentious, human dimensions.

Victoria agreed to write a script for the performance. As she conceived it, the narrator's role went to the sprawling, old *algarrobo* tree, the oldest surviving witness on the grounds of the chacra to the events that had transpired there. During the performance, moments of history unfold in the tree's presence, as if evoked by its long memory, and personal dramas of the famous—and not so famous—are reenacted. One of the characters is a young woman, María Telle Echea de Pueyrredón, the general's wife, who married him when she was fifteen, knowing neither how to read or write. As she overhears parts of the hushed conferences between her husband and San Martín, she longs to be able to share with someone the thoughts and feelings she finds so difficult to define. Technical discussions of war and politics elude her, but she understands intuitively—even better perhaps than the generals—what they are fighting for: "How sad it makes me," she says, "to feel them so distant when they come into the house and greet me almost without seeing me! They come back from the river's edge without seeing that the river has turned rose-colored, like the clouds that look down on it. And they don't see that the river is painted across my heart and that I don't know what to do with so much rose-colored river in the afternoon. Is what I feel looking at the river," she wonders, "the thing they call the fatherland?"[3]

Victoria's sympathetic portrayal of the general's wife was, in part, a translation of her own reactions as a woman living in a world still governed by men. Spanish colonialism and Spanish Catholicism had bequeathed to both women a legacy of social taboos that denied them freedom of expression. A century had passed between them, but few things had changed for Argentine women.

Another character in Victoria's script was Victoria Ituarte Pueyrredón, the general's niece and Victoria's great-grandmother. The beauty of the Ituarte women was legendary, and she was no exception. Many eligible bachelors sought her hand, including Godoy Cruz, an influential commander on San Martín's staff. But Victoria Ituarte was interested in only one man: Manuel Hermenegildo de Aguirre, whose family came originally from the Spanish province of Navarre. In 1817, Pueyrredón entrusted Aguirre with the diplomatic mission of sailing to the United States as a confidential agent to plead for official recognition of the new Argentine republic. Generals San Martín and Bernardo O'Higgins also charged him with purchasing ships and weapons for their campaigns in Chile and Peru. Aguirre went to Washington and spoke with John Quincy Adams, then Secretary of State, but his petition on behalf of the Argentine republic was denied by President Monroe; the United States was in the process of working out a delicate treaty with Spain and an alliance with a former Spanish colony could have upset negotiations. Although Aguirre returned to Argentina with only half of his mission accomplished (he bought the arms and two frigates with his own money, for which he was never fully reimbursed), he was consoled to find Victoria Ituarte still waiting for him. They were married soon thereafter. On more than one occasion Victoria has compared her great-grandfather's trip to the United States to her own sense of mission on Argentina's behalf. She has also said that, like him, she had to learn to live with defeat.

While writing the Sound and Light script and delving into her own family's history, Victoria uncovered several skeletons in the family closet, stories buried for generations that had never been told to her as a child. They had been ignored or conveniently forgotten. It seems that Irala, the conquistador of Asunción, followed the colonial Spanish custom of having Indian concubines. During his tenure in Asunción, he had seven Guaraní mistresses, and with them, nine natural children. More noble than most of his companions in conquest, Irala legally recognized each of his offspring in his final will and testament. One of his children was born to Agueda, the only name recorded for that Guaraní tribeswoman who lived by his side. The child, Isabel de Irala, and her mother are related to Victoria on her mother's side, but Victoria was in her sixties before she learned of Agueda's existence. Master-slave relationships of this sort — similar to the one between Hernando Cortés and the Aztec woman Malinche—were not discussed in proper society. Women of any class who bore children out of wedlock were kept out of sight, often in another town, another country, or perhaps even in a convent. When Victoria learned about her ancestor Agueda, she proclaimed aloud the truth her forefathers had tried to hide. Discovering Agueda was a vindication for them both: Victoria could rescue Agueda from "history's back room," as she referred to the place where so many women's stories had been traditionally shunted, and Agueda, in turn, could provide Victoria with a blood link to Pre-Columbian America that complemented the spiritual link she had felt all her life. Recognizing Agueda was, for Victoria, an act of justice. With regard to Irala's attitude toward his Indian concubine, Victoria simply said, "As far as I'm concerned, I side with the servant, not the master."[4]

Another long-hidden story that illustrates the persistent double standards of Hispano-American morality involved a relative on the Ocampo side of Victoria's family. Apparently, her grandfather's brother, a hot-headed young man named Carlos Ocampo, shot to death a young widow in her twenties, Felicitas Guerrero, because she had turned him down in favor of another suitor. After killing Felicitas in the parlor of her home, Carlos either shot himself or was shot by one of her relatives. According to reports in an important newspaper of the time, aristocratic society matrons blamed Felicitas for the tragedy: if she had been content to remain a widow, as was the accepted custom, Carlos would not have been driven to kill her in a fit of jealousy. The moral onus was placed not on the murderer, but on the "coquettish" woman. It might have been a plot for one of the tragic plays of the Spanish Golden Age, so little had South American society changed in almost three hundred years. Victoria was so outraged when she learned of it that, like a modern Calderón or Tirso de Molina, she wrote a screenplay based on the incident. Thus far, however, it lies on a shelf, unpublished and unproduced.

Clearly there was no shortage of generals and statesmen in Victoria's family. This inheritance may well explain her sense of commitment to country, her spirit of adventure, and her love of challenge. But where in her family's history were the poets, artists, or literary geniuses who could have bequeathed her the kind of sensibilities that favor the pen over the sword, poetry over politics? The patriarchs who dominated Argentine society for generations valued achievement in war and government over achievement in the arts; history books are therefore heavily one-sided in the talents they record. Still, some clues do survive.

Prilidiano Pueyrredón, the son of General Pueyrredón and María Telle Echea, was one of Argentina's outstanding painters. After studying in France, he returned to the banks of the Plate to paint Argentine landscapes, still lifes, and portraits, among them the portraits of Victoria's great-grandparents which hang in Villa Ocampo. He also proposed the idea that Buenos Aires should imitate Paris by planting shade trees along its avenues and flowering gardens in its plazas; a century later, Victoria tried to encourage the same beautification with only moderate success. The rapport she feels with Prilidiano Pueyrredón is not just based on his love of nature and things French, however. He also had progressive ideas about women's education. According to Victoria, he was "a feminist *avant la lettre*," and that, she adds, "transformed a blood relationship (which is usually of no value) into a spiritual relationship (which is worth everything)."[5]

The only known writer in Victoria's family was a second cousin of her great-grandmother, Victoria Ituarte de Aguirre: his name was José Hernández. Hernández's major contribution to Argentine letters was the well-loved gaucho poem, *Martín Fierro* (1872), now considered a national masterpiece. Although not a gaucho himself, Hernández sympathized with the popular gaucho poets whose work had been derided by European-oriented literary circles in Buenos Aires. *Martín Fierro* was written in defense of traditional, indigenous poetry. As an evocation of gaucho life, it was so authentic that the gauchos themselves would recite it around campfires on the pampas.

What a curious irony it is that the only ancestors Victoria can claim who were famous for their artistic and literary contributions to Argentine history were two men of such opposing viewpoints: Prilidiano Pueyrredón, the *afrancesado*, or French sympathizer, and José Hernández, the nativist. One looked to Europe for inspiration, the other to America. The cultural polarity they epitomized has been a characteristic phenomenon of Argentine life since the early nineteenth century. Certainly it has existed in other Latin American countries where the search for a national identity has involved similar controversies between "nationalists" and "foreignists" — but not to the same intense degree. Argentina's remote geographical location, its less significant status among the Spanish colonies in America, its scant indigenous population and large immigrant population, and its history of conflict between Buenos Aires and the rural provinces are possible explanations for this controversy. Economic, social, and political factors make it a complex historical problem which is yet to be resolved.

A famous Argentine who spoke out publicly in favor of more contact with Europe and North America was Domingo Faustino Sarmiento, friend of Victoria's great-grandfather. During the time Sarmiento lived outside the country as an opponent-in-exile under the Rosas dictatorship in the 1840s, he roundly criticized the isolationist policies of the tyrant's regime. Rosas, he said, by alienating artists and intellectuals who went abroad seeking freedom of thought and speech, was inadvertently fostering the enlightenment of future generations who would return home one day and revitalize Argentina.[6] The exodus and return did not cure all the nation's ills as Sarmiento had predicted, but considerable liberalization occurred during the era that followed Rosas's fall. Sarmiento himself returned from exile to help reconstruct the nation, first as minister of education, then as governor of San Juan province, foreign minister to the United States, and finally as president of the republic from 1868 to 1874. Author, educator, and statesman, Sarmiento was a tireless reformer, optimistic about Argentina's future, and convinced that foreign immigration and public education would be the keys to national success.

Sarmiento died on the eve of Argentina's period of maximum growth and prosperity. At his funeral in Buenos Aires on a rainy day in 1888, Victoria's parents caught their first glimpse of one another. Within a year, Manuel Ocampo and Ramona Aguirre were married, thus joining two of the most aristocratic and historically prominent families in Argentina.

An Intersection in the Gran Aldea

A picture of Victoria's father taken in the gardens of Villa Ocampo shows that he was indeed, as she describes him, a handsome and distinguished man. Sitting jauntily in a lawn chair, newspaper and walking stick in hand, he gazes at the camera with a touch of aloof skepticism. Here is a man of wealth and social standing, a man with ample reason for self-satisfaction. Manuel Silvio Cecilio Ocampo Regueira, born in 1860, was one of the most respected architectural engineers in Argentina. He was a specialist in building roads and bridges in the interior provinces, particularly bridges for the British-financed railway system, begun in 1857.

One of nine children himself, Manuel Ocampo was a traditional, late Victorian father: conservative and patriarchal, but nonetheless devoted to the well-being and happiness of his children. He could be taciturn and pessimistic at times, but he also had a streak of humor that would quickly brighten the household when he was in a good mood. Although Victoria talks favorably and even affectionately about him, one senses in her a reluctance to go into details of their relationship, as if embarking on it would bring up things she would rather not discuss. When pressed to describe him in depth, Victoria protests, putting her hand up to her face to illustrate her point: she is still too close to his memory to be able to see him objectively. One of her sisters suggests that Victoria was closer to her father than to her mother; even so, there appears to have been a distance between father and daughter, especially in Victoria's adolescence, brought on by a conflict between his traditional attitudes and her rebellious temperament. When Victoria talks about her father, she prefers to emphasize what she admired most in him: he was a gentleman, she says, with a strong sense of moral honesty. Once someone asked him if a certain trusted employee in his business was an honest man, whereupon he replied: "Do I even know if *I* am?" Apparently he was a very intelligent man, though not an intellectual.

Victoria's mother, Ramona Máxima Aguirre, was a typically "feminine" woman. She was charming, affectionate, vivacious, accomplished at gardening, playing the violin, and other domestic talents. Ramona Aguirre was attractive, with her warm dimpled smile, but she was not what might be called a real beauty of her time. One of eight children, she was born in 1866 and nicknamed "la Morena" (generally meaning dark-haired, but in this case, her auburn hair was not the motive for the name; it was simply a *sobrenombre*, common among Argentines). Like her husband, she grew up in a well-to-do, large household, but unlike the Ocampos, the Aguirres were very *criollo*. The colonial house on Mexico Street where she spent her childhood and adolescence later became the property of the Argentine Writers' Society, an organization her daughter was to preside over as president and from which she would receive a prize of honor. Not as intelligent as her husband, but more sensitive than he to nature and music, Ramona Aguirre did not approve of women who led bohemian, artistic lives. She had very rigid notions of what was morally and socially correct, of how women should behave in private as well as in public. Not only was she religious; she was puritanical, as were many women in the Victorian age. Her devout Catholicism, according to Victoria, was her greatest strength and her greatest weakness. It made her the backbone of the family in moments of crisis, but it also made her intransigent in her manner of bringing up children. Conventions and traditions mattered to her just as did her daughter's regular attendance at mass. Victoria apparently loved her mother deeply but found herself constantly at odds with her, to the point where she preferred not to express herself and thus avoid censure or misunderstanding.

Victoria's parents had been married eleven months when their first child was born at home on April 7, 1890 and baptized Ramona Victoria Epifanía Rufina. The first name was for her mother, the second for a great-aunt (there were Victorias on both sides of the family), and the last two for her patron saints. Victoria or Victorita, however, was what she would be called.

Victoria Ocampo: a name with natural rhythmic flow, triumphant-sounding. Oddly enough, a map of downtown Buenos Aires drawn around 1810 shows that the intersection in the heart of the city near where Victoria was born—where Viamonte crosses San Martín—used to be the intersection of two streets called "Victoria" (in honor of the Argentine victory over the British) and "Ocampo" (for Victoria's ancestors). Today the intersection is no longer a residential area but a busy commercial district a block from Florida Street, the main shopping thoroughfare where vehicular traffic is prohibited. The colonial house at 483 Viamonte in which Victoria was born has since been torn down. Only the familiar church and convent of Las Catalinas stands at the intersection as it did in 1890, its colonial facade marred by an unflattering renovation. Yet, despite years of urban metamorphosis, one could say that the intersection of Viamonte and San Martín still belongs to Victoria: on the corner opposite Las Catalinas, at 494 Viamonte, stands a modern, ten-story office building, the home of *Sur*, Victoria's review and publishing house.

Victoria Ocampo was born during a time of transition in the Argentine republic, transition from an agricultural to an industrial-based economy, from a society dominated by a few powerful families to one more attuned to the needs of the middle classes. Symptomatic of this was the so-called Revolt of 1890 which took place a few months after she was born. It was a short-lived uprising of the middle sectors against the entrenched Conservative government of President Juárez Celmán, but it signaled the beginning of a new era in Argentine political life.[7] Thereafter, increasing support for the Radical and Socialist parties among the urban middle classes would bring about the ousting of the Conservatives in 1916 and the election of Hipólito Irigoyen, the Radical candidate for president. One could say, in fact, that Victoria Ocampo and Argentina came of age together.

In 1890, however, the oligarchy was still in control of the country, even though in numbers it represented only one percent of the population.[8] At that time Buenos Aires was a city of approximately 600,000 people (compared with a population of over 9,000,000 in Greater Buenos Aires today), and it was commonly referred to as the "Gran Aldea," or Big Town, by porteños. It was not a particularly lovely city, not dramatically framed by nature like Rio de Janeiro or Santiago de Chile, nor was it able to claim a rich Pre-Columbian culture like Mexico City or Lima. Then, as now, Buenos Aires conveyed an impression of unrelieved flatness, a flatness magnified a hundred-fold by the pampas that lay beyond the city limits. In Buenos Aires, one had to look for another, less classic kind of beauty. Perhaps in the very openness of the river, the land and the sky, there was a beauty one couldn't find elsewhere.

Originally built along the river's edge, Buenos Aires gradually turned to face more and more inland. Its broad avenues and parks, buildings and monuments, made the city resemble some of Europe's capitals. In the late nineteenth century, as now, the Avenida de Mayo leading from the *cabildo*, or colonial town hall next to the Plaza de Mayo, to the more modern Capital building similar to the one in Washington, D.C., divided the city into an older residential section on one side and a newer, commercial area on the other. Then, as now, the port of Buenos

Aires was filled with ships that had sailed 150 kilometers up the world's widest river to dock along the canals below the Plaza Colón. In those days, ships' holds carried large numbers of European immigrants, enough to double the city's population in less than fifteen years. Traffic heading for Europe was equally heavy; ships carried Argentine agricultural products bound for European markets as well as parties of wealthy porteños heading for a season of entertainment, or perhaps study, abroad. Buenos Aires was quickly changing from a Gran Aldea to a metropolis. By the early twentieth century, its reputation as a modern and progressive Latin American capital had been definitively established.

The Early Years

Victoria and the five sisters who followed her into the world in the next fourteen years—Angélica (1891), Pancha (1894), Rosa (1896), Clara (1898), and Silvina (1903)—were surrounded from infancy with the indisputable advantages of wealth and privilege. They became accustomed early in life to having servants to wait on them, large houses to play in, and indulgent relatives to spoil them.

In the winter months, their lives centered as much around the home of their four unmarried great-aunts as it did around that of their parents. Each day they were bundled off to great-grandfather Ocampo's home a block away where they were pampered, entertained, and allowed to have the run of the three interior patios filled with plants and flowers. The four elderly maiden sisters who lived there hovered lovingly over the tiny girls, assuming parental roles when called upon, though they were loathe to scold or punish. Victoria and Angélica were inseparable playmates. They loved those daily excursions. Of the two, Victoria was the more aggressive and assertive, so she was the acknowledged leader of the pair. In return, when mischief was being plotted, Angélica was a faithful and willing accomplice. With no brothers to bully them or steal their infantile glory, the little sisters were treated like princesses in their great-aunts' household.

By her own repeated confession, Victoria's favorite relative was her great-aunt Victoria, whom she called "Vitola." There was a special bond between them that lasted throughout Victoria's childhood and adolescence. Vitola was a kind of secondary mother figure, an older woman who guided and encouraged Victoria. There is no doubt that Vitola was the first to inspire her to dream of doing great things with her life.

In the summer months of December through March, the whole family would move out to the *quinta* or country home in San Isidro—to Villa Ocampo, the house that grew with Victoria. It was a big house, modern for its time, with running water and its own electric generator, though it had no central heating. In those days, the Ocampos owned an enormous tract of land stretching from Avenida Libertador on the barrancas down to the river's edge. The property actually belonged to Francisca Ocampo de Ocampo, Victoria's great-aunt and godmother, who left the house to Victoria's parents in her will with the provision that it become Victoria's upon their deaths. Francisca (or Pancha) had seen more of the world than most women of her time. She had traveled with her husband to Europe, Russia, Egypt, and North America. They had even visited Niagara Falls on the recommendation of their friend, Sarmiento, who had also encouraged Pancha to buy books wherever she traveled and to donate them to the public libraries he was trying to build in Argentina. Another of Victoria's married great-aunts, Adela Ocampo de Hermendahl, had also been abroad many times. Known in the family as "tante Adèle," she returned one year from France with a portrait of herself, wearing a pink-plumed hat, painted by a young artist named Pierre Auguste Renoir. The quinta built on the barrancas of San Isidro reflects the European tastes of this generation of Ocampos.

Of course Victoria was not aware of any of this when she was a small child bent on teasing the swans that lived in the pond that graced the front lawn of the mansion. She loved going out to San Isidro for the pure joy and adventure of it. There were gnarled ombus to climb around, the barrancas to play hide-and-seek in, lazy days and warm nights. She loved to go out to her grandfather's estancia for the same reasons. Trips there were less frequent, however, so she never grew to feel as naturally at home at the ranch in the pampas as she did in the house by the river. In San Isidro there was never the kind of constriction that was imposed upon her freedom in the city, where the houses had iron grillwork on the windows and gardens inside rather than out. She remembers being horrified when her mother once told her, as they were going to mass at Las Catalinas, that there were women who actually spent their whole lives behind its walls.

One of the great adventures of Victoria's young life—an experience that would leave a deep imprint on her—was the trip the family took to Europe in 1896. It was to be a grand tour lasting more than a year. For a six-year-old child, too young to comprehend what it meant, the anticipation of the event must have been both awesome and thrilling. Parents and relatives who had been to Europe time and again must have described to her the wonderful things she would see and do. They probably showed her maps pointing out the route from Buenos Aires north to the much smaller continent they all raved about. To her fertile young imagination, their stories must have been as fascinating as the fairy tales of palaces, knights, and kings that she pleaded to hear before going to bed.

It was a mass exodus, via German steamer, in a turn-of-the-century style characteristic of the affluent. In addition to her immediate family, a great-aunt, and several servants, they embarked with substantial provisions and foodstuffs, including cases of live chickens and two cows to supply milk for the children en route. The voyage itself took almost three weeks, a long time for small children to be kept confined. The days went by uneventfully, except that one of the cows took sick and had to be sacrificed to the crew for dinner. Finally they landed in Cherbourg, and for the next year Victoria was delighted by experiences that, if they bore only a slight resemblance to her imaginings, were no less wonderful and entertaining. One after another but at a leisurely pace, they visited all the fashionable cities: Paris, London, Geneva, Rome. They stayed in luxurious hotels and toured all the famous sites. It was a trip done in the kind of grand manner that gave South Americans a reputation in Europe for being extravagantly rich, if not also exotically mysterious. Few Europeans knew anything factual about them or the lands they came from.

Like most cultured South Americans in Europe in those days, Victoria's parents preferred, whenever possible, to adopt the language and customs of the country they visited. Thus, during their stay in Paris—the longest segment of their trip—the children had their own French governess who spoke to them, sang to them, scolded them, and played with them exclusively in French. Since Victoria was just beginning to learn how to read, her first lessons and readers were in French. Soon she was speaking better French than Spanish. It was an amphibianlike adaptation that only small children can undergo without self-consciousness. Indeed, just as Victoria was becoming aware of herself as an independent human being and just as she was storing up memories that would affect her as an adult, France and the French language became her natural habitat. In her own words:

> France began for me when I began to be conscious of my own existence. The alphabet I learned to read in was French and so was the hand that helped me to trace my first letters and the slate on which I learned to write my first numbers. All that happened overlooking Avenue Friedland. Ever since those days when I used to spin a top on the Champs-Elysées and chase frogs in the Pré Catalan, France has left an indelible mark on my life.[9]

Victoria has always maintained that part of her belongs to France in the same way that another part of her belongs to Argentina. As a child her spirit was nourished there, and the spirit knows no physical boundaries. A child's fantasies, including the scenario in which those fantasies are enacted, inevitably influence his or her formation as an adult. As she puts it, "We are of the same stuff our dreams are made of because we are of the same stuff that our childhood—which is pure dream—was made of."[10]

She has a similar affection for England, though it is not as intense because the family spent less time there. In London the children had a "nanny," but Victoria didn't have the time to adapt to English as completely as she did to French. Most vivid in her memories of that visit are the sweet-smelling round soaps she would play with in the bathtub and the guards in front of Buckingham Palace who looked like toy soldiers. Even the aged Queen Victoria, riding by their hotel balcony in a royal jubilee procession, looked to Victoria like a fairy-tale character. (Years later the last vestiges of her idealized image of royalty vanished when she discovered that the Queen had been unremittingly opposed to women's suffrage.) When she studied English a year or two later in Buenos Aires, it was again accomplished by direct exposure to the language. Her English governess would entertain her and her sisters by reciting nursery rhymes like "Pat-a-cake, pat-a-cake, baker's man," or "Fe, fi, fo, fum, I smell the blood of an English man," with all the attendant gestures and inflections. "I loved this sort of incantation," Victoria recalls, "I held my breath to hear it and demanded its repetition over and over again. I think England owes to *Pat-a-cake* the first victories she won over me . . ."[11]

Whether through nursery rhymes, lullabies, or fairy tales, learning French and English were natural processes whose earliest stages became blurred in her memory. They blended into the fabric of childhood recollections along with other experiences of that wonderful year abroad. Thereafter, when evoking scenes of her early years, she found it just as natural to speak about Paris as about Buenos Aires, in French as well as in Spanish. And going back to Europe when she was older would always feel rather like going home again.

Childhood and Schooling

Everything Victoria has written about her childhood—and, significantly, she has written much more about this part of her life than about her adolescence or early adulthood — conveys an impression of near-idyllic innocence and happiness. Being part of a large and loving family and growing up in an atmosphere of material comfort had a great deal to do with her positive impressions. Only much later would she realize the price she paid for so much attention and affection. Of course, she experienced the fears and anguish that all children feel, but, as she once put it, "I was so vital that what came uppermost was joy."[12]

Citing Baudelaire's words, she has often referred to "le vert paradis des amours enfantines, l'innocent paradis, plein de plaisirs furtifs." (the green paradise of childhood loves, the innocent paradise full of furtive pleasures) with the nostalgia of one who cherishes it as a time of visionary purity, a time when there were no barriers to the intuitive perception of reality. Children are able to see worlds of meaning in the merest trifle, and they respond to outside stimuli with untrammeled directness. This is the quality, says Victoria, that characterizes what is called creative genius in adults: "Wise men, poets, painters—in a word—artists and thinkers[. . .] possess genius only in the measure to which they are individuals ill-cured of their childhood and their loves. Individuals for whom life's trifles always have marvelous allusions, becoming tiny magic wands before which they are engrossed Rabdomantes."[13] More than the simple indulgence of physical delights, childhood innocence permits the experience of an instinctive spirituality, a quasi-mystical understanding of one's divine origins and destiny, a thought expressed symbolically by Wordsworth in his ode, "Intimations of Immortality":

Our birth is but a sleep and a forgetting:
The soul that rises with us, our life's star,
　　Hath had elsewhere its setting,
　　And cometh from afar;
　　Not in entire forgetfulness,
　　And not in utter nakedness,
But trailing clouds of glory do we come
　　From God, who is our home.
Heaven lies about us in our infancy;
Shades of the prison-house begin to close
　　Upon the growing boy,
But he beholds the light, and when it flows,
　　He sees it in his joy;
The youth, who daily farther from the east
　　Must travel, still is Nature's priest,
　　And by the vision splendid
　　Is on his way attended;
At length the man perceives it die away,
And fade into the light of common day.

　　Because childhood holds special meaning for her, Victoria has never ceased to explore, in Proustian fashion, what she calls the labyrinth of her memory searching for threads of knowledge that might explain the path her own life has taken. There have been those, she acknowledges, like her friend André Malraux, who preferred to avoid writing about their childhood. They may have chosen not to dwell on what was unpleasant for them, she speculates, but they weren't able to erase the conscious and unconscious impact of those years: "Childhood governs our life and colors it to such an extent that we can't avoid it. Poets and novelists haven't needed psychoanalysis to feel and express that. No one has ever succeeded in escaping from his childhood."[14]

Victoria enjoys remembering hers and is intrigued by the very apparatus of memory itself. Why, she asks, do two sisters like Angélica and herself, so close in age, retain different memories of the same childhood experience? Can modern psychoanalysis offer logical explanations for this, or is there some deeper reality that man's mechanistic language is insufficient to describe? In her opinion, each person has an unconscious psychic structure of inborn vital preferences that influence whatever memories — voluntary or involuntary — are retained from childhood. These vital preferences distinguish us as individuals. "I have always believed," she has written, "that we have the memories we deserve. Our will does not intervene in this choice. We must inevitably resemble what we remember best since *that* is what has engraved itself most deeply."[15] For this reason, she has considered her abundant writing about her childhood a means of achieving self-knowledge. It also explains why autobiographies and personal reminiscences are her favorite type of reading.

When writing about her childhood, Victoria returns time and again to the locale of San Isidro and the family quinta. There, in her youth, she evidently found an environment that suited her exuberant temperament and allowed for its fullest expression. She remembers how she and her sisters, especially Angélica, would fish on the banks of the river, play croquet, swing from a homemade trapeze (that delighted her and scared her sister), watch the train that passed through the lowlands, or *bajos*, and occasionally even ride horseback when their father allowed it. If they wanted playmates, they would call on the sons of the black servants, Juancito and Alfredo, who were more like members of the family because their parents and relatives had been part of the household for years. Victoria recalls playing with them day after day, oblivious to the differences between them except for the frustration of being teased for being a girl and having to wear dresses. She also remembers carnival time in February, when they would all choose costumes; her favorite, she confesses, was a devil's outfit.

The setting of the quinta in San Isidro must have struck a deep resonance, awakening in her a telluric sensibility that others have noticed and reacted to in her presence. It is as if contact with the energies of nature brings out energies of her own. After a few days in the man-made forest of New York skyscrapers, she is liable to say to a friend with a car, "Let's go where there are some trees!" Once there, she will be happy just to walk silently among them. Her sensitivity to nature is instinctive and thus necessary to her well-being; from it she derives aesthetic and spiritual nourishment.

San Isidro, then, appealed to her in her youth as a symbol of physical freedom. More than her other sisters, Victoria needed the environment of the quinta as an outlet for her immense vitality. Sometimes her aggressiveness made her misbehave; she had a reputation in the family for being the most quick-tempered and impatient of the children when things didn't go her way. When she was in a rebellious mood, the only one who could command her instant respect was Vitola. At times, Victoria was so willful and difficult to deal with that the servants in her great-aunts' house would call her "la Infanta." It wasn't so much disdain for others or haughtiness that made her impetuous and demanding. Nor was she hyperkinetic or hyperenergetic. Certainly she was naughty out of sheer contrariness at times, but more than that, it seemed to be her nature to function at a higher level of intensity than other children her age. "La Infanta" was definitely a child with a vigorous mind of her own.

After the family returned from Europe in 1897, no time was lost in making arrangements for the girls' schooling. For advice, Victoria's parents turned to Vitola, who had experience in such matters by virtue of having known Sarmiento, the father of modern education in Argentina. Sarmiento had said that women deserved as complete an education as men, and he proceeded to establish schools for them modeled on those he had seen in the United States. Vitola and Victoria's parents believed in the importance of a good education, but they also felt that young girls of prominent families should be educated in the traditional manner—in the home. Not only did they believe, as did many wealthy Victorian parents, that they could provide a better education with private instructors, they also felt that it was proper for young girls to remain within sight of watchful eyes. The old Spanish custom of the *dueña*, or chaperone, was still rigorously observed in upper class Latin America. It was taken for granted that girls were being trained primarily to become good wives and mothers, so the domestic environment was appropriate in every sense.

With Vitola in charge, great care was taken in selecting tutors or governesses for Victoria and her sisters. Above all, they had to be respectable women (only one music instructor was a man) who would maintain rigid standards. Once employed, they would have full control of their charges, arriving early in the morning and leaving late in the afternoon during winter and most of summer. The subjects chosen were almost exclusively in the areas of the humanities. Starting with piano lessons at seven in the morning (painful for all concerned), classes included modern languages and literatures (French, English, Spanish, and Italian), history, religion, and basic math. Even when they were older, there was no biology, chemistry, economics, philosophy, or classical languages; those were boys' subjects. When they were in the city in the winter, the daily routine of classes took place at the home of their great-aunts. In summer, classes were held upstairs in Villa Ocampo in the room that has always been Victoria's. From there, over the top of her Hachette primer, she would steal furtive glimpses of the barrancas and the river in the distance. Many times she was scolded for not paying attention and not studying hard enough. It wasn't that she disliked learning; it was just that she was inclined to be lazy about doing assigned work, preferring to read books she enjoyed or daydream about being outdoors. One governess was in the habit of calling her a "wild pony," warning her that unruly behavior did not become a young lady.

Victoria credits what she finally learned—and learned well, however limited the subjects—to the unflagging diligence and devotion of her governesses. The struggle they had to wage against her recalcitrance was, she has said, like a battlefield campaign, but one that was fought with as much affection as authority. In retrospect, she admired them even more for having accepted the obscurity of a profession that offered only minimal prestige and negligible material benefits. Two of her governesses in particular, Mademoiselle Alexandrine Bonnemaison from France and Miss Kate Ellis from England, were classic examples of this nearly extinct species of women. In Victoria's words:

> . . . I wonder if decorated and dazzlingly-uniformed diplomats and luxurious embassies have rendered their countries as much service as these poorly-dressed, determinedly faithful, at times maniacal, at times self-effacing, anonymous, hard-working women who held in their hands delicate human material that was often rebellious and exasperating even when its good quality deserved watchfulness and sacrifice. Frankly, I doubt it. [. . .] And those women never dreamed about meriting the kind of monument that drums and bugles bring to the mind of the least ambitious soldier. Those feminine voices that ordered us to wash our hands or read Dickens, to sit up straight or conjugate a verb, always to say "if you please" or "s'il vous plaît," or to recite fables,—they made their white-pinafored (at times betraying an ink or food stain) army march without drums or bugles. It never occurred to them to want a monument, and so there will never be one worthy of them.[16]

Their diligence at imparting the culture of France and of England was only excelled, it seems, by their chauvinistic dislike of one another. In the eyes of their charges, they were two utterly different personalities who embodied, as the children later realized, the opposing characters of their rival nations. How strong an impression they made on Victoria! If at times their classes reminded her of happy times spent in Europe a few years earlier, at other times their strictness made the class hour seem like purgatory:

> I still remember with nostalgia those distant hours of daily classes, and with

an echo of the old anguish, my two morning hours of struggle with Mademoiselle Bonnemaison, our French instructor. What differences were there between the two teaching systems or between the two women? [. . .] Mademoiselle knew very well what she knew (her grammar, her geography, her arithmetic, her little bit of history, her selections from the classics), and she proposed to put all that into our heads. To a certain point, she succeeded (I refused to be burdened with arithmetic, like the llamas who won't budge if you pile too much weight on them. By my own internal laws, I had decreed that the science of numbers would be of no use to me). But Mademoiselle was demanding, and her demanding, if she was not satisfied, always led to punishment. Without pity. To all my complaints or excuses (I should have avoided being insolent with her) she answered with an invariable series of axioms or affirmations whose repertory is engraved on my memory:

— Vous ne savez pas? Il fallait savoir.

— Eh bien, vous le copierez vingt fois.

— Il n'ya pas de *mais*.

— Vous mériteriez le bonnet d'ane.

— Vous me conjuguerez le verbe "répondre."

— Je vous le répète pour la dernière fois.

— Vous appelez ça savoir?

— Vous etes un fiéffée paresseuse.

— "Impossible" n'est pas français.

As one can see, in those days when nationalism was not spoken of as much as today, it already existed.[. . .]

Miss Ellis, much less learned than Mlle., had better manners, was a more delicate woman, weaker with her students (who took advantage of her indulgence or softness by not studying . . . I, anyway). She belonged to a different social class from Mlle., who was, no doubt, the daughter of farm people from the Pau district. Reading de Maupassant years later, I met the churlish family in which Mlle. must have been born. Miss Ellis, who was from St. Leonard, was infinitely better brought up than she was educated. She gave us vague notions of English grammar and history. After the *Nursery Rhymes*, she made us learn some poems by heart. [. . .] Not much more. Most important and unforgettable were the hours she spent reading aloud to us. From the *Graphic Reader* to *David Copperfield*. How impatiently we used to wait for her to finish drinking her ritual glass of milk which always arrived a few minutes before reading hour!

Miss Ellis' anger, moderate like her person, might extend to causing her to say: "You'll never be a lady!" I never saw her, as I did Mlle., tear up a book out of pure impotent rage (how much I must have tested her not very abundant patience!).

Both of them had complete authority over us. If an argument broke out, we knew all too well that our parents wouldn't take our side.

And so we lived, in my childhood years, governed by England and France. From an early age I learned to distinguish between England and

France, perhaps rather unjustly for the two countries since the distinction I established was, at first, an instinctive one, born of the characteristics and peculiarities of the two women. Miss Ellis was England, Mlle. was France. I felt great affection for both of them, except during the moments when I detested them — especially Mlle. — and wished that some prolonged though not mortal sickness would befall them (I didn't want any remorse to cloud my happiness).

Naturally, if my secret offensive against France was more frequent and active than against England, I also took France more seriously than her traditional enemy. Mlle. had drilled into us that French grammar *existed*, with inviolable and ferocious rules. While in England, I thought, one never knows the reason for the spelling. I only needed to remember certain capricious combinations of letters in words that were pronounced in a way that had nothing to do with the combination. If in matters of spelling the British Empire inspired less respect in me than the French Republic, in matters of clothing, Miss Ellis, with her immaculate blouses, her smell of lavender and talc, her tweeds and even her umbrella, awakened in me the echo of a world that I preferred to that of Mlle.[. . .]

Coming from two different worlds, Mlle. and Miss Ellis pulled us in opposite directions. They looked at one another like cat and dog. The French woman would speak of perfidious Albion (Joan of Arc, etc.). The English woman would say—even to Mlle.'s face one day—that "la marine française est adonnée à l'opium." Not knowing about that drug and its evil effects, these rumors didn't impress us. But Mlle. attributed them to the Machiavellianism of British politics. What could one expect after the Transvaal?

What we owe to those hours of class, to the sometimes hated company of the two governesses, is perhaps one of the most precious of all gifts to those who love books as an important part of life: the privilege of entering directly, without an intermediary — as into our own home — the master-pieces of the two literatures, two of the richest literatures of the world.[17]

Under the benevolent command of these two women, Victoria learned to read, write, and speak both French and English perfectly, even to the finest nuances of meaning and pronunciation. Later, when she traveled abroad, people would mistake her fluency for that of a native speaker. More than any of the assets of her wealth or social position, it was this ability to speak fluently in other languages that ultimately opened the doors to freedom and adventure in her life. Of course she had no inkling of this in the days when Mlle. Bonnemaison and Miss Ellis scolded her for her mistakes.

Looking at the neatly ruled notebooks she used when she was thirteen, notebooks filled with meticulously penned compositions entitled "le Chien" or "Amitié," one would never guess that Victoria had been anything but a model student. When she decided to apply herself, her aptitude was remarkable. One day while she was still quite young, she overheard her father comment that it was a pity she wasn't born a boy so she could use her talents in a career. Her reaction at the time was a measure of her innocence: "How fortunate he doesn't expect anything of me! Now I can keep on playing and doing just as I please!" It did not occur to her until many years later to challenge the assumption that women didn't have careers like men. By then, she realized that she would have to teach herself what had been left out of her education.

CHAPTER TWO

CHARTING THE COURSE

Victoria believes that our preferences in life are determined by inborn vital needs. We have certain preferences just as we have certain memories of our childhood, not because we arbitrarily pick them but because they are expressions of our own unique nature. They may vary in level of intensity—from simple predilections to passions—but we all have them. "Whoever has no preferences," says she, "is not alive."[1]

Books and Heroes

For Victoria, reading has been a passion all her life. As a child she read voraciously in three languages, devouring what was given to her by others and saving her money to buy more. In her eighties, her hunger continues unabated. Her bedroom and study in San Isidro and in Mar del Plata are cluttered with the books she is reading, has just read, or is about to read. There are books on her bed, on her night table, and on chairs and sofas, in addition to those that fill the hundreds of shelves. What gives the appearance of disorder is actually a kind of arrangement she alone understands and remembers. Woe unto the one who takes a book and carelessly sticks it back on another shelf! Each book has its own place where Victoria can find it instantly. Even when she is traveling, reading material must go with her; books and magazines are piled on every available surface in her hotel room, no farther from her fingertips than from her mind.

When a book appeals to her, she can't bear to be interrupted. On one transatlantic journey, she took *War and Peace* out of the ship's library and was still reading it when the boat docked in New York. Hailing a taxi, she went directly from the pier to a bookstore on Fifth Avenue to buy a copy of her own to finish that night.

The profusion of books that share her habitats is not there as the tools of a writer's or publisher's trade. They are "presences," as she has called them, intimate friends that keep her company from the hours before dawn when she awakens until late at night. Their pages are sometimes folded back or dotted with remarks and underlinings — the kind of abuse tolerated by good friends who know that it is born of loving curiosity and concern. Of all her possessions—with the possible exception of the letters she has saved over the years ("presences" of another kind)—nothing is more valuable to her than her books.

When she began to read at six or seven, Victoria discovered that it gave her a new sense of freedom and the keys to a more fascinating world of fantasy. Reading fables and fairy tales and later the Comtesse de Ségur, Conan Doyle, Dickens, Jules Verne, de Maupassant, Poe, and many others, she found a feeling of liberation that only playing out of doors when she was younger and listening to music when she was older could equal.

In spite of all the advantages of her way of life, as she approached adolescence she became increasingly aware of how much she was circumscribed by the conventions and taboos to which her parents adhered. Of course, the boxes of clothes that came seasonally from Paris for her and her sisters were beautiful, but why must she be so rigidly limited in her comings and goings, her reading material, and her friendships? She chafed at the bit she was forced to wear, a wild pony reluctant to be tamed. Intellectual and emotional energies pent up inside her were channeled into the rich fantasy life that her reading reinforced.

For the youngster who seeks it out, reading is a form of self-expression, albeit a vicarious one. Certain characters awaken his sympathy and he or she identifies with them. According to Norman Kiell in *The Universal Experience of Adolescence,* "Characters in books may serve as useful objects for identification and imitation in terms of incorporating certain qualities into the adolescent's ideal self. . . . Through reading he may bring his own feelings to the surface, enabling him to recognize and identify himself in what he has read and thereby helping to bring about the reintegrated personality and self-actualization he is seeking."[2] Looking back on her own experience, Victoria would agree, though she would suggest that the "ideal self" is less a product of will than of destiny, something akin to the Hindu concept of *dharma* or the role one has been assigned to play in life by divine moral order. As she wrote in 1937:

> All children who possess vivid imagination and sensitivity are captivated by certain heroes and invent for themselves stories in which, in relation to

those heroes, they play an important role by being pursued, loved, betrayed, saved, humiliated or glorified by them. Later, once that stage has passed, they generally live out in their lives the scenes they rehearsed so many times in their childhood; the wonderful or awful moment finally presents itself and the response is immediate: impossible to change, impossible to mistake. . . . The rehearsals have been too frequent for any other response to be chosen. There never was any choosing. *Every person carries inside himself the same scene, the same drama, from the time he achieves conscious awareness until the end of his life.* He plays out his scene, his drama, no matter what plots or characters he meets until he eventually finds *his* plot and *his* character. He may never even find them. But that doesn't stop him from playing out his scene, his drama, and giving the plots and characters that seem the least suitable for his play the form of the plot and character that are most his own. This is because he has been born to play out *one* scene and *one* drama only, and he can't help repeating them as long as he lives.[3] (Emphasis added)

Although she has not defined precisely what she believes to be her drama in life, Victoria has identified her adolescent heroes. Not surprisingly, they were all characters in her favorite books, and all of them were men. For a young girl of exuberant nature who dreamed of worldly excitement and adventure, female role models were singularly uninspiring at the turn of the century. Both in life and literature, the Victorian age fostered the notion that a woman should be chaste and long-suffering, a Griselda-like creature of infinite patience and self-abnegation. In part, this was a legacy from chivalric and romantic ages that idealized woman as an untouchable goddess or muse intended to be a passive source of moral and aesthetic inspiration for man; but it was also a reaction to the threat of women's suffrage that was gaining ground, particularly in Victorian England. The typical nineteenth century literary heroine has been described as a "drooping lily," not at all the kind of role model that would have suited Victoria's temperament.[4]

Nor was she inclined to identify with either her mother or her great-aunts. Victoria was devoted to her female relatives, but she sensed that there was something inside her that they lacked or had never developed: a kind of vibrancy of spirit so acute that she seemed to experience life with double the vigor and ardor of others. Not even her sisters seemed to feel as she did.

If she looked to her father for encouragement she was disappointed. A traditionalist when it came to preparing his daughters for life, he couldn't respond to the side of Victoria's nature that was outspoken and aggressive. The Victorita he loved was the affectionate and sensitive girl with big wistful eyes whose exceptionally lovely features were taking on more definition and making her stand out as the handsomest of all his daughters. He must have watched her approach womanhood with mixed feelings. Was her aggressiveness a form of pride that would sour her relationships with others? This is what he indicated to her when she asserted herself so strongly. She, in turn, resented his inability to understand her. But she loved him and her mother too much to provoke them repeatedly, so she began to keep her feelings to herself. Inside her, the need to cling to her family clashed with an equally strong need to rebel against the conservatism they represented. Like most adolescents, she may not even have been aware of it at first. Evidently, she buried much of her emotional energy in her passion for reading.

As she read the mountains of books she accumulated, she identified most naturally with male heroes. One of her favorites was Captain Hatteras, the protagonist of a pair of novels by Jules Verne. Hatteras, the son of a multimillionaire Englishman, is driven by an *idée fixé*: he must reach the North Pole and plant the British flag before the Americans get there. His character is an ambivalent one; in one sense, he is a courageous patriot, in another, an unscrupulous madman capable of sacrificing others to satisfy his needs. Above all, he is a man of action with boundless energy and self-confidence.

Another of her literary heroes was Sherlock Holmes, the fanatical sleuth, invariably capable of solving the most uncanny crime. Holmes too is obsessed and, like Hatteras, driven to the point of being ascetic in his personal habits. He is indifferent if not hostile to the opposite sex. Yet Holmes awakens a reader's sympathy by his devotion to the finer points of his craft and his versatility. He has, without a doubt, a superb mind.

Still another of her heroes was the dramatic and enigmatic Steerforth, David Copperfield's school chum who meets an untimely death in a shipwreck. Steerforth, so disarmingly attractive, seems to possess a diabolical charisma. Davy succumbs to it at first, but manages to escape in time, whereas poor Emily is helpless to resist. She follows him and repents later. Steerforth's evil power over others cannot be defined easily; one must have wisdom and self-control to recognize it. Agnes calls him a "bad Angel." If so, he represents the antithesis of a mind such as Sherlock Holmes's. Hatteras, one might say, is a combination of the two. All three heroes have in common a powerful ego. They are also rebels and thus, inevitably, loners in a conventional world.

Victoria's choice of male literary heroes as the objects of her adolescent hero-worship is understandable. Her heroes were the embodiment of her own conflicting feelings: the reckless adventurer and the ascetic perfectionist, the willful and the disciplined sides of her nature. In the context of her own definition of youthful hero-worship, this is an important clue to the drama of her life that was beginning to unfold.

Dreams and Frustrations

When Victoria was about ten years old, she was given her first taste of the literature of the classic French theater. Mademoiselle Bonnemaison culled some verses from Racine's *Phèdre* — the play in its entirety was evidently too risqué — and asked Victoria to memorize and then recite them. It was an assignment she relished. Here was an opportunity to express herself with all the dramatic flair that was instinctively hers. Standing before Mademoiselle and Angélica, her first audience, she transferred her own feelings to the role of Hippolytus as he defends his moral integrity against his father's wrath. She remembers the experience:

Nothing was more consoling to me than reciting in class, whenever the occasion presented itself, Hippolytus' response to Theseus, a response that I thought suited my complaints perfectly. I became Hippolytus, the victim of false accusations. Of course no one had suspected me of murder or incest (and anyway, I had no idea what the latter term meant), but I had often been punished for answering back, as if answering were a premeditated crime and not an involuntary movement, like blinking your eyes. Standing in front of Mademoiselle with my hair parted in two tight braids, my starched pinafore and my ink-stained fingers, I wasn't reciting a lesson but a plea, an appeal, a prayer that seemed to rise from the core of my being:

D'un mensonge si noir justement irité
(Actually, Mademoiselle, you accuse me of insolence because I answer back, but that's not insolence.)
Je devrais faire ici parler la vérité
Seigneur; mais je supprime un secret qui vous touche,
(No, I'll not tell you how much I detest you right now.)
Approuvez le respect qui me ferme la bouche
Et sans vouloir vous-même augmenter vos ennuis
(I'll never ever learn all the multiplication tables, Mademoiselle. It's no use doing them.)
Examinez ma vie et songez qui je suis
Quelques crimes toujours précèdent les grands crimes.
Quiconque a pu franchir les bornes légitimes
Peut enfin violer les droits les plus sacrés.
Ainsi que la vertu, le crime a ses degrés.
(It's true that I once kicked a door and broke it when someone wouldn't open it but I was innocent because I didn't know the door was so fragile or my kicks so powerful.)
Mais jamais on n'a vu la timide innocence
Passer subitement à l'extrême licence.
Un seul jour ne fait point d'un mortel verteux
Un perfide assassin, un lâche incestueux.
(I'm neither treacherous nor cowardly. All the servants can tell you that, Mademoiselle, if you doubt it.)

Elevé dans le sein d'une chaste héroïne
Je n'ai point de son sang démenti l'origine
Pitthée, estimé sage entre tous les humains,
Daigna m'instruire encore au sortir de ses mains.
(I'll bet Pitheus was easier than you, Mademoiselle.)
Je ne veux point me peindre avec trop d'avantage,
Mais si quelque vertu m'est tombée en partage,
Seigneur, je crois surtout avoir fait éclater
La haine des forfaits qu'on ose m'imputer.
Actually, Mademoiselle, I never intended to be insolent; I only needed
to answer, and it's no use making me conjugate *répondre* because the need
won't disappear.)[5]

Not long after that, Vitola took Victoria and her sisters to the theater
for the first time. It was a play by the classical Spanish playwright, Lope
de Vega, performed by two well-known actors, María Guerrero and Díaz
de Mendoza. Victoria applauded until her hands ached. The theater soon
became another of her passions.

Since few plays passed parental censorship, opportunities for attend-
ing performances were rare. Victoria had to be content to read as many
plays as she could and memorize parts of them to recite at home. The idea
of reciting before others never threw her into a panic; she looked forward
to it, much as she looked forward to the release she found in reading. It
was a way of externalizing thoughts and feelings she often recognized as
her own, though she wouldn't have confessed openly to having them. Her
instructors praised her talents, and Victoria tried hard to absorb everything they taught her about the art of diction. In those days, many young
girls studied recitation as one of the social refinements they were expected to cultivate, like playing the piano or doing embroidery. But to
Victoria it was much more than that. Without telling anyone, she dreamed
of standing on a stage, playing a part in a real performance. As a young
teenager she couldn't have been fully aware of how dim the prospects
were for the realization of her dream. A life in the theater was considered
taboo for young ladies of respectable Latin American families. Associating
openly with theater people was tantamount to being dissolute.

When she was fifteen an unexpected event brought her hopes to a
peak. A French acting company under the direction of Constant Coquelin
arrived in Buenos Aires with its repertory of classical and modern French
theater. One of its members, Marguerite Moreno—not yet the star she
would become later in life—immediately impressed Victoria as a great
actress. Watching her perform made the theater come alive in a special
way. Victoria was transfixed by her talent: "I only had eyes and ears for
her. She was thin, pale, fragile, and tubercular (so they said), like the

heroines of Poe's tales. And she was ugly, but hers was an expressive and fascinating ugliness. Besides, she had an impressive voice and she recited verses better than anyone. That's what I thought when I heard her, and I wasn't mistaken. In those years, they used to laugh at me when I said there was no actress comparable to her in the troupe. My opinion didn't count." [6] When she saw the famous Sarah Bernhardt a few years later, her opinion didn't change. To her, Moreno was a thousand times better: her diction was far superior to Bernhardt's and so was her acting. Moreno's later success and acclaim confirmed Victoria's judgment, though the Bernhardt legend is better known.

Moreno became Victoria's hero—her first female hero. After seeing Moreno on the stage, Victoria would memorize the same verses and try to recite them with her idol's diction and intonation. She attended as many performances as her parents would allow. When she learned that Moreno had decided to stay on in Buenos Aires for a few years, she conceived a daring idea. Gathering up her courage, she approached her parents and pleaded with them to let her take French diction lessons from Moreno. Although they disapproved of her fascination with the theater and of theater people in general, they finally gave in, with the proviso that classes be properly chaperoned and that Victoria have no illusions about any further involvements. Nothing more specific was said, but the implications were clear.

Twice a week, Victoria studied with Moreno, and as the time went by, she became more and more convinced that the theater was her true calling. In a letter to her friend Delfina Bunge on August 3, 1908 she wrote:

> I was born *to act*. I have the theater in my blood. I am a great artist and, without the theater I can have no joy or peace. It's my vocation. The *far niente* to which I am condemned kills me.

Under Moreno's expert coaching, she developed a repertoire of poems and dramatic verses that she would occasionally recite for family and special friends. They were recitations, not performances, though she knew many roles well enough to do on stage. The more she studied with Moreno, who became a close friend, the more she was tortured by contradictory feelings. All her instincts on one side told her that the theater would be a natural and fulfilling career; on the other side, even stronger instincts told her that such a decision would be a crushing blow to her parents, a blow she was not prepared to deal. Gradually, it dawned on her that if she had been a boy, her departure from the family would not have been a problem. This realization only made it more painful for her to suppress her urge to leave. "I dreamed of devoting myself to the theater," she later wrote, "and for years that desire tortured me. But the magnitude of the catastrophe that such a dream would have meant to my parents inhibited me and kept me from going ahead with it, as it was my nature to do."[7]

Finally, she had to renounce her dream. It was a decision forced on her by her weakness, but it was weakness she could not overcome. The thought of making her parents unhappy made her physically sick; migraine headaches often plagued her. She felt a kind of loyalty to her parents that had nothing to do with filial duty but rather with an emotional commitment. Though she despised herself for giving in to it, she felt powerless to do otherwise; it was a kind of involuntary faithfulness. While she knew it was not premeditated on their part, she hated her parents for having instilled this weakness in her. She resented their narrow-mindedness and their blindness to her needs — yet she loved them in spite of it.

She was nearly twenty when she accepted the decision as final, but it was many years before she could be as philosophical about it as the following statement suggests:

> There's some good in every evil. Perhaps not having been able to be an actress was a blessing in disguise. At least I'd like to think so. The theater would have absorbed me and prevented me from doing other things. Temporarily, it would have kept me far from my country, as I couldn't imagine my acting in any language but French. Now that all that is long past, I will say that the only thorn still pricking me is the certain knowledge that I could have made a career on the stage, maybe even a brilliant one, with an authentic vocation.[8]

She doesn't say it vainly. It was simply a fact she never doubted because her rapport with the theater was instinctive, and she knew her own capabilities matched her instinct. Professionals in the theater who have heard her give recitations—an art she never renounced though she shared it with others only on rare occasions—confirmed her opinion. One friend recounts that he was present in Paris when Victoria recited some verses for the great actor and teacher Jacques Copeau with the idea of studying under him. When she finished, Copeau rose, bowed to her, and said, "Madame, I have nothing to teach you."[9] Another friend recalls that when the French actors Lugnè Poe and Suzanne Déprès heard Victoria recite, they agreed that the theater had lost a great artist.[10]

Letters to Delfina

In the process of making her decision and coping with the self-betrayal she felt, Victoria turned to another outlet she had discovered as a child:

"I'll have to content myself with writing," she thought. "Writing, from the time I first learned to trace letters has always been a passion of mine. I used to be a great letter-writer—to my mother, my aunts. I was sure I could be a writer, but I doubted my success in that field."[11] This doubt explains, in part at least, why it took her many years to publish her first prose pieces. She was never sure they were good enough, and she had no one close to her who could convince her otherwise.

When she was much younger, she and Angélica had briefly tried their hand at editing a household magazine; Victoria did the writing and Angélica the imaginary ads. Her first serious effort was a piece for that magazine. Like so many of her later essays, it was written in reaction to an injustice: Miss Ellis had punished her undeservedly; in retaliation, Victoria took up her pen and wrote an impassioned defense of the Boers in the Transvaal War against the British. She has confessed that her knowledge of the subject at the time was far less developed than her sense of outrage. The only other writing she did as a youngster was a series of dialogues imitating the tales of the Comtesse de Ségur, transcriptions, as she recalls them, of conversations with family and friends that allowed her to express dramatic talents as well as a creative impulse. Other than this, writing meant letters and diaries. These she produced in abundance, all of them in French.

Most of her adolescent writing has been lost or destroyed over the years with the exception of a collection of letters that Victoria wrote between 1906 and 1910 to her friend Delfina Bunge. Delfina, the daughter of another wealthy Argentine family, was herself a budding writer, several years older than Victoria. Their paths parted amicably after Delfina married Manuel Gálvez in 1910, but Victoria's letters, contrary to her expressed wishes and expectations, were never destroyed. Delfina eventually had them bound in leather in a single volume and returned them to her friend. These letters, which number in the hundreds, have never been published. If they were, they would be acclaimed as a unique personal journal, comparable in sociohistorical interest to the diary of Marie Bashkirtseff, a young Russian woman of the late nineteenth century who died of tuberculosis at the age of twenty-four. Victoria had read Bashkirtseff's diary, published posthumously, and had felt they were kindred spirits: young women with artistic ambition and drive who were unable to express themselves freely in a hostile environment. If they were both narcissistic, it was because they were forced to retreat inward, though in Victoria's case, fantasy never replaced reality in her search for meaning in life.

Several times a week, sometimes daily, Victoria would write pages and pages of letters to Delfina, always in French and always on fine vellum stationary with an elegant monogram, *RVO* or simply *Nike* (Greek for Victoria). Delfina was her emotional and artistic lifeline. With her—a woman and a writer—she needn't hold back the feelings she hid in the presence of others. She could pour out hopes, fears, and frustrations, and she could even send Delfina some of the verses she had written which were inspired by her favorite French poets. They were letters meant for Delfina's eyes only—passionate, intimate letters bearing a private self that Victoria didn't dare expose to public scrutiny.

The Victoria Ocampo of the letters to Delfina would have shocked both her family and her casual acquaintances. To them, she was a rather difficult, domineering, and unemotional person, not at all the vulnerable creature her letters reveal. Although she took part in the normal family obligations and social pastimes, she was always somewhat enigmatic when she was with others, as if she disdained the goings on around her. She did, in fact, feel superior to her milieu and resentful of the restraints it imposed on her. She despised the materialism that motivated most of porteño society and the shallowness of the people who spent enormous sums on clothing, trips, furnishings, and art objects without caring or wanting to know the meaning of true culture. To a certain extent, her own family was guilty of these superficialities as was she by association. To speak openly, however, would have been to invite acrimony, and the realization of this drove her further inside herself. As she confessed to Delfina in October 1908:

> You can't imagine how tormented and weary I am. Oh! It seems to me that I'm becoming wicked, hard, egotistical by dint of being shut up inside myself. . . . It seems to me that my heart is about to burst at times. I'd like to weep, to cry out my love, to be, in short, the creature of tenderness and love that I am . . . and yet, I can't. This bruising, daily incomprehension, this misunderstanding, this coldness, this uneasiness that reigns inside me and in those around me embitters my sensibility in a frightful manner.

Earlier, in June 1907, she had written to her friend:

> What you say is true. I am hardly satisfied to be able to say to myself that four or five people think or feel as I do; I'm hardly satisfied to know that two or three people understand me more or less. What I feel crying inside me is, as you say, an immense and imperious need for universal comprehension.
>
> I'd like to be able to photograph my soul as I see it, that is as I feel it . . . I'm tired of feeling misunderstood. I wish I could be known *for what I am* . . . A person "who thinks," a person who analyzes herself unceasingly or who analyzes her neighbor. An intensely vibrant and passionate creature can't be joyful more than two minutes . . . if that. To be truly and sincerely

joyful, a woman must be giddy, a being without brains or reflection; or else she must have enviable *courage,* a serene and generous will power.[. . .] The only thing that does any good, the only thing that makes me forget how detestable life can sometimes be, is art. Art in all its forms . . . *I adore it.* You say that my heart suffers because it's hungry for love. Oh, how right you are!

I've made up my mind to have only one great love: Art! It's foolish, I know. Art won't always be enough for me . . . the proof is that the need to love always torments me. I was made to love, to suffer . . . when I don't love, when a giant enthusiasm doesn't raise me toward a celestial region, I feel only discouragement and bitterness.

I expected too much from humanity . . . the world I wanted to live in didn't exist. I'm a stranger down here! I've fallen from a strange and divine country . . . down here nothing will ever satisfy or please me completely.

In February 1908, she revealed to Delfina that one of her greatest enthusiasms was for the author and social critic Anatole France. His works consumed her to the point that she wrote him an anonymous letter: "I admire you; I think I understand you, and I love you." It was Victoria's first case of literary hero-worship.

At about the same time, two of her poems were published anonymously in a Buenos Aires newspaper and she won a prize in a French magazine, *Femina,* for another.[12] In March 1908, she confided in Delfina:

I cannot judge my poems. Once they're written, they only interest me half-heartedly, so inferior do they seem to those that are written in my soul. I'm happy that they pleased you.

Literary ambitions? . . . My dear friend, if you only knew where I'm aiming, how far I'd like to go, whom I'd like to equal . . . and all without knowing how to go about it! *I feel* that I can demand a great deal of myself. *I adore literature* frantically. *I feel* that I have something unusual inside me. I'll have to work, persevere, arm myself with patience and resignation if I want to achieve the aim I've set for myself. But God knows I'll have to *struggle* because patience, perseverance, etc., are things that are quite contrary to my impetuous and versatile nature.

In July of that same year, Victoria suggested to Delfina that they try to publish some verses together in one volume—anonymously of course— but the idea was never followed through.

As Victoria clearly recognized, her passion for literature and art could not take the place of her craving for another kind of love. The subject of men and romance came up regularly in her correspondence with Delfina. But Victoria was never so carried away as to forget that the two kinds of love she sought might be mutually antagonistic. She had apparently discussed with Marguerite Moreno her concern that marriage might interfere with her aspirations, and Moreno had warned her that no man would understand her unusual intelligence. On July 8, 1908 she shared these startlingly modern and perceptive thoughts with Delfina:

> What am I? What would I be and what would become of me if I were to weaken one day before the sadness of another and my own need for tenderness. Can you see me burying myself with domestic cares? Because, needless to say, someone will have to take charge of the house. Can you see me leading that colorless life? That would be a true suicide of the intellect, of "the self." Never, never in my life will I be able to resign myself to abdicating my personality. And I understand that one must make this sacrifice for love. But not me, I can't. So I will only give myself in part, because my intelligence will remain mine, intact and powerful, ready to combat the *other* intelligence. It's useless; I'll have to say goodbye to all my beautiful dreams. It's the best thing to do. Oh, Delfina! If you knew how I feel my brain open to all great ideas. If you knew how I have the effervescent feeling of my young intelligence on guard. I would have to be face to face with an almost impossible-to-find man in order to feel subdued admiration. I'm not a fragile plant that likes to be protected by the shade of a vigorous tree. I have too much love in me, but I'm also too intoxicated with freedom and intellectual strength! Delfina, for the first time perhaps, I feel happy with this intelligence that upsets my life. I feel I have the courage to sacrifice everything to it! It's so beautiful to understand everything . . . and so sad at times. If I could only stifle this cursed heart that never ceases to play its tricks on me.

At eighteen, Victoria could analyze herself with more clear-headedness than most adults. She could look at the liabilities of romance objectively while the very craving for it tormented her. The gifts of intelligence and foresight allowed her to develop a feminist consciousness that was extremely rare in her time, especially in Latin American society.

Victoria was as emotionally susceptible to romance as any adolescent female. She had had a crush on a young man when she was thirteen, but she had never done more than look at him from afar. After that she had been attracted to older friends of her cousins, but they had never noticed her. The fact was that male companionship was virtually impossible on any natural basis because a young woman of good family was constantly under surveillance. Chaperones hovered nearby whether she was on a tennis court, a golf course, or a dance floor. Any possibility of romance was limited to brief conversations or remote glances. Certain things were strictly prohibited: dancing more than one dance with the same partner, talking to a boy on the telephone, or allowing him to visit without the proper social pretext. It was the era of the tango in another part of Buenos Aires, but in the aristocratic homes on Florida Street or in the Barrio

Norte, no respectable young porteña was permitted even to see, much less partake in, such an indecent form of recreation. In this restricted atmosphere, a young woman's imagination had to make up for whatever society's taboos denied her.

Most of the young men she knew, Victoria told Delfina, were tedious bores. Some appealed to her weakness for good looks, but they failed to excite her intellectually. She knew that many of them were attracted to her, mistaking her indifference, or even her rebuffs, for coquettishness. True, she enjoyed being admired, but she was not a premeditated flirt. The more they pursued her, the less she was interested in them.

In 1907, a darkly handsome, blue-eyed man of twenty-five, Luis Bernardo de Estrada, stopped by the Ocampo quinta in San Isidro one day with Victoria's cousins while she was playing tennis. Afterwards they all sat under the trees and talked. There was something elegantly proud and disdainful about "Monaco," as everyone called him. He had studied law, traveled abroad, and came from a well-known family like her own. Among other things discussed that day, Monaco voiced the opinion that most Argentine women did not recite well in public—an observation with which Victoria was inclined to agree. Then someone singled her out and asked her to oblige, so she recited Coppée, Rostand, and some verses of her own for the group, whereupon Monaco had to confess that Victoria was certainly an exception to the rule. It was a promising beginning.

Monaco Estrada was more refined and restrained than most of the young men Victoria knew. In addition to his handsome features and sharp mind, there was a subtle irony in his gaze that captivated her. It seemed to her that he understood her own disinclination to follow the crowd. To Delfina, she confessed that he appealed to her more than anyone she had ever met.

When she thought—even abstractly—about marriage, however, she remained wary. In November 1908, she recounted to Delfina a conversation she had with another girlfriend, Lía Sansimena, who had "liberated" ideas like her own:

> We were pretty much of the same opinion in our rebellion against our slavery and in our faith in the position that women will obtain in future societies. The more we talked, the more we became indignant about the *injustice* that is done to us. Here, it's perfectly acceptable for a man to continue his bachelor existence after marriage . . . A woman must put up with everything, without complaining. You know, that's too much! Marriage is a pact that ought to be equal on both sides. If the man abandons the woman, it's stupid and unjust for a woman not to do the same to him. Do I scandalize you, Delfina? What do you expect? This brutal injustice revolts me beyond my powers of expression.

Ah, the man! The egotistical brute who *abuses* his liberty, and knowing the power social prejudice gives him over his wife, is content to treat her with the consideration one has for a pampered pet or a costly object. Ah, Delfina! And to say that when one loves, one forgets everything, one weakens, one allows oneself to be enchained, one becomes reduced to slavery by love!

There are two contradictory forces struggling eternally inside me when it comes to love as well as religion: the mind and the heart.

Victoria was determined never to accept the double standard most women took for granted. It outraged her to think her own grandmother had proudly worn a bracelet, a gift from her husband, that was inscribed: "Chained and content."

A Gilded Cage

This was Victoria's state of mind on the eve of her departure for a second lengthy stay in Europe. It was November of 1908. The whole family—this time with six daughters, the youngest being five years old—set sail once again for the Old World with the usual complement of servants and provisions. A new addition to the household, a young Spanish woman named Fani, was brought along especially to tend to the girls' needs. More than ten years had passed since their last trip to Europe, yet in many ways, Victoria felt spiritually closer to the old continent than she did to her own. Years of instruction under Mademoiselle Bonnemaison and Miss Ellis, years of speaking French and English as if they were her own languages, had made the culture of Europe an integral part of her life. Now she was ready to absorb as much more of it as she could. She was eighteen, almost an adult, and she was hungry for new experiences.

She would have been delighted at the prospect of the trip if it weren't for having to leave Monaco—even though they saw each other only rarely in Buenos Aires. There is no doubt that Victoria was seriously considering him as a possible husband, but romantic visions of him were often shattered by practical doubts. On April 5, 1909 she wrote to Delfina from Paris:

"There can be no disparity in marriage, like unsuitability of mind and purpose." These words of Dickens are always on my mind . . . It's the truest thing in the world, or so I imagine at least, as I've never been married . . . Oh, Delfina, you do well to pray for me, because I really need your prayers!
[. . .] When one loves without knowing (and one almost always loves that way), what hasn't one the right to expect? That's why, Delfina, I sense that what has drawn me toward M. can also blind me; I feel I can only know in him what I want to know; I love his eyes more than the words he says to me; I'm too disturbed in his presence to keep any vestige of mental lucidity.

That's why I'd like to close my eyes, cover my ears, and *no longer a woman myself or he a man*; no longer subject to being panic-stricken by his reproaches or overcome by tenderness and sweetness, I'd like to say to him: "Tell me who you are are, what matters to you and what you think." I'd like to come to an agreement with him intellectually without being blinded by crazy imaginings. I'd like to say to him: "I understand certain things in life this way. And you?"

They were valid considerations, and the fact was that Victoria didn't entirely regret the distraction of a trip to Europe so as to have a chance to think them over. For the two years she was abroad with her family she and Monaco kept up an irregular correspondence.

When it was decided that most of the trip would be spent in Paris, Victoria began to dream of the things she would do there to make up for the cultural isolation of Buenos Aires. It was the "Belle Epoque" in Paris and the city was thriving; Art Nouveau, Cubism, and Modernism were the new trends in arts and letters. Of course, she would go as often as she could to the Louvre, to the Comédie Française, to the quays filled with bookstalls and the cafés of the Left Bank, just as she would naturally return to the places she remembered from her childhood, like the Bois de Boulogne, the Tour Eiffel, and the Arc de Triomphe. But what she really dreamed of was the opportunity of meeting some authentic literary people, people who wrote and studied literature not because it was "snob" to do so, but because they were truly committed to it as a vocation. Maybe she would even catch a glimpse of a famous author or two. *They* were her real heroes now; the days of fictional heroes had passed.

After the family was settled in the Hotel Majestic on the Avenue Kléber, Victoria's hopes were not disappointed. Her parents agreed to let her attend some university lectures provided she was properly chaperoned. So she hastened to plan a schedule of classes at the Sorbonne and the Collège de France. Among other subjects, she studied English and ancient Greek literature, the origins of Romanticism, the history of the Orient, and the works of Dante and Nietzsche. The lectures devoted to these last two authors must have offered her a provocative contrast: the philosophy of medieval Italian Catholicism on the one hand and the philosophy of nineteenth-century German Heroic-Vitalism on the other, the power of religion versus the religion of power. Whenever she could, she attended the lectures of Henri Bergson, whose classes in philosophy were among the most popular at the Collège de France. Paris had become an intellectual banquet. If the legendary City of Lights had filled her senses as a child, it was now a feast for her hungry mind and spirit.

Her dreams of meeting literary heroes were not entirely realized, but there were some exciting moments: through a friend, she was introduced to Anatole France's personal secretary, who encouraged her to write. In Edouard Champion's bookstore one day, the famous Joseph Bédier signed her copy of the recently published *Tristan*. She never actually met Edmond Rostand, author of *Cyrano de Bergerac* (the great dramatic success of 1897), but she did become friends with his son Maurice who was staying with his parents in the same hotel as the Ocampos. Maurice had quite a crush on Victoria and he sometimes composed verses in her honor, but to no avail; she was far more interested in his father's work. Two older Argentine friends of hers, Enrique Larreta (a writer) and Carlos Reyles (the novelist's son), visited her in Paris and regaled her with stories of the literary world. However vicariously, she relished being involved with the culture of Paris.

In addition to her university courses, Victoria took piano and voice lessons. Through her voice teacher, Mlle. Germaine Sanderson, she learned to appreciate the modern music of Fauré and Debussy, who, along with Chopin and Wagner, became her favorite composers. Her preferences in music were as strongly defined as her preferences in reading; when she discovered a combination of chords or a melody she particularly liked, she would play it over and over again. What she found most wonderful about Debussy was the way in which one could recite so effectively, rather than sing, the poems he set to music. When it came to applying the right inflection to these musical recitations, she was in her element.

From their base in Paris, the Ocampos took several trips to other parts of the continent including the fashionable resort of Biarritz, where Victoria apparently found too many idle rich Argentines to suit her taste. She much preferred a journey she took with her aunt and uncle to London and then to the highlands of Scotland. The solitary, wind-blown heaths appealed to her romantic moods far more than the crowded French beaches.

Portraits and photographs taken of Victoria during these years abroad attest to her extraordinary beauty as she approached her twentieth birthday: a classic oval face, slightly arched nose, well-proportioned mouth, and large expressive eyes. Many Parisian heads must have turned to take another look at the tall (1 m., 76 cm.), auburn-haired mademoiselle as she walked along the boulevards with her sisters or went into Rumpel-mayer's to buy the chocolate she found so hard to resist. With her long legs and statuesque figure, the tailored suits and simple coiffures she chose to wear were more eye-catching than the fussier styles so popular at the time. In 1909 she posed for several drypoint etchings by Helleu, who captured her exquisite loveliness and a sensual, yet unyielding look in her eyes. An informal photograph taken of Victoria and her uncle the same year in Scotland reveals a similar romantic, slightly mysterious creature looking not unlike a heroine of a gothic novel. For a 1910 oil portrait by Dagnan Bouveret, Worth, the famous French couturier, came personally to fit a formal white gown he had designed for her. It was a regal portrait, but almost too posed and perfect. One thing was certain: the artists who painted her and the couturiers who dressed her lavished on Victoria the kind of attention reserved for women who were not only rich and elegant, but who were also rare, natural beauties.

Despite all the compliments and attention, she continued to feel like a caged bird. It didn't matter that the cage was a gilded one other women might have envied. What Victoria wanted most of all was to be free, free to explore the worlds of literature and art that her parents' way of life denied her. But she was incapable of going against their wishes, so she kept her longings to herself, exasperated as much by her emotional dependency as by their restrictions.

An Error and Its Penalty

The year of Argentina's centennial celebration—1910—marked a national reaffirmation of faith in the fatherland, then at the height of its prosperity, and a resurgence of the controversy between "nationalists" and "foreignists" over the proper course for the country's future. Among the oligarchs (who were often abroad, as was Victoria's family all during that year) and the *nouveau riche* (who made their fortunes in the economic boom of the last two decades), there was strong nationalistic sentiment. But it was motivated more by a desire to retain economic and political control over large numbers of immigrants in Argentina than by an intention of turning away from Europe as a source of cultural or economic reinforcement.[13] The consequences of this attitude, which denied immigrants certain political rights and cultural freedoms, would have to be borne by later generations.

Shortly after the Ocampos returned to Buenos Aires early in 1911, Victoria's eleven-year-old sister, Clara, contracted incurable diabetes and died after a brief illness, leaving the family stunned with grief. It was Victoria's second encounter with death in less than a year. Her great-aunt, Vitola, had passed away suddenly while they were in Paris, and Victoria, whose affection for her had been very deep, was particularly saddened by the loss. Clara's death was even more cruel and unexpected. How could Victoria help but reflect upon the tenuous quality of life and the unpredictability of the future as she lived through the long months of mourning when no social gatherings, unnecessary visits, or excursions were permitted?

During the family's bereavement, a friend asked permission, as custom required, for Monaco Estrada to call on Victoria. Ostensibly, it was a gesture of sympathy, but other sentiments, rekindled by her return to Argentina, must have also been expressed. Three or four more visits followed. One day, Victoria's father called her into his study and asked if she planned to marry Monaco. If not, he said, she ought to realize that his visits were becoming too compromising. She understood that her father's words were meant to caution her, not to push her into marriage. The decision was hers to make. It was true that Monaco was on the verge of proposing, so she pondered how she would answer.

Whether she liked to admit it or not, his physical attractiveness was an important factor; she couldn't fall in love with a man who was aesthetically displeasing to her. Beyond this, Monaco was intelligent, well-read, and sophisticated. From another perspective, it worried her that he was conservative and moralistic in outlook and that he tended to be jealous of her attentions, sometimes overly possessive. Perhaps marriage would eliminate this problem. At any rate, she was convinced that her influence would transform him into the husband she wanted. One thing was clearly true: if she were too cautious about choosing a husband, she would be trapped forever, like her unmarried great-aunts, in her parents' home. The thought was intolerable. She was past twenty-one. It was time to make a decision that had seemed inevitable since her childhood. Of course, she had no intention of making the mistakes other women did by becoming the slaves of their husbands. She would never abdicate her will, never live through another person. The reservations she had gradually gave way to her strong desire for freedom.

On November 8, 1912 she and Monaco were married. In December they left for a long honeymoon in Europe.

It was a mistake from the beginning. No sooner were they abroad than Victoria discovered that she had merely exchanged one form of captivity for another. The freedom of expression she had anticipated in marriage was illusory. Wherever they went, Monaco criticized and reprimanded her for being too independent, too interested in other people, too provocative, and too inattentive to his needs. At first he was protective, then he became tyrannical, accusing her of infidelities. According to Victoria, what he saw in her as coquettishness was largely the fabrication of his own jealousies. True, she could be willful and impetuous, and she was anything but submissive, but that had always been her nature; disloyalty was not. In, this, he misunderstood her and she resented it deeply. When he demanded that she be the conventional wife his traditional upbringing had prepared him to expect, she refused. It gave her small consolation to think that she could now read books that her parents had censored or go to shows like Diaghilev's Ballets Russes that they had labeled too risqué. Nor was there much satisfaction in finding herself the center of attraction in the most talked-about salons and spas of Europe where decadent aristocrats from all over the world lounged with ostentatious abandon. Even the excitement of being in the audience during the tumultuous debut of Igor Stravinsky's *Le Sacre du Printemps*—a work she immediately liked and played, as best she could, on their hotel piano— was clouded by her marital unhappiness. She and Monaco were hopelessly unsuited to one another.

Several arrestingly beautiful photographs of Victoria taken in 1913 show her as others must have seen her: a young and glamorous South American matron. One, taken in Rome, is a demure portrait of innocence recaptured: Victoria is wearing a broad-brimmed hat and delicate lace collar. In another she is posed provocatively in a chinchilla-lined cape and a velvet turban: the Victoria of Parisian soirées and nightclubs. A year later, Prince Paul Troubetzkoy, a noted sculptor, did a bronze statue of her in the same pose. Nowhere is there a hint of the anguish within her.

All the glamour and excitement of Europe couldn't compensate for the misery she felt in Monaco's company. Their incompatability had reached painful proportions. His efforts to control her met with explosions of outrage, doors slamming between them, and protracted silences. What angered her most was Monaco's hypocritical posturing, his obsessive concern with what others would think. It was precisely this kind of obeisance to social pressure that had kept them virtual strangers until their marriage. Had she known Monaco better beforehand, she said later, she would never have married him.

Within a year, they began to lead separate lives, though they continued to share the same residence for more than eight years. A total estrangement was impossible, not only because appearances were extremely important to Monaco but because Victoria couldn't bear to break her parents' hearts with the truth. In Catholic Argentina, divorce was neither recognized nor legally permitted (nor is it to this day). Marital separation under the same roof was often a fact of life, a necessary evil that was endured but not publicized. A broken marriage could mean social ostracism for a woman; for her family, it was an unmitigated tragedy. Victoria didn't care about the consequences for herself, but she knew that the news would have destroyed her parents' happiness, perhaps even affected her father's precarious health (he had just had a leg amputated), so she kept silent. In the summertime, she and Monaco would visit her parents in Mar del Plata in their newly built chalet, imported piece by piece from Scandinavia. They would stay in separate rooms, barely talking to one another, while her parents either ignored or pretended not to see the reality of their relationship.

Exactly what caused the irrevocable separation that made Victoria so bitter and so reluctant thereafter to discuss her marriage is not clear. It may simply have been the cumulative effect of months and years of altercation. More likely, the clash of their wills and personalities reached a point of physical violence — violence on her part as well as his.[14] Although Victoria had a fiery temper she found hard to control, she abhorred her weakness and condemned it in others. Any physical violence between her and Monaco would have ended their marriage once and for all as far as she was concerned.

After their return from Europe in 1914, they lived in a large house on Tucumán Street in the Barrio Norte, communicating only on social occasions that couldn't be avoided. Finally Victoria found the hypocrisy of their situation intolerable. Opening the door to the cage that had held her prisoner in one form or another since childhood, she declared her freedom and independence. In 1922, she rented out the Tucumán residence (which belonged to her) and moved a few things into a smaller apartment on Montevideo Street. They eventually obtained a legal separation.

Art for Life's Sake

Between 1913 and 1922, then, Victoria lived with the private knowledge that her marriage was over and that she would have to reconstruct her life on her own. To have confided in her parents would not only have been painful but pointless; the values they lived by and respected had ceased to have meaning for her. Nor did religion provide her with a refuge. Catholicism as she knew it did not correspond to the image of God that she carried inside her; the narrowness of its dogma and the pettiness of its clergy, in her experience, did not reflect what she felt was God's truth. She could not accept the impersonal liturgy of church services or the concept of intermediaries between man and God. Although she was not able to define exactly what her beliefs were, the intense need she felt for God was very real to her. She was a believer without a religion; in the lonely unhappiness of those years, she felt more and more pressed to find spiritual guidance.

A curious and revealing document survives from this period of her life. In August 1914, an Argentine historian and graphologist, Roberto Levillier, analyzed a sample of Victoria's handwriting with no prior knowledge of her. His analysis, originally written in French, is uncannily accurate. It is too detailed to quote in full, but one paragraph describing her religious sentiments merits quoting:

> The religiosity perceptible in her is not so much the need to believe as that of a love of nature, of beauty in all its forms. She is not irreligious, she is

indevout. Mystery exercises a secondary attraction for her; she does not like half-tones or indecision; she loves radiant light, vibrant strength and joy. That is why she can be vehement, impulsive and even brutal, and yet she can experience to a very high degree the most delicate and shaded sentiments. She is capable of the greatest and most constant abnegation — by nature not by reflection or sense of duty. She does not have the sense of duty. She is rebellious, independent and does not like or accept any yoke.[15]

However Levillier had accomplished it, he managed to capture the essence of Victoria's personality.

Living in the shadows of half-truth until 1922 was a constant torment for Victoria. She felt adrift on a dark sea, off course, alone. With the exception of a very few close friendships, she had no outlet for the turmoil she felt inside her, no source of guidance, no direction. So, as in her youth, she turned to writing:

In my childhood, adolescence and first blush of youth, I used to live in books what I couldn't live in life, because life was full of absurd taboos for a young girl in those days. Later, I lived in life what I had read about earlier in literature, and the literature paled in comparison. There was no alternative but to tell, in a more or less direct manner, what I had lived. What I had lived brought me to write and to read, not vice-versa. At the beginning of my life, I discovered that writing was a kind of unburdening. Later, I found that it was a way of learning and ordering my inner world. I don't know what "art for art's sake" is. I do know what life for life's sake is. And art for life's sake, or as a translation of life (although a book may be called fiction). I don't know how to write novels or stories because I never "invent." Everything I live is an "invention" from which I've never been able to escape. Nor do I know who has invented me; since I'm not capable of inventing, someone is inventing for me: someone is inventing me.[16]

For Victoria, life is a drama—as Calderón and Shakespeare also suggest— whose ultimate significance cannot be known though it *is* possible to recognize the nature of one's own role and play it authentically or falsely.

Her earliest essays—first-person commentaries on reading that had captured her interest and echoed thoughts of her own—were published in 1920 in *La Nación*, one of the two most respected daily papers in Buenos Aires. Making her debut as an author was a fitting way to celebrate her thirtieth birthday. Despite her excitement, however, she didn't tell her parents about it beforehand: "For a single much less a married woman to publish an article, let alone a book," she has said, "was looked upon with disapproval here, as in the era of the Brontë sisters. There was no better way of getting pilloried and so no parents dared to wish that fate on their daughter."[17] When her father and mother learned of her first publication, they reserved judgment, still apprehensive about her future. "My parents were as afraid for me of the road that I proposed to follow," Victoria remembers, "as they would have been for a son intent on exploring a country of cannibals. They expected something else of me and I was disillusioning them by substituting my dream for theirs."[18]

To be published in *La Nación* in those days was no mean feat, even for a man. As the Argentine author and critic David Viñas has said: "To write for *La Nación,* to become 'a man of *La Nación,*' was an ideal in life that was beginning to catch on and a special kind of social validation for intellectuals. A 'literary career' was confirmed only by a newspaper job or at least by a position as correspondent."[19] Of course, no one talked of becoming "a woman of *La Nación.*" At that time, the Argentine literary world was dominated by men; women who wrote were a rarity and were generally not accorded membership in the "society" of serious profes-sional authors. It is not clear whether it was with a tone of conciliation or of condescension that the editors of *La Nación* commented in parentheses above Victoria's first article, published on April 4, 1920, on her "explain-able but unjustified reserve" in not sending them some of her work sooner. The article, they said, revealed talent.

In one of those first articles, Victoria described the unique empathy that she felt toward certain books and authors:

> Certain books awaken us suddenly to the sense of finding a treasure that belongs to us. This is why we ingenuously cry out: "How good it is! It's exactly what I think!" This doesn't mean that one knows as much as the author. It means that there existed dormant in us—and certainly on a less intense level—thoughts and feelings that the author has had the intelli-gence, the passion, the power and the talent to drag out from the dark and dreamy recesses of his heart and spirit in order to explain them to himself first, and then to us.[20]

One of the books that led to what would become for her a treasure beyond calculation was Dante Alighieri's *Divina Commedia.* Her first encounter with it—more an emotional than an intellectual experience—left a deep impression on her as an adolescent:

> I had just turned sixteen when my Italian teacher made me read some passages of the *Inferno.* The impression which that reading made on me is only comparable to what I felt as a very young child when, bathing in the ocean for the first time, I was caught up and tumbled down on the sand by the magnificent force of a wave.[21]

Later, while searching for spiritual comfort and guidance after the failure of her marriage, she returned to the sonorous verses of the exiled Floren-tine, remembering that he too had lost his way in the dark woods of life and feared for his soul's salvation. She read and reread how he had been guided to the ultimate truth, first by Virgil, then by Beatrice, a symbol of love's spiritually redeeming power. Dante understood that the hunger for wholeness which passionate physical love inspires can only truly be satisfied by another kind of love, "l'amor che muove il sol e l'altre stelle," a love that goes beyond the disillusionments of human imperfections and seeks refuge in divine peace and harmony.

His poem motivated her to write her first published article, "Babel," in which she discussed a concept that had long preoccupied her: the equality and inequality of human beings. Legally, all people should have equal rights and opportunities in society, she affirmed. This was the true meaning of a democracy. However—and she cited Dante as her authority — not all people are born with equal talents. Dante acknowledged in Canto XV of the *Purgatorio* ("quanto natura a sentir te despuose . . .") the necessary existence of different levels of perfection. "This means," Victoria wrote, "that nature puts more sensitivity in others than in you, and yet, in others, less."[22] Dante's viewpoint can be linked to a tradition as old as Plato's *Republic* or the Hebraic concept of "messiah." Although Victoria didn't say so, the Florentine poet furnished her with the intellectual reinforcement she needed to justify her own sense of "differentness." She was, she had felt since adolescence, more sensitive than most people, more given to expressing her own preferences, on the one hand, and admiring those of her heroes, on the other. She knew that she was a nonconformist—certainly in comparison to other young women around her—and she sensed that it came largely from demanding more of herself, from having a greater desire for perfection (*voluntad de perfección*). Where this desire came from she did not know; it must be part of the preordained script that determines each individual drama.

After "Babel," Victoria decided to write a longer interpretation of the whole *Commedia*, tracing its major theme as she understood it. She didn't intend it to be a lengthy, erudite treatise, but rather a brief "Baedeker" or guidebook for common readers who had not yet discovered Dante's masterpiece. In fact, she meant its writing to be as much a learning tool for herself as a service to others. It would be ready, she hoped, in time to coincide with the six-hundredth anniversary of the poet's death.

The title of her short book, *De Francesca a Beatrice*, indicates the direction and focus of her study: how Dante, in the course of his journey from encountering Francesca in hell to joining Beatrice in paradise, undergoes a critical development in his understanding of the "intelligence of love" (*la inteligencia de amor*). From the earthly, physical passion of Francesca, whose soul is forever tormented by floating aimlessly beside Paolo on the winds of desire, to the transcendent, spiritual love of Beatrice, which has the power to redeem the repentant sinner, Dante discovers the various kinds of love that exist in the universe. He learns that the spirit can triumph over "false appearances" (*falso imaginar*) and thereby achieve freedom and the knowledge of truth.

When she finished her book, it occurred to Victoria that she might ask her father's friend Paul Groussac, the director of the National Library and a notoriously severe critic, for his opinion. So she took a portion of her manuscript to him, fully expecting his blunt criticism. What she didn't expect, however, was his complete misunderstanding of her intentions as a writer: he advised her to write about a less pedantic, more personal subject. She was shocked. Nothing could have been more personal for her at the moment than the *Commedia,* her spiritual companion. But Groussac was unable to see this, blinded as he was by the conventional notion that women should devote themselves to only certain kinds of writing (novels, poetry, memoirs) provided they were appropriately "feminine" in inspiration. The implication, of course, was that no woman — and certainly not one lacking scholarly training — could possibly have anything worthwhile to say about such profound subjects as Dante's *Commedia.* No one liked a *marisabilidilla* (a know-it-all), and as the Spanish saying goes: *Mujer que sabe latín, ni tiene marido ni buen fin* (A woman who knows Latin won't find a husband or a happy ending). This, essentially, was Groussac's criticism.

Victoria knew his reaction was prejudiced and unfair; just the same, it made her have second thoughts about a literary career. Fortunately, a friend whom she loved, *not* a writer himself, provided the encouragement she needed to persevere. She made up her mind to keep going, against all odds if need be, ignoring the criticism of those who treated her as Groussac had. Her writing would certainly be personal, but not in the sense he suggested; she would not limit herself to so-called feminine subjects. She would personalize her writing by saying honestly and directly what she believed and how she felt about her discoveries. She would be a witness. She would testify.

CHAPTER THREE

WIDENING HORIZONS

The Groussac episode was Victoria's initiation into the hazards of being an author in the often unpredictable and sometimes unjust world of literary criticism. Her resolution to continue writing her own way was an act of self-affirmation. She wasn't disillusioned about all men just because one of them had misjudged her; that would have been an error of the same magnitude as Groussac's. Male authors continued to be her literary heroes and mentors to whom she looked for knowledge and self-improvement. As she once explained, it was the only way she knew of approaching literature: "There are people who cannot live without admiring and for whom admiration means hero-worship."[1] Good literature was what she admired most and most writers were men, so it was inevitable that they would become the heroes she idolized in her own fashion.

Three authors —José Ortega y Gasset, Rabindranath Tagore, and Count Hermann Keyserling—became Victoria's heroes during the 1920s. Each one had a profound influence on her personal and literary development. Directly or indirectly, they helped her achieve insights that her upbringing and education had denied her. Her personal relationships with them—developed largely by her own initiative—opened her eyes to fundamental problems of the dialectic between the sexes in a way that her previous experience with men had not revealed to her.

They were friendships, not sexual relationships. During the time Victoria came to know these authors, she was very much in love with another man, a lawyer by profession. Because she was not legally divorced, she told almost no one about him; a man whom she has called her only true husband, he understood her literary needs and encouraged her to fulfill them, whether it involved writing, reading, or having close friendships with other men. Their relationship continued for many years and meant a great deal to Victoria, especially after the disastrous failure of her marriage. Her devotion to this man during the years she met Ortega, Tagore, and Keyserling precluded, as far as she was concerned, any other sexual liaisons. Even after he and she had amicably parted ways in the 1930s, no other man ever inspired in her the same complete love as she had known with him.

All three authors were attracted to her beauty, character, and intelligence, and expressed their feelings for her in their writing. She touched their lives as they did hers. For them, Victoria Ocampo was not only a lovely and talented woman; she was a feminine archetype, a muse. Unlike other legendary muses of history, however, Victoria has left written testimony of her friendship with each one of them and how it affected her.

José Ortega y Gasset

In 1916 when he came to Buenos Aires for the first time on a lecture tour, Ortega had already established his reputation as an intellectual leader in Spain. Born into a family of journalists and politicians, Ortega was educated in Germany in the neo-Kantian school of philosophy. From 1910 until the outbreak of the Spanish Civil War in 1936, he occupied the Chair of Metaphysics at the University of Madrid, though he was better known to the public as a prolific essayist who wrote for numerous newspapers and magazines, some of which he himself founded. The most notable was his review, *Revista de Occidente*, with a publishing house of the same name. In 1914, he published his first major book, *Meditaciones del Quijote*, which influenced the thinking of an entire generation; his later works included *España invertebrada* (1920), *El tema de nuestro tiempo* (1923), and *La rebelión de las masas* (1930).

If his contemporary, Miguel de Unamuno, was recognized as the philosopher of a Spanish-oriented Spain, concerned primarily with the eternal question of man's relationship to God, Ortega y Gasset was the philosopher of a European-oriented Spain who proclaimed that the Old Spain was dying and a New Spain would have to be created under the influence of foreign ideas. Renovation was a word he used frequently, and progressive intellectuals who were bothered by Spain's official neutrality during the War of 1914 listened.

In his early works, Ortega began to outline a philosophy that has been called Perspectivism by some, Existential Relativism by others. He spoke of the interplay between man and his circumstance; life does not just happen, he said, it must be created by each individual who has the vital responsibility to build it and choose its direction in accordance with his own authentic reality. Neither purely subjective nor deterministic, Ortega's philosophy emphasized the importance of creative individual action. Although he had not fully developed all of these ideas in 1916 when he addressed large Argentine audiences, Ortega's message of intellectual liberalism created a stir that had long-range repercussions. Those who heard him speak knew that they had not only been fortunate to hear one of Europe's exceptional minds but also one of its most expressive and persuasive public speakers.

It was after his lecture tour was concluded that he and Victoria were introduced at a dinner party in Buenos Aires. As they faced each other for the first time, Ortega was the one who had to look up at the Amazon-like beauty who greeted him with polite reserve. Victoria has recalled that she was only vaguely interested in meeting the famous Spanish professor, who was cordial but rather proud in manner—a typical Spanish trait, she thought. "I had heard continuous praise of him as a speaker and a thinker, but to tell the truth," she later confessed, "none of that captured my curiosity. I was involved in something else (or so I thought). I felt no particular attraction at that time to Spanish literature. French and English monopolized me." [2] When Ortega began to speak with quiet assurance and eloquence, her attitude changed. Listening to him that evening, and on many occasions thereafter before he left for Madrid, Victoria realized that a foolish prejudice had blinded her:

> In him I discovered Spain. A dazzling Spain. It was too late to listen to his lectures, as the series had ended. I couldn't believe I had missed them! But I had occasion to talk with Ortega, or rather, to hear him talk, and I've never heard anything like it since. I was *médusée* by his talent, which I noticed right away, though he didn't seem to believe it [. . . .] "Folded up inside myself," Ortega later described me. I should say so! After a short while, I wanted to disappear. I was inhibited by the surprise of finding myself with someone like that and would have liked to hide in a corner like Cinderella and listen to him from there. [3]

Ortega's eloquent command of Spanish had the effect of a revelation that was not without its irony: he was a Spaniard who advocated the Europeanization of Spain, yet he convinced her that her own Europeanization might be depriving her of part of her native heritage. Her education, which had neglected Spanish in favor of French and English culture, had caused her to be unjustly biased against the language of her own country.

Victoria was only one of a whole generation of middle and upper class Argentines who were raised with a distinctly cosmopolitan outlook that reflected the international flavor of their capital and the large numbers of immigrants who were flocking to it at the turn of the century. Among some wealthy aristocrats it was even suggested that anything "native" was inferior, though certainly this was not what Sarmiento had in mind when he encouraged more European and North American influence in Argentina.[4] The idea of enriching the national culture by replacing it with another was an easy step for some snobbish Argentines; Victoria's family had never gone this far. They did believe, however, as did the parents of many future writers such as Ricardo Güiraldes or Jorge Luis Borges that a European education was an undeniable asset and that fluency in foreign languages was essential to being well-educated. Families who could afford it took their children to Europe; as a result, as children, Güiraldes spoke French and Borges English, better than Spanish. Later in life, both of these writers found themselves hailed for their profoundly Argentine literature, for works of art that would undoubtedly have been impossible without their earlier international experience.

Victoria was the product of the same cultural attitudes, though many of her compatriots who have "forgiven" Güiraldes and Borges their "foreignness" have been less sympathetic toward her. Possibly it was because she never wrote a national best-seller. Perhaps it was because she was wealthier, a woman, and eventually, a kind of literary high-priestess. It may have been a combination of all of these. In any event, Victoria was accused of being *extranjerizante*, a "foreignizer," because she preferred to write in French. It was a habit that began to take hold in her childhood and had become ingrained by the time she was an adult. Whenever she and her friends got together in Buenos Aires, they discussed literary and artistic subjects in French; they would also write one another primarily in French. Because Spanish was neglected on an intellectual level, Victoria didn't have the ability to use it with as much nuance as French. Except in practical conversations, Spanish sounded stiff and artificial to her. "Any attempt at writing Spanish," she said, "was like the writing of a left-hander who is forced to use his right hand."[5]

It was her contact with Ortega in 1916 and the admiration she felt for his eloquent Spanish that made her understand what she has described as a uniquely American (Latin American) drama with its own tragic irony:

> What I am most interested in saying must be said here in my country and in a language familiar to all. What I write in French is not French in a certain sense, in terms of its spirit. And yet—this is my drama—I feel that Spanish words will never come to me spontaneously, especially when I am moved emotionally, when I need them most. I shall always be a prisoner of another language whether I like it or not, because that is where my soul became acclimatized. This circumstance has produced strange effects. I fear that if I were to succeed in yanking out of my memory all the French words, I would

also yank out, attached to them, the most precious, most authentic, and most American images I possess.[6]

There is a Proustian flavor to those lines written in 1931: one's language, like one's memory, is connected emotionally and psychologically to the milieu in which it is formed. Victoria's French had as much of Buenos Aires as Paris in its associations.

The passage of time has eased this problem for her, but it was a painful process just the same. After years of writing in French and later translating her work—or having someone else translate it and feeling that part of herself had been lost in the translation—she began to write in Spanish in the 1930s, not all at once but bit by bit. As a result, her way of writing and speaking Spanish is intensely personal, a hybrid cultivation like herself. Whenever she feels that an expression in another language will convey her idea more accurately, she won't hesitate to use it. On the other hand, she is a faithful defender of "Americanisms," indigenous words that neither Ortega nor the Spanish Academy would condone as pure Spanish. "She's a true criolla," said her friend, María Rosa Oliver, and other Argentines who know her, or are beginning to understand her more fully, agree.

After their first meeting, Ortega visited Victoria's home on Tucumán Street on several occasions, usually for dinner and hours of conversation. Their growing friendship also precipitated an exchange of letters in which they shared further thoughts and reflections. Some of Ortega's letters contained eloquent declarations of affection which Victoria found very flattering but not irresistible. They were close friends; she wanted nothing more. When Ortega persisted, Victoria admitted to him that there was another man in her life, and then Ortega said something petulant that offended her. At the time, she thought his remark unpardonable. Reflecting upon it nearly fifty years later, it seemed insignificant, a natural occurrence between two people who cared for one another.

In her anger at the time, however, Victoria tore up the letters Ortega had written to her while he was in Buenos Aires. From Spain in July 1917, he sent her a long letter of explanation, trying to coax her forgiveness. Part of the letter contained a reminiscence of a special evening they had spent together. A less implacable heart than Victoria's might have relented at these words:

The hope or dream of drawing you into a special friendship would never have come to me spontaneously, of its own accord. Similar reasons prevent me from thinking that the canvas painted by Leonardo [the Mona Lisa] could ever be here in my room, hanging in front of my desk. But that night there were two incredible moments . . . One: in your library. I was standing there and you were also standing nearby. Full of curiosity, I took a glance at your books—and, at the same time, I caught you looking at my glance—not at me, Victoria, at my glance. Like a seed that opens and begins to germinate, I suddenly had this unexpected thought: "But what is this? . . . This woman! . . . one could say she has understood me, profoundly understood me!"—The other moment: at the end of the evening, when I was leaving, there you were leaning on a chair with the "Double jardin" in your hand. I don't quite know what it was about you, but I do know that I said to myself: "There's no room for doubt! This Mona Lisa has understood me completely, to my very roots . . . She will never ever confuse me with anyone else . . . How strange it is! She *knows* me by heart . . . She likes my way of deforming the banality of things that life throws at our feet, my way of giving them a new life, dancing and rhythmic . . . She has discovered that to Live, for me, is a matter of style . . . and that she could all of a sudden design with her *finger* the movement of *my* style."

In my hotel room the whole night long, it seemed to me that a dream pearl was giving forth its pale, thoughtful brilliance. . . .

Still, Victoria would not forgive his indiscretion: "He was put out by it, and so was I, but since I was younger, more impulsive and more intransigent, I was more upset. Fully aware of what I was losing by losing a friend of his importance, I nevertheless determined to show him my frame of mind by maintaining a total epistolary silence."[7] Her silence, despite generous overtures from Ortega, lasted eleven years.

Ortega made another conciliatory gesture, albeit indirectly, by publishing in one of his essays a portion of a letter Victoria had written to him while he was in Buenos Aires. The essay concerned the Spanish author "Azorín" (José Martínez Ruiz), and his way of giving the small things of life new meaning. In her letter, Victoria had consulted Ortega on the subject of literary criticism, confiding to him that she could never interpret a book impersonally because she only responded to books that helped her understand herself. Ortega answered her in his essay; without identifying her by name, he praised her inclinations, but he also alluded to their misunderstanding and chided her privately by saying:

Señora, your way of reading is not unjust or unlawful, but there is no need to assure you of this. In the first place, because a woman capable of writing and thinking with so much gracefulness certainly does not get upset when she commits an injustice. In the second place, because it is, in effect, the only way to read that exists. The rest . . . is erudition.[8]

Then, referring to the concept of *sinfronismo* (an expression coined by Goethe meaning a coincidence of feeling, tone, or style between persons or circumstances of any era) that he had been developing in relation to

Azorín, Ortega reassured her with this generous comment in his characteristic metaphorical style:

> . . . I know well that you are an intrepid huntress of resonances and affinities—of *sinfronismos*, and that, like Diana in every way, you travel the world, rapidly and elegantly, inciting the greyhounds of your feelings.[9]

When Victoria read this essay by "the Spectator," as Ortega called himself, she understood the combination of positive and negative provocation to be his way of communicating with her. Still, she did not reply.

It was well known in literary circles that Ortega was inclined to be protective and encouraging toward young authors whom he considered promising. He would watch over them, offer paternal advice, and help them publish their work when it met with his rigorous standards.[10] This may explain, in part, why in 1924, Ortega's Revista de Occidente press published Victoria's monograph on Dante, *De Francesca a Beatrice,* and why, two years later, he also published a dramatic fairy tale she had written titled *La laguna de los nenúfares* (The Water-Lily Pond). These were acts of unsolicited generosity on Ortega's part that were all the more noticeable considering Victoria's stubborn silence. On January 6, 1921 Ortega had written a letter to an Argentine friend, Sra. Isolina G. de Zubiaurre, who was on her way to Spain:

> If you will be as kind as always, I shall ask you to bring me clippings of all the articles that Sra. Ocampo de Estrada has published after her "Babel." Her extraordinary style is, without a doubt, the only one that is capable of intriguing me by suggestion in the midst of the terrible literary inertia that the world is suffering today.

This confession leaves little doubt that Ortega was genuinely impressed by Victoria's literary talents.

When he published *De Francesca a Beatrice* (translated from the French by Ricardo Baeza), Ortega took the unusual step of appending an epilogue he had written to Victoria's text. It was like an open letter to her, not an essay of literary criticism, and it occupied nearly a third of the book's pages. His opening words were:

> Señora: The excursion has been delightful. You have guided us marvelously through this triple avenue of trembling tercets, placing here and there, with a delicate gesture, an insinuating accent that gives a new perspective to an old spectacle. Of course, sometimes our glance left Dante's figures to contemplate your gestures which, after all, was what the poet often did with his own preferred guide. What can one do! A possibly immoderate appetite for the present made me prefer over the old spectacle, genial but bloodless, this new one that is the reflection of the other in you. I don't think that even

Dante reincarnate would find reason to censure me. He was too much a doctor of voluptuousness to overlook the double delight which, at times, means not looking at the world head-on but rather obliquely, reflected in the variations of another countenance.[11]

The memory of Victoria's beauty and sensitivity was more vivid to Ortega than the poetry she wrote about. In spite of her rejection, he could not help complimenting her effusively: "You are, Señora, an exemplary apparition of femininity. In your person the rarest perfections converge with radiant grace."[12] As he evokes her, Victoria becomes another Beatrice—a norm, an ideal, without which, says Ortega, no man can function as a vital human being: "To a human being, excitation or stimulation is primordial. All else depends on it to the point that one could say: To live is to be stimulated."[13]

This leads Ortega to a discussion of the role of the female in history, a subject that for him, as for many intelligent men of his time, was predicated on the belief that the male and female possessed attitudes and aptitudes totally distinct from one another. Ortega was undoubtedly influenced by the neo-Kantian theories of Otto Weininger's *Geschlecht und Charakter* (Sex and Character) (1903), an enormously popular and influential German work that rejected an empirical approach to the study of sex roles in favor of identifying the ideal type of Man and Woman as archetypal abstractions, defining them in terms of traditional philosophical dualisms: male-female, subject-object, logos-eros. Weininger, intransigently patriarchal in matters of sex, often confused his notion of Woman as an absolute with his assessment of women in general; moreover, he refused to examine social or economic factors that might have been responsible for women's subordinate role in society.[14]

With similar dualistic definitions, Ortega points out in his epilogue that the male's highest function is *doing* (*hacer*) while the female's is *being* (*ser*), activity versus passivity, public achievement versus private inspiration.[15] Although he acknowledges that all human beings possess a combination of masculine and feminine traits, Ortega has little sympathy for masculine women; Salome, who asked for and got the head of John the Baptist, was, Ortega wrote a few years earlier, "a deformation of femininity," since the essence of femininity is to give oneself to another person, "because the woman normally imagines and fantasizes less than the man, and thus her easier adaptation to the destiny that is imposed on her."[16]

According to Ortega's epilogue, "progress for woman consists in making herself more perfect, creating in herself a new type of more delicate and more demanding femininity," for her "supreme mission on earth is to demand, to demand perfection from the man."[17] Ortega's theory, reminiscent of the Neoplatonic concept of love as an ennobling force, is that woman must represent an ideal to which man can aspire; she must be the soul, he the body, though to Ortega, "soul" was to be understood in the emotive, not the intellectual sense. Intellect (espíritu) is a masculine trait, he wrote in another essay in the same year: "If, among adults, we compare woman to man, it is easy to see that in her the soul predominates, followed by the body, but rarely involving the intellect."[18] He believed that a woman has an intuitive "magical power to enchant" whereby she can inspire and mold the ideal man. With this intangible power, he says in the epilogue, more tangible ones are unnecessary:

> It is incredible that there are minds so blind as to admit that woman might influence history by means of the electoral vote or the university doctoral degree as much as she influences it by this magical power of illusion that she possesses.[19]

The demanding woman, with her "magical power," can bring about an apocalyptic rebirth in the course of history. As Ortega dramatically describes it:

> . . . the hearts of men will begin to beat to a new rhythm, unsuspected ideas will awaken in their minds, new ambitions, projects, undertakings will furrow vital spaces, all of existence will begin to march in rhythm and, in the fortunate country where that femininity appears, a historic spring, a whole "vita nuova," will bloom forth triumphant.[20]

Naturally, such heroic undertakings will be the province of men. Women, on their pedestals, must be content to be silent partners, inspirational goddesses.

The potential of each country can thus be enhanced, in Ortega's opinion, by the ideal aspirations of its women. Argentina, with women like Victoria Ocampo, "a Mona Lisa of the Southern Hemisphere," as Ortega calls her, could rectify the "bad hygiene of ideas" in vogue and create a new type of man by stimulating a "new health" whereby the body (man) serves as a counterbalance to the soul (woman): "I believe that the integration of feeling, this effort to join the soul with the body," he concludes, "is the mission of our age."[21]

Ortega's mystical, almost religious concept of the role of woman in history was evidently the outcome of a powerful combination of cultural and historical influences: a Spanish upbringing and a German education. Women's existence, he felt, should be devoted to the service of man, to the embodiment of a transcendent ideal which, mirrorlike, would reflect the perfection of man. The ideal woman, as he described her, had no independent reality: "The radical perfection of man — not just his improvement in the sciences, the arts or politics—has customarily come to him by looking at the infinite through a feminine soul, a crystalline medium where great concrete ideals are reflected."[22]

Victoria's reactions to Ortega's epilogue were decidedly mixed. She was grateful that he had published her monograph and had chosen to add an epilogue; she knew it was a gesture of friendship and an expression of his faith in her abilities. It was evident, however, that he saw her potential more as a *femme inspiratrice* than as an author, and it bothered Victoria to think that, once again, a valued critic's judgment might be clouded by an unconscious sexist attitude. The role Ortega assigned to women was offensive to her, but she also knew that he meant what he wrote in the epilogue as flattery, not as deprecation. In the end, she may have been relieved that they were not on speaking terms. She steadfastly maintained her silence until Ortega's second lecture tour of Argentina in 1928, at which time their friendship was renewed.

In 1931, she finally decided to reply to Ortega's epilogue. Knowing how sensitive he was and how easily his masculine pride could be wounded, she avoided the kind of direct confrontation that might have alienated him. Instead, she focused on what he had referred to as "a bad hygiene of ideals" in the world and the need to strike a new balance of body and soul. She agreed with his assessment, she said, but she suggested that the desired objective could best be accomplished by ensuring that relationships between men and women were based "on mutual respect and mutual independence."[23] Possessiveness, jealousy, oppression — tyranny in all its forms — must cease; today's excessively corporeal vision of the world must give way to a more healthy morality.

Two years later, Victoria wrote another essay, originally delivered as a lecture in Buenos Aires and later in Madrid. In it she attacked Ortega's antifeminism more directly. It was a lecture on the work of the French poet, Anna de Noailles, whom Ortega had identified as an exception to the general rule that women lacked the aptitude for great poetry. By nature, he said in an essay lauding Mme. de Noailles in 1923, women were not given to expressing themselves openly and sincerely, as poetry required: "That mechanism of sincerity which moves one to poetry, that tossing outwards of what is intimate, is always forced in a woman, and if it is effective, if it's not a fictitious confession, it has a cynical flavor."[24] (He made no effort to explain why women in general might be less inclined to public openness. It was merely a fact, as far as he was concerned.) Referring to this opinion of Ortega's, but also thinking of his epilogue, Victoria let some of the thoughts that had been smoldering inside her rise to the surface in 1933:

> What I gather to be on the tip of the Spectator's pen does not seem to me to have the indestructible force of conviction. This is not because I doubt for a

moment the power of the scrutinizing glance that Ortega casts over the most diverse kinds of topics, but in this particular case, isn't he at a slight disadvantage? In the first place, because he's a man, and secondly, because, although he may be a European by virtue of his privileged intelligence and a citizen of the world by virtue of his roots, he is Spanish by instinct. Thus, to the fatalities of his sex are added those of his nationality. Let's not forget that there are motives behind the Spanish expression: "A queen of Spain must not look out the window." One can very well think that there should be no more queens in Spain without thereby ceasing to believe that queens must not look out of windows. But this contains a contradiction that would bother me if I were more given to discourse. I wish it would bother Ortega so he would be obliged to clarify the point for us. I fear that, in a certain sense, all women are, for him, queens of Spain.[25]

When he learned of her remarks, Ortega communicated through a third party that he was sorely wounded by them. His reaction calls to mind Virginia Woolf's metaphor of the looking-glass: if a woman criticizes a man and begins to tell the truth, "the figure in the looking-glass shrinks; his fitness for life is diminished. How is he to go on giving judgment, civilising natives, making laws, writing books, dressing up and speechifying at banquets, unless he can see himself at breakfast and at dinner at least twice the size he really is?"[26] As a concession to their friendship, Victoria deleted the passages that offended him when the Revista de Occidente published her essay on Mme. de Noailles in her first volume of essays in 1935. Privately, she confided to a friend that Ortega's views on women were disturbingly similar to those of the Fascists who were gaining more and more power in Europe.[27]

Ortega's second visit to Argentina in 1928 was even more of an event than his first, and this time Victoria was more closely involved. It occurred during a period of intense national introspection brought on in part by South American disenchantment with the recent war in Europe and its after-effects, and in part by an increasing threat of influence from the Colossus of the North. Ortega, with his provocative and often blunt outsider's assessment of Argentina, acted as a catalyst for many South American writers who began to publish works reacting to his ideas or their diffused impact. In the philosophy of this highly respected Spanish thinker—a philosophy that stressed the interaction between man and his circumstance—the Old World had once again brought enlightenment to the New. As one intellectual historian put it:

The implications of Ortega's fundamental position were tremendous in the context of the Spanish American intellectual scene of the 1920s. Budding philosophers could take heart in the knowledge that their efforts now had a validity undreamed of a few years earlier; and the careful investigation of the 'circumstance' — in all its aspects — acquired fresh significance and greater urgency.[28]

During both his visits to Argentina, Ortega was more impressed with the qualities of Argentine women—judged according to his standards of perfection — than with those of Argentine men. In 1916 he had seen a symbol of the vitality of the Argentine nation and its potential for self-realization in Victoria and her women friends. As he wrote in his epilogue in 1924:

Eight years ago, Señora, when I was concluding my stay in Argentina, I had the honor of meeting you and your women friends [Lía Sansimena de Gálvez, Bebé Sansimena de Elizalde, Nina Sansimena, and Julia del Carril de Vergara]. I shall never forget the impression made on me at finding that group of essential women standing out against the background of a young nation. There was in you such enthusiasm for perfection, such excellent and demanding taste, so much fervor for acquiring knowledge that each one of our circular conversations left a kind of moral weight on my spirit.[29]

Ortega developed these ideas further in two essays published in 1929 after his second visit: "La pampa, promesas" (The Pampa, Promises) and "El hombre a la defensiva" (Man on the Defensive). In both, he specifically charged Argentine men with being shallow and insincere, qualities he attributed to a feeling of insecurity brought on by the nature of the ever-receding horizon of the pampas that surrounded them. His interpretation of the men he met on his visit, an interpretation as highly generalized as that of the women, to be sure, was uncompromisingly frank:

We do not perceive in them a spontaneous existence. Their conduct seems to us in part too childish and in part too affected to be sincere. All in all, we note a lack of authenticity. Their words and gestures are not produced as if emanating directly from an intimate vitality but rather as if manufactured expressly for external use.[30]

Ortega's criticism provoked a furor of resentment in the Argentine public. To be criticized by an outsider was difficult to accept; criticism from a Spaniard was almost unbearable. The press gave considerable attention to his essays and suggested that he had betrayed the warm welcome Argentina had shown him wherever he went. When Ortega learned of this negative reaction—Victoria was the first to inform him—he wrote another essay, published, like the other two, in *La Nación*, explaining that his criticism was motivated by his love for Argentina and his desire to be constructive:

The Argentine must be called to achieve his authentic self, he must be brought back to the rigorous discipline of being himself, of immersing himself in the hard task set forth by his individual destiny.[31]

This Germanic rather than Spanish tone of warning to Argentina reflected a fundamental tenet of Ortega's philosophy: there can be no authentic life without dedication to an authentic vocation. It was what he called man's "vital imperative."[32] Argentina would never achieve realization as a nation, he believed, until certain unpleasant truths about the Argentine character were faced and dealt with openly. Only then could a philosophy suitable to the Argentine reality be formulated and dependence upon Europe ended.

Perhaps because she had a similar breadth of vision, free from xenophobic sensitivities, Victoria was one of the first Argentines to acknowledge publicly the justice of Ortega's criticism and to respond to it with an essay probing the Argentine character. Entitled "Quiromancia de la pampa" (Palmistry of the Pampa), it was written in December 1929. It is one of her earliest and best essays, not only because it is so characteristic in its frankness and its perceptive observations, but also because it expresses the strongly Argentine side of Victoria, the side often overlooked by those who called her a "foreignizer." She wrote it after returning from her first trip abroad in many years. While in Europe, she confessed, she felt like "the owner of a soul without a passport, a soul that I would leave upon entering any conversation just as I leave my umbrella at the entrance of museums."[33] Her familiarity with the languages and cultures of the Old World notwithstanding, she acknowledged that she felt "different" there and that Ortega's criticism helped to explain why. Most Argentines, she observed, don't recognize the source of the problem:

> It is rare that a talented Argentine doesn't realize in his first encounter with Europe that he occupies a significantly inferior level to that attained by a European who is less talented but more energetic and clearly more disciplined than he. This discovery is upsetting and depressing. By reaction, we accuse the Europeans of injustice toward us. Actually, we are the ones who are unjust with ourselves because we don't try to deserve the gifts that fortune has given us gratuitously.[34]

She reminded her fellow Argentines that Ortega was not the only foreigner to visit them in the last year or so with important truths to share. The North American writer, Waldo David Frank, had just completed a triumphant lecture tour of South America, and Victoria had responded to his message as eagerly as she had to Ortega's. Now she called for more enlightenment of the same kind: "We need to be brought clarity, come from where it may, from ourselves or from our neighbor."[35]

Not all Argentines shared her receptivity to foreign influences. Some who called themselves "cultural nationalists" said Argentine culture would be diluted and eventually weakened by importations from Europe and North America. To them, then and many times thereafter, Victoria replied that excellence in any area of national culture becomes, by definition, international and enduring. "I also believe," she has said, "that there's no reason to fear the influence of wisdom from other lands if we're capable of digesting it and converting it into our own substance."[36]

Ortega's constant concern for her personal and professional welfare is reflected in his correspondence with Victoria during this period. Both the tone and content of his letters show that he considered her not only a friend whose letters delighted him with their descriptions of people and places—to the point that he wished he could publish one or two—but that he also considered her a committed intellectual and a talented writer. His letters to her are masterpieces of their genre, at times poetic, often humorous, always stimulating and eloquent. Ortega never tired of encouraging "Niké" or his "gigantic criolla," as he would affectionately call her, to develop her potential to the fullest. One letter, addressed to her in Paris in 1930 when she was mulling over the considerable challenge of founding a literary review, stands out from the others for its classic statement of his philosophy. Understanding her anxieties at this critical juncture in her life, he offered her the following advice:

It frightens me to embark on this theme [her life] because it is enormous. It is enormous because what is characteristic of that which we call Life, Yours, Mine, each Person's — Life is a reality which must essentially belong to Someone—is that it means existing in an inexorably given world, in this one here and now. Your Life depends on what happens in the world and on what the world is like. You are no more than one of the two important ingredients in your Life: the other is the World. If you wish to be successful in your Life, you must be successful in your ideas and presumptions about the World. Thus I cannot talk to you seriously about your Life without talking to you about the World. But the World, what there is around us, our *circumstance*, has layers like an onion, and the most external or superficial ones are less real, less *authentic* than the internal ones. A life is successful when it is lived *toward*, *with* and *from* the most authentic and substantial part of what is *existing* and *occurring* in today's world. It's useless trying to be admirable if you don't live the substantial part of your era. To do this, your life must cease to slide over the world (being amused, seeing, hearing, entertaining, being capricious); on the contrary, it must be anchored to it [. . . .] *Today's life is in its last hours and a radically different type is forming rapidly.* But, of course, precisely because it will triumph tomorrow, that new life cannot be found in the street or in store windows. To find it requires work, effort, dedication, *vocation* — not diversion.[37]

In the Orteguian sense, publishing a review would be more than just a profession, it would be a moral commitment.

After many years of mutually enriching friendship, a friendship that was expressed not just in letters but in visits wherever their paths crossed, neither Victoria nor Ortega saw one another in the same idealized proportions as when they first met. He had dazzled her in 1916 with his eloquence and brilliance, qualities that she never ceased to admire in him, and she was indebted to him for his generosity toward her as a young writer, but his antifeminism and other aspects of his political beliefs made him less than a hero in her eyes.

Similarly, Ortega, who had initially seen Victoria as an otherworldly symbol of feminine perfection, eventually came to appreciate her as a dynamic professional woman committed to a demanding vocation, one whose hazards and pitfalls he knew well. His affection for her, however, remained as warm as ever. Once during his second visit to Argentina he wrote her a note of thanks en route to Mendoza, enclosing fifty pesos for a banquet bill she had paid without telling him:

> I owe you an enormous debt, as big as these Andes that I see in front of me at this moment that make me want to give them a pat on the back as one does with an elephant in the zoo. This gigantic debt is you yourself . . . the simple fact that you take the trouble to exist . . . I've been carrying around this debt for so long, I'll never be able to repay it to you . . . Let me pay you instead this other minimal and very Argentine one. (Is there anyone who doesn't owe fifty pesos to someone else?) This way, the other debt will stand by itself, pure, alone, — like a monument.[38]

Over the years, Ortega's image of Victoria took on more physical substance, though his virtuosity as a master of the metaphor could still transform her into a symbol, as when he wrote these lines to her in 1937 in Mar del Plata where she was spending the summer: "I don't know why, but I think that in those summer months and in that existence under the sun and next to the sea, the vegetal subsurface that we all have but that you, so superlative, must have in the proportions of a tropical forest, rises and inundates your whole person."[39] In his imagination, Victoria the Goddess had become Victoria the Earth Mother.

Rabindranath Tagore

Victoria first encountered Tagore in 1914, a year after he was awarded the Nobel Prize for Literature. It was a purely spiritual encounter—ten years would pass before the Indian poet himself would stand before her on her own Argentine soil. Nevertheless, it was a momentous occasion when she first read André Gide's French translation of *Gitanjali*, Tagore's most famous collection of poems. In the poetry of a man who was raised as a Hindu and inspired by the philosophy of Buddha, she found a religious spirit akin to her own. In the words of the *Gitanjali*:

> . . . I stand under the golden canopy of thine evening
> sky and I lift my eager eyes to thy face.
> I have come to the brink of eternity from which
> nothing can vanish — no hope, no happiness, no
> vision of a face seen through tears.
> Oh, dip my emptied life into that ocean, plunge it
> into the deepest fullness. Let me for once feel
> that lost sweet touch in the allness of the universe.[40]

Victoria has described the effect Tagore's poetry had on her in 1914:

> God of Tagore, said I to myself, you who do not want to shelter me from anything and do not mind the oblivion in which I hold you, how well you know me! Hidden God who knows that I shall always seek him! Merciful God who knows that the only path to him is the path of freedom!
>
> I remember the moment and the exact spot where this took place, I was leaning against a white marble fireplace in a room upholstered in light grey silk. The house no longer exists. Neither do those I was afraid of hurting, or those who were hurting me. Nor does the Poet who was bringing me the gift of tears, as not even the closest friend would have been able to do. The images which now live only in my memory will cease to exist together with it, as easily, as irrevocably as all that has preceded them into nothingness.
>
> But the *Gitanjali* over which I was weeping will remain.[41]

If, in the *Divina Commedia*, she found the companionship of a soul in despair struggling, as she felt she was, toward the truth, in the *Gitanjali* she discovered the feeling of joy and fullness that comes with the perception, however fleeting, of that truth. This was Tagore's gift to her—a sense of the "lost sweet touch" she had longed for. Where Dante's God was the more distant, vengeful punisher of souls, Tagore's was compassionate and forgiving, a God who understood and tolerated his creatures' shortcomings. Ultimately, both Dante and Tagore aspired to achieve "allness," "wholeness," the union of finite and infinite. Both sought the liberation of the soul from the body's earthbound desires. In both, Victoria found the same answer: love. As she leaned against the fireplace reading the verses of the *Gitanjali* on that long-ago day, she realized that the Bengali poet was no more foreign to her understanding than the Florentine. The differences of language or culture that separated them were insignificant in the realm of the spirit.

During the ten years that passed between this first acquaintance with Tagore in 1914 and their unexpected meeting in Buenos Aires in 1924, Victoria, who was living through what was undoubtedly the most difficult part of her personal life, kept Tagore by her side in spirit. She also followed the news of the struggle for home rule in India, which was reaching a crisis in the 1920s. Again and again, she was drawn to the reports of a pathetic bespectacled figure in sparse native dress who preached nonviolent resistance and who endured imprisonment and physical self-denial to prove his conviction. After reading Romain Rolland's biography of Mahatma Gandhi early in 1924, she was even more impressed by the magnitude of his virtues, virtues she admired all the more knowing that she herself was given to being violent and physically indulgent. When she heard that the British press had denounced the Mahatma as a fanatical agitator, she decided to write an article for *La Nación* (published in March 1924) explaining his philosophy to the Argentine public. It was the first of many things she would write over the years about India and its leaders.

Without knowing that she was soon to meet Tagore, Victoria was aware of feeling a contrasting, but not conflicting, admiration for him on the one hand and Gandhi on the other. For Gandhi, she felt more than admiration. He seemed to be the living incarnation of the ethic of the Christian Gospels: by his own sacrifice and suffering—not by the death of others — he was determined to conquer the oppressive force of British imperialism. The meek shall inherit the earth, said the Bible she had read as a child and as an adult; by his example, Gandhi made it clear that meekness did not mean cowardice. To practice nonviolent resistance required the strength of an unshakable will and determination. Brute force, he preached, was the law of animals. To Victoria, this seemed the kind of heroism that verged on sainthood. Yet, there was a side of Gandhi with which she couldn't sympathize: his extreme nationalism (noncooperation) and his belief that sexuality, except for procreation, was immoral. Jawaharlal Nehru, a follower of Gandhi, also imprisoned for his opposition to the British, felt similar reservations about parts of the Mahatma's philosophy, but his commitment to him was total nonetheless. Despite his unimpressive appearance Gandhi awakened a fervent devotion in those who followed him. Victoria sensed this on the one occasion in 1931 when she saw the Mahatma and heard him speak. It was in Paris, after his visit to the Second Round Table Conference in England. Softly and calmly, before a sometimes unruly and unsympathetic group of listeners, Gandhi spoke of self-knowledge, self-perfection, and the unity of peace and truth — principles that governed the Eastern way of life, as opposed to the Western laws of force and aggression. Although she had entered the lecture hall with some skepticism, Victoria was immediately captivated by the aura of Gandhi's person. He seemed to radiate a moral and spiritual energy; it was what Henri Bergson must have had in mind in 1911 when he defined the importance of great men who leave their mark on an era:

> . . . it is the moral man who is a creator in the highest degree—the man whose action, itself intense, is also capable of intensifying the action of other men, and, itself generous, can kindle fires on the hearths of generosity. The men of moral grandeur, particularly those whose inventive and simple heroism has opened new paths to virtue, are revealers of metaphysical truth. Although they are the culminating point of evolution, yet they are nearest the source and they enable us to perceive the impulsion which comes from the deep. *It is in studying these great lives, in striving to express sympathetically what they experience, that we may penetrate by an act of intuition to the life principle itself.* To pierce the mystery of the deep, it is sometimes necessary to regard the heights.[42] (Emphasis added.)

This, so eloquently expressed by Bergson, is what Victoria sensed as she listened to the Mahatma. He was, she wrote years later, a hero truly worthy of worship:

> This surrender before a superior, which doesn't imply the denial of our *dharma*, our destiny, but a reverence for a being with all his singular qualities, *this* is what I believe Nehru and Tagore have felt before Gandhi as I did. Neither of them was totally in agreement with him, but there was something more important than agreeing or disagreeing. What can one call that something that tips the scale? Soul? Devalued though it may be, it's still the only appropriate word. Spiritual energy is what Bergson would call it. If one believes in electrical or atomic energy, I don't see why one shouldn't accept this other obvious (for me) form of a hidden power within us.[43]

Rabindranath Tagore was, to be sure, a great teacher, poet, dramatist, and novelist but he was not a saint. Victoria admired him for other qualities of mind and heart—the qualities that made his poetry so moving. For her, there could be no identifying with Gandhi, except on the level of aspiration. In Tagore, however, she saw something of her own delight in nature and art, in the sensual and aesthetic pleasures of life — flowers, birds, children, sunlight, and clouds. In different ways, both men were spiritual examples:

> Gandhiji on one side, Guredev (the teacher-poet) on the other. I saw clearly that one of them sought perfection in the object, the work of art, his creation (that is, outside himself, in the manner of an artist); the other sought perfection exclusively in his acts, in his conduct, in the consonance between thought and action (in the manner of a saint).[44]

In September of 1924 word reached Buenos Aires that Tagore would be passing through Argentina on his way to attend a commemorative centennial celebration in Peru. Traveling with his secretary, Leonard Elmhirst, Tagore planned only a brief stopover in Buenos Aires. Nonetheless, Victoria was charged with enthusiasm. She immersed herself in his books, reading as much of his work as she could to prepare for the occasion. As part of her ritual whenever such enthusiasms took hold of her, she composed imaginary letters to the poet filled with her own interpretations and reactions to his works. She then shaped these into an article for *La Nación*, aptly entitled "The Joy of Reading Rabindranath Tagore" (published in November 1924).

On Thursday, the sixth of November, the ship carrying Tagore and Elmhirst docked in Buenos Aires. Apparently, the poet's rigorous schedule of lectures and world travels had finally caught up with him, for he disembarked suffering from a case of the flu. The doctors who examined him, fearing the possible effects of his illness on his already weakened heart, prescribed a complete rest. Further travel was impossible. When Victoria heard what had happened, she went to the hotel where Tagore and Elmhirst were staying. Speaking first to Elmhirst, then, shyly, to Tagore, she offered them the peace and quiet of the suburb of San Isidro, which they gratefully accepted. She had originally hoped to convince her parents to lend Villa Ocampo to her; when they refused, she leased a nearby quinta called "Miralrío" (River View), and sold a diamond tiara to pay for it. She would stay at her parents' house a kilometer or two away, but her household staff (including Fani and several others from her home in the city) would go to Miralrío and take care of Tagore. In two days, she told her guests, everything would be ready.

Finally, the great moment arrived:

> The day of Tagore's departure for San Isidro, November 12, came at last. I had not seen him again. On that day he was having lunch with "important" people who always managed to get hold of interesting travellers, treating them like stage stars. I imagined with irritation that some of the guests would be sure to plague the Indian Poet with absurd questions; I felt on edge and ashamed. When I went to fetch him by car, at about three o'clock, violent squalls were sweeping the streets. Dust enveloped us in a swirl, driving young leaves torn from plane trees and any bit of paper trailing on the pavement. The sky, yellowish in some parts, leaden in others, threatened imminent rain. This lasted during the whole of the drive of a little over half an hour. By contrast, entering the house became all the more pleasant. The silence of the rooms, deepened by the noise of the wind in the trees (transformed into the noise of waves), the flowers, with which I had flooded the house, and solitude welcomed us as soon as the door was closed.

On that afternoon the sky continued to darken in some places and at the same time became more golden in others. I had never seen such heavy, menacing and radiant clouds. These sulphurous yellows and leaden greys made the greens of the banks and the trees all the brighter. The river, true interpreter of our sky, was giving in its own way and in its own language the image of what it saw above. Tagore and I looked from the balcony of his room on the landscape where everything, the sky, the river and the earth, decked in "embroidered clothes," the willows weeping more tenderly with their new curly leaves, was bathed in the diffused illumination of an abortive storm.

"I must show you the river," I had told Tagore leading him on to the balcony. And everything conspired with me to make the scenery a striking one. The heavy clouds were hemmed with glowing light.

That balcony was to become his own. He was to watch from it "evenings veiled in rosy vapours," like that other poet [Baudelaire] who gazed at them from another balcony, facing another river, the narrow Seine. He would later remember it: "I haven't been able to shake off my weakness . . . In this state of physical feebleness my mind often wanders back to that balcony in San Isidro," he wrote me from Santiniketan. "I still vividly remember the early morning light on the massed groups of strange flowers, blue and red, in your garden, and the constant play of colours on the great river which I was never tired of watching from my solitary balcony."

I had instinctively led Tagore to that balcony immediately upon his entering Miralrío, certain that if he was to take anything away on leaving it, it would be this: the memory of the landscape that would meet his eyes morning and evening, with its changing light. That landscape was the only gift worthy of him. [45]

During the two months Tagore spent at Miralrío recovering his health amid the luxuriant trees and flowers of a San Isidro summer, he was surrounded with as much solitude and tranquility as Victoria could create for him. She guarded his repose by limiting the large numbers of curious visitors to brief stays and by leaving him alone to read and write when she would have much preferred to sit by his feet, as a picture taken of them in the garden shows her doing. She had no intention of monopolizing him or profiting in any way at his expense; her hospitality—a hospitality she has shared with so many other writers and artists since then—was simply an expression of her devotion to him. As Krishna Kripalani, Tagore's biographer, wrote, "[the poet] was very content and happy to watch the river from the balcony of the villa and be looked after by so charming and devoted a hostess. It was a real devotion, the devotion of a young and ardent spirit to an ideal and not the 'fussing' of a society lady eager to capture a lion." [46]

Certainly there was something approaching the religious in her devotion to Tagore. He was Gurudev, the prophet-teacher and spiritual father-figure, dressed in flowing white robes, with abundant white hair and beard and handsome features—a truly patriarchal countenance. To Victoria, his eyes possessed an "enslaving sweetness," but if her devotion was slavelike, it was born of her own bountiful will to please her hero.[47] As the weeks passed, she gradually came to know Tagore the man — his moods, his preferences, his anxiety over the problems of his homeland and Europe — but she rarely ventured to converse with him on these subjects. Her shyness was painful for her, as there was so much she would have liked to say. Fortunately silences can be as eloquent as words, and this Tagore understood. As Kripalani put it, "Even God is moved by such devotion—so the saints assure us. Tagore was only human. He was deeply touched and grateful."[48]

In Victoria's eyes, Tagore was a literary hero and a guru. She had steeped herself in his poetry, wept over its beauty and felt uplifted by its message. To be by his side, like a pupil beside a guru, was a purifying experience, one in which the ultimate goal of self-knowledge and spiritual insight demanded a submissive, yogalike trust in and respect for the wiser teacher. Victoria knew enough of Eastern philosophy to be aware of this Hindu custom even if she did not think of herself precisely in the same context. In the presence of a literary hero, she was instinctively reverential. Having read all Tagore's books, and absorbed his every word, she felt she knew him intimately. But he, she believed, had no way of knowing her as well, so she was convinced that their relationship was unilateral:

> . . . there was a difference between his position with regard to me and mine with regard to him. I knew who Tagore was and his books had told me about him things that his actual presence now made complete. But Tagore could know nothing of the speechless creature I was except by intuition. "I know you, O woman from a strange land! Your dwelling is across the sea . . ." Did my silence really tell him my thoughts? I am afraid it did not and that our knowledge of each other was extremely one-sided.[49]

From her point of view it was one-sided, but not from his. What Tagore saw before him in Argentina—with no prior knowledge of her— was a beautiful, vibrant young woman of thirty-four who was evidently accustomed to wealth and to an atmosphere of refinement. In the hours they spent in each other's company along the banks of the River Plate, he must have perceived her love of nature and her aesthetic sensitivity, her spiritual inclination, and her enthusiasm for learning. As she suspected, he responded intuitively. In her, he undoubtedly identified what the Indians call *shakti*, a nourishing vitality and intangible charm, as Tagore himself described it:

> This ineffable emanation of woman's nature, has, from the first, played its

part in the creations of man, unobtrusively but inevitably. Had man's mind not been energized by the inner working of woman's vital charm, he would never have attained his successes. Of all the higher achievements of civilization—the devotion of the toiler, the valour of the brave, the creations of the artist—the secret spring is to be found in woman's influence.[50]

Tagore's definition of *shakti* and Ortega's description of woman's "magical power" are variations on the same theme of woman as man's inspiration—the catalyst that precipitates *his* creative abilities.

Despite this similarity, it would be unfair to suggest that Tagore was as much of an antifeminist as Ortega. He did believe, with Ortega, that women and men were essentially different in aptitudes and attitudes (i.e., woman = emotion, man = intellect); however, he showed far more concern with the problems of women in his novels and plays and was much more progressive than Ortega in his concept of women's role in society. For example, his novel, *The Home and the World* (1915), depicts the theme of tyranny in marital relationships and speaks for a woman's need to have the freedom to develop her own personality. Tagore rejected the Indian custom of *purdah* just as he opposed fanatical nationalism (noncooperation with foreigners), believing that both represented the cult of power inherently destructive to human development. Although he was sympathetic to women's rights to a certain extent, calling for a larger role for women in society to counterbalance men's aggressiveness, he still felt that women should stay close to the home: "It is because she has not found her true place in the great world," he wrote in 1926, "that she sometimes tries to capture man's special estate as a desperate means of coming into her own. But it is not by coming out of her home that woman can gain her liberty. Her liberation can only be effected in a society where her true *shakti*, her *ánanda*, is given the widest and highest scope for its activity."[51] How this was to be accomplished, he did not elucidate.

Tagore may not have known many particulars about Victoria's life, but he was clearly moved by her presence to write several tender love poems during his stay in San Isidro. They were later published in Bengali with other poems of the same period under the title *Puravi* (the name of a lovely evening mode in Indian classical music), and the volume was dedicated to "Vijaya," as Tagore called Victoria, her name in Sanskrit.[52] While he was still in Argentina with her, he translated three poems at her request. This is one of them, written in November 1924 in San Isidro:

Tempt me not to load my boat with debt,
  but give me leave to go away empty-handed,
lest the price of love that you recklessly pay
  should only reveal the poorness of my heart.

I can but litter your life with the torn shreds of my pain,
   and keep you awake at night with the moan
   of my lonely dreams.
It is better that I remain speechless
   and help you to forget me.

While walking on my solitary way
   I met you at the dusk of nightfall.
I was about to ask you to take my hand
   when I gazed at your face and was afraid.
For I saw there the glow of the fire that lay asleep
   in the deep of your heart's dark silence.

If in my frenzy I waken it up into flames
   it can only throw a glimmer on the brink of
   my emptiness
I know not what sacrifice is mine
   to offer to your love's sacred fire
I bend my head and trudge on to my barren end
   provisioned with the remembrance of our meeting.[53]

This poem and others included in *Puravi* suggest that Tagore felt deeply attracted to Victoria. Whether it was more than a spiritual sentiment is not clear, though it appears that he at least considered extending his visit in Buenos Aires to be with her longer. According to Tagore's biographer, the poet habitually avoided deep emotional commitments, feeling that his duty lay in his service to God.[54] Then too, he was thirty years older than Victoria—the same age (sixty-three) as her father—and he may well have feared hurting her or taking advantage of her youthful devotion.

   On January 4, 1925 Tagore and Elmhirst sailed for Europe in staterooms personally arranged for them by Victoria, including the gift of a special armchair that Tagore had enjoyed sitting in at Miralrío and that now stands in his home-museum in India. From on board ship he wrote to Victoria this explanation of his departure:

> I have often said to you that I am not free to give up my freedom—for this freedom is claimed by my Master for his own service. There have been times when I did forget this and allowed myself to drift into some easeful captivity. But every time it ended in catastrophe and I was driven by an angry power to the open — across broken walls.[55]

   Many times during the ensuing years Tagore felt nostalgia for the rare peace and beauty of San Isidro and for Victoria's company. He evidently came to realize that his compulsion to return to his duties may have been an error in judgment. In August of 1925 he wrote this to Victoria from India:

> You express regret in your letter that I could not continue to stay at that beautiful house near the river till the end of the summer. You do not know how often I wish I could do so. It was some lure of duty which drove me from that sweet corner with its inspiration for seemingly futile idling; but today I discover that my basket, while I was there, was being daily filled with shy flowers of poems that thrive under the shade of lazy hours. I can assure you, most of them will remain fresh long after the time when the laboriously built towers of my beneficent deeds will crumble into oblivion.[56]

On the eve of his death, sixteen years after leaving Victoria and San Isidro, he composed a poem which shows that he was haunted by the same thought:

> How I wish I could once again find my way to that foreign land where waits for me the message of love! The dreams of yesterday will wing their way back and, fluttering softly, build their nest anew. Sweet memories will restore to the lute its lost melody. . . . Her language I knew not, but what her eyes said will forever remain eloquent in its anguish.[57]

Tagore's poems and letters prove that, if their relationship was unilateral in one sense, Victoria nonetheless left a deep impression on him which time and distance could not eradicate. She and the tranquil haven she had offered him by the broad River Plate became symbols in his mind of a paradise lost. More than that, she had been an inspiration to his poetic spirit, a muse in his waning years. Whether she chose to acknowledge it or not, Victoria had once again been idealized by a writer's pen.

Although they corresponded fairly frequently, she and Tagore saw each other only one more time, in Europe in 1930. That year Victoria decided to organize an exhibit in Paris at the Galerie Pigalle to introduce to the art world Tagore's unusual drawings which she had discovered in San Isidro and had encouraged him to continue. They had originally been doodlings on manuscripts: "He played with the erasures, following them from verse to verse with his pen, making lines that suddenly jumped into life out of this play: prehistoric monsters, birds, faces appeared. The cancelled mistakes in Tagore's poems gave birth to a world of forms that grinned, frowned or laughed at us in a mysterious and fascinating way."[58] Thus Victoria described her discovery of the painter in the poet. Parisian critics agreed with her discerning eye, praising Tagore's "pure painting, absolutely sincere and wholly uninfluenced by our studio customs."[59]

While they were in Paris, Tagore urged Victoria to accompany him to Oxford, where he was to deliver a lecture, and then to India. This time, the one sorely tempted was Victoria. Her devotion to Tagore and Gandhi had made her feel close to India despite its distance and its exotic culture. Unlike André Malraux, for whom India held the fascination of "otherness" as if it were a mysterious woman, Victoria was drawn by what she felt was India's "likeness," spiritual qualities that transcended cultural contrasts.[60] In the end, however, she did not accept Tagore's invitation to England or to India because she had promised to go to New York to discuss with Waldo Frank the details of founding a literary review. It was too important a commitment to abandon.

Even after the death of both Tagore and Gandhi, India was never far from her mind. Jawaharlal Nehru, who carried on in his predecessors' footsteps, became Victoria's next spiritual link with India. Twice they met, briefly, in Paris and in Washington, and the invitation to come to India was renewed. "I never made up my mind to go," she wrote after Nehru's death, "and now I repent to no avail. Still, Nehru was, I believe, the last living man whom I wanted to know personally (the ones that are in books, for always, don't require a long journey); I wanted to know him with the fervor of my lost adolescence, always in search of hero-worship."[61] (In 1968 while she was prime minister, Nehru's daughter, Indira Gandhi, visited Victoria at Villa Ocampo.)

In 1962, the Argentine minister of foreign affairs asked Victoria to accept the post of ambassador to India. Again she refused. She could offer the legitimate excuse that she was in her seventies and no longer able to tolerate a tropical climate, exotic food, long journeys, or the rigors of diplomatic obligations ("officialdom" and formal social occasions have never appealed to her). She was, as she liked to say, an "aged eagle," referring to T. S. Eliot's line from "Ash Wednesday."

Another explanation may lie in the fact that the India that mattered to her was already a part of her intimate knowledge. "The true face of a country," she has said many times, "has only been revealed to me through the men who are its spiritual landscape."[62] The spiritual landscape of India, thanks to Tagore, Gandhi, and Nehru, required no traveling. It was as close to her as her bookshelf. The "other" India, the land of maharajahs and the Taj Majal, could never equal, much less surpass, it.

Count Hermann Keyserling

The following description of Orlando in Virginia Woolf's 1928 novel might just as easily have described Victoria in that very year—prior, that is, to her face-to-face encounter with Count Keyserling:

> . . . as Orlando, we have said, had no belief in the usual divinities, she bestowed her credulity upon great men—yet with a distinction. Admirals, soldiers, statesmen, moved her not at all. But the very thought of a great

writer stirred her to such a pitch of belief that she almost believed him to be invisible. Her instinct was a sound one. One can only believe entirely, perhaps, in what one cannot see.[63]

As Orlando found out when she invited Mr. Pope to tea, famous writers are not necessarily great or honorable men:

> A woman knows very well that, though a wit sends her his poems, praises her judgment, solicits her criticism, and drinks her tea, this by no means signifies that he respects her opinion, admires her understanding, or will refuse, though the rapier is denied him, to run her through the body with his pen.[64]

With Count Hermann Keyserling, Victoria learned the same painful lesson.

An aristocrat of Russo-German background, Keyserling was a self-styled philosopher, author, linguist, and world traveler. To promote his philosophical approach, which was fashioned on theories of mass psychology, popular mysticism, and intuitive deduction, Keyserling founded the School of Wisdom in Darmstadt, Germany, to which he invited noted thinkers from all over the world for lectures and discussions in the 1920s. Vital problems, not abstract ideas, he said in his book *The World in the Making* (1927), must be the subject of contemporary philosophical inquiry, and because "every man is an integral part of mankind, serving it as an organ, [. . .] the best method by which man can find out the truths which apply to all is to study his own mental processes."[65] Wholeness, he proclaimed, was the object: "the attainment of complete self-consciousness and complete self-realization."[66] His own egoism, he therefore believed, had a larger human significance and moral value because it was essential for achieving a deeper form of consciousness. As Victoria later discovered, Keyserling's ego was as imposing as his physical presence.

Victoria's introduction to Keyserling occurred in 1927 when she first read some of his work in Ortega's *Revista de Occidente*. (Coincidentally, Keyserling had met both Ortega and Tagore on his world travels.) Following her usual custom, she proceeded to devour all of his books published or translated into English with growing enthusiasm. In them she recognized thoughts of her own in the Count's eloquent if sometimes ponderous prose. She was particularly taken with a two-volume work published in 1925, titled *The Travel Diary of a Philosopher*, in which Keyserling recounted his world travels and his impressions of the contrasts between Eastern and Western cultures. Here she found not only the confirmation of many thoughts she had developed in her reading about India, but also the vitality, curiosity, and aspirations of a kindred spirit. As was her custom, she underlined passages that touched a responsive chord. For example, vast expanses of nature, Keyserling wrote, produce in us a feeling of exaltation and a sense of self-extension beyond the limits of the finite world: "Our ego expands, and we then recognize our individuality as an insignificant portion of our true selves."[67] Victoria knew this experience from looking at the Argentine landscape: "Our pampas and our river stretch toward the infinite on the horizontal line," she wrote to a friend at about the same time she was reading Keyserling's work, adding, "I believe that our soul is destined to express itself similarly."[68] Keyserling warned however that nature can only be an inspiration: "Nature, no matter how rich she may be, cannot rise to the heights of spirituality. They can only be reached (creations) by the man who through personal effort rises above the sphere of his own origin."[69] Not all men have the capacity for sustained creativity, he said: "A profound recognition discovered and expressed by an imperfect being may benefit the whole of humanity."[70] This theory, which he borrowed from Goethe, of the "fecundity of the insufficient" appealed immensely to Victoria, who thought of herself as one who had yet to achieve wholeness and thus depended on others for stimulation. Keyserling understood her reaction or so it seemed as she read his words: "Man always experiences joy when someone else makes clear to him his own experience."[71]

Victoria was so fascinated by what she read, so eager to know the Count himself, so sure that knowing him would have a transcendental effect on her life—her fortuitous contact with Tagore had convinced her of the value of knowing an author in person—that she decided to get in touch with him through friends in Spain (one of them was Ortega) and invite him to give a series of lectures in Argentina as soon as possible. The answer was transmitted to her from Germany that due to his heavy schedule no trip would be feasible until 1929 (two years later). In her characteristically impetuous manner, Victoria cabled a reply: "Impossible to foresee if enthusiasm will last until that date." What Keyserling thought when he received this is not recorded, but he must surely have been intrigued by such bluntness coming from a woman he did not know in a part of the world he had never seen. Tropical climates, he had noted in his *Travel Diary*, generally produce less imaginative and less vital types of individuals because growth in these regions is not a struggle but rather a normal part of life. Who, then, was this very aggressive woman? A letter followed, and thus began a correspondence that lasted a year and a half and produced virtually kilos of letters.

At first, many of their letters had to do with the Count's proposed lecture tour to Argentina. It was part of his eccentric and demanding nature to insist, before accepting the invitation, that certain perquisites be agreed upon to provide for his comfort and well-being. Victoria, acting as an intermediary between him and the groups to whom he would speak, relayed his wishes, acquiescing to them more than she might have, had her enthusiasm for him been less exuberant: "The institutions who were paying for the philosopher's trip didn't look happily on this, but I used all my diplomacy to make them accept, like it or not, the conditions of the founder of the School of Wisdom. They maintained that they interpreted wisdom otherwise."[72] She could do no less, after all, for someone she regarded as a hero.

By her own confession, her letters were openly adulatory. She wrote frequently and fervently, and Keyserling responded with growing interest and encouragement. It was an intoxicating experience. One must take into account all the literary passions that motivated her to believe, as she claims, that she was naively unaware of the complications that her letters might provoke. Never, she has said, did she make any romantic statements in her letters or even insinuate any intentions of the sort; nonetheless, Keyserling apparently assumed that her outpouring of devotion implied romance. As the piles of letters grew on both sides of the Atlantic, so did a misunderstanding that neither one identified as such until they met. As Victoria recalled:

> I was in my element when it came to corresponding. Not because my style sparkled from being polished (I've always been careless in this respect), but for the inexhaustible pleasure that that type of dialogue gave me. And so I poured oceans of ink in the direction of Darmstadt. There, Keyserling, with his Baltic eyes and Mongolian ancestry, read my letters and interpreted them as he pleased. He reproached me for my lamentably conventional handwriting when I complained that his was indecipherable. But did he really read my letters or did he examine them almost unconsciously as one looks at ink blots in a Rorschach test? And when he thought he was analyzing the ink blot I was to him, he was only doing what those who take the Rorschach test do: projecting himself.
>
> What can't be read into the letters of a devoted reader, an unknown woman from another continent and another race? What can't be read into those of a correspondent admired as an author and unknown as a man? One need only loosen the reins of imagination.[. . .]
>
> I would write to Keyserling about all the subjects that interested me at the moment and more particularly about his books and all they suggested to me. Happy and fulfilled because I existed for him to the point that he deigned to answer me, I expressed my thanks in fervent terms. He was for me more or less what Houston Chamberlain was for him at a time when his uncle Edward Keyserling compared the young Hermann to a child dazzled by a Christmas tree. I too was a child before a tree, and he was the tree full of lights that I stared at with my mouth open.

You should come to Europe, Keyserling began to write me. And then: you must come to Europe so that we can talk about the lecture tour, so that you can teach me to speak Spanish, so that we can meet one another. And soon: it's essential that you come. This coincided with my own vivid desire to return to the old continent. But in spite of my dream of finally meeting Keyserling, I began to feel, at the simple idea of the meeting, an uneasiness in the pit of my stomach as one feels the night before an exam or a visit to the doctor whose diagnosis one fears.[73]

The meeting was arranged, at Keyserling's suggestion, for January 1929, after which he would go to Argentina to give his series of lectures. It had been more than fifteen years since Victoria was last in Europe. Emotional ties had kept her from leaving home during that time, but more and more she craved the intellectual and spiritual sustenance of the Old World. Finally, it was her enthusiasm for Keyserling—following upon her enthusiasm for Ortega and Tagore — that convinced her to loosen those ties, ties that could never give her all the fulfillment she required.

When it was decided that she would make the trip, Ortega and other friends who knew Keyserling warned Victoria that he was not an easy person to get along with. Even *he* wrote her saying, "My vitality is such that there are some people who can't stand me for three days in a row."[74] Unfortunately, her eagerness to make the trip, coupled with her own tendency to be exuberant and demanding, made her take these warnings lightly. It was even agreed between them that Keyserling's lodging for a month in Versailles, where they would meet, would be at her expense because his tour of Argentina was to be discussed. Never one to deprive himself of any luxury, the Count asked for and received first-class accommodations. Victoria intended to stay at a rented flat in Paris and visit him daily, as he had requested, along with other stipulations:

Above all, he wanted me to visit him as frequently as possible during the months of his stay in Versailles, he also didn't want me to lead a mundane life (as if that would have occurred to me), a life that might distract me from our conversations; nor should I count on him as being sociable for any kind of get-togethers; I should invite him to dine in Paris once or twice with a select group of Argentines, champagne, oysters, *idem*; the women should wear evening dress and the men tuxedos. These demands struck me as innocent and attributable to a disturbing kind of *gourmandise* of the eyes and the palate. I have always detested champagne, oysters, dinners for which one had to "dress," but I understand that others may like them.

I knew all the details of this pact by heart when I arrived one afternoon at the Hôtel des Réservoirs. Keyserling was waiting for me in the little room that would become his study. Snow was falling or had just fallen on that drowsy winter Versailles that I like so much. The Hôtel des Réservoirs, where I had reserved rooms for Keyserling in accordance with his instructions, was a very old hotel with a quintessential French charm. The building had admirable proportions and in it one felt one was in the heart of France. An explosive giant, the founder of the School of Wisdom (whose stature I had underestimated) came toward me with his hands extended. In just one of them he could have crushed both of mine; my two hands or even my two feet. In the little square room whose windows looked out on the *pavé du Roi*, he seemed to fill the whole space. Two names came into my mind: Genghis Khan, Tamerlain . . . the Genghis Khan and Tamerlain of letters this time.[75]

Later, two other names came to mind when they sat down to dinner: Bacchus and Pantagruel. It was precisely this very physical side of his nature, a side she could not know from his letters, that took her by surprise. He devoured his food and consumed quantities of wine. Naturally she would have preferred him to be somewhat more restrained in his acknowledged vitality, but being a person of strong physical expression herself—a lover of good food, though not a drop of alcohol—she could not object to similar weaknesses in her hero. After all, she reasoned, it was the intellectual and spiritual side of him that mattered to her.

Keyserling, however, had other ideas. Hadn't this beautiful and desirable woman written him reams of letters and hadn't she come almost half-way around the world to see him? There was no doubt in his mind that her devotion was amorous and that what she wanted was to have an affair with him, the man of her dreams. Philosophically, according to his theory of wholeness, it was the logical corollary to their spiritual attraction. In fact, the book he was writing in Versailles at the time, *America Set Free*, specifically states that for a cultured man to achieve the essence of his being (wholeness), he must seek to unify spirit (male) with flesh (female). The act of possessing the woman he loves is sacred, says Keyserling, because it can lead to the birth of an immortal soul (as in the Christian concept of "the word made flesh").[76]

For Victoria, meanwhile, the initial thrill of their meeting had been replaced by disillusionment, disagreement, and irritation. She evaded his advances with polite refusals. Finally there was no alternative but to reject him once and for all. His reaction, she recalls, was volcanic and vindictive; he accused her of leading him on and then demoniacally betraying him, "of gloating over my destruction [of him] as I had gloated over my 'idolatry.' "[77] She protested that her enthusiasm for him had no such ulterior motives, sexual or otherwise. Surely both of them were to blame for being imprudent. It had been a painful collision of wills—one as strong as the other—but it might eventually be forgiven, if not forgotten.

Although she was upset by what had occurred, Victoria did not renege on her invitation to Keyserling to lecture in Argentina, reasoning that she could deal with him in public and remain friendly albeit at a distance. But Keyserling, his masculine pride sorely bruised, was not content to keep their disagreement private. During his stay in Buenos Aires, tension mounted, tempers flared, and there was another explosion. This time, Victoria demanded the return of all her letters, most of which she burned in disgust.

The story of their misunderstanding does not end there. Count Keyserling was not just an ordinary man of wounded pride. He was a writer—a very subjective one at that—and in due time his resentment, transformed by psychological and philosophical manipulation, took literary shape in a book entitled *South American Meditations*, published in 1932. It was a work in which Keyserling gave free rein to his tendency to fantasize and mythologize, a habit Victoria referred to as his "interpretative elephantiasis." [78] In reaction to the disturbing experience in Versailles and the later visit to Argentinia, Keyserling formulated a grandiose interpretation of the psychology of an entire continent, full of generalizations and misconceptions. When she read it, Victoria might have agreed with Orlando that a male writer, however flattering he may be to a female, will not refuse, "though the rapier is denied him, to run her through the body with his pen." Keyserling attacked indirectly, not mentioning her by name, but the intent was clear.

South American Meditations develops, in extensive subjective discussion, Keyserling's theory that South America is the continent of the Third Day of Creation. There, he writes, "I gained access to the stratum of the Third Day of Creation within my own being. That is the layer in which Life, such as man is capable of re-living and re-experiencing in imagination, first wrested itself from the dead gravity of First Matter. In these deeps there is no liberty, there is only bondage absolute; their psychic part is ruled by the exact correspondence of the material force of gravity. There man experiences the Earth, not Spirit, within him." [79] South America, according to Keyserling, is the primordial continent, "the earthly womb of all Life," where "man involuntarily sees the Magna Mater face to face." [80] Consequently, in South America, one finds primordial woman, the quintessential female:

Primordial woman is completely unchecked by spiritual or ethical motives. She is entirely rooted in the world of the Third Day of Creation. This is why beauty with woman means so much as opposed to the little it means with man. This is why woman is originally devoid of moral instinct. This is why the real element in her life is disguise and deceit. This is why her womanhood dwindles in every world of exclusively determinant truthfulness, such as the North American world of today; this is why man becomes enmeshed and enslaved by primeval woman, by "Carmen," by "She," and by her alone, for she catches him there where Spirit and Freedom do not reach down to.[81]

Although Keyserling had very little of a positive nature to say about South American men, he reserved his most outrageous insults and generalizations for South American women:

> . . . they desire to be violated; they want to be able to remain entirely passive, completely irresponsible.[82]
>
> Among women, endowed with remarkable gifts of mind, I have met with few strong personalities who were not self-centered, authoritative and greedy of power to a degree rarely found even among South American caudillos.[83]
>
> No woman on earth makes such masterly use of all the possibilities of passivity and deceit. None has so spider-like a way of catching men in her net; none abuses the indissolubility of marriage so slyly and unscrupulously with the view of harassing him. Nowhere else does loyalty so often mean nothing but sloth. [. . .] Nowhere else do the emotions of the women so easily turn into their opposite on the slightest provocation.[84]

So brutal and venomous an assault on South American women can only be understood as a reaction to a personal crisis. By Keyserling's own confession, his encounter with them and with South America, the primordial feminine, nonspiritual world, was an unpleasant, though valuable, psychological experience: "My pilgrimage to South America meant for me a descent into the nether world. But since I came from Spirit, the darkness in which I was enmeshed served to clarify what was not clear before."[85] "Then did I realize: among other things, I am Earth and pure force of Earth. I am Earth not merely understood as material: this non-ego is an essential part of that which I experience myself to be."[86]

This explanation was sufficient for many readers who praised the book, evidently blind to its glaringly flawed method of stereotyping a whole culture from a few unsystematically recorded experiences— personal experiences only.[87] Even in South America, there was surprisingly little objection to it. Among the few Argentines who spoke out in denunciation, Eduardo Mallea, a writer and one of Victoria's closest friends, was perhaps the most eloquent. In 1935 he wrote:

> [the book is] a kind of erroneous intransigence, a delirious, howling negation of our continent; a kind of absurd mental terror like the cry of a weak-hearted man at night in the desert. This Baltic Count who drowned himself in torrents of champagne and consumed entire menus of food in one of the main salons of a certain luxury hotel in Buenos Aires, was a giant with a sparse beard, a Mongolian skull, and steely eyes, cold and small, who had founded his School of Wisdom in a city in Germany and who traveled in an

inebriated rapture throughout the world maintaining that one of the pillars of the creative "motus" in the consciousness of the Spirit was the way his imagination transformed the universe.[88]

In *South American Meditations*, Keyserling only told part of the story of his psychological crisis. Several recently published letters that he received from the Swiss psychoanalyst C. G. Jung, who had lectured at the School of Wisdom in 1927, shed more light on the full nature of that crisis, as he and Jung interpreted it. Apparently Keyserling wrote to Jung after his altercation with Victoria in Versailles, describing their misunderstanding, its traumatic effect on him, and asking for Jung's professional opinion of its significance. In his letters of reply, Jung identified Keyserling's experience with Victoria as an encounter with his own anima, the unconscious feminine part of his psyche, which he had repressed until meeting Victoria in whom he instinctively saw his own soul image.

In Jungian theory, the concept of the anima and the woman's role in bringing it to man's consciousness represent a necessary step toward achieving psychic wholeness or what is also called the "individuation of the self."[89] In symbolic terms, Jungian philosophy defines the anima in men and the corresponding animus in women as contrasexual archetypes, or that part of each person that represents qualities characteristic of the opposite sex; in Jung's words:

> No man is so entirely masculine that he has nothing feminine in him. The fact is, rather, that very masculine men have — carefully guarded and hidden — a very soft emotional life, often incorrectly described as "feminine." A man counts it a virtue to repress his feminine traits as much as possible, just as woman, at least until recently, considered it unbecoming to be "mannish." The repression of feminine traits and inclinations naturally causes these contrasexual demands to accumulate in the unconscious. No less naturally, the imago of woman (the soul-image) becomes a receptacle for these demands, which is why a man, in his love-choice, is strongly tempted to win the woman who best corresponds to his own unconscious femininity—a woman, in short, who can unhesitatingly receive the projection of his soul.[90]

Jung's letter to Keyserling on December 20, 1929 interprets the Versailles episode as a classic animus-anima confrontation:

> Your excellent description of the fateful intermezzo with X. [the editors identify Victoria only as a "well-known South American writer"] clearly shows that it is an encounter with an "earth woman," fraught with meaning. Concealed and revealed in it is one of the most beautiful animus-anima stories I have ever heard. Unfortunately poetic stories usually end in disappointment because, when one meets one's own soul, one never recog-

nizes it but confuses it with the poor human creature who has functioned unconsciously as a symbol carrier. X.'s longing for identification refers to the animus which she should like to possess in you, but she mixes it up with you personally and then of course is deeply disappointed. This disappointment will be repeated, always and everywhere, until man has learnt to distinguish his soul from the other person. Then his soul can return to him. This lesson is a hellish torture for you both, but extremely useful, *the* experience one would have wished for you, and assuredly the most fitting torture of all for X., who is still possessed by her earth demons. Perhaps she prefers to be torn to pieces by the titans, as happens to many such anima figures. Hence you should always remember, with reverence and devotion, what has been revealed to you in the human shell of X., so that your soul may remain inalienably with you, and your access to the earth may never be blocked. Let us hope the same for her, that besides tigers and serpents and eternal spirits there is still a human being in her who can remember with gratitude the revelation of her own spirit in you.[91]

Jung's assessment of Victoria's situation with respect to Keyserling is less than sympathetic. Naturally, he had heard only one side of the story but one senses in his interpretation a bias on the masculine side.[92]

Some time later, Keyserling sent Jung a portion of his unfinished manuscript of *South American Meditations* to show him how he was trying to incorporate what he had learned of his unconscious anima into his conscious self. In Jung's answer, dated August 13, 1931, there is a note of warning along with praise for Keyserling's effort:

Your manuscript is rich and significant in content. You are inaugurating a new and contemporary style of "sentimental journey," though it is considerably bloodier than its predecessors. South America has also brought you face to face, plainly and honestly, with the dark underworld, the chthonic unconscious. [. . .] That was an encounter with the daemonism of the earth and it has never yet been described better.

I wish you all luck with the continuation, but would advise you to cut down on "cultural speculation" as much as possible, otherwise you will blur what is most impressive about your work—the personal experience with its exemplary subjectivity.[93]

Paying little heed to Jung's closing advice, Keyserling let his self-centered imagination run rampant. The very subjectivity Jung had praised in the Count for its confessional value, would be, without the check of prudent consideration, responsible for a pseudorational cultural analysis that bore scant relationship to reality. To justify the crisis of his conflict with Victoria, he mythologized the attributes of an entire continent. Because it was a painful experience, he called South America "the Continent of Sorrow."[94] In the end, however, his suffering had made possible the personal triumph of psychological growth. What it had done for South America was of less concern to him.

When *South American Meditations* appeared in 1932, Victoria refrained from publishing a rebuttal, as she would have liked, for the simple reason that her relationship with Keyserling had been difficult enough without provoking further hostility. Privately, she was horrified by what she read, not only because his conclusions were incorrect and insulting for the most part, but also because in page after page she recognized topics that they had discussed in Versailles, now deformed by the Count's unbridled fantasy. Above all, she was outraged by his description of South American women as deceitful and immoral. Still, she bit her tongue and kept silent.

The last time she saw Keyserling, on a visit she made at his sister's request to Darmstadt in 1939, his life had changed considerably. Hitler had taken away his passport and forbidden him to lecture. The School of Wisdom had closed. Over a long evening of conversation, Keyserling described to her the horrors of living under the Nazi regime and the persecution he and his family suffered. Before they parted that night, Victoria spoke her mind frankly. Keyserling remained intransigent in his opinions. "Let's agree to differ" was their final understanding.

Ironically, Keyserling had been dead four years when his spirit, so to speak, came back to haunt her, convincing her that she must publish a public response to his misinterpretations. In 1950, Keyserling's widow sent her a copy of his memoirs that were about to be published. They contained a chapter entitled "Victoria Ocampo." Although she might be disturbed to see herself portrayed as a symbol, said Frau Keyserling, those who had read that chapter—not knowing Victoria—thought it was one of the best in the book.

As he described Victoria, through the prism of his own ego, Keyserling made both a confession and an accusation. He acknowledged that the Versailles experience was "the most fairy-tale-like situation in my life," and that he felt himself "in the thrall of the most other-worldly woman whom I have ever encountered."[95] She had sought him out as a deity-worshipper, he said, but her "matter-of-factness" made her unreceptive to his teaching that the spiritual must be combined with the earthly.[96] He confessed that he tried to "fictionalize" her (his euphemism for "sleep with"), but "the resistance which Victoria showed against being fictionalized by me provoked me to particularly emphatic, even occasionally violent fictional distortion."[97] Thereupon, he said, he called her an iconoclast—his way of pointing out that their relationship was "abnormal" and "even more eccentric than that between Beatrice and Dante."[98] In her rejection of him, he admitted that there was probably a measure of

disappointment on her part over not finding in him the spiritual fulfillment she had sought. Yet this did not deter him from characterizing her as
a schizoid personality. Her resistance had only one possible explanation
for him: "she was someone who, in extremely intense life experiences,
embodied the medieval split between spirit and flesh."[99] The chapter
closed with this curious statement, both aggressive and defensive, as if
anticipating future criticism:

> I know very well: no one has seen Victoria Ocampo as great as I have. Few of
> those who know her well, among them perhaps she herself, will possibly
> read my description without shaking their heads. But who really had
> something from her, they or I? Who did justice to her in the deeper or
> higher sense, *I*, the transcendor, or the registrar of facts without sense for
> their meaning? *One* woman really opened up a world hitherto unknown to
> me — within me as well as outside of me — and provided therewith the
> impetus for a decisive transformation.[100]

In Keyserling's vocabulary, "to do justice" was apparently synonymous with "to use for one's own benefit." The ultimate accomplishment
for a woman, as he saw it, was to be an anima figure, a mediator between
man's ego and his unconscious, an "evocative woman." Earlier, in 1934, he
had written a brief introduction to an Argentine publication dealing with
Victoria Ocampo; it read in part:

> And thus I believe that what will *remain* of Victoria is something much
> more important than what her South American friends and admirers be-
> lieve. It is known that the true influence of the great instigators of political,
> social and religious movements is completely different from what they
> intend it to be and what their contemporaries see. The same thing happens
> with women of great caliber. It doesn't matter in the end what they are or
> believe themselves to be or what they seem or even what they do—what
> matters is their *evocative force*. And I do not believe that at this moment in
> history there exists a more evocative woman than Victoria. She is not
> inspirational—nor can she be, as she is too involved in herself. But without
> a doubt, this woman has evoked more — without the majority of her
> "objects" knowing it—than almost all the women one hears about. This is
> because Victoria is the most strongly telluric woman that exists.[101]

Although Keyserling was right about Victoria's "evocative force"—witness
Ortega and Tagore's reaction to her—he was supremely presumptuous (as
was his nature) and supremely unjust to say "it doesn't matter in the end
what they are or believe themselves to be or what they seem or even what
they do." It matters enormously to the individual herself, even if she is
one of history's great instigators.

This was what Victoria set out to express in a small book entitled *El*

viajero y una de sus sombras: Keyserling en mis memorias (The Traveler
and One of his Shadows: Keyserling in my Memoirs) written in 1951. In
her characteristically straightforward, almost conversational style, with
more than a touch of sarcasm and ironic humor, she tells the story of their
stormy relationship from beginning to end. As the literary testimony of a
woman confronting the problem of the psychology of the sexes on the
basis of her own experience, it is a book that can stand alongside those of
Colette, Woolf, de Beauvoir, and Lessing—the precursors, one might say,
of today's heightened feminist awareness in literature. Victoria describes
in Keyserling what Virginia Woolf referred to as "a spot the size of a
shilling at the back of the head which one can never see for oneself,"
performing what Woolf called "one of the good offices that sex can dis-
charge for sex."[102] Too few women have done this service for men, she
said, and done it effectively, without anger.

These pages of clarification are necessary, says Victoria, because "V.
O. is not a character in a novel that an author can mold as he chooses."[103]
Nor is she a symbol of South America to be fantasized as Keyserling did
the *puna* (an Andean altitude sickness) or the llama:

> Circumstances may have decreed that Keyserling encompass me in his
> vision of South America in the company of the puna and the llama. But the
> truth is that if I didn't disappoint him as puna, I certainly did as llama. It's
> well known that the llama refuses to walk if it's burdened with more weight
> than it can carry. That was my only resemblance to it, to my misfortune. And
> thus I warranted being punished for Andean schizophrenia.[104]

How rarely, she reflects, are male writers—and men in general—
capable of putting aside their masculine pride in order to understand the
true nature of a woman's interest in them (or lack thereof):

> [Bernard] Shaw seems, in his [autobiographical] writing, to be considera-
> bly lacking in this complex. He begins by saying that if he remained
> sexually continent until the age of 29 (a rather extraordinary case!), he
> never connected sexual activity with delinquency (an uncommon attitude
> to have even in our day). From the moment he began to dress well, he says,
> he began to have success. Women sought him out. But his success as a
> well-dressed man coincided with his literary success, which allowed him
> that luxury. So one can't ascribe all his success to clothing. Here, miracle of
> miracles!, is what he writes about the women who hovered around his new
> (or old) glory: "Not all my women pursuers wanted to have sexual relations
> with me." And I say: miracle of miracles!, because a statement like that on
> the part of a world-famous author is more unusual even than his having
> been continent until the age of 29; also the perceptivity that such a state-
> ment implies is as contrary to masculine nature as a miracle is to the laws of
> nature itself. But his perceptivity goes even farther (oh Montherlant!):

"Some were willing to buy my friendship in the currency of pleasure, since they had learned by varied experience that men are made in that way. Others . . . etc. No two cases were alike."

A woman may have various reasons for prostituting herself (if one gives that name — as one should — to sex without love in exchange for some material or practical benefit). It's not only a question of jewels, furs, comfortable apartments or one's daily bread. There are other kinds of ambitions: the movies, the theater, politics, marriage, even literary glory, for all I know! [. . .] But in those not-infrequent cases, let's get it straight: Adam is the one offering the apple, Adam the one who talks first to the serpent. We know all too well that "the little scheme between the Woman and the Serpent destroyed the bases of the original plan" when it came to the creation of the First Author. But, if it's true that the mix-up of that plan didn't start with the man, he has certainly made up for it in destruction of another kind. He has no reason to be modest. And a lot of women would like to say to him now and then: Give me back the apple, take your rib, and let's forget it![105]

When she refused to bend to Keyserling's will, when she denied him the satisfaction of a "conquest," he could only see her attitude as abnormal. According to her:

When a woman is captive of an intellectual enthusiasm or a spiritual devotion to such and such a thinker, writer, sage or hero, there's no reason that it must end, fatally, in amorous passion. But it's true that the majority of thinkers, writers, heroes and even wise men, whether they admit it or not, often put their self-love (rarely their love) into conquests in that area. Even if only to prove their power to themselves and satisfy a very natural but not admirable instinct for domination. I suppose it must be pleasant to feel oneself adored as a thinker, writer, hero or wise man; it must be more flattering to feel oneself desired as a man. Thinkers, writers, heroes and geniuses generally detest it when women incorporate them into the calendar of saints. They don't admit that a normal woman can do so without suffering from a certain imbalance, a rare phenomenon which they attribute to some pathological state or other that they choose to diagnose. Blind and deaf to all reality that they themselves do not dictate as creators, that they see in that imperfect and indocile creature: "the incarnation of the sharpest split between nature and spirit."[106]

Keyserling's theory of Man as Spirit and Woman as Flesh—not uncommon in philosophical circles both in Darmstadt and elsewhere — was, according to Victoria, the result of a man's need to rationalize his own "weakness of the flesh":

. . . I have never admitted (although it may be the opinion of every philosopher and prophet) that man, as the carrier of spermatozoa, was the representative of the Spirit on earth, while woman, as the carrier of ovaries, was the representative of telluric forces. To the contrary, I believe—and I repeat it again—that if men have seen in woman the representative of said telluric forces, it is through a phenomenon called projection. The reaction caused in them by the woman as woman made them attribute to her the feelings that they had in her presence. They pronounced her emotional because she awakened their emotion. They pronounced her animal because her proximity acted on certain glands in them. And since, in the first and last analysis, they sought in woman, consciously or unconsciously, agitations of that order, they generally left Spirit in the closet, like an unnecesary umbrella, and ended up (or began) believing themselves the true representatives of the Spirit that they naturally did not find in her for lack of an organ to perceive it (the organ had stayed in the closet).[107]

Thus Victoria redefines—as Simone de Beauvoir did a few years earlier—the myth of Woman as Nature, as the "Other." In de Beauvoir's words:

Man seeks in woman the Other as Nature and as his fellow being. But we know what ambivalent feelings Nature inspires in man. He exploits her, but she crushes him, he is born of her and dies in her; she is the source of his being and the realm that he subjugates to his will; Nature is a vein of gross material in which the soul is imprisoned, and she is the supreme reality; she is contingence and Idea, the finite and the whole; she is what opposes the Spirit, and the Spirit itself. Now ally, now enemy, she appears as the dark chaos from whence life wells up, as this life itself, and as the over-yonder toward which life tends.[108]

Keyserling had felt this ambivalence and had transferred it to Victoria, labeling her as the embodiment of "the medieval split between spirit and flesh." It was, then, largely a projection of himself that he saw in a mirror named Victoria Ocampo.

In addition to this explanation for Keyserling's behavior toward her, however, Victoria sensed that there was another psychological motive behind his extravagant projections. Delving further into his memoirs, she found a chapter he wrote about his mother in which she learned that Keyserling harbored deep resentment over a childhood crisis involving his mother's second marriage to a man he despised and considered her inferior. Moreover, he blamed himself for not having aggressively insisted that she remain true to her first husband's memory. His mother, whom he associated with nurturing and thus with the earth, became identified in his mind with the monstrous and satanic. To avoid thinking of his own inadequacy, he unconsciously suppressed this association while consciously cultivating his spiritual nature. His encounter with Victoria—the Earth Woman in his eyes—and with South America—the Magna Mater—brought these repressed associations back into his conscious awareness.

Unknown to Victoria when she wrote this analysis in her book was Keyserling's correspondence with Jung, and in particular, a letter in which Jung responded to Keyserling's confession of negative feelings toward his mother. According to Jung: "Such feelings are always an affront to nature, unnatural. Hence distance from the earth, identification with the father, heaven, light, wind, spirit, Logos. Rejection of the earth, of what is below, dark, feminine."[109] It is significant to note that this letter was written in August 1928, five months before Keyserling met Victoria in Versailles. Thus, as Victoria points out from another perspective, the tables were turned: Keyserling himself was suffering from a deep division in his own psyche that had prompted much of their misunderstanding.

Finally, one aspect of their relationship requires some clarification and further analysis because it is a pivotal factor in Victoria's relationship with Ortega, Tagore, and other men she admired. Ever since her adolescence, Victoria has been, by her own repeated confession, an incorrigible hero-worshipper, but she has qualified what it means to her: "If it's true that hero-worship can include another kind of love, it's also true that it can exist without it, and that's one of its characteristics. In this last form, not in the other, is how I've known hero-worship."[110]

In contemporary Western culture, the concept of hero-worship has had more negative than positive connotations because it has frequently been linked to the nineteenth-century antidemocratic, protofascist philosophies of Carlyle and Nietzsche. Dictators and demagogues from Napoleon to Hitler have cultivated the blind devotion of the masses they ruled, and therefore hero-worship has come to be associated with political fanaticism and the suppression of individuality by the state. The romantic view of the hero as a solitary, superior being — beyond the bourgeois values of good and evil—was appealing to both elitists seeking to preserve the status quo and to revolutionaries who despised the materialism of the industrial age. Precisely because hero-worship can be interpreted in so many ways, it has intrigued philosophers of both the right and the left. In fact, its roots can be traced back to a mixture of political, social, religious, moral, and aesthetic theories ranging from Plato's ideal state to the medieval divine right of kings to the Renaissance humanist's notion of the perfect prince.

The concept of a natural aristocracy was common to all these theories, though the limits of individual freedom may have been defined differently. In a democratic-oriented society, "aristocracy" is a word with negative associations; however, as Eric Bentley points out in his study of hero-worship, Thomas Jefferson saw it as a nonsocial, nonpolitical hierarchy that no democracy could afford to deny: "For I agree . . . ," wrote Jefferson in 1813, "that there is a natural aristocracy among men. The grounds of this are virtue and talents. . . . The natural aristocracy I consider as the most precious gift of nature, for the instruction, the trusts, and government of society."[111] This is how Victoria has understood and interpreted the notion of an elite or an aristocracy of individuals from whom she singled out personal heroes to worship. Nothing could be more abhorrent to her than tyranny disguised as Heroic-Vitalism, that is, immorality rationalized by social or political elitism.

Nor does Victoria define hero-worship as acquiescence to the patriarchal custom of female subservience. When Keyserling protested that her worship and idealization of him had been an injustice for which she should have expected to pay the consequences (i.e., his desire to "fictionalize" her), he was merely expressing what has been a common attitude in Western culture for centuries.[112] He assumed, as did Ortega and Tagore, that a woman's highest function in life was to be a muse whose "magical power," "shakti," or "evocative force" existed for man's benefit. What they were saying made perfect sense to *them*: a woman should feel honored to put herself docilely and passively at the service of a man—she as the mediator, he as the creator. A man could worship a woman and be free to choose whether she should stand in regal chastity on a pedestal or lie voluptuously beside him in bed. But the idea that a woman might need a male muse, an inspiration for her creative energies, was rarely entertained. The possibility that she might admire a man on a level that had nothing to do with sexual attraction did not fit into a man's stereotypical image of her. Ortega, Tagore, and Keyserling saw the "myth" of Victoria Ocampo—valid in its own context—but they found it much more difficult to see the "reality" of her as she interpreted it.

C. G. Jung spoke somewhat nebulously of a woman's animus, a woman's need to project her "masculine" qualities onto a male in order to achieve her own psychic development. One of his female disciples has clarified what he tried to say: "Projection of the animus occurs when its qualities of discrimination, creative contact with meaning, articulation, and penetration are seen either as embodied in a succession of men with whom the woman falls in love *or as the teacher with the truth*."[113] (Emphasis added.) Jungian theory, even if it does retain sexist symbolic language, at least recognizes a woman's need to find her own kind of creative imagination.

When Victoria became passionately enthusiastic about the work of Ortega, Tagore, and Keyserling and about them as authors, she was looking for stimulation and incitation comparable to what they sought in her. Keyserling himself had preached the ethic of fecundating (as had Ortega), and Victoria responded to it: "I remember having talked at length with him [Gabriel Moner, in 1928] about *Wiedergeburt* [Moner was translating passages from the German for her] in the preface to which Keyserling had written: 'In *Symbolic Figures* I established my conviction that *no one can do anything but incite*, that there is no ethic superior to fecundity.' Well, it was as an inciter that I saw the power of Keyserling."[114] Victoria looked at her heroes as they looked at her—as one looks in a mirror seeking a clearer picture of oneself. But unlike them, she did not practice "looking-glass vision," she did not see herself enlarged or enhanced by comparison with them. The writers she worshipped as heroes were "teachers with *the* truth," intellectual and spiritual mentors, guides on an Augustinian or Dantesque pilgrimage in search of wholeness. Her passionate enthusiasm for them was an expression of her own acute feeling of intellectual inadequacy (thus the appeal of the idea of "the fecundity of the insufficient") which may, in turn, be explained by a stronger than average ambition, a stronger vitality, and equally strong realization of how great the gap was between her starting point and the destination she had in mind. One could also see it as the expression of frustrated genius. Since she felt herself superior to her environment, limited by its taboos and conventions, a sense of rebellion drove her to look for heroes, or mentors, elsewhere.

Her conflict with Keyserling—like the earlier conflict with Groussac —was a major turning point in her life. It forced her to recognize her tendency toward hero-worship for what it was: a projection of her own creative aspirations. One might say it was a weakness born out of strength that had both positive and negative aspects. In her words:

> I've lived all my life peering into books, peering into those magic windows:
> "... magic casements, opening on the foam
> Of perilous seas, in faery lands forlorn ..."
> I don't regret it, in spite of the disappointments with which my "cult of authors" has tended to reward me. I have also known, through it, great delights. I owe one of them to the reading of Keyserling, and I won't deny it. Nor will I deny my meeting (or clash) with him. It was a lesson to me, and I no longer regret having lived through it.[115]

Perhaps, she thought, her "Keyserlingian misfortune" was a kind of expiation for what Charles de Bos called "an almost monstrous and almost continual superabundance of religious emotion spent on profane objects," an emotion she referred to as "my lot in this life."[116] Secular divinities, sometimes all too accessible to their worshippers, have a very human way of resisting the distortions that divinization entails. This applies to female as well as male deities.

After 1929 there was a dramatic change in the course of events in Victoria's life. She began to take a more active role in the world of literature and the arts, carving out a career for herself that she has never abandoned. After that her heroes would never command the same slave-like devotion from her, nor would they be limited to men. Thanks to three men in particular she was able to understand her own myth and reality more fully, and she was now ready to express herself with more conscious awareness as a woman. Many years later, when she was chosen as the first woman to receive the prestigious Vaccaro Prize in Argentina, she concluded her speech of acceptance with these remarks:

> I have always dreamt that a woman might be for you, my men friends, an equal and a companion. I have never made pacts with those who didn't want this, whether they were friends or enemies. The Victorian situation seemed to me as humiliating for men as for women. To see men diminished by persisting in this injustice has been painful, because I like to admire them and love them. Only in admiring and loving have I found happiness. Admiring and loving lead us to accomplish work (whatever its nature) which is like the palpable demonstration of how we admire and love. I know that my work is nothing but this, nor does it have another meaning or reason for being. It's the result of a very intense and always renewed need to admire and to love. If there had not been in the world men (and I repeat, men) worthy of this admiration and love of mine, my life would have been very different. They have helped me in my struggle and I haven't even always needed their physical presence. With the living and the dead I was not only in communication but in communion. *Never have so few been responsible for the pardoning of so many things done by others*.[117] (Emphasis added.)

Victoria's inclination has always been to treat men as allies, not as adversaries. To reach out, to love and admire, has been her way of life, but she has had to acknowledge that appearances can be deceiving, that reaching the truth, as Dante pointed out, requires developing "the intelligence of love." Ortega, Tagore, and Keyserling—all of whom she loved and admired in different ways — helped her refine that "intelligence" without which the other kind of intelligence is ultimately meaningless.

CHAPTER FOUR

BARRIERS AND BRIDGES

"Machona!" men would shout at her as she drove a late-model Packard through the streets of Buenos Aires in the early 1920s. For a woman to sit nonchalantly behind the wheel of a roadster in those days was an open act of rebellion that jolted male egos and scandalized proper society. "There was Victorita," her maiden aunts hurried to tell her mother, "driving without a chauffeur—and in short sleeves!" The fact that Victoria was an adult and no longer living in her parents' home didn't lessen the enormity of the transgression. It simply wasn't acceptable behavior for a lady, particularly a lady of wealth and position. "That episode," Victoria has said, "repeated itself over and over in my life in Argentina. I have always been reproached, in different ways and for different things, for driving without a chauffeur and in short sleeves."[1]

At about the same time in another part of Latin America, a woman named Teresa de la Parra was writing a semi-autobiographical novel about a rebellious young woman of the upper classes in Caracas: María Eugenia Alonso had studied in Europe and returned to Venezuela to live with her grandmother and maiden aunt who criticized her incessantly for being too outspoken and too unladylike. Gradually her defiance diminished under the onslaught. As the novel ends, María Eugenia is about to marry a man she doesn't love and with whom she will spend her life, brainwashed into traditional domesticity. *Ifigenia* (1924) describes a way of life that was adhered to by aristocratic women throughout Latin America. In her awareness of its injustices, the author, like Victoria Ocampo, was way ahead of her time.[2]

When Victoria dared to drive a car in public, smoke in a Buenos Aires tea room, or live in her own apartment in the 1920s, she had to face the same kind of relentless criticism that broke María Eugenia's will. But Victoria did not succumb. In fact, she turned her back on proper society and cultivated a private world that reflected her own rebellious way of thinking.

A *Clearer Vision*

As Victoria was still establishing her intellectual identity on the periphery of the cultural world in the 1910s and 1920s, a small number of writers and artists in Buenos Aires were shocking traditionalists and offending orthodox taste with their innovative aesthetic trends. Influenced by Latin American Modernism (Ruben Darío had lived and published in Buenos Aires) and by the European vanguard (Surrealism, Cubism, Dadaism, etc.), these young Argentine writers—among them, Jorge Luis Borges, Guillermo de Torre, and Eduardo González Lanuza—called themselves "Ultraists," indicating that their work was the most avant-garde on both continents. They saw themselves as a creative elite, a minority of intellectual and artistic purists with unique talent and outlook. Although Victoria was not a member of this group, her own aesthetic sensibilities were close to theirs. She too was essentially at odds with what most Argentines considered "good taste," as her interests and friendships at the time reveal.

An Argentine author of her own generation, who nonetheless collaborated with some of the younger Ultraists, was one of her closest friends during those years. His name was Ricardo Güiraldes. From a well-to-do family and educated in the European mold, Güiraldes shared, among other things, Victoria's passion for France where he had spent part of his childhood. He and his wife, Adelina del Carril, would visit Victoria frequently on Tucumán Street and later on Montevideo Street. (This was long before Güiraldes became a national hero with the publication of *Don Segundo Sombra* in 1926, the story of a young orphan's fascination with a mysterious gaucho and the change in the boy's life under his influence.) Over lunch and tea and in the hours in between, they would talk endlessly about French symbolist poetry, about the literature of the vanguard, and about Paris. They would laugh and joke with each other like brother and sister. Sometimes, Güiraldes would take out his guitar and play Argentine melodies; other times, they would dance with friends to the plaintive strains of porteño tangos, so popular at the time. Since they lived only a few blocks from one another, many late evening conversations were carried on into the early hours of the morning in the form of hand-delivered letters.

Along with their devotion to France and French literature, Victoria and Güiraldes shared a feeling of being outcasts in their own society, cultural exiles from Europe in America where their preferences were rarely appreciated. However, they also confessed to one another their love for the expansive beauties of their own country (he preferred the pampas, she the river), and they knew that in Europe they would have to endure another kind of nostalgia. These contradictory sentiments were not understood by most of their contemporaries who ignored or criticized Güiraldes's early publications. As Victoria has explained:

> Outside of Argentina, it's not easy to imagine the isolation and hostility that accompanied the early efforts of a young writer in the late 1910s or early 1920s. (Things have improved a bit since then.) A writer or an artist, especially if he belonged to Ricardo's social class — in a certain sense, the country's aristocracy — was considered lazy by the people of his class, a *poseur* or a snob by the intellectuals, and a pervert by the majority. Deprived of sympathy, deprived of conscientious criticism, that is, of points of reference, the writer, the artist, had the sensation of not hearing his own voice any longer. Sound is not generated in a vacuum. Ricardo suffered terribly from this at the beginning of his career.[3]

So they turned to one another for support. When Güiraldes wrote the tragic prose-poem, *Rosaura*, in the space of merely twenty days in 1918, he read it aloud to Victoria before sending it off for publication. In a later work, *Xamaica*, he modeled the protagonist, Clara Ordóñez, after her and asked her permission to use one of her letters to him in his text. Güiraldes's premature death in 1927, barely a year after the resounding success of *Don Segundo Sombra*, was a great blow to Victoria, who cherished his friendship in a very special way:

> You called me sister; you gave me that title when writing me. It's not by chance that in religious orders this relationship, transported to the realm of the spirit, is a symbol of a sacred tie between individuals and of an attitude of the soul. Happy are they who can reach those heights where our worst enemies become our brothers. I aspire to that blessed state, but I'm no doubt too weak to merit it yet. One effect of this weakness is the need for brothers like you to keep alive in my heart the most difficult of the three theological virtues: Hope.[4]

She wrote this final letter to Güiraldes twenty-five years after his death at a time when she was deeply depressed by the state of affairs in Argentina and shortly before she herself was to become a victim of government oppression.

Another close friend of hers during the 1920s was the Swiss musician, Ernest Ansermet. He had come to Buenos Aires in 1924 after directing the orchestra of Diaghilev's Ballets Russes (whom he had accompanied to Argentina for the first time in 1917) with the object of conducting a series of concerts by Argentine musicians who had formed the first national symphony orchestra, a disparate group functioning on a shoe-string budget. Excited by the quality of the performance she attended, Victoria sought out Ansermet and invited him to lunch at her home. Before long, she had convinced him that he should come back to Argentina on a regular basis to conduct the symphony; in order to insure that there would be a symphony to conduct, she also convinced the president of the republic (who happened to be her friend, Marcelo T. Alvear) to allocate a govern-ment stipend to help the orchestra survive.

When Ansermet returned to Buenos Aires the following season, he brought with him the finest contemporary music being written in Europe at the time — works by Stravinsky, Honegger, and other avant-garde composers. Although it didn't always please conservative Argentine audi-ences, it thrilled Victoria. At home, Ansermet would play it for her on the piano, or they would listen to recordings and he would explain them to her in detail and tell her about composers and artists he knew. They also shared a passion for North American jazz.

During the years Ansermet conducted regularly in Buenos Aires—until 1927 when a conservative group on the symphony's board insisted on inviting a new conductor—Victoria was immersed in music and dedicated to upgrading the musical taste of the uninitiated Argentine public. As a result, she made her own debut on the stage, not as an actress as she had once dreamed, but as a dramatic narrator. It was on August 29, 1925. Victoria performed the narrator's role in Honegger's new oratorio *Le Roi David*, conducted by Ansermet. The role, originally recited by Jacques Copeau, had never been performed by a woman. When Ansermet first thought of doing the piece in Buenos Aires, he intended to have a male narrator read the role in Spanish translation. Then Victoria suggested to him that a woman might do the recitation just as effectively in the original French. Ansermet was skeptical until Victoria added that she could take the part if he wished. After the performance, he confessed that she had taught him a lesson:

> You can't imagine [he wrote to her], how, at the beginning, the principle of a man's voice reciting in the audience's native tongue seemed an absolute necessity to me. It's a sign that, in me, abstract logic (always false outside mathematics) imposes itself over the aesthetic sense. From my background and teaching habits, I've remained something of a "pedant" and also some-thing of a "foot-dragger." In this adventure of *Le Roi David*, even before you knew the piece well, you had a sharper and clearer vision than I. Still more: you made the whole work have more meaning for me than it ever had before.[5]

Ansermet saw something in Victoria that it would take the Argentine public much longer to recognize and respect: her gift of vision.

Music and musicians have been almost as important in Victoria's life as books and authors. Through Ansermet, she later met and became a close friend of Igor Stravinsky, her musical idol since the first time she heard his *Sacre* in Paris. In 1936, Stravinsky was her guest in Buenos Aires where he had come to conduct his *Perséphone*, composed around a poem by André Gide and originally performed as a ballet-recitation in 1933 by Ida Rubenstein. The Teatro Colón wanted a re-creation of the original version, but at Stravinsky's insistence, the recitation was performed by Victoria, who later accompanied him to Rio de Janeiro to repeat the performance. In 1939, she recited the role once again in Florence under the maestro's baton.

The artists whom Victoria was instrumental in bringing to Argentina were not always as well-known or as appreciated by the Argentine public as was the composer of *Perséphone* in 1936. Many were still considered avant-garde in their own countries; some had only been recognized by a minority in European circles. Even when the quality of something or someone new *had* been noticed abroad, it took a special talent in the 1920s and 1930s—before mass cultural communication on an international level became as common as it is today — to single it out from a distance of thousands of miles with an ocean in between. Victoria had that talent, that vision that Ansermet had praised. But one person's vision may well be another's eyesore. Such was the case when Victoria became enthusiastic about modern architecture.

In 1927, after studying many books and illustrations of the New Architecture of the Bauhaus group, particularly Gropius and Le Corbusier, Victoria made up her mind to have a house of similar, modern design built for her in Mar del Plata. On a lot high on a hill overlooking the Atlantic, she had a local builder of horse stables construct a white, cube-shaped house with large windows, starkly modern and functional inside and out. Much to the horror of other residents of the resort community, it stood out like a pristine beacon of rebellion in the midst of the conventional chalets and villas. People would go out of their way to gawk at what was commonly referred to as "the ugliest house in Mar del Plata." But Victoria was not fazed.

A year later, eager to undertake a more ambitious project, she sold the house in Mar del Plata and put the money towards building a larger home in the Palermo Chico section of Buenos Aires. The house stands today, as it did then, right across from the Plaza Francia on a tree-shaded street named Rufino de Elizalde. Inspired by Le Corbusier in its plain white, geometric exterior and uncluttered, white-walled interior, the

Palermo Chico house still attracts attention because it is so unlike the Beaux Arts mansions and modern high-rises that were later built around it. The architect, who had drawn up plans to Victoria's specifications, refused to place his name on the cornerstone as was customary in Argentina. Neighbors petitioned municipal authorities to have the house torn down, but to no avail.

For decades, Argentines had favored a traditional, undistinguished style of European architecture that had turned Buenos Aires into a city that had practically obliterated its colonial heritage and come to resemble the Old World more than the New. It was one of the reasons the city was referred to, as early as 1910, as "the Paris of South America." Ironically, the native colonial architecture that was demolished had a great deal in common with Bauhaus architecture in its unadorned, functional design constructed to fit human needs and dimensions. They were both styles that suited a free and open American environment.

Hoping to reeducate Argentines to this viewpoint, Victoria was one of the prime movers in convincing Le Corbusier to come to Buenos Aires in 1929 to deliver a series of lectures on modern architecture. During his stay, he went to see the house in Mar del Plata and visited her in the new one in Palermo Chico. Both houses delighted him, and he congratulated her, whereupon Victoria brought up the possibility of transforming the face of Buenos Aires with examples of his architecture. Le Corbusier was more than willing to cooperate, but, as Victoria explains:

> I couldn't find people who were enthusiastic enough about Le Corbusier's projects to risk money on them. It was a bitter disillusionment for him and for me, and a wasted opportunity for Buenos Aires to begin opening itself like a fan facing the river, toward which it constantly and unattractively turns its back.[6]

She would have liked Le Corbusier to design at least a small resort community on the banks of the river near San Isidro on some property that belonged to her mother, but even her mother could not be convinced.

Three years before his death in 1965, Le Corbusier wrote a tribute to Victoria whom he had come to know well after their mutual disappointment. "Victoria," he said, "you have led a courageous combat. My respect and my friendship."[7] By then, they had both been vindicated, but as far as she was concerned, it was a battle that was never won.

When her parents died (her father in 1931, her mother in 1935), Victoria was confronted with having to make a choice between staying in her new home or moving to the family quinta that she inherited in San Isidro. Materially, she preferred the house in Palermo Chico, but emotionally and spiritually her ties to Villa Ocampo were too strong to sever. Nostalgia—in which no intellectual preferences play a part—brought her back, once and for all, to the barrancas overlooking the River Plate.

Federico García Lorca had not yet written about another house, *La casa de Bernarda Alba* (nor had he yet visited Villa Ocampo as he did in 1933), when Victoria met a Spanish woman who was very unlike the symbolic characters in that tragic Andalusian play about women's oppression. María de Maeztu, author, teacher, and founder of a college for women in Madrid, first came to Buenos Aires in 1926, invited by the Spanish Cultural Institute to deliver a series of lectures. She had been one of the few women students at the University of Salamanca, where she received her doctorate; later she went to Madrid to study with Ortega y Gasset, and then to Marburg, Oxford, and Paris for further specialized studies. Her primary field was pedagogy, though she was trained in literature and philosophy. As a lecturer, she was brilliant, according to one knowledgeable listener:

> Her lectures are a bit of theater, because María de Maeztu evokes ideas with such dramatic force—treating them like people, carrying on dialogues with them, while looking at, gesturing toward and questioning that place in the proscenium where (no doubt!) Plato himself, stands—that the public is breathless watching those spiritual movements in march, watching those centuries that stand up and come on stage, watching those tremendous ghosts of philosophers that cross the hall, conjured up by the miracle-worker. [8]

Considering the culture in which she was born, it was almost miraculous that Maeztu had succeeded in achieving such intellectual credibility.

When Victoria first met Maetzu in 1926 (and later when they met again in Madrid and finally in Argentina, where Maeztu sought refuge from the horror of the Civil War in Spain that had claimed the life of her brother, Ramiro, a well-known writer), the two women spoke again and again of a woman's right to have the same educational opportunities as a man. Maeztu had proven that it was possible for a woman to reach the highest levels of academia; she had taught at Spanish, Argentine, and North American universities and colleges (Wellesley, Bryn Mawr, Smith, Johns Hopkins). Nevertheless, her experience had convinced her that women needed more opportunities for higher education, so she founded the Residencia de Señoritas in Madrid in 1915, modeling it after the Institución Libre de Enseñanza founded in the same city in 1876 by Giner de los Ríos and the colleges for men she had seen in Great Britain. Giner's college had been inspired by the educational philosophy of C. F. Krause in Germany; *krausismo*, as it was called in Spain at the end of the last century, stood for educational reform, schools free from church or state control with a strongly humanistic and liberal approach to learning. Maeztu's college for women also interpreted educational reform to include the serious training of young women. It functioned successfully until the Civil War forced it to close its doors. In addition, Maeztu was also one of the directors of a coeducational primary school founded in 1918, another pedagogical innovation in Spain. If women were to contribute fully to society, she believed that society was obligated to prepare them to do so. As she once wrote:

> I am a feminist. I would be ashamed *not* to be one, because I believe that every woman who thinks must feel the desire to collaborate as a person in the total endeavor of human culture. And this is what feminism means to me. First of all: it is, on one side, the right a woman has to participate in cultural work, and on the other, society's duty to offer it to her. [. . .] To deny it to her would be immoral, like seeing her as an object, an extra-human being, unworthy of work.[9]

Victoria's long conversations with Maeztu in 1926 gave her the opportunity to articulate the feminist ideas she so rarely shared with anyone. When Maeztu left Buenos Aires that year, the tenor of their discussions stayed with Victoria as an inspiration. There was no question that she, like Maeztu, was committed to the principles of the struggle for women's equal rights. However, she had no intention at the moment of becoming involved with organized feminist activities. Her first objective was to educate herself, and that, as she saw it, would be a full-time occupation.

Rediscovering Europe

In the winter of 1928–29, when she decided to meet Keyserling in Versailles, Victoria returned to Europe for the first time in fifteen years. It had been a long separation from the continent that gave her so much intellectual nourishment, much longer than she would have ever imagined when she last left its shores. Although her hunger for European culture had been temporarily satisfied by visitors and travelers from abroad (Ortega, Tagore, Ansermet, Maeztu) and by enormous quantities of letters, books, and magazines, she longed to meet other writers there and immerse herself in their literary and artistic milieu.

Since the end of the First World War, Paris had become a haven for writers and artists of all nationalities, many of whom went there seeking a freedom of expression denied to them at home. Joyce, Picasso, Stravinsky, Pound, and Hemingway were a few of those who, in Valéry Larbaud's words, were welcomed as "real Parisians" because they contributed to "the material activity and the spiritual power of Paris."[10] Paris radiated creative vitality in the 1920s. As a center of culture it was unmatched by any other world capital. It was truly a mecca for the cultural pilgrim.

As would be her custom on all her trips (until 1955), Victoria traveled with Fani and later Pepa, her personal maids. For the first trip back to Europe in 1928, she also took along Fani's brother, José, her butler. In Paris, she lived in a rented apartment on the rue d'Artois. She also had a car and chauffeur to take her out to the Hôtel des Réservoirs or wherever she might please. Her way of life, abroad as at home, was elegant if not opulent. Her clothes were made to order by the finest couturiers. She took frequent trips to the Riviera, Italy, or England, indulged in the French food she adored, and bought tapestries by Picasso and Léger for her new house in Palermo Chico. Money was no object in those days, so keeping track of it or its value was never a concern.

During that first trip in 1928–29, her craving to meet writers and artists was amply satisfied. Besides Keyserling, she was introduced to Paul Valéry, Maurice Ravel, Gabriel Miró, Benjamin Fondane, Léon-Paul Fargue, Lev Chestov, Nikolai Berdiaeff, and Pierre Drieu la Rochelle. Drieu, a young writer and later director of the *Nouvelle Revue Française*, became an especially close friend. (It was he who introduced her to André Malraux and Aldous Huxley.) She met Drieu la Rochelle early in 1929, at about the same time she was visiting the Count in Versailles. Compared with the German's volcanic temperament and egomania, the Frenchman's low-keyed and refined manner, even his self-deprecation, was refreshing. Three years later, Drieu also came to South America at Victoria's invitation, and he too wrote a book with a South American setting, *L'homme à cheval*, (The Man on Horseback), in which one of the characters, Doña Camilla, was modeled after Victoria (a far less recognizable portrayal of her than Güiraldes's Clara Ordóñez). Driven by his own sense of weakness, partly from his experiences during the War of 1914, and by his disillusionment with the promises of democratic governments, Drieu gradually became an avowed Fascist and a Nazi sympathizer. In 1945 he committed suicide as the Nazis faced defeat. His last letter was addressed to Victoria who had remained his friend when others forsook him in spite of her total disagreement with his political philosophy and with his candidly sexist attitude toward women.

How could she, a believer in nonviolence, accept Drieu, who endorsed the use of force and totalitarianism, as her friend? The explanation lies in her own awareness of the contradictions inherent in human nature, contradictions that she knew tormented some individuals more than others. It was clear to her that Drieu's fascination with totalitarianism was largely a reaction to the inadequacies he hated inside himself and that, physically and spiritually, he was a victim of his own self-destructiveness. Unlike Keyserling, Drieu had never tried to impose his ideas on her or mold her to his liking; he was thus, in her opinion, a tragic and misguided man, but still a friend:

> If there's nothing more sweet and comforting than the companionship of a friend, there's perhaps no experience crueler or richer than suddenly finding in a friend we respect ideas we don't respect. I say this experience is rich because it teaches us to control our indignations, our impatiences, our angers, in fact, all the violent reactions that are born of mutual disagreements, mutual ignorances, mutual irritations. And besides, it also teaches us respect for an adversary.
>
> If the greatest happiness we can have in life is that of counting on friends worthy of our love, the greatest fortune is that of fighting against adversaries worthy of our respect.[11]

When she encountered enemies who were not worthy she could be implacable.

One of the first places any literary pilgrim to Paris visited was the rue de l'Odéon on the Left Bank, where there were two small bookshops with a reputation as gathering places for those who wrote and those who loved to read the latest literature. One was presided over by a Frenchwoman, Adrienne Monnier, who called her shop "La Maison des Amis des Livres." Across the street was an English-language bookstore called "Shakespeare and Company," run by Monnier's North American friend, Sylvia Beach. Together they were responsible for much of the literary activity on the Left Bank: they sponsored readings in their shops, set up lending libraries, brought authors together, helped translate their works, and even took on the thankless task of publishing, as Beach did with Joyce's work, for example. Monnier also wrote pieces for various journals including her own monthly review *Navire d'Argent* (1925–26), named (ironically, as it turned out) after the emblem of Paris, a ship that never sinks.

When Victoria arrived in Paris that first winter, she went to the rue de l'Odéon to see for herself what Güiraldes had told her was one of the landmarks of Paris, "La Maison des Amis des Livres." In the ample person of its proprietress, Victoria found a woman who felt the same passion she did for books and authors and who devoted herself religiously to creating a literary home for them. They became fast and dear friends. Monnier's more diminutive friend, Sylvia Beach, was equally dedicated; both of them were as generous to the often destitute writers who frequented their shops as their limited means would allow. Indeed, few of their clients were as wealthy as Victoria; she must have stood out among the relatively impecunious habitués of rue de l'Odéon, though she herself probably never gave the incongruity a second thought. If she was looked at with some wariness at first, she was soon accepted as an *amie* by those who met her there.

It was Beach who, in 1929, first recommended to Victoria that she read the works of the English novelist and essayist Virginia Woolf, especially a little book published that year entitled *A Room of One's Own*. The discovery of this eloquent and ironic commentary on women and literature was a revelation for Victoria. Here was a kindred spirit, someone who understood what it was like to be hobbled by being an intelligent woman in a patriarchal society. Like Woolf, Victoria was more blessed than most women who wanted to write, for she had money, a room of her own, and the freedom to pursue her objectives. But what she lacked, as *A Room of One's Own* expressed so well, was the feeling of confidence and self-assurance that centuries of male tradition provided to the most ordinary of male writers. This book, which said so effectively what Victoria had only thought to herself, instantly became a precious literary treasure, its author one of her heroes.

Through Adrienne Monnier, some years later, Victoria met a young Parisian woman of German-Jewish background who had just completed her studies and was beginning her career as a photographer. Gisèle Freund remembers Victoria at their first meeting in 1938 as "a towering figure," a beautiful, aristocratic woman who was extremely generous to young writers and artists. One evening in 1939, Freund, Denis de Rougement, and Roger Caillois were having dinner with Victoria and Adrienne Monnier at the latter's apartment. Apparently, Victoria invited them all to Buenos Aires, at which they all protested jokingly that they hardly knew where Buenos Aires was. Within a few years, all of them, excepting Monnier, would flee occupied France and find refuge at Villa Ocampo. In fact, Victoria was responsible for getting Freund out of France just before the Nazis arrived, having sent money for her trip to Argentina and a visa when Freund was without funds or anyone else to turn to for help.

In Buenos Aires in the early 1940s, Freund photographed Victoria (as she had in 1939 and would again in later years), and added her portrait to the stunning collection of those she had taken of writers and artists all over Europe. In those days, Victoria presided like a queen over a cultural court in Buenos Aires, many of whose members were voluntary and involuntary exiles from France, Spain, or other countries in Latin America. The plenitude of life there in the years before Perón was a sharp contrast to the deprivation of war-torn France. As an expression of solidarity with the French writers suffering under the occupation, Freund conceived the idea, which Victoria immediately championed, that the

Argentine cultural and business communities sponsor a shipment of clothes, food, and other rationed items to Adrienne Monnier, who would distribute them to writers at "La Maison des Amis des Livres." With money raised principally by Victoria and Gisèle Freund, three tons of provisions were sent to France in 1945, and thanks to Malraux's intervention, trucks were waiting in Marseilles to escort the shipment to the rue de l'Odéon. As a return gesture of appreciation, the French writers sent copies of their books to Argentina. When Victoria went back to France after the war in 1946, Adrienne Monnier organized a tribute to her at which she read a short speech that began:

> Dear Victoria Ocampo.
>> We are happy, very happy to have you among us.
>> You are truly an extraordinary person. I am sure that there is not, in all of Argentina, a woman or man who is more *Argentine* than you. You are of your country to the point where symbols are born.[12]

André Gide, whom Victoria had met in 1930, also spoke in her honor at the Bibliothèque Doucet:

> I must begin by making a confession to you which will help explain the great pleasure that we here joined together feel at having you among us and with what impatience I awaited your coming: I was beginning to believe that the name of Victoria Ocampo, which has become so dear to all of us, stood not just for a real person, but for a myth, a myth that incorporated everything Argentina could offer that was kind, intelligent, generous and charming. . . .[13]

By the end of the war, the legend of Victoria Ocampo was as well known in Europe as in Latin America. Yet ironically, as Gide's words indicate, she was received with more unqualified warmth and affection in the Old World than she was in the New. Her friendships in Europe had become legion. Jean Cocteau, Jacques Lacan, Paul Claudel, Paul Eluard, André Maurois, Louis Jouvet, and René Etiemble were just a few of those who would have agreed that, in Larbaud's terms, Victoria was a real Parisian.

One prominent woman Victoria had hoped to meet in Paris in 1929 was Countess Anna de Noailles, Princess of Brancovan, a poet and novelist whose work had been widely read in the early 1900s and highly praised by younger writers such as Proust, Ortega, and Cocteau. Victoria had memorized her verses when she was fifteen; so it was with considerable excitement that with an introduction from Keyserling, she went to visit the Countess late one afternoon. Dramatically swathed in veils and reclining in bed, the Countess greeted her guest warmly, remarking that Victoria's small handwriting had not prepared her to expect such a large young woman; since she herself was so tiny, she added, side by side they would look like Russia and Belgium. As Victoria listened, the voluble Countess enveloped her in talk on all kinds of subjects. She was as charming and intelligent as Victoria had imagined. But there was one topic to which she returned, directly or indirectly, that impressed Victoria more than any other: the relentless criticism of her own sex. Women of intellectual accomplishment like herself, she believed, agreeing with Ortega, were the exceptions that proved the general rule that women were inferior to men. As they conversed in the half-light of the Countess's bedroom, so filled with furniture and *objets* that little space was left to maneuver a way through them, Victoria felt stifled by more than the physical atmosphere. Anna de Noailles was a confirmed antifeminist, a woman as prejudiced in her views as the most biased man. When Victoria learned that Napoleon had been one of her heroes since childhood, she was not surprised; as she later wrote in an essay about the Countess, with bittersweet recollections of their first meeting: "Only an antifeminist could express a preference for the Bonaparte responsible for the civil code that established the legal disqualification of women in so many areas of life."[14] It seemed to Victoria that an attitude like Madame de Noailles's could only be explained as an excess of pride and vanity that prevented her from admitting that women in general might be as talented as men. Clearly, the struggle for women's rights would require educating women to recognize that by supporting the prejudices of the past they were as guilty as men of the oppression other women suffered. (Witness Lorca's Bernarda Alba.) Worse yet, they had become collaborators in a form of tyranny of which they themselves were the victims.

A Soul Without a Passport

If Victoria anticipated that in Europe in 1928–29 she would feel a stronger sense of belonging than she did at home, she was mistaken. Despite her education, despite her fluent French and English, she soon discovered that in Europe she was "the other" just as she had been at home in Argentina. This time, however, the "otherness" was not a sense of alienation brought on by sexist or socioeconomic prejudice; it was the realization that, for Europeans, South America was not another continent but another world, a world of which they had little knowledge or understanding. Most of them were ignorant not only of its geography but also of its people. Was Buenos Aires in Brazil? she was asked. Were the natives civilized? How did she stand the tropical heat all the time? Argentina might just as well have been Mexico, for all many people knew of the differences between the two. Considering the misconceptions they had about her country—the result, Victoria believed, of an ingrained attitude of superiority toward America, North and South—how could she hope to feel totally at home there? The thought of staying and living in Paris had crossed her mind more than once, but this realization dissuaded her. She was comfortable and happy with friends in Europe; it was a cultural climate in which she thrived. But she acknowledged to herself and to a few friends that, however nourished she was there, the setting her soul craved was one Europe could not provide.

It was after her return from Europe in 1929 that she met Waldo Frank through his translator, Eduardo Mallea, then a writer for *La Nación*. North American author of novels, essays, and the highly acclaimed book, *Virgin Spain* (1926), also published in Spanish by Ortega's Revista de Occidente, Frank had been invited to South America to share his messianic vision of a New America united by a spirit of hemispheric solidarity. Two "half-worlds," he proclaimed, could become one mystical organic whole, coexisting in harmony and combining the best qualities of the materialistic North and the spiritual South. Frank was a short, stocky, mustachioed man, unpretentious and sincere; he spoke like a prophet and awakened the sympathy of his audiences by addressing them as "sisters and brothers." His tour was an enormous success. In Buenos Aires, he was feted at banquets and cheered by crowds in the streets. Some said that he had an appeal not unlike that of Charlie Chaplin, of whom he spoke in his lectures. But Frank was a master of words, not gestures. In a speech in Buenos Aires in 1929, he spoke of the challenge to create a New America:

I am here, friends, primarily because I am an artist. I have not come to preach, or to pray, or to pry. I have come because what interests me more than all else in the world is *creation*: aesthetic, spiritual creation. And I have felt for long that there was something here which I needed, in my own terms and in my own humble way, to create. America is a potential organism: a potential Whole. Actually, up to now, it has been little more than a word. And America will be created by artists. By artists of all kinds: artists in thoughts, in words, in architecture, in plastic form, in music—artists in law, in relationship, and in action. Only artists can create America: and only to the extent that artists have created America, can the peoples of America experience America and enjoy it. And this, to me, is the ultimate goal: an America that will be realised, experienced, and enjoyed by the many American peoples.[15]

Coming from a Yankee, who, though extremely patriotic, was not afraid to identify what he disliked about the United States, these words found a deep resonance among Argentine intellectuals who felt—as Victoria did —that their country had to develop an awareness of its own authentic identity apart from but not necessarily at odds with that of Europe or North America.

In their discussions together with Mallea, Frank seemed to understand the feeling Victoria had had in Europe of being "like the owner of a soul without a passport."[16] As Victoria wrote to Tagore in 1930:

> He [Waldo Frank] has experienced in the North what we have been suffering in the South. And when we found out that we shared this orphan-feeling, we also thought that it could be stopped some day or other through the whole continent . . . because so many people shared it. We miss Europe terribly, both of us, and yet when we reach Europe and live in it, we both feel she cannot give us the kind of nourishment we need. We feel, in one word, that we *belong* to America, crude, uncultured, unformed, chaotic America. America that means suffering for us, but for whom we are ready to suffer, even against our will.[17]

Frank listened sympathetically when Victoria described the sensation of being treated like an exotic bird by Europeans. Worse yet, she told him, if a South American attempted to define him or herself, there was still the problem of having to describe his environment. The vastness and monotony of the South American landscape offered no recognizable reference points, no familiar associations for Europeans; "even if I had a gift of expression powerful enough to describe that hopelessly unpicturesque soul," said Victoria, "it would remain temporarily invisible to the majority of European eyes, accustomed as they are to other sights."[18] The pampas, the jungles, the mountain ranges, the rivers of America were so vast, she believed, that the South American was unable to see himself mirrored clearly in the landscape of his country, and thus was unable to explain himself to others.

The sense of alienation that Victoria expressed to Frank was reiterated by Mallea in a book published a few years later, entitled *Historia de una pasion argentina* (Story of an Argentine Passion) (1935), in which he wrote of the "visible" and the "invisible" Argentina, the latter being the authentic national character, and the former being an inauthentic, irresponsible, parasitic attitude of dependency on Europe. In an effort to explain why Argentines or South Americans in general had failed to realize their potential as young nations, other authors wrote similar introspective studies, influenced not only by Frank but by Ortega as well. According to Ezequiel Martínez Estrada in *Radiografía de la pampa* (X-Ray of the Pampa), published in Buenos Aires in 1933, the problem lay, as Victoria had suggested, in the isolation of South America imposed by its geography and by its lack of historical continuity. Physical distances had created psychological distances between peoples on the continent;

they had also produced an atmosphere of sterility due to a lack of communication between man and his environment. Almost two decades later, in an effort to analyze a similar alienation and insecurity among Mexicans, Octavio Paz wrote *El laberinto de la soledad* (The Labyrinth of Solitude) (1950), in which he spoke of the otherness of Latin Americans who had existed for generations as objects acted upon, not subjects acting and molding their own identity. Because they had lived a lie superimposed from without (from Spain, Europe, or, more recently, the United States), they felt alienated from their own as well as the foreign reality. Alienation, according to Paz (who cites Toynbee), is an archetypal experience common to those who break ties with the past and prepare to create a new future; no separation or solitude can be permanent, however, without becoming a death sentence. For there to be growth, he concludes, there must be organic solidarity. The studies of Mallea, Martínez Estrada, Paz, and many other Latin American essayists have been echoed by modern Latin American novelists who have also written of unfulfilled potenital, of alienation and insecurity, i.e., Carlos Fuentes's *La muerte de Artemio Cruz* (The Death of Artemio Cruz), Julio Cortázar's *Rayuela* (Hopscotch), or Gabriel García Márquez's *Cien años de soledad* (One Hundred Years of Solitude). What Victoria sensed and wrote about in 1929 became a hemispheric preoccupation.

Waldo Frank understood Victoria's need to make a more definitive commitment to literature and culture in Argentina, her need to become more involved in her circumstance, as Ortega had also observed. Surely, he saw before him in South America in 1929 a woman overflowing with creative energy, a woman of intelligence, of taste, and of aesthetic and spiritual sensitivity. In addition—and importantly—she had wealth and influence. Victoria, along with Mallea who was equally committed, would be the perfect one to give concrete shape to the New America in the form of a literary review. She must accept the challenge, he told her, and Mallea agreed. The review, possibly in Spanish and English, would be a cultural bridge between the Americas, a forum for the best thinkers of both continents. Day after day the three of them talked about the project, and time and again Victoria protested that she had no idea of what was involved in publishing, that other reviews put out by more experienced writers like Borges and Güiraldes had run aground on the shoals of criticism, disagreement, or financial insolvency after being launched with high hopes and purposes. But Frank and Mallea argued that she had to do it, that she was destined, in fact, to publish a review of her own. The more she demurred, the more they insisted. Finally, she agreed to consider it and to discuss the idea with friends in Europe; she would test the water, get their reaction, and then meet Frank in the United States the following spring to make final plans.

The reaction in Europe in the winter of 1929–30 was favorable, albeit guarded as to prognostications for the review's chances for survival. She could count on cooperation from friends like Drieu, Ortega, Ansermet, and others she met that year like Stravinsky, Gropius, Cocteau, and Leo Ferrero. Gradually, she began to envision a review that would link not only South and North America, but also the Americas and Europe. It would be published only in Spanish because its readers would be primarily South Americans, but it would welcome contributions—in the form of prose or poetry, fiction or nonfiction—from authors of any country who took an interest in America and whose work was well written. As Victoria wrote to Ortega in 1930: "This is what I propose to do: publish a review devoted principally to American problems, in various aspects, to which Americans who have something to say can contribute as well as Europeans who are interested in America. That will be the *leitmotiv* of the review, but naturally it will address itself to other topics as well."[19]

When the time came for the trip to New York, Victoria reluctantly turned down Tagore's invitation to go to India. At the time, India intrigued her more than the United States—a country which many of her European friends disdained to visit—but she had promised Frank that she would come, and that was what she would do. As the ship sailed into New York harbor, she was still skeptical. No sooner was she installed in the Sherry-Netherland on Fifth Avenue overlooking Central Park, however, than her doubts dissolved into delight and amazement at what she saw. From skyscrapers to griddle cakes, she couldn't get enough of New York. With Frank and other friends she went to Greenwich Village, Harlem, Wall Street, the Hudson River, and everywhere she was struck by the openness of the people she met and the dynamic pace of North American life. Despite the recent stock market crash, she was impressed by the spirit of energy and growth in New York and, in particular, by the spiritual intensity of the black culture in Harlem, a thriving community in those days, not yet reduced to slums. With Frank, she went to the Cotton Club to listen to Duke Ellington's orchestra. On another occasion, Frank took her to the home of friends of his in Harlem where she met Taylor Gordon, a Negro spiritual singer and author of *Born to Be*. That night they went with Gordon to the Savoy, a Harlem jazz club. When Gordon learned of Victoria's passion for jazz and Negro spirituals, he invited her and her friends (including Serge Eisenstein, the Russian filmmaker whom Victoria had met at the estate of Otto Kahn on Long Island) to attend a revival meeting at a Harlem church the next evening. It was a fascinating experience and it moved her to write an essay which she later read as a lecture to Maeztu's College for Women in Madrid in 1931. Some people who heard about it remarked on the incongruity of an aristocratic

Argentine woman talking to Spanish college women about Negro life in New York, the implications being that Victoria had romanticized what she witnessed and neglected to see the real problems of urban blacks. Of course, Victoria saw what she preferred to see and wrote about what she liked most, but no one who had been with Waldo Frank in Harlem could have been ignorant of the less uplifting aspects of the black experience in America. To her critics, she had this to say:

> I believe they have reported, in I don't know which newspaper, that what interested me about New York was the negroes. Said that way, it sounds absurd. New York, with or without negroes, is the most extraordinary and intriguing spectacle that can be seen in our day. Only the blind or the envious would deny this fact.
>
> With regard to the negroes, I confess that I feel great sympathy toward them. Perhaps the roots of that sympathy can be found in my childhood, as I said before. At that time, two of my playmates were negroes. I also remember four negro faces of four servants whom I loved in my great-grandfather's house. But, surprisingly enough, I had never established any relationship between those family servants and the negroes who populated the book of Mrs. Beecher-Stowe.
>
> One day Ansermet and I were discussing why the negro race, so fertile in musical composition in the United States, hadn't produced anything in Argentina. And I said to him, "Doubtless because here [in Argentina] they suffered less."
>
> In the interminable croquet games I played when I was about ten with the two negro children, I often got angry with them because they won . . . But the idea never crossed my mind to oblige them to lose because I had white skin. Everything happened on an equal basis between us.[20]

She meant it without condescension. If she failed to see that things may not have been entirely equal from the black children's point of view, it was a lack of experience, rather than insensitivity that caused the oversight. In New York, she wrote about the revival meeting because, to her, it was a deeply moving experience, not just local color.

During the few short weeks in May 1930 that she spent in New York, Victoria met Alfred Stieglitz at his studio, "An American Place." The suggestive power of his photographs seemed to her to possess the quality of hope and faith in America that she also felt. Standing beside Stieglitz, looking out over the Manhattan panorama below, Victoria recalls:

> Stieglitz pointed out the city to me with a gesture, saying, "I have seen it growing. Is that beauty? I don't know. I don't care. I don't use the word beauty. It is life." I listened to him, smiling, with one of those strange urges to cry that take hold of one (and that one is ashamed of) when one is surprised by a happiness one was no longer expecting.[. . .]

An American Place . . . This modest apartment (where the first Cézannes, the first Matisses, the first Picassos came after disembarking on this side of the Atlantic) had served as a refuge, they tell me, for those who, having lost the old gods, felt painfully the need to look for new ones.

Wasn't that in a certain way what I had sensed from the moment I entered the room with white walls? Wasn't I also one of those looking for refuge? Men and women who suffer from the desert of America because we still carry Europe inside us, and who suffer from suffocation in Europe because we carry America inside us. Exiles from Europe in America; exiles from America in Europe. A little group disseminated from the North to the South of an immense continent and afflicted with the same sickness, the same nostalgia, that no change of place would definitively cure.[21]

It was this feeling that had brought her to New York to discuss final plans for the review with Waldo Frank. In her eagerness to devour all that the city offered, Victoria hadn't the chance to talk about as many details as she had intended, nor did Frank give her all the advice he had hoped to. But the new review was taking shape in the manner Victoria envisioned, and it was hers, not his, despite his role as a kind of godfather at its birth. She could count on him for whatever she might need, he told her, urging her not to give up under any circumstances. As her boat sailed for South America, Victoria felt strengthened by her North American visit. As was so often to be the case, she thought about what she had seen and done in New York, and with the new perspectives she had acquired, she understood her own relationship with Argentina better.

Back in Buenos Aires in the summer of 1930, she set to work preparing the first issue.

Sur

When Victoria's father learned that she planned to publish a literary review, his reaction was like that of many others in Buenos Aires: he predicted she would never make a success of it. "You'll go broke," he said. That was in 1931, the year *Sur* was born and the year her father died. Four decades later, though the founder was admittedly poorer financially for her efforts, the review was still being published.

Two years of planning and preparation went into the first issue that appeared early in 1931.[22] Compared to other Latin American reviews of the same period it was an unusually handsome publication, printed on fine paper in bold type and containing several illustrations. Victoria had spared no effort or expense to produce the final product she had in mind. The name of *Sur*, or South, in large block letters on the cover, was chosen by Ortega when Victoria consulted him by transatlantic telephone; in view of the encouragement he had given her over the years, it was only appropriate that he should have had a baptismal role in her debut as an editor and publisher. The simple wide arrow pointing south that adorned the cover was Victoria's idea. Four thousand copies were printed of the first issue, which was quickly sold out; it did particularly well in Paris and Madrid.

From the start, *Sur* was both a collaborative effort and a one-woman enterprise. Victoria was the founder, director, guiding spirit, and financial backer. Without her determination—or stubbornness, as she has called it —*Sur* might have met the fate of other short-lived reviews. At the same time, *Sur* was never a dictatorship. Eduardo Mallea selflessly contributed his editorial skills, and Guillermo de Torre acted as secretary; they were the two people who helped her most from the time *Sur* was conceived and put together in Victoria's home to the days when it moved into an Ocampo storage deposit on Viamonte Street, its first offices. In addition, there was an editorial board of Argentines that included Jorge Luis Borges, Eduardo González Lanuza, Eduardo Bullrich, Oliverio Girondo, Alfredo González Garaño, and María Rosa Oliver. A board of foreign consultants included Drieu la Rochelle (French), Ortega y Gasset (Spanish), Alfonso Reyes (Mexican), Leo Ferrero (Italian), Ernest Ansermet (Swiss), Pedro Henríquez Ureña (Dominican), Jules Supervielle (Uruguayan-French), and Waldo Frank (North American), all personal friends of Victoria's.

The spirit of the review was then, and remained thereafter, international and ecumenical, an attitude that Victoria has often insisted is not incompatible with being Argentine. As she wrote in an open letter to Waldo Frank at the head of the first issue:

> Waldo, in a just sense, this review belongs to you and to all those who surround me now and in the future. It belongs to those who have come to America, to those who think about America and to those who are native Americans. To those who have the will to understand us and who help us so much to understand ourselves.[23]

Sur was founded as a symbolic reaching out to encourage communication through literature and the arts across national borders. This openness to the world—an American attitude in Victoria's opinion—was unusual at the time *Sur* was created. According to María Luisa Bastos, the review's editor from 1961 to 1967:

> . . . *Sur* "discovered" Europe and the United States long before the northern hemisphere "discovered" Latin America. That is to say, circumstances caused *Sur* to anticipate an inclination toward literary internationalism that French or North American reviews only achieved many years later. *Partisan Review*, the current *Nouvelle Revue Française*, and the more agile *Lettres Nouvelles* bear a resemblance — except for the distance of time — with the *Sur* of the 1930s and 1940s.[24]

The "circumstances" to which Bastos refers were created from within not without. It was Victoria, and the small group around her, who believed in literary internationalism contrary to the mood of the times in Argentina. Among most intellectuals, narcissistic nationalism was the order of the day.

The fact is that Sur came into being shortly after the military coup of 1930 put an end to the moderate, middle-sector regime of Hipólito Irigoyen who, although maintaining a neutral political stance in foreign relations, had allowed Argentina to remain dependent on foreign capital and foreign business enterprises, thus heightening the impact of the economic depression that struck in 1929. From 1930 to 1943, an alliance of the military and the Conservative Party in Argentina signalled a shift away from a *laissez-faire* economy toward a system of legislative controls over foreign investment and a corresponding attitude of cultural protectionism that became overtly and fanatically nationalistic in the 1940s under Perón. Sur's internationalism, therefore, ran against the tide that began rising as the review was founded, a tide that eventually engulfed and suffocated intellectual freedom in Argentina.

The very first issue of Sur in 1931 established a precedent that future issues upheld: not only was there a mixture of American and European contributors, but there was also a combination of articles about both continents. Drieu la Rochelle wrote a letter to South American readers, Borges wrote about Colonel Ascasubi, Frank contributed a piece on Brazil, Eugenio d'Ors wrote about Picasso, Ansermet studied the problems of American composers, Walter Gropius wrote about the modern theater, and Alberto Prebisch analyzed the work of Le Corbusier.

Another precedent was set almost simultaneously with the appearance of the first issue: critical reaction in Argentina unfavorable to the review's spirit and content. On the one hand, critics attacked Sur's foreign contributions; on the other, they objected to photographs of American scenery included in the issue, saying that such gestures proved Sur was catering to the curiosity of foreign readers. The fact that many of the critics themselves, let alone other Argentine readers, may not have ever seen the places in question was beside the point. Such controversy surrounded Sur's debut and continued to greet subsequent issues.[25]

Considerable fuel was added to the fire of criticism by Victoria's candid assertion that the review was founded as an elite publication, an effort at building cultural bridges between small minorities of readers on both continents. The elite she cared about, as she explained, were not those normally identified with the word, whose connotations she deplored, but those who recognized the value of the finest literature and who knew how to read it with appreciation. She was thinking of an intellectual elite. Several members of the review's board had already been identified as elitists of the literary vanguard; they had published reviews of their own in the 1920s *(Prisma, Proa,* and *Martín Fierro),* but these reviews had not survived.[26] By publishing an elite review like *Sur,* Victoria also hoped to encourage inexperienced readers to educate themselves and learn the difference between "reading" and "knowing how to read" in the full sense of the experience. If quality and excellence were demanded from a soccer star or a movie actor, why shouldn't similar standards apply to literature? As Victoria observed:

> The fundamental thing in a literary review conceived in the way ours was is to support and defend the *literary standard*. There's no room for equality or charity in art. To reward a mediocre work because its author lives in difficult circumstances is inconceivable. The work is well or badly written, well or badly thought out (even though the tastes and ideas of the author may not coincide with ours. An example in my case: Jean Genet). There's no passport other than talent. Of course there are grades of talent and one cannot very well expect an unpublished Shakespeare to come along every day. But the demand for quality to which I refer is more and more resisted in the world today. It is *unpopular*, and that says it all.[27]

Unpopular because to enjoy it requires more effort than watching a soccer match or a movie; unpopular because an intellectual, however authentic his or her qualifications, functions at a level of understanding that is often beyond the grasp of the general public. What's more, it was particularly unpopular in Argentina in 1931 to hear about intellectual elitism from a member of the oligarchy who was also a woman. If Victoria had been a more traditional intellectual — say, a middle class male, a struggling writer, trying to make ends meet—or if she had repudiated her origins to the point of being politically committed to social and economic change, perhaps *Sur* would have been greeted more charitably, at least in some circles. Without her wealth and influence, of course, *Sur* might have folded. Even her father feared that.

After meeting the first wave of criticism in 1931, Victoria shared her discouragement with friends abroad; to María de Maeztu, she wrote, "I have the painful impression of having spent a year working the desert, for the desert. I don't know what the people who matter most to me think of the review . . . I'm depressed. And you can't imagine how much I've worked against the wind and the tide."[28] Similar thoughts were shared with Waldo Frank, who kept abreast of the situation from New York. A friend of his, Samuel Glusberg, whom he had introduced to Victoria, had ended up criticizing *Sur*'s "foreignism," a flaw, he suggested, that was Victoria's as well. On February 15, 1931 she complained to Frank: "Of necessity, *Sur* is like me. And if *Sur* is like me, it's irremediably more interested in the quality than the nationality of a thing. That's my way of being Argentine and it's what I need. I'd suffocate otherwise." Frank was dismayed by Glusberg's criticism. Calling *Sur* "absolute Americanism," he wrote to Victoria in a letter dated February 25, 1931:

> One's Americanism has nothing to do with generations — it is a matter of spirit. Glusberg is not less American because you are the daughter — the glorious daughter of the Conquistadors. There are doubtless other daughters of the Conquistadors in whom the spirit of a New World does *not* live. And there may well be a son of immigrants in which that spirit does live. It is the deed, not the talking about it, and the shouting America, that shows the real stuff. You, bien chère, were American, sans le savoir! Your house, your spirit, your sorrow, your struggle, your malaise with your friends (my friends, too) in Paris—all were signs of your Americanism—but you did not know it. *Sur* is deeply American, through the very look of its pages, and every accent of your Carta, and all I have read in your book is American too.

Frank also understood that for a woman like Victoria to hold a position of authority was an affront to many Latin American male egos. Three months later, on May 12, 1931, he wrote to her:

> . . . I am sorry too, that you are being subjected to petty and unworthy attacks for *Sur*: but there is doubtless a strong undercurrent of feeling in Buenos Aires against a woman of your strength and independence—above all, a woman of your light. You will be hurt, but you must grin and bear this, in the public lists.

Again, on July 25, 1931 these words of encouragement:

> You must, as quickly as possible, make a personal adjustment so that you profit by the attacks — to the extent of extracting from them all possible instruction; being careful however never to swerve from your own due course. And this, I feel certain, you will do; for you are strong, Victoria, and capable (if you really want to pay the price in time and effort) of being the leader — the leader whom almost everyone at some time appears to abandon or betray. The day will come when you will realize that you have learned more from opposition than from support: not spiritually, but technically.

That day has long since come, and Victoria might well say that she has been fortified spiritually too by having to confront relentless opposition.

Politics has never been one of her passions, and she has never believed in mixing politics and literature, so *Sur* remained free of political allegiances that might have limited the variety of its contributions. Authors of the right as well as the left and center were published in its pages over the years. The list—a testimony in itself to the review's high literary standards — is truly impressive and includes, among others, Thomas Mann, Jacques Maritain, Henry Miller, T. S. Eliot, Paul Claudel, Karl Jaspers, Denis de Rougement, Aldous Huxley, Simone Weil, Lewis Mumford, André Gide, Nathalie Sarraute, Martin Heidegger, Ezra Pound, Evelyn Waugh, Lawrence Durrell, Thomas Merton, Jean Piaget, and André Breton. Many articles were original contributions; others were reprints of works published recently in reviews abroad. Translations were done by experienced linguists who were often authors themselves. Occasional issues were devoted to special topics such as the works of one author (i.e., Shakespeare, Gandhi) or the literature of one country (i.e., England, Germany, Canada, Japan). One issue, that of July 1942, contained a special "Vindication of Borges" when the Argentine author failed to receive a national prize for literature which the editorial board of *Sur* and other noted intellectuals believed he merited. It was an unusual editorial decision, unique in the review's history. The passage of years has proven its validity; *Sur* was notably ahead of its time in recognizing Borges as an exceptional talent.[29] Other authors, like Roger Caillois and Albert Camus, to name just two, were also published in its pages before they received worldwide acclaim.

In order to increase profits and defray the expenses of the review, Victoria decided to follow Ortega's advice and add a publishing house to the *Sur* enterprise in 1933. Although she published many books by Spanish-speaking authors (i.e., Mallea, Alfonso Reyes, Borges, Lorca, José Bianco, Ernesto Sábato, Silvina Ocampo, Adolfo Bioy Casares, and her own books), one of her major objectives was to bring out translations of the best foreign literature available at the time. She was the first to publish Aldous Huxley in Spanish (*Point Counterpoint* in 1933), the first to publish D. H. Lawrence (*Kangaroo* in the same year), André Malraux (*La Condition Humaine* in 1936), C. G. Jung (*Psychological Types* also in 1936), and Virginia Woolf (several books in the 1930s, two of them, *A Room of One's Own* and *Orlando*, translated by Borges, who, by the way, was not enthusiastic about Woolf). Other titles included works by Joyce, Mann, Chestov, H. G. Wells, Faulkner, Sartre, Mailer, Nabokov, Kerouac, Bataille, T. E. Lawrence, Camus, Graham Greene, and Dylan Thomas. The last four authors were translated by Victoria herself. In the publishing house as in the review, the selection of authors did not depend on their politics but on their literary quality. Consequently, Victoria was attacked from both the right and the left—some calling her a Communist, others a Conservative. As she once explained:

What mattered to me was talent, not politics. Each person held the right to think as he wished in that zone. Of course those who put themselves at the service of a party and made "propaganda" for it dropped immediately to another level. There's no reason to name names. And let it be noted that I refer to propaganda, not to an honest expression of opinions (even though they may appear mistaken to us). The bad thing about politics is that it changes the writer into a propagandist and makes him vacillate and lose quality. If this doesn't occur, it's because his sights are higher, from whatever position he occupies in the ideological struggle.[30]

Even those who should have been above politics sometimes let their true colors show by ostracizing or insulting Victoria for decisions to publish certain authors. (The Curia of the Church, for example, let her know indirectly in the early 1930s that her participation as a *récitante* in a benefit for Catholic charities would not be welcome.) Undaunted, Victoria continued to believe that free speech and thought were the only safeguards of truth and justice. When Fascist totalitarianism threatened Europe with the suppression of all freedom, *Sur* spoke out in moral, not political opposition. As an editorial of 1939 put it: "Politics does not interest us except when it is linked to spiritual values. When the very foundations of the spirit appear threatened by a political situation, then we raise our voice."[31] For Victoria, the distinction between morality and politics was clear wherever intellectual and religious freedom were concerned.

In 1951, after twenty years of publication, statistics showed that *Sur* had published more North and South American writers than all the French, English, Spanish, Italian, and German authors combined. Still, the criticism in Latin America persisted. In the early 1950s, the Chilean poet Pablo Neruda, a declared Communist, accused *Sur* of publishing the work of "international spies" and "colonialists" and of promulgating the pernicious influence of such authors as Faulkner ("full of perversity"), T. S. Eliot ("a false mystic reactionary"), and Heidegger ("an ideological Nazi").[32] When *Sur* rebutted Neruda's wild accusations in a brief statement, Neruda replied with a poem mocking what he believed was *Sur*'s decadent, bourgeois mentality and Victoria, whom he referred to as "Madame Charmante." The poem, so evidently political in motivation, did more to vindicate Victoria's position vis-à-vis politics and literature than it did to confirm Neruda's talents:

Now the Danube Sings (I)

Old Rumania, golden Bucharest
how you resembled
our infernal and heavenly

republics
of America.

You used to be pastoral and shady.
Thorns and rugged terrain hid
your terrible misery,
while Madame Charmante
rambled on in French in the salons.
The whip would fall
on the scars of your people
while the elegant literati
in their review "SUR" (no doubt)
studied Lawrence, the spy,
or Heidegger or "Notre petit Drieu."
"Tout allait bien à Bucarest."
The oil
would leave burns on our fingers
and blacken our nameless
Rumanian faces,
but there was a chorus
of sterling pounds
in New York and London.
And thus
Bucharest was so elegant,
and the ladies so delicate.
"Ah quel charme monsieur."
While hunger
hovered about carrying
its empty fork
through the black suburbs
and the wretched countryside.
Ah yes, gentlemen, it was
exactly like Buenos Aires,
like Santiago or Lima,
Bogotá and Sao Paulo.
A few people were dancing in the hall
exchanging sighs,
the Club and the literary reviews
were very European,
the cold was Rumanian,
the hunger was Rumanian,
the lament of the poor people
in the communal charnel-house was Rumanian,
and so life went on
from one generation to another, as on my continent
with the prisons full
and the waltzes in the gardens.

Oui, Madame, what a world
it was, what an irreparable
loss for all
the distinguished people!
Bucharest no longer exists!
That taste, that style,
that exquisite mixture
of putrefaction and "patisserie!"
It seems terrible to me.
They tell me
that even the local color,
the picturesque ragged clothes,
the beggars twisted like poor roots,
the girls who, trembling,
would wait at night
at the entrance to the dance—
all that, horrors, has disappeared.

What shall we do, chère Madame?
Somewhere else we shall start
a review "SUR" for cattle ranchers
profoundly concerned
about "métaphisique."[33]

In the 1960s Neruda changed suddenly from a critic to an admirer. At a
P.E.N. club meeting in New York, he made a point of praising Victoria,
evidently retracting what he had said earlier in a moment of political
fervor.

Other noted Latin American authors have openly testified to the
important role that *Sur* and its director played in their intellectual and
spiritual formation as young writers in the 1930s and 1940s. For many of
them, Victoria Ocampo's name stood for literary integrity and freedom of
thought; a volume of testimonies to this effect was published in her honor
in 1962 containing tributes from friends abroad as well as fellow countrymen. One of the most eloquent testimonies came from Octavio Paz, the
well-known Mexican essayist and poet, who wrote:

The name and person of Victoria Ocampo evoke a column, a caryatid or a
tall commemorative monument in the center of a large plaza. Sun, light,
and a space governed by a noble architecture. These images are not capricious nor fortuitous. For almost all Hispanic American writers, the life and
work of Victoria Ocampo are inseparable from the review *Sur*. And *Sur* was
for us a temple, a house, a place of meeting and confrontation. How could
one not see in its director the Pillar of the house of letters? Pillar, support or
caryatid, Victoria is something more: the founder of a spiritual space.
Because *Sur* is not just a review or an institution; it is a tradition of the
spirit. I published something in the review for the first time in 1939, invited

by José Bianco [editor of *Sur* from 1938 to 1961[34]] [. . . .] Since then, to write for *Sur* has never meant to me collaborating in a literary review but rather participating in an undertaking which, if it is not the true spiritual life, neither is it literary life in its common form. What the *Nouvelle Revue Française* was for Europeans, *Sur* was for me: literature conceived of as a world of its own — not apart from or facing other worlds, but never subjected to them. The literatures of freedom always depend on one or another idea of freedom; *Sur* is the freedom of literature in the face of earthly powers. Something less than a religion and something more than a sect [. . . .] Victoria Ocampo is a Pillar, but she is not a mythological creature; she has arms and hands, will and imagination, anger and generosity. And with all this, she has done what no one before had done in America.[35]

In the same year that Paz first contributed to *Sur*, a young French writer, Roger Caillois, came to Buenos Aires at Victoria's invitation to give a series of lectures. When the war broke out in Europe, a three-week visit turned into a five-year stay. Caillois was deferred from military service, so during this time he worked at the French Institute in Buenos Aires, and he also edited *Lettres françaises*, a literary review in exile for writers of Free France, sponsored by *Sur*. Returning to France after the war, Caillois took with him a considerable knowledge of Latin American literature as well as the friendship of many authors. Through his encouragement and participation, French translations of the best contemporary and classical Latin American works began appearing with more regularity. Caillois became the director of a new collection of translations called "La Croix du Sud" published by Gallimard and of another series, mainly works of history, published by UNESCO. Any Latin American author published by "La Croix de Sud" was virtually assured of being recognized and translated in other countries as well, such was its prestige.[36] Authors who thereby became familiar to readers in other parts of Europe and in the United States included Borges, Mallea, Julio Cortázar, Alejo Carpentier, Miguel Angel Asturias, and Juan Rulfo, to name but a few.

    Sur's survival for over forty years despite critical opposition, economic inflation, and political upheaval in Argentina, is an accomplishment that few other publications in Latin America can match. When Columbia University awarded Victoria and *Sur* the coveted Maria Moors Cabot award in 1965, Victoria, in New York to accept the award, had this to say about *Sur* in retrospect:

The life of a purely literary magazine, determined to preserve a high level of contributors and to brook no compromise in matters of quality, is a hard one and generally it is a life with no material aid. At least in some countries. This was one of the early lessons that had to be learned — and we had to resign ourselves to a struggle for life: a struggle to exist economically — a struggle to withstand the temptations of means that would ensure greater circulation but at the cost of commercialization—a rejection of all undesirable backing, regardless of the advantages offered — a struggle against the invasion of political elements that creep in everywhere and reward the surrender of minds but punish any independent stand—a struggle to exist in freedom and to welcome all valuable thought, even if it happened to be different from our own.

If the Maria Moors Cabot award is the acknowledgement of that line of conduct which *Sur* followed—of that daily and constant skirting of obstacles through troublous times, then the magazine and all those who have unselfishly worked for its growth do deserve this signal honour. [37]

For future generations, *Sur* will be an essential reference guide to the intellectual history of Argentina and Latin America. As Boyd Carter wrote in a study of Latin American literary reviews:

> . . . *Sur* is a true repository of treasures. It is a publication that does honor to Latin American intellectualism and literary invention, making its values known abroad and informing its readers of what is best and most significant in the thought and writing of other countries. And this outstanding achievement is due, above all, to the perseverance and faith of its founder, señora Victoria Ocampo. [38]

Virginia Woolf and Gilded Butterflies

As *Sur* became better known in the early years of its publication, Victoria's reputation grew apace. Although the review could easily stand on its own merits, the legend of Victoria Ocampo undoubtedly reinforced the attention it received at home and abroad. Wherever she went, journalists wrote about her as if she were a fabulous creature: "Nike of all the oceans, with her tunic to all the winds," "one of the most beautiful women in the Argentine," "the imperious autocrat of Argentina's intellectual life," "a goddess," "an exceptional mentality," and "a champion of the feminine spirit." Her effectiveness as a speaker was widely praised, and invitations to give lectures and recitations flowed into *Sur*'s offices. On one occasion in the mid-1930s when the hall of the Jockey Club in Buenos Aires was filled to capacity to hear her give a reading of French poetry, one reviewer explained: "Spectacles like this aren't often seen in Buenos Aires. And that's because it isn't easy to find, united in one person, harmony of gesture, purity of voice, and especially a clear intelligence that, in reciting old verses, gives them new life." [39]

In the fall of 1934, Victoria and Eduardo Mallea were invited by the Italian Inter-University Institute to give a series of lectures in several Italian cities. When Victoria pointed out to the Institute that she didn't sympathize with the Fascist regime of Benito Mussolini, her hosts responded that it did not matter to them; they were still eager for her visit. Italy and its people had long held an interest for her so she accepted. The tour was a great success. To enthusiastic Italian journalists, Victoria was "the intellectual ambassador of a new people."[40] Her fluent Italian was commented upon in all the papers.

Mussolini was then at the height of his popularity. Italian troops had not yet invaded Abyssinia, though Fascist militarism was on prominent display. Still, the Allied powers refused to condemn "il Duce"; in the United States he was called "a regular guy" by Will Rogers, and Cole Porter wrote a song that said "You're the tops, you're Mussolini."

While Victoria was in Rome, her hosts asked her if she would like to meet the Duce. She accepted immediately, curious to know what the man behind the myth would be like. On September 24, 1934 she was ushered into the immense Sala del Mappamondo of the Palazzo Venezia where Mussolini greeted her, escorted her to a chair beside his desk (the only furniture in the gigantic hall), and insisted on standing beside her as they conversed. Victoria had read that he considered a woman's foremost duty to the Fascist state was to bear as many children as possible; on Christmas Eve, 1933 he had rewarded ninety-three of Italy's most prolific mothers with a visit to the Palazzo and a ceremony in their honor. So her initial question to the Duce was about women. They could contribute to the State, he answered, with their fertility. And by the way, he asked, did she have any children of her own? She did not, she replied, but perhaps he would like to read her little book on Dante, and she handed him a copy inscribed: "To Benito Mussolini, the work of a student in search of her soul." "Have you found it?" he inquired. "You're teasing me," she answered. They spoke for half an hour about women, literature, and Italy. When she left, Victoria couldn't help thinking that there was a certain charm about the Duce in spite of the things she detested in him. What she feared most, she recorded in an essay written after the interview, was that he would lead Italy into war, a war in which women, as producers of future soldiers, would be crucial tools in the hands of the State.

After concluding the tour in Italy, Victoria headed north to Zurich where, in October 1934, she knocked on the door of the famous psychoanalyst who had counseled Keyserling after their fateful intermezzo in Versailles. She wanted to see Jung to arrange for the rights to translate his *Psychological Types*, a book that had had a profound impact on her own thinking, but she also wanted to invite him to give some lectures in Argentina. "Why?" he responded, "They wouldn't be interested. They wouldn't understand." And Victoria wondered whom he meant: the Latins? the Catholics?[41] There wasn't time to ask.

A month later she was in London. One day her friend Aldous Huxley (whom she had visited in Sanary on the French coast the previous June) invited her to the opening of a Man Ray exhibit in Bedford Square. Virginia Woolf might be there, he told her, knowing she had long wanted to meet the famous Bloomsbury author. It was November 26, 1934; Virginia Woolf noted their meeting in her diary, remarking on the opulent beauty of the Buenos Aires millionairess whose pearl earrings reminded her of clusters of moth eggs. She also recorded that they had an engrossing discussion about Victoria's recent interview with il Duce (a "rat," Woolf thought, for being so nice to her on purpose). Victoria remembers that the inquisitive novelist also asked her about her childhood, her life in Argentina, her travels, her favorite books—a veritable barrage of questions that she was only too happy to answer.

From her diary entry, it seems that Woolf, too, was impressed by their meeting. She had an admitted propensity for the glamorous and the aristocratic ("Thus I seem to have arrived at the conclusion that I am not only a coronet snob; but also a lit up drawing room snob; a social festivity snob. Any group of people if they are well dressed, and socially sparkling and unfamiliar will do the trick; sends up that fountain of gold and diamond dust which I suppose obscures the solid truth" [42]). Victoria, though not a coronet aristocrat, would certainly have appealed to Woolf in this sense. The fact that she was also a South American must have further piqued Woolf's curiosity and imagination.

Despite the rapport they established at their first meeting, Victoria felt that it was an unequal relationship. After all, Woolf was a great writer whom she had admired for years and whose books she had read over and over. On the other hand, Woolf hardly knew who Victoria was or where she came from. Nor did Victoria feel that her explanations had much effect on the novelist's imaginative fancies. During the ensuing years, whenever they met or exchanged letters, Victoria had the impression that, in Woolf's eyes, she remained something of a *rara avis*, a creature who took flight in Woolf's imagination and never quite came down to earth. Quentin Bell has acknowledged this side of his aunt's character and the problems it caused for others:

> This was one of the difficulties of living with Virginia, her imagination was furnished with an accelerator and no brakes; it flew rapidly ahead, parting company with reality, and, when reality happened to be a human being, the result could be appalling for the person who found himself expected to live up to the character that Virginia had invented. [43]

When it came to South America, Woolf had already shown that she had only the vaguest notion of what it was like. In her first novel, *The

Voyage Out (1915), she chose a fictitious coastal city in South America for a setting. There, in her vivid imagination, crimson and black butterflies fluttered amid olive trees set in a red, purple, and green landscape. Shortly after she and Victoria met, when Victoria was preparing to return to Buenos Aires, Woolf wrote to her on January 22, 1935:

> And you are about to voyage to the land of great butterflies and vast fields: which I still make up from your flying words. . . . Therefore, do not let me drift into the fog. Tell me what you are doing, whom you see, what the country looks like, also the town, also your room, down to the food and the cats, dogs, —what time you spend on this and that. And please never never think me cold because I do not write. I get so tired of writing.

Evidently, Victoria's explanations were not at all successful at reining in Woolf's unbridled fancies; on October 29, 1935 a letter from London contained the following:

> How remote and sunk in time and space you seem, over there, in the vast, —and what did you call them—those immense blue gray lands with wild cattle and the pampas grass and the butterflies. Each time I go out of my door I make up another picture of South America: no doubt you'd be surprised if you could see yourself in your house as I arrange it. It is always grilling hot and there is a moth alighted on a silver flower. And this too in broad daylight.

No wonder Victoria urged Virginia and Leonard Woolf to accept her invitation to visit her in Buenos Aires. They said they were tempted, but the distance of the voyage and the delicacy of the novelist's health probably dissuaded them. From "the land of great butterflies" Victoria could only send her friend what she so frequently envisioned: some brightly colored South American butterflies mounted in a glass case which the Woolfs hung on the wall of their home in Tavistock Square. When an all-expense paid trip was offered to Virginia Woolf by the International P.E.N. club, inviting her to address the 1936 meeting in Buenos Aires, she declined, confessing in a letter to Victoria that that sort of thing was "not my line."

Victoria was right about the unequal basis of their relationship. For her, each visit to 52 Tavistock Square was a kind of pilgrimage. She would arrive, that first winter, in a white car driven by a liveried chauffeur (Woolf called it her "white chariot"), go upstairs with her hostess to the sitting room decorated by Vanessa Bell's paintings, and savor the hours she spent in the company of the more loquacious novelist. More than once, Woolf's imaginary biography of Flush, Elizabeth Barrett Browning's dog, came to

Victoria's mind while they talked together over a cup of tea, the Woolfs' dog resting at their feet:

> Often, after the foggy cold of the street, I entered the comfort of that room, and above all, of that presence. As soon as Virginia was there, all else disappeared. Virginia, tall and slender, wearing a silk blouse whose blues and grays (was it Scottish silk?) harmonized admirably with the silver of her hair. Virginia, made even more slender by a very long, black velvet skirt. Virginia, sitting in an armchair, her dog asleep on the floor. Was it hers or was it Elizabeth Browning's?
>
> Virginia Woolf was as capable of speaking marvelously as she was of writing marvelously. With this I am confessing to you that I could not, without effort, leave her side. The hours that I stole from her work, from her reverie, from who knows what or whom, filled me with remorse. But I kept on stealing. During those hours, Elizabeth Browning's dog snored so loudly between us that mentally I scolded him: "Flush," I thought, "how can you make that disrespectful noise! We're talking about serious things. About women, literature, America. About how your mistress manages to write in such a way as to change the modern novel. Flush, be quiet! Let me listen! I've come from too far away and have too little time to allow you to distract me. Flush, please don't snore so loudly while she's talking!" But even if I had spoken these reproaches out loud, it would have done no good. Virginia was at her most expansive between snores and Flush must have had special dispensation to snore since God knows when. Perhaps since the time when Elizabeth Barrett of Wimpole Street became Elizabeth Browning. . . .[44]

Now and again in their conversations, Victoria would detect a tone of condescension in Woolf's attitude toward South Americans, though not toward her. It was a transference, she thought, of a social and cultural snobbism that not only Woolf, but many other Europeans had expressed, intentionally or unintentionally. Sometimes it took the form of a joke; other times sarcasm was barely disguised. Woolf herself once wrote in a playful but serious essay on her own snobbism: "I have visited most of the capitals of Europe, it is true, I can speak a kind of dog French and mongrel Italian; but so ignorant am I, so badly educated, that if you ask me the simplest question—for instance, where is Guatemala?—I am forced to turn the conversation."[45] When Victoria told Woolf that she was anxious to have several of her works translated into Spanish and published by *Sur*, Woolf's first reaction was one of skepticism if not disbelief: Why would South American readers be interested in her books? What could they possibly have in common with them?

Clearly, however, she and Victoria shared many of the same ideas about women and literature. Although she never read more than a few pages of Victoria's work — pages Victoria sent her that she had written about *To the Lighthouse* — Woolf gave her constant moral support and encouragement. Less than a month after they met, on December 22, 1934 Woolf wrote her these words: "I'm so glad you write criticism not fiction. And I'm sure this is good criticism — clear and sharp, cut with a knife not pitchforked with a rusty old hedge machine (I see one going across the meadow) [. . . .] I hope you will go on to Dante and then to Victoria Okampo [Woolf often misspelled her name]. Very few women yet have written truthful autobiographies. It is my favorite form of reading." Later, when Victoria wrote her that she had just given a lecture in Buenos Aires devoted to her work, Woolf answered on September 2, 1937 with characteristic candor and wit: "I suspect you are one of those people — they are almost unknown in England—who can make a lecture exciting. Is it your Latin blood? I would rather sit in a cellar and watch spiders than listen to an Englishman lecturing."

For the first time Victoria felt understood, intellectually, by someone who knew what it was like to be an aspiring woman writer. How *much* Woolf could help her, she must once have said, later explaining lest she be misinterpreted: "When I told you you could help me I meant that by being *yourself*, what you are, and by letting me feel that through your *présence réelle* (as the Catholics would say) you were helping me enormously. That is the sort of help I need." [46] Such undisguised hero-worship may have made Woolf somewhat uneasy—it certainly was not in keeping with the understated British way of doing things. But how could she not respond to the Argentine woman, only eight years her junior, who had grown up in circumstances in many ways similar to her own and who had struggled, as she had, to overcome the obstacles that had vanquished so many other women writers in the past? Not only was Victoria a writer, but, like Woolf, she was a publisher as well.

Better than anyone, Woolf must have understood Victoria's hunger for female solidarity. No male author could entirely comprehend what a woman writer faced: her feeling of insufficient preparation, her lack of a feminine literary tradition. Nor could a woman trust a man's encouragement without wondering if other interests might be clouding his vision. How could Woolf not respond to this note from Victoria, so unabashedly direct in its appeal:

> If there is anyone in the world who can give me courage and hope, it is *you*. By the simple fact of being who you are and thinking as you think. I would be ungrateful if I said that I have never been encouraged, etc. I have some friends (men) who think I am gifted to the point of genius and who have said so and written so. But these declarations have always left me cold and unbelieving inside myself. They are impure. You understand what I mean

. . . Men always (or almost always) judge a woman according to *themselves*, according to the reactions they experience in contact with her (even spiritually). Above all, if she is not deformed or unpleasant-looking. It is their particular fatality. Especially if they are *Latins*. Then they cannot *honestly* serve as guide marks.[47]

When she wrote this, she must surely have been thinking of Keyserling. Even though Victoria knew that both she and South America were also distorted by Woolf's imaginative fancy, she wasn't angered by it because she felt an essential solidarity with Woolf that all her imaginings could not affect: they understood each other as women and could communicate authentically on that basis, respecting one another's individuality. Another note Victoria wrote to Woolf early in 1935 makes her point very clearly:

Dear Virginia,
   I think I will stay in London till next week, though I just received a letter from Madrid where they are waiting for me since the first days of November. You see I must publish a book there this very month [her first volume of *Testimonios*]. But as I shall not be able to *come back* to London now, it's better for me to stay some days more. As long as I possibly can!
   Of course, I know quite well there are lots of interesting people to talk to in London. The same happens in Paris. But very few (at least in Paris where I know nearly every writer worth knowing) of them are interesting to me in the way you, or André Malraux, are interesting. I mean in a *vital* way!
   Valéry is a good friend of mine. So is Drieu (even more). So was Anna de Noailles. And Fargue is quite amusing. And Giraudoux is delightful. And Morand is quite nice, etc., etc. But they give me nothing *vital*. And I must say that is the thing I most crave for.
   Please, Virginia, don't think for an instant I am trying to flatter you. *I hate it*. When you spoke yesterday of K. Mansfield and I said you were not to be compared with her (or others, such as I know them) it is because, though I can perfectly see their charm, they *mean* very little to me. I don't like to eat and not be nourished. I am a very *voracious* person. And I believe *hunger* is all. I am not ashamed of being hungry. Don't you think love is our hunger to love? (I am speaking of love with a capital).
   [And she continues in French]
   I mean to say that *our hunger* is a very important element. That things don't truly exist for us until, and because, we are hungry for them and then only in proportion to the intensity of that hunger. The secret of a Picasso is that he has a hunger (a lion's hunger) of painting. That's why he says: "I don't seek, I find." It's his hunger speaking.
   What frightens me in Europe (France, Spain, Italy) is a kind of failing appetite in people. Where I'm from, there's appetite . . . But nourishment is still lacking! And so we come here, famished.
   Lord, how many things I have to say to you and ask you!

Virginia Woolf (who significantly reminds Victoria of her own mother in appearance), was, of all her heroes over the years, the one who offered her the most substantial and enduring nourishment for her hunger. Victoria herself realized this shortly after she met Woolf. Less than a month after their meeting, she wrote a "Letter to Virginia Woolf" that she placed at the head of the volume of her own essays which was published in Madrid in 1935. The letter, which Woolf probably never read, is a public statement rather than a private message. It acknowledges Woolf as a prophet of a new era in women's literature. Referring to A *Room of One's Own*, Victoria writes:

> You say it is important for women to express themselves, and to express themselves in writing. You encourage them to write "all kinds of books, hesitating at no subject however trivial or however vast." You say that you give them this advice out of egotism: "Like most uneducated Englishwomen, I like reading—I like reading books in the bulk," and masculine output is not enough for you. You find that men's books inform us rather imperfectly about themselves as well. In the back of our heads, you say, there is a spot the size of a shilling that we cannot see with our own eyes. Each sex must assume the responsibility of describing that spot for the benefit of the other. In that respect we cannot complain about men. From ages back, they have rendered us that service. It would therefore be suitable that we not show ourselves to be ungrateful and that we repay them in kind.
>
> But here we come to what I, for my part, would like to confess publicly, Virginia: Like most uneducated South American women, I like writing. And this time "uneducated" should be pronounced without irony.
>
> My sole ambition is to one day write more or less well, more or less badly, but *like a woman*. If I could have a magic lamp like Aladdin and, by rubbing it, could have the power to write like Shakespeare, Dante, Goethe, Cervantes, or Dostoevsky, I truly would not take advantage of it. Because I believe that a woman cannot unburden herself of her thoughts and feelings in a man's style, just as she cannot speak with a man's voice.[48]

Women must build a feminine tradition in literature to counterbalance a masculine tradition that has told only half of the human story. Moreover, Victoria agreed with Virginia Woolf that modern society was dangerously one-sided because rational ("masculine") faculties had been cultivated to the exclusion of intuitive ("feminine") faculties. No one, she believed, had expressed as well as Woolf the concept of psychic wholeness, as symbolized by the androgynous mind described in A *Room of One's Own* and *Orlando*. Out of her own hunger for it, she had responded to this concept in the works of Dante, Tagore, Keyserling, Frank, and Jung, but it was in Virginia Woolf that she first found it expressed from a woman's viewpoint.

The news of Woolf's suicide in March 1941 reached Victoria while she was vacationing in Mar del Plata, far from the hideous war that had made Woolf and her husband, who was of Jewish background, fear for their lives. Even before the devastating news arrived from London, Victoria had spent a painful time knowing that friends in France and England were in danger. (She would later learn that two of them, Benjamin Fondane and Benjamin Crémieux, died in concentration camps.) As she reflected sadly on her friendship with Bloomsbury's most famous author, Victoria regretted that there had not been a more complete understanding between them and that she was never able to give as much to Woolf as she received from her.

It seemed to Victoria that her tendency toward hero-worship had even marred their last meeting in 1939. Did Woolf ever really forgive her for her impromptu idea to bring Gisèle Freund along so that the Woolfs could see a screening of Freund's photographic portraits? Victoria hadn't realized how much Virginia Woolf disliked being photographed (yet the next day, Woolf permitted Freund to come for a two-hour session of photographs and, according to Freund, she appeared to enjoy it). Victoria had only wanted to have the beauty of that fragile face preserved for posterity. The magnificent photographs, which she saw for the first time when Freund came to Buenos Aires in 1941 and which Woolf herself never saw because the war intervened, only partially consoled her. Regrets lingered in her mind. Some years later, she shared them with Vita Sackville-West whom she had met through Woolf in Paris in 1939. They had become fast friends, and Victoria particularly admired her naturalness and lack of snobbishness, which was all the more remarkable in light of her coronet-studded ancestry. Writing to Victoria on July 7, 1954, Sackville-West reassured her about Woolf:

> I don't think it is in the least true to say that you had no real existence for her, because she often talked to me about you even before I had met you. It is true that there was a certain unreality about her unless one knew her very intimately. One always felt that she might take flight at any moment and disappear.

When, earlier in 1943, Victoria confessed to her that she planned to write something about Virginia, Sackville-West approved wholeheartedly, saying, "No one could do it with more feeling."

Since then Victoria has written about Virginia Woolf in many essays and talked about her on many occasions. In 1954 she wrote *Virginia Woolf en su diario* (Virginia Woolf in Her Diary) à propos of Leonard Woolf's publication of excerpts of his wife's diaries. It is a short book but one in which Victoria articulates many of the thoughts and feelings that she was unable to share with Woolf. In the process of writing it, she came to

understand Woolf even more fully than she had before, just as Woolf felt
when she wrote about her deceased friend, Roger Fry. According to
Victoria, "Reading Roger Fry after his death in order to write his biography, she [Woolf] felt a more intimate friendship grow between them
than the one that joined them in his lifetime [. . . .] In the same way, I feel
closer today to Virginia Woolf; I can talk about this and that with her more
freely, *laugh at gilded butterflies* with her and peer into the mystery of
things *as if we were God's spies*."[49] More important still, writing about
Woolf in retrospect gave Victoria the chance to understand how symbolically important their relationship had been in the process of her own
development.

CHAPTER FIVE

THE EYE OF THE STORM

The Argentine woman whose name has been most familiar to the world in recent decades has not been Victoria Ocampo but Eva Perón—"Evita" as she was called by the *descamisados*, or shirtless ones, who idolized her from the time her husband became the undisputed leader of Argentina in 1946 until she died of cancer at thirty-three in 1952. That Eva Perón and Victoria Ocampo should have become legendary figures in the same country and that Evita's name should have eclipsed Victoria's up to the present is not only an irony of history but also a vivid illustration of forces in conflict in twentieth-century Latin America.

There is no question that they have been the two most influential Latin American women of this century, one in the political and the other in the cultural sphere. Nor is there any question that they were antagonists though they never exchanged a word. Surely they recognized each other that one time their paths crossed in front of an elevator in a Buenos Aires clinic, the glamorous, blond, former radio actress from the provinces thinking, perhaps, that the wealthy aristocrat thirty years her senior was no longer to be as envied as she, the wife of Juan Domingo Perón. So *that* was "Evita," thought Victoria, and all she could see before her was an unscrupulously ambitious young woman who had proclaimed herself the fanatical disciple of a demagogue.

Two women, two opposing forces: one the daughter of the working classes, the other, of the oligarchy. One was minimally educated and unread, the other a member of the cultural elite. The historical incompatibility of their backgrounds predisposed them to repudiate one another. And yet, ironically, they had things in common, not the least being their reputation as feminists, leaders in the struggle for women's liberation in Argentina. Both professed commitment to this goal. The fact that they were incapable of joining forces to achieve it, however, cannot be explained solely by the social, economic, and cultural differences between them. There was another, more intrinsic difference between Eva Perón and Victoria Ocampo.

The Beginnings of Argentine Feminism

In the mid-1800s Domingo Faustino Sarmiento had proclaimed that one could judge a country's level of civilization by the social position of its women. Citing Fénelon and Rousseau, he said that a nation's men could only be as great and virtuous as the women who raised them, but he also went on to suggest that women might have a political destiny of their own, as more progressive voices in Europe were urging at the time.[1] Whatever the future might hold, said Sarmiento, equal education for women must be the starting point, and under his guidance, teachers were brought from the United States to start the first schools for women in Argentina. The advancements made in public education during his presidency were indirectly responsible for bringing about the first organized feminist activities in the country in the early 1900s. Women who had studied for university degrees at the turn of the century decided to unite and combat the discrimination they had met as students and later as professionals in a society that stubbornly insisted that a woman's place was in the home. As Nancy Caro Hollander has pointed out:

> Although one would never know it by perusing the majority of books on Argentine history, women make up approximately one-half of that nation's population. Yet the history of Argentine women parallels the history of women in most countries to the extent that it is largely unwritten.[2]

The same could be said for all the countries in Latin America, but Argentina's omission is all the more noteworthy considering the fact that Buenos Aires was the fastest growing industrial capital on the continent and women had played an important role in its development. The Buenos Aires census of 1887, for example, reported that women constituted 39 percent of the total paid work force of the city; by 1914 that figure had dropped to 22 percent due to the availability of cheap, male, immigrant labor, though it rose again in the 1930s when immigration to Argentina declined.[3] During the first decades of the century, women were consistently exploited, economically as well as politically. According to Hollander:

> While it was true that the number of women who were wage earners

increased yearly in certain economic sectors this fact alone did not define the degree to which women were able to achieve any qualitative change from their traditional secondary status in Argentine society. Women were still subject to the control of their fathers and husbands due to their total juridical dependency on men inherited from Spanish legal tradition. Women's husbands still maintained the right to dispose of their earnings because legally, the adult married woman was reduced to the status of a minor. Furthermore, women still did not have the right to vote or to be elected to public office. These restrictions on women underscored legally the idealized image of women in Argentine culture, which remained that of the housewife-mother: the lovely decoration, weak, not very intelligent, and totally dependent on the male for her source of identification and status. Paradoxically enough, often the very men who spoke of women as the "weaker sex" in need of male protection found no inconsistency in their positions as owners of industry in which women of the working class were so exploited.[4]

In an effort to organize women in their own defense, Cecilia Grierson, Argentina's first female doctor, founded the National Women's Council in 1900. Later, in 1904, she and another doctor, Julieta Lanteri, began an organization of university women to promote higher education for women. Women activists from these and other groups were responsible for organizing the First International Feminist Congress which took place in Buenos Aires in 1910 with representatives from all over the Americas and Europe; the delegates, ignored by the Argentine government at the time, voted to fight for civil and economic equality for women, reformation of the school system (Sarmiento's advice had only been partially heeded), and a divorce law. The first feminist party in Argentina was founded by Lanteri in 1919. In the same year, Elvira Rawson de Dellepiani, a doctor and a teacher, founded the Women's Rights Association, urging women of all backgrounds to struggle for equal rights. Dellepiani, Sara Justo, and Alicia Moreau de Justo, leading feminists working through the Socialist Party, were responsible for winning some advancement in protective legislation for working women and minors from the Argentine Congress early in the century. However, according to Señora Moreau de Justo, herself a doctor, working women still had to confront skepticism and hostility from men. When she first started her practice, she recalls, no one wanted to accept her as a bona fide physician.[5] In her nineties and still an ardent feminist, she believes that the efforts of the early feminist organizations in Argentina were at least partially successful in changing the status of working women.

Considerable progress was made under the Radical regime in the 1920s. The Argentine labor movement, "the most vigorous on the continent" from the years before the First World War until the Depression, won some important victories, among them, more protective legislation for women working in commercial and industrial establishments.[6] But this only affected the working conditions of women in the large cities; it failed to legislate improvements for women employed in rural agriculture or domestic situations. Nor did it tackle the issue of the unequal wages that women were still forced to accept; in fact, during the 1920s the gap between the wages paid to women and men for the same work *increased* rather than decreased.[7]

A major step toward achieving equal rights for women in Argentina was taken in September 1926, when congress passed Law 11357. The law changed the civil status of women—married women, in particular—who had previously been considered no more than legal wards of their husbands. Under Law 11357, a married woman was given the right 1) to exercise any profession without the permission of her husband; 2) to dispose of her earnings as she wished; 3) to enter into civil or commercial agreements without her husband's authorization; and 4) to exercise authority over her children and their goods in case of a legal separation from her husband, whether or not she remarried; in marriage, however, the law stipulated that the husband was dominant, following the traditional, patriarchal custom of *patria potestad*. Although there was no guarantee that this new law would be observed in the privacy of Argentine homes, it did bring the country into the mainstream of twentieth-century progress toward equal rights for women.

The Argentine Women's Union

The world economic disaster of 1929 and the subsequent military coup of 1930 in Argentina represented a significant setback for the labor movement in Argentina. The new Conservative government regime, trying to avoid economic collapse, tightened its control over labor and industry while encouraging national industrialization to counteract the loss of foreign trade. The repression of labor in the 1930s meant a halt in the progress of the women's movement as well; the more reactionary elements in power were less receptive to women's demands for equal treatment. In fact, there seemed to exist a fundamental contradiction in attitudes toward women; on the one hand, the potential for industrial growth and profits caused employers to hire larger and larger numbers of women at low wages, while on the other, there was a strong reaffirmation in Argentine society of the traditional notion that a woman's primary role must be that of wife and mother.[8]

Despite this, young women, fleeing from dreary and demeaning jobs in the interior provinces, flocked to Buenos Aires hoping to find steady work and perhaps some glamour and excitement. For every fifty men that migrated to the capital, a hundred women did the same;[9] most of them were lonely, uprooted women disappointed in their dreams, who felt neglected and exploited by their employers. One of them, María Eva Duarte, managed to break out of the mold and scale heights of power and wealth that even she probably never envisioned.

Eva was born in a small town in the province of Buenos Aires in 1919, the illegitimate daughter of a working-class woman and a landowning father who deserted them when Eva was three.[10] In 1935 at age fifteen Eva left home with only a primary school education, and went to the capital hoping to become an actress. Racine and Molière meant nothing to her; the theater she had in mind was the kind she had read about in cheap magazines or had seen at the movie house. She wanted to be a star, and she was prepared for a struggle. At first, she only got bit parts on the stage and in fourth-rate films, but by 1942 she had maneuvered herself into a desirable position as head of a radio soap opera program. It was said that she got what she wanted through the men with whom she had affairs; apparently, her performances as an actress were dreadful.[11] In any event, her success was unique compared to the fate of most other young women from the provinces. María Eva Duarte was clearly driven by ambition.

As women of all backgrounds became more visible in the urban workforce, traditionalists and conservatives in Argentina took to warning of the dire consequences of this trend:

> During the thirties and early forties, the increasing public employment of women elicited interesting responses from political economists and intellectuals which revealed Argentine attitudes toward women in general. In an almost hysterical fashion, many viewed the process with alarm and detailed the tragic consequences for Argentina of this change in the traditional role of women. Indeed, many insisted that it was because women were working outside the home that Argentina was suffering from a series of crises such as a declining birthrate, the decreasing moral significance of the family, the increasing unemployment rate among men due to "unfair" competition of cheap female labor, and the consequent decline in the dominant position of the father within the family structure.[12]

An organization called Catholic Action was behind much of the insistence on the threat to morality and cohesive family life that working women represented. Founded in Argentina in 1928 and modeled after a similar organization in Fascist Italy, Catholic Action was devoted to propounding the view of the Church hierarchy on matters of contemporary concern and to bringing pressure to bear on government officials who depended on the Church for support.[13] This group and *Criterio*, a journal edited by Catholic intellectuals, publicly stated their sympathy toward Fascism and undoubtedly influenced Argentine sentiment in that direction. Praise for Mussolini and, in particular, for Fascist attitudes toward women appeared in Argentine newspapers; and some Argentines even suggested that there be financial aid programs to encourage an increase in the birthrate and the exclusion of women from the paid work force.[14] When the 32nd International Eucharistic Congress was held in Buenos Aires in 1934, the Church's position with regard to women and their proper role received even more widespread attention. A reactionary fervor was building that threatened the liberal legislation of 1926.

In 1935, a notoriously corrupt Conservative regime proposed that Law 11357 be reformed. Article 333 of the reform bill stipulated that a married woman would no longer have the civil rights granted to her under the 1926 law, that she would, in effect, be reduced once again to the same legal status as a minor or, for that matter, a demented person or an unborn child. Essentially, it threatened to undo what little progress had been made in women's rights in Argentina thus far. Not surprisingly, the proposal's implications were not widely publicized by those who favored it. Word of the reform bill managed to reach Victoria through her friends María Rosa Oliver and Susana Larguía, who were more politically involved than she and who had learned of it from Socialist women law students. While they were infuriated by the proposal, the women were equally incensed by the legislators' underhanded tactics.

Victoria had just returned from Europe where she had been dismayed by Mussolini's antifeminism and, in turn, heartened by Virginia Woolf's encouragement to express her womanhood in literature. The subject of women's rights was very much on her mind. For years she herself had felt discriminated against as a woman; when she occasionally found sympathetic understanding from friends, generally not Argentines, she experienced, as she wrote to Waldo Frank in a 1929 letter, a kind of joyful liberation: "My friend, to understand my joy, you'd have to know what my life has been like in this country, among people who have never understood me, never accepted me. By whom I feel myself outraged and denied, denied, denied. Denied to the point of feeling myself poor in all my wealth, made miserable by my useless wealth. You don't know what it's like to be a woman in South America." The wealth she referred to was spiritual and intellectual, as well as material.

Between her own experience and the spectre of renewed oppression that she sensed in Europe, Victoria was moved to write more and more frequently about the concepts of justice and equality which she feared were becoming perverted in modern society. It was a preoccupation that had haunted her back in 1920 when she wrote her first article for *La Nación*. A few months before learning of the proposed reform bill, Victoria had written these words in an article about André Gide's *Pages de Journal*:

> It is difficult to live and work intellectually in a country where hierarchies are falsified, in a country where they exist only rarely and then poorly (even though it may annoy Lucifer, paradise is hierarchical), in a country where, consequently, nothing is in its place. This is what is happening now in the most civilized countries (or should I say cultured?). And doesn't the terrible state of nausea in the world today come from the intoxication produced by that extreme disorder? [. . .]
>
> I am against equality and against leveling out. That was what I tried to say the first time I published an article fifteen years ago. But I am also against privileges and favoritisms, against all that Gide attributes, rightly or wrongly, to "the errors of capitalism to which our western world is still tied and which is driving it to ruin."
>
> I was born into this world on the side of privileges and favoritisms; but when I see them for what they are, I detest them, and when I become conscious of them, I repudiate them. It's a gradual process of stripping away. I have no illusions about making rapid progress on this road.
>
> When I say I am against equality, I express myself inexactly. How can one be *against* what does not exist? Men are not equal. I even believe that centuries of effort would not succeed in equating them. Fortunately so. How much less beautiful nature would be if all the flowers, all the trees, all the greens were alike!
>
> I can say, on the other hand, that I am against artificial inequality. I believe that *that* kind of inequality impoverishes and debilitates humanity — including those who are on the side of privilege.
>
> To find an order that will correct such a situation and a rule of conduct so as to live well within it is something that I ardently desire. I need it as much morally as the world's disinherited need it materially.[15]

The retrograde attitude that motivated the proposed reform of Law 11357 was a perfect example of efforts to establish "artificial inequality," as Victoria called it. To lump women together in a category determined by their sex and to deprive them of equal rights under the law is a clear case of privilege and favoritism on the part of men. Artificial inequality based on socioeconomic distinctions is a deplorable injustice; in her opinion, however, exploitation on the basis of sex is even worse than the exploitation of one class by another. She reemphasized her priorities in a recent interview: "Don't talk to me about our [women's] duty to help the triumph of Marxism, or whatever, with the promise that its success will furnish us the enjoyment of all our rights. . . . No, no, no. First the status of women must change in the world. Later the other changes will arise from this, not vice-versa."[16]

Together with other friends who denounced the proposed reform bill, Victoria, María Rosa Oliver, and Susana Larguía founded the Argentine Women's Union in March of 1936. Their objective was to stop the bill's passage in congress through the united opposition of women from all walks of life. At the first general meeting elections were held, and as Oliver recalls in her memoirs, "Victoria Ocampo, who had always been outraged by any tacit or open discrimination against women, had recently returned from Spain and was enthusiastic about the rights of women recognized by the code of the new Republic; she was elected president of the Union."[17] The members of the Argentine Women's Union must have recognized that, as a crusader for women's rights and as a figure of national prominence and influence, no one could equal Victoria Ocampo. She had never been active in feminist groups before nor had she joined any political party, but she was widely recognized as a rebel and a free thinker —a woman willing to fight for democratic principles. María Rosa Oliver also recalls that many wealthy women of Victoria's own class refused to join the Union and mocked Victoria, saying she was "crazy for getting mixed up in something like that" when she was so well off herself.[18] By this time, Victoria was used to such criticism. It only annoyed her to think that, when battle lines were drawn, she would have to contend with female as well as male adversaries.

The Union's first order of business was to set up offices and organize activities to raise the consciousness of as many people as possible—male and female — with regard to the meaning of the proposed reform bill. Naturally, women were the ones to be affected by the bill, so they should be the major force in organizing and voicing opposition to it. They drew up a plan of action that included frequent general meetings, the establishment of various subcommissions to deal with special topics of concern, the publication of an official bulletin to report the Union's activities, the distribution of pamphlets and fliers to the public, the gathering of legal and statistical information to support their position, and interviews with legislators, journalists, jurists, and church officials who backed the regressive reform. Affiliate organizations were founded in other cities.

It was through the subcommissions and public pamphlets that the members hoped to reach large numbers of supporters, especially women of the working classes. Subcommissions were charged to gather and distribute information on such topics as (1) civil and political rights for women, (2) expanded protective legislation for women who were industrial, domestic, or agricultural workers, (3) maternity, (4) child protection, (5) cultural and spiritual development for women, (6) world peace, and (7) the curbing and prevention of prostitution. Each subcommission held open meetings and sponsored lectures for the community at a nominal charge. Typical lectures were entitled "Women in a Democracy," "The

Civil Rights of Women," "Women and Culture," "Women and Science." One of the most popular pamphlets, printed by the thousands and sold for a few pesos on the streets of the capital, was written by Victoria and entitled "Woman, Her Rights and Her Responsibilities." One morning, two young women hawking the pamphlet in the street were picked up by the police and later released without explanation. When the incident was made public, a judge named Hector Lafaille, who backed the reform bill, made a speech condemning the pamphlet in which he said that no woman who belonged to the Union could rightfully call herself a member of the Catholic Church. He concluded his remarks by saying that he would have had the girls arrested and thrown in jail if it weren't for the fact that 20,000 women supporting the Union were behind them.[19] The Union had evidently made its mark, much to the chagrin of its critics.

Hostility to the Union and what it represented was expressed in many quarters. Both men and women felt threatened by it. Many women, both rich and poor, felt that the traditional influence they wielded in domestic situations might be eroded and that the preordained status quo was some sort of divine will. After all, this was what their husbands, fathers, and parish priests seemed to believe, and they knew no higher symbols of authority. Men particularly objected to the Union's efforts to stop prostitution and close the bordellos for which Buenos Aires was internationally famous. For years, prostitutes had been imported from the provinces and from as far away as France, and books were written about a "white slave trade" that had become notorious.

When Victoria, or other Union members, expressed the membership's viewpoint in interviews with influential men, they were often greeted with flippant remarks or even rude insinuations. In one interview, a priest of considerable public stature accused her of encouraging immorality by seeking protection for unwed mothers. In another, the chief justice of the Argentine Supreme Court asked her why in the world she had gotten involved in the Union in the first place since the proposed bill would not affect her status (Monaco Estrada had died in 1933, so she was a widow). Susana Larguía, the Union's first treasurer, remembers still another interview during which Victoria paced furiously, "like a lioness," barely able to control her rage when a legislator suggested that a husband should have the exclusive right to seek an annulment if he discovered his wife was not a virgin. "The things they said were unbelievable," Victoria recalls. Even at a distance of forty years, she adds *"qué brutos!"* with an accent of undiminished contempt.

In an effort to achieve the widest possible diffusion of the Union's message and to reach the largest audience, it was decided that a major radio broadcast would be an effective form of publicity. Because Victoria was the organization's president and its most accomplished speaker, she wrote and delivered the address in August 1936 over network radio on a program simultaneously broadcast in Spain. She called it "Woman and her Expression." Remarking on the new technology of voice transmission that had conquered the distance between the Old and the New Worlds, permitting dialogues where only monologues used to exist, Victoria called for a similar end to the distance that separated men and women. Women must break the silence of centuries and join in dialogues with men. In order to do this, they must have the ability to express themselves to the fullest, not just as mothers but as professional women. For this, equal educational opportunities were essential. She must have been inspired by Virginia Woolf when she said:

> Until the present, we have heard principally from male witnesses concerning women, witnesses that a court of law would not allow since they would be considered suspect, male witnesses whose testimony is biased. The woman herself has scarcely uttered a word. And it is up to the woman not only to discover this unexplored continent that she represents, but also to talk in turn about men in her own capacity as a suspect witness.
>
> If she manages to do this, world literature will be enriched beyond calculation, (and I don't doubt that she will).
>
> I know by my own experience how unprepared the present-day woman, and particularly the South American woman, is to achieve this victory. She has neither the necessary training, the freedom or the tradition. And I wonder what can be accomplished by genius alone without these three things; can it produce something of value? The miracle of a work of art is produced only when it has been silently prepared for during many years' time.
>
> I believe that our generation and the following one, and even the one about to be born, are destined not to achieve this miracle but to prepare for it and make it imminent. I believe our work will be painful and unrecognized. I believe that we must resign ourselves to it with humility, but also with a profound faith in its greatness and its fecundity.[20]

The immediate aim, she concluded, must be to build solidarity among women of all nations, a solidarity based not just on mutual interests but on mutual feelings — a "subjective solidarity," as she called it. "Such an aspiration may seem exaggerated or absurd," she added, "but I cannot resign myself to less."[21] To be truly effective, feminism must transcend the boundaries imposed by time and space and become a universal state of mind and heart.

The pressure exerted on legislators and the public finally brought about the defeat of the proposed reform bill. But the work of the Union didn't end with that victory. For several years it continued to function in

Buenos Aires and other Argentine cities, pursuing the other objectives of the various subcommissions. A major focus of the group's efforts was the support of legislation that would grant women the vote. Proposals to this end had been submitted to the congress regularly since 1919, most recently in 1932 and 1935, but without success. Women's suffrage—already a reality in England, the United States, and Latin American countries such as Ecuador, Bolivia, Panama, Uruguay, Cuba, Costa Rica, and the Dominican Republic — was still not guaranteed by law in Argentina, perhaps the most progressive and economically advanced nation on the continent. In 1938, 1939, and 1942 repeated petitions were made by feminists, generally backed by Socialists in the legislature, but to no avail. Apparently, the preservation of Law 11357 was considered concession enough to the rights of Argentine women.

After serving two years as an officer and active member of the Union, Victoria decided to resign and withdraw her membership, a move she regretted but found morally unavoidable. Her decision had nothing to do with the basic purpose and objectives of the Union itself as it was originally conceived. What she could not accept was the intrusion of partisan political motives into the Union's management and direction; she felt that Communist members were manipulating the organization for their own political benefit by linking the goal of women's rights to the class struggle they were advocating in a climate of economic unrest which had been aggravated by the government's intransigence and corruption. To Victoria, the cause of women's liberation was a cause as morally right and just as human slavery was morally wrong and unjust; it was a universal truth beyond the sphere of party politics. Feminists must have recourse to political means to achieve the ends they seek, but politics cannot be an end in itself, nor can the goal of equal rights for women be compromised by any other objectives.

Prelude to Perón

In a letter written to María de Maeztu shortly after Mussolini declared war on Abyssinia and just as the Spanish Civil War was beginning, Victoria said succinctly, "If Fascism triumphs in Spain, we're done for in America." By the time the war in Spain was over, Maeztu had fled her native country to seek refuge in Argentina as had many other Spanish intellectuals. However, for those who had witnessed the growth of Fascism in Europe and were familiar with its telltale signs, Argentina in the late 1930s must have been a less than comforting place. Xenophobic nationalism and militarism were on the rise; according to one historian, "Nativism (*criollismo*), defense of national economic and political sovereignty, anti-British, pro-German and Hispanist ideas were advocated, and right-wing para-military groups paraded in the streets and occasionally engaged in acts of anti-Semitism."[22] When the Nazi aggression in Europe became blatant and France was threatened with invasion, Victoria found more European friends seeking refuge at her doorstep, confident that in the atmosphere around *Sur* and its founder they would have intellectual freedom and companionship. Meanwhile, she did everything in her power to express solidarity with the Allied cause; it was a personal mission, an ongoing statement of moral commitment made more urgent by the fact that Argentina, under the influence of its military leaders, remained officially neutral during the war and refused to align itself with the Allied cause until Germany's defeat was almost certain. Besides the moral and material support Victoria gave to refugees in Argentina and writers in France, and besides *Sur*'s sponsorship of Caillois's *Lettres françaises*, she was also one of the founders in 1940 of Argentine Action, an organization formed to counteract Nazi-Fascist infiltration in Argentina. Notably, she was the only woman on the original executive committee.

Many Argentines refused to acknowledge the existence of Fascist tactics in their own country. One particularly unpleasant incident, in which Victoria was personally involved, occurred in 1942, when Waldo Frank was concluding another lecture tour in Argentina. The morning he was packing to leave the country, a gang of five thugs forced their way into his apartment, attacked him physically while shouting anti-Semitic abuse, and threatened his life if he didn't leave Argentina immediately. Apparently a mistranslation of a crucial word critical of Argentina in his farewell article had unleashed the violent resentment of some Nazi sympathizers. Frank was a Jew and a pro-Communist; his words were no longer so widely applauded as they had been in 1929. Luckily, neighbors heard his screams and the attackers fled. Victoria was quickly notified and when she arrived on the scene, she found the walls of Frank's room spattered with blood and Frank lying on the bed with an open head wound. The attack was reported to the police, but no official action was taken. It was clear that Frank was *persona non grata* as far as the government was concerned. Unfortunately, many of Frank's Argentine friends turned their backs on the incident for fear of reprisals. Victoria and María Rosa Oliver were the ones who saw to it that his injuries were treated, and twenty days later, they alone accompanied him to the airport. Watching Frank board the plane, Victoria again wondered if she wouldn't be safer and happier outside Argentina, in a place where fanatical nationalism was not mistaken for patriotism. But to abandon the land, the river, and the barrancas of San Isidro that she loved in an irrational, visceral way would have been a betrayal of herself and her country. To register her protest internationally, however, she publicly condemned the attack in the August 1942 issue of *Sur*.

Since her last, and only, hasty visit to the United States in 1930, Victoria had wanted to return. Her first impression had been extremely favorable; now that the United States was engaged in the war effort in both Europe and the Pacific, she was particularly anxious to observe the effects of national mobilization and write her impressions for Argentine readers. In addition, she wanted to establish more contacts for *Sur* in the United States and invite some young North American writers to contribute to a special issue of the review devoted to the literature of the States (which was published in 1944). In May of 1943, therefore, she accepted an invitation from the Guggenheim Foundation to tour the United States and give a series of lectures. Breaking with her custom of traveling by sea, she decided to make the trip of more than 6,000 miles by air. In those days, the planes were only minimally equipped for passenger comfort, so Victoria went dressed in slacks, which she had begun to wear frequently in public contrary to the accepted custom of the time. It was an arduous trip with many intermediate stops where passengers were sometimes bumped to make way for high-priority cargo — a journey exhausting beyond the comprehension of today's travelers who make the trip in less than eleven hours, nonstop. Even the relentless drone of the propellers could not put her at ease; she was never able to relax on any plane (prop or jet). In fact, it was a journey that many of her fellow countrymen would have refused to make — but not necessarily for these reasons.

Relations between Argentina and the United States had been strained ever since the first Pan-American conference held in Buenos Aires in 1936 to deal with the general problem of the maintenance of hemispheric peace and the threat of territorial aggression from Nazi Germany. Roosevelt had called the conference in the spirit of the Good Neighbor Policy and was pleased with its outcome when all the Latin American nations joined the United States in a "declaration of principles of inter-American solidarity and cooperation."[23] Argentina had signed the document, but unenthusiastically. Two years later, at another conference of American states in Lima, the Argentine foreign minister showed his country's lukewarm attitude toward the business at hand by taking a tour of the Chilean lake region while the most critical sessions of the conference were being held. The concept of American solidarity had appealed to Argentines less than to other Latin Americans because Argentina had traditionally been oriented toward Europe; restrictions placed by the United States on the importation of Argentine beef were also a source of friction. The growing influence of Nazi-Fascist sentiment in Argentina was yet another wedge between the Colossus of the North and the would-be Colossus of the South. Interestingly, in the United States, the sentiment in favor of solidarity was so strong that when a poll was taken in February 1941 to determine how many were ready to fight for the defense of the Caribbean area and even of Argentina or Brazil, 86 percent of those questioned replied affirmatively.[24] Argentina's indifference seemed not to be a deterrent to the general desire for hemispheric solidarity.

Victoria was warmly welcomed in the United States in the spring of 1943, and her reaction to what she saw was predictably favorable. After living in a country divided by political and economic unrest, the unified spirit of the Yankee war effort was impressive. Victoria made a point of looking into the role of women in both the war industry and the armed forces. In an article on this subject for *La Nación,* she wrote:

> Some criticism, masculine and South American in origin, had reached my ears about the excessive number of women who were abandoning their femininity to enlist in the army or work in factories. It's always the same thing: damned if you do and damned if you don't. Men don't make the effort to be logical nor to examine the facts dispassionately when it comes to censuring the conduct of women. I'm speaking in particular about Latin men on account of their tendency to imagine (and this is what English-speaking Americans call "wishful thinking") that the weaker sex (?) has all the duties and only a few rights, while the stronger sex (its strength is revealed, no doubt, in this form of determining roles) has all the rights and only a few duties. For these and other reasons, I was interested in seeing the Wacs and the Waves for myself.[25]

What she saw convinced her that women were essential to the war effort (morally justifiable in view of Axis aggression) and that they were as effective as men in their jobs, at no risk to their femininity.

A few years later, when the war in Europe was over, the English government asked if she would like to fly to Nuremberg on an RAF transport to witness part of the trials of Nazi war criminals. Again, the subject of women and war was on her mind while she watched the proceedings:

> Everything in this room proves to me that this is a matter to be aired among men only. The Nuremberg trial is like my Dakota [RAF plane], equipped strictly for the transport of troops. Female presence was not expected in either one of the two cases. This tribunal and that plane did not anticipate carrying women on board. Both have been built and organized with the intention of doing without them.
>
> Evidently women cannot participate in that masculine sport whose consequences they suffer.
>
> The Hitler conspiracy was an affair of men. There are no women among

the accused. Is that, however, any reason not to include them among the judges? Wouldn't it rather be a reason for having them? If the results of the Nuremberg trial are going to affect the destiny of Europe, wouldn't it be fair to let women say something about it? Were they spared the war? Were they unworthy companions in the moment of danger? Would they be so in the moment of making decisions that will affect the future of the world? Up to now, the failure of men in the area of the suppression or prevention of war crimes, and of war itself—which is always a crime—has been resounding. To ask women what they think about these matters and to allow them to intervene in them carries no danger, and it can offer unsuspected advantages.[26]

She would not accept the idea that war was inevitable; if women were more involved in the affairs of state from the outset, they might exert a beneficial moral influence that would deter men's aggressive instinct. A truly balanced rule of law, she believed, would be one in which the male and the female had equal representation and authority.

Feminism and the Perón Regime

In July of 1943, while Victoria was still in the United States, the Argentine army responded to the climate of increasing discontent provoked by economic mismanagement and social injustice by overthrowing the civilian government of Ramon S. Castillo. It was a bloodless coup that brought to power the GOU (Group of United Officers), a highly nationalistic, pro-Axis "colonels' clique." By 1944 Juan Domingo Perón had become its most visible leader.

Early that year, Perón had met Eva Duarte at a fund-raising benefit held at Luna Park for the victims of an Argentine earthquake. Since moving to the capital from the provinces nine years before, Eva had scrambled, struggled, and finally engineered a career for herself that brought her reasonably close to having the glamour and recognition she sought. She had a sharp eye for useful contacts and for men of influence. A few months after she met the widowed Colonel Perón, then head of the Ministry of Labor and Welfare as well as the Ministry of War, they began living together and she started doing a daily broadcast of political propaganda extolling the benefits that Perón's labor legislation had brought to urban and rural workers.[27] Far from keeping a low profile as the colonel's mistress, Eva was openly presented to Perón's friends as if she were his wife, and she was often included in his daily meetings at home with politicians and fellow officers.[28] Their relationship became the talk of Buenos Aires, a topic of scandalous proportions in conservative social circles.

It was evidently a match that satisfied ambitions on both sides. Eva

Duarte had met the man who would make her final climb to the top a reality, while Perón had found a woman with the qualities he needed to help him rally popular support for his own push to occupy the seat of power in Argentine government. Her working-class background, her public experience as an actress, and her energy and drive could be molded to suit his own political purpose. Whether or not he revealed his intentions to her, the interest he showed in her abilities and the role he gave her to play by his side must have satisfied her own cravings. The feeling of having been rejected by her natural father and by the wealthy, landowning classes with whom she associated him was counterbalanced by Perón's companionship; he was twenty-three years her senior and the leader of a political program that championed the working classes against the power of the oligarchy. Within a year of their meeting, Eva Duarte, radio actress and cabaret girl from the provinces, had been transformed into the political comrade and confidante of the most powerful man in Argentina. It was a better story than any radio script-writer could have invented.

By the end of the 1944, Perón had added the vice-presidency to his list of political posts, but he had also succeeded in alienating other officers of the GOU because of his radical programs and demagogic tactics. In October 1945 there was a confrontation, and he was forced to resign. Within a few days, however, strikes and demonstrations by workers in the capital and other cities of Argentina brought him back from exile and arrest. Delirious crowds heard him speak from the balcony of the Casa Rosada on the triumphant night of October 17. Six days later, he and Eva were married. In February 1946, Perón became the elected president of Argentina.

Once in office, Perón vowed to destroy the oligarchy through a coalition of the rural and urban working classes; in this aspect, his authoritarian system differed from other forms of European Fascism.[29] He called it *justicialismo* or social justice, but behind the slogans and speeches designed to arouse the xenophobic passions of the *descamisados* by condemning the *vendepatria* (sell-the-country) economic policy and European outlook of the oligarchy, he was a virtual dictator with control over every aspect of public life. If the post-Radical regimes of 1930–1945 were often corrupt and mismanaged, tangled in bureaucracy and subservient to upper-class interests, the Perón regime that lasted from 1946 to 1955 was, according to one historian, much worse:

> The dictator methodically destroyed most of what remained of the democratic processes and procedures achieved under the Radicals. The judiciary, which under the Radicals had won national and international respect for integrity, was destroyed as *antiperonista* judges were purged.

For extended periods of time the country was declared to be in "a state of internal war" and consequently subject to control under legislation that had the effect of martial law. The press and the radio were gagged. Imprisonment and torture were commonly employed. Political exile was freely resorted to. An elaborate spy system was developed to intimidate the populace. Elections were deceptions. Voting could be held in an ostensible atmosphere of freedom because the terms under which the opposition was permitted to campaign left no doubt as to the final results.[30]

In spite of this, Perón undeniably had the support of the working classes which had been ignored or abused under previous regimes. To them, the dictator was a hero and his wife a storybook princess who handed out gifts and peso notes to her adoring public:

It was hardly any wonder that working people looked upon her as a beautiful goddess. Wherever she went in Argentina men knelt in the dust to spell out Evita in flowers for her to walk upon. She appeared before them at monster demonstrations, a young woman in her twenties, dressed in the latest Paris fashions, draped in mink and glittering in diamonds. "You, too, will have clothes like these some day," she promised them.[31]

If Eva thought that as the wife of the president she would be able to command the respect of the upper-class women she despised, she was mistaken. Their rebuff in denying her the leadership of their charity organization, a courtesy accorded to wives of presidents, seemed to make her intensify her devotion to Perón. She began wearing simpler clothes, working longer days, and cultivating the image of the self-sacrificing motherly intercessor between the workers and their benevolent *patrón*.

A large measure of Perón's support came from the women of the working classes to whom he gave the social and political dignity that society had traditionally denied them. It appears to have been a calculated political move that began to take shape at about the time he met Eva. She may have contributed to it, but to ascribe its genesis to her is an unconvincing argument considering that she had no experience in politics or in the movement for women's rights before she met him. On October 3, 1944 Perón broke an established tradition by creating a special Women's Division of Labor and Assistance in the Ministry of Labor and Welfare he then headed; in a speech that day he called for more material and moral recognition for the over 900,000 women who were part of the paid work force in Argentina.[32]

What he said and what he did broke official precedents. After the 1943 coup, the GOU had been markedly antifeminist. The hiring of women in industry, commerce, and government was discouraged as were any activist women's associations; one pro-Allied fund-raising group, the

Committee for Victory, was forced to disband.[33] When Paris was liberated from Nazi occupation in August 1944, many women (including Victoria) were among those celebrating and demonstrating their support for the Allies in the Plaza Francia in Buenos Aires; police on horseback came and chased them away, knocking many down, and later the government accused extremist groups and women in particular of having provoked the clash. Politically active and aware women were anathema to the pre-Perón regime.

Before reaching the presidency, Perón called for suffrage for women in Argentina. On July 26, 1945 he made a speech before congress, pledging his determination to work toward that end. He evidently wanted to be seen as the lone paladin of women's rights, the knight in shining armor who would defend women's political honor. Interestingly enough, he made no mention of the many previous attempts to gain suffrage for women in Argentina. In view of the fact that the suffrage proposal was not a politically expedient move at the time, historians generally interpret it as part of a long-range plan that Perón knew would work to his benefit.

Perón's proposal struck Victoria as blatantly self-serving. There was no doubt in her mind that he was a Fascist at heart and that his feminism was merely a guise for political motives: granting women suffrage would virtually assure him of a large percentage of the female vote when elections were called. Above all, from her point of view, there was a moral principle at stake: to accept the vote from a *de facto* totalitarian government would be tantamount to ratifying its policies and its very existence. In 1936 she had urged Argentine women to fight for their rights; this time she would urge them to do the same, not by fighting for, but by fighting against suffrage granted under what she considered immoral conditions. On September 3, 1945 Victoria made a speech before a women's group, the National Women's Assembly. Not mentioning Perón by name nor specifying her objections to his policies, she limited her remarks to a discussion of the immorality of totalitarian governments and the danger of accepting the rationale that ends justify means. She was careful to make the following disclaimer, but in the end, her political sentiments were quite clear:

> I am not speaking in the name of any political group because I don't belong to any party, not even to the Communist Party as some people persist in saying, perhaps because I have never considered the Communists "untouchables," not even in the eras when they were most vilely persecuted. Now that the party has been legalized, I can allow myself the luxury of declaring publicly that I am not and never have been a Communist. On the other hand, I *am* strongly anti-Nazi and anti-Fascist and have always been so. Therein lies the nuance.

Nor do I belong to the body of the Catholic Church in which I was born, for reasons that are not pertinent to the present discussion.[. . .]

I have never involved myself in what is popularly called politics. And if I were to—something that is not among my aptitudes or inclinations—it would be to maintain that things relegated, as it were, to the region of abstract morality must become an immediate part of politics for the salvation of a world devastated by the greed of some and the apathy of others; by violence and lies and satanic pride in its various disguises: that of totalitarianisms, for example, with no exceptions. They must become part of politics through the mediation of women who should not sanction any other concerns, weapons, or strategies.[34]

Those who knew anything about Victoria Ocampo understood the symbolic import of this speech. No woman in Argentina wanted equal political rights for women more than she, but to be granted them by an unjust and illegal regime would be worse, she felt, than not having them at all.

The case for symbolic opposition was doomed to defeat. On September 23, 1947 the Argentine Congress passed the bill granting women the right to vote. It was not Perón but Evita who greeted the crowds of women celebrating in the Plaza de Mayo:

On that date there were mass demonstrations in Buenos Aires in celebration of the event. Women from all social classes, including workers, who left their jobs to join the demonstrations, filled the streets in jubilation and listened to Eva Perón speak to them about the significance of that day for women and for Argentina. She described the struggles that they had had to wage with the representatives of the oligarchy in Congress for the passage of the law. She asserted that the vote which women had won was a new tool in their hands. "But our hands are not new in struggle, in work, and in the repeated miracle of creation," she said, urging women to use the vote with the same consciousness that they had historically demonstrated fighting and working by the sides of their men to build a great Argentina.[35]

In the elections of 1951, women in Argentina cast their newly won vote overwhelmingly in favor of Perón.[36]

Evita was never given an official post in the government, but her importance to Perón as a liaison with the working classes was immense. Acting as an extension of Perón himself, she had offices in the Ministry of Labor where many would come to plead for her intercession with the president. Wherever she went, often representing Perón at official meetings and union rallies, the crowds adored her. She, in turn, seemed to thrive on giving speeches and public broadcasts in which she would make use of all her dramatic and rhetorical talents. Whipping the crowds to a peak of emotion, she would denounce the oligarchy and harangue her listeners, urging them to declare their willingness to die for Perón as she was prepared to do. If Perón was the nation's hero, then she was his principal hero-worshiper.

Evita's appeal to the people was a valuable asset to her husband, yet precisely because she was a woman and his wife, she was no direct threat to his power. When it was once suggested that she run on the same ticket, as his vice-president, Perón's disapproval was enough to quash the idea, though there is evidence to indicate that Evita would have liked the nomination.[37]

Under Perón's guidance, Evita assumed the leadership of a special women's branch of the Peronist Party in 1949. The idea behind this ostensibly autonomous organization was to give women a forum for developing their own program of interests which would receive equal consideration with that of the men's branch of the party. Responding to Evita's invitation to join the struggle for women's rights, which was identified as part of a larger struggle of the working classes against economic and social injustice, many women took part in the Peronist Women's Party, discussing issues and proposing candidates for the 1951 elections. Behind whatever decisions were made, however, lay the presence and ultimate authority of Perón himself; it was acknowledged from the beginning that the General was the true leader of all Peronist parties and that he had the final say in every instance.[38] In fact, women's political independence under Peronism was only superficial, just as Evita's feminism was subordinated to Perón's interests. As she proclaimed to the first national assembly of the Peronist Women's movement, "For women, to be a Peronist is, before anything, to be loyal to Perón, subordinate to Perón, and blindly confident in Perón!"[39]

If Evita understood the inherent contradiction between the goals of authentic feminism and Peronism, she never seemed bothered by it, nor did she ever seem to resent being used by Perón as a political drawing card. His wish was apparently her command, or so she openly stated in her official autobiography *La razón de mi vida* (My Mission in Life). By her own confession, her involvement in the cause of women's rights was originally his idea:

> In this, as in everything, he showed me the way.
> The world's feminists will say that to start a woman's movement in this way is hardly feministic . . . to start by recognizing to a certain extent the superiority of a man!
> However, I am not interested in criticism.
> Also, recognizing Perón's superiority is a different matter.[40]

The ideology of Peronist feminism, as Evita explained it, was a curious mixture of freedoms and dependencies. On the one hand, she said that women should have political, social, and economic freedom, while on the other, she affirmed that women's highest mission in life was homemaking. At times, the things she called for (women in the great centers of power, world peace, a monthly salary for homemakers, a return to spiritual values, the cultural improvement of women) sounded like the program of the Argentine Women's Union and even like many of Victoria's own ideas on the subject of women's liberation and its potential impact on human society. Yet, as one reads *My Mission in Life* and other statements made by Evita, it becomes clear that all the apparent freedoms that Peronism offered to women were predicated on the continuation of a basic dependency — the conventional roles of the worldly male and the domestic female. Perón was well aware that most of his constituency, out of habit, ignorance, or fear of change, was not sympathetic to any real alteration in the stereotypical sex roles. Feminists who favored total equality for women were ridiculed, as this passage of Evita's autobiography makes clear:

I confess I was a little afraid the day I found myself facing the possibility of starting on the "feminist" path.

What could I, a humble woman of the people, do where other women, more prepared than I, had categorically failed?

Be ridiculous? Join the nucleus of women with a grudge against woman and against man, as had happened to innumerable feminist leaders?

I was not an old maid, nor even ugly enough for such a post . . . which, from the time of the English suffragettes down to today, generally belongs, almost exclusively to women of this type . . . women whose first impulse undoubtedly had been to be like men.

And that is how they guided the movements they led!

They seemed to be dominated by indignation at not having been born men, more than by the pride of being women.

They thought, too, that it was a misfortune to be a woman. They were resentful of women who did not want to stop being women. They were resentful of men because they would not let them be like them; the "feminists," the immense majority of feminists in the world, as far as I could see, continued to be a strange species of woman . . . which never seemed to me to be entirely womanly!

And I did not feel very much inclined to be like them.

One day the General gave me the explanation I needed.

"Don't you see that they have missed the way? They want to be men. It is as though to save the workers, I had tried to make oligarchs of them. I would have remained without workers. And I do not think I should have managed to improve the oligarchy at all. Don't you see that this class of 'feminists' detests womanhood? Some of them do not even use makeup . . . because that, according to them, is womanly. Don't you see they want to be men? And if what the world requires is a woman's political and social movement . . . how little will the world gain if the women want to save it by imitating men! We have done too many strange things and made such a mess of everything that I do not know if the world can be arranged anew. Perhaps woman can save us, on condition that she does not imitate us."

I well remember that lesson of the General's.

His ideas never seemed to me so clear and bright.

That is how I felt.

I felt that the woman's movement in my country and all over the world had to fulfill a sublime mission . . . and everything I knew about feminism seemed to me ridiculous. For, not led by women but by those who aspired to be men, it ceased to be womanly and was nothing! Feminism had taken the step from the sublime to the ridiculous.

And that is the step I always try to avoid taking![41]

Reassuring her readers lest they doubt what that mission might be, Evita continued:

. . . And the world really needs more homes every day, and for them more women willing properly to fulfill their destiny and their mission. That is why the first objective of a feminine movement which wishes to improve things for women—which does not aim at changing them into men—should be the home.

We were born to make homes. Not for the street. Common sense shows us the answer. We must have in the home that which we go out to seek: our small economic independence — which would save us from becoming women with no outlook, with no rights and no hope![42]

Just as she never challenged the rightness of Perón's every word, Evita never doubted that women's true place was in the home.

The Perón approach to politics was strictly paternalistic. By extension of this traditional posture, Evita liked to refer to herself as "the mother of my people."[43] To enhance this image, the Eva Perón Foundation was created in 1950, a private social aid foundation with recourse to substantial funds controlled entirely by Evita. Some say it was also Evita's way of putting the charity organization run by the matrons of the oligarchy, who had snubbed her, out of business. In any event, it was another effective political maneuver and one which gave Evita a vehicle for carrying out the maternal role that Perón had designed for her.

When she died prematurely, after struggling to go on with her duties as First Lady despite the cancer that weakened her, Evita was portrayed in newspapers and magazines not only as the mother of her people but as a secular saint. In death she achieved her final apotheosis.

Ironically, the man who had created the legend of Eva Perón did not last more than three years in power without her. As his position became more precarious, he became more and more of a demagogue. In 1955, the armed forces that brought him to national prominence drove him from office and into exile. Not surprisingly, when he returned to Argentina less than twenty years later to head the government a second time, another woman—but this time a much weaker one—was by his side, not just as his wife, but as his hand-picked vice-president.

In 1970, eighteen years after Evita's death, Juan Domingo Perón had these telling words to say about his former wife. They capsulize his attitude toward her and toward women in general:

> *Eva Perón is my product. I prepared her to do what she did.* I needed her in the social sector of my movement. And her work there was extraordinary. In a woman one must awaken the two extraordinary strengths which are the basis of her intuition: sensitivity and imagination. When those attributes are developed, the woman becomes a marvelous instrument. Of course, one must also give her a little bit of knowledge. (Emphasis added.)[44]

The second time around, his product was not at all extraordinary. After Perón's death in 1974, Isabel Martínez de Perón led Argentina to the brink of economic collapse. Again, the armed forces stepped in, finally putting an end to Perón and his women if not to the problems that his regimes had engendered.

A Victim of the Regime

During all the years Perón was in power, Victoria understood that, unofficially, she was considered *persona non grata*. Everything she represented was anathema to Perón and his movement. In 1951, when crosses were painted on the entrance to Villa Ocampo to brand her as an oligarch and a dissenting intellectual, she protested vehemently to the local police station, but she was not intimidated. Friends abroad urged her to pack up and leave Argentina for her own safety—as they would again in 1973 when Peronists set fire to her house in Mar del Plata—but she refused, not wanting to give the impression she was either fearful of threats or guilty of any wrongdoing. If she felt any apprehension, it was for the safety of her personal papers and her collection of correspondence. Were her house to be peremptorily searched, as had happened to other writers who were harassed or arrested by the government, her papers might be confiscated or destroyed. So she took the unusual precaution of packing them in various suitcases and valises which she circulated among members of her family and close friends. Letters destined for friends abroad had to be cautiously worded and entrusted to someone she knew who was planning a trip and could mail them outside the country.

Anything written for Argentine consumption and anything published in *Sur* was, of necessity, apolitical. A direct reference to the dictatorship was an invitation to trouble. Although she never engaged in any political activities while Perón was in power, it was public knowledge that she and *Sur* were adamantly opposed to his regime. As a forum for intellectual freedom that had a reputation for being a bastion of the cultural elite, *Sur* was as unwelcome as Victoria. Perhaps because its reputation was not only national but international and its list of contributors and subscribers so influential, Perón never tried to interfere with its publication. Perhaps it was also because *Sur* could not threaten him politically as did the daily newspaper, *La Prensa*, which he hounded and finally expropriated for government use.

Victoria hated what she saw taking place around her. Whatever positive steps were taken by the regime, such as the construction of many new schools, were negated by the oppressive tactics applied to the conduct of daily life, such as the official school books full of Peronist ideology. If she could not speak out without putting herself and her family in jeopardy and if she would not flee across the river to Uruguay as many of her dissenting compatriots did, the only viable recourse was to carry on with her normal activities: writing, publishing *Sur,* and remaining a thorn in the dictator's side.

The subject of tyranny and the forces of evil in the affairs of government was very much on her mind when she discovered a new play called *Caligula* by a young French writer, Albert Camus. Impressed by the timeliness of its message and the skill with which it was dramatized, she immediately asked for the rights to translate it. She did the translation herself and published it for the first time in Spanish in the March 1946 issue of *Sur*. Later that year, she met Camus in New York and they became good friends. In 1949, he accepted her invitation to visit her in Argentina. As Perón was at the height of his power, Camus, who had fought against colonialist oppression in Algeria and against the Nazis in the French underground, refused to make any public appearances or give any lectures during his brief stay. His silence was his way of repudiating the censorship that had prevented Argentine intellectuals from speaking freely in their own country. While in Argentina, he remained secluded in San Isidro with Victoria and a few writers and other intellectuals who went there to meet and talk with him. As the storm threatened without, Villa Ocampo remained a haven, an oasis of intellectual freedom.

Living in Argentina during the final years of the Perón regime was, according to Victoria's description, like living in a jail without bars:

One felt it, I repeat, at home, on the street, everywhere, and perhaps with a more sinister quality because it was covert. Of course, no jailkeeper watched us sleep [. . .]. Beyond the jails there was no jailkeeper, but our sleep was infested with foreboding nightmares, because life itself was a bad dream. A bad dream in which we couldn't mail a letter, however innocent it might be, without fearing that it would be read. Nor could we say a word on the phone without suspecting that it was being listened to and perhaps recorded. We writers didn't even have the right to speak our intimate thoughts in newspapers, journals, books or lectures—which, moreover, we were not allowed to give—because everything was censorship and prohibited zones. The police had all the rights and could dispose of our papers and, if they chose to, read letters that had been written twenty years before the 1953 bomb plot at the Plaza de Mayo: a plot they suspected us of participating in by sole virtue of being "objectors." One could say without exaggeration that we lived in a state of perpetual violation. Everything was violated: correspondence, the law, freedom of thought, even the human person. [45]

The bomb plot she mentions occurred on April 15, 1953. Two bombs exploded near where Perón was speaking to a crowd in the Plaza de Mayo. That evening gangs of angry Peronists retaliated by burning the famous Jockey Club on Florida Street, destroying its valuable library and art collection. For generations, the Jockey Club had been the symbol of the power and traditions of the oligarchy; it was they whom Perón held responsible for the bombing, and thus the club was his target in retribution.

When this incident took place, Victoria was living in the seclusion of Villa Victoria, her summer home in Mar del Plata. She had been there since December, seeing only a few close friends and avoiding public appearances, including visits to the casino where in years past she had indulged a weakness for gambling. Early on the morning of May 8, 1953 six police agents came to the gate of Villa Victoria and asked to see the señora. They had tried first to find her at Villa Ocampo at three in the morning, and the gatekeeper there, a Peronist sympathizer, had told them she was in Mar del Plata. Victoria was writing in bed that morning, as was her custom, when the police commissioner's visit was announced. She told her maid to show him and his inspector into her room. Considering her quiet existence far from the capital, she was not expecting any kind of trouble, so she was shocked when the commissioner told her he had orders to search the house and asked her to come with him. No further explanation was offered. Thinking it was a matter of minor import, she made no effort to resist. Her immediate concern was the insult of having the personal letters and papers she had with her scrutinized as if they were public documents; in the end, the only thing consfiscated was her address book. When she was dressed, she went with the commisioner to the local police station where she was fingerprinted and made to wait for several hours. Finally, she was told that the results of the search were negative but that it would be necessary for her to go with an agent to an unspecified destination in Buenos Aires. She protested, but to no avail. Stopping at home to pack a small overnight valise, she told her distraught housekeeper, Abelina, not to worry, only to telephone her lawyer and her sister, Angélica. Then a police car took her to town where she and an agent boarded a bus for the capital.

For a day and a half, no one in her family knew her whereabouts. First, she was taken to the central police station in Buenos Aires where she spent the night sitting on a hard wooden chair. Then, the next day, she was interrogated repeatedly about the April bomb plot, the insinuation being that she had prior knowledge of it. This she vehemently denied; the first news she had had of the bombings was from servants in her house who had heard the report on the radio, but the police were not quickly convinced. They asked her many questions: what she lived on, what her income was, what properties she owned, what contacts she had with Communists. She answered everything and then suggested that they respect her age—she was then sixty-three—and leave her in peace. The response was laughter and the comment that she didn't look at all aged.

By that time, her family had found out where she was being detained and had sent her some food, the only gesture they were allowed to make. Later that afternoon and without explanation, a police van transported her to the women's prison of Buen Pastor located in the San Telmo district of Buenos Aires, one of the older sections of the city. Buen Pastor—still in use, though there is talk of building a new women's prison—is a two-story colonial building less than a block in size. It is flanked by the church of San Telmo, run by Jesuits. To this day, the prison's dreary gray facade is guarded by unseen armed police inside a watchbox above the entrance. Two guards led Victoria into Buen Pastor, identified her as a political prisoner, and handed her over to the nuns who tended the prison and its inmates. For twenty-six days, without ever being informed of the charges against her, Victoria was one of those inmates. Officially, she was listed as Victoria Ocampo de Estrada on the detention register; ignoring her protests, the police insisted on using her married name (an example of bureaucratic stubbornness that so enraged her that she later went through years of legal efforts to obtain a formal court authorization to use her maiden name, as she had in fact been doing since 1922).

Most of her time in prison was spent in one large room shared with eleven other women, all political prisoners. The room, once an infirmary, was dank and noisy, connected on one side to a prison corridor and, on the other, to an open patio where the prisoners were allowed to walk for an hour in the mornings and afternoons. Aside from these brief airings, they were kept under constant lock and key, eating and sleeping and even washing themselves in the same small adjoining washroom that had no ventilation and only broken-down sanitary facilities. Each prisoner was expected to wear a regulation blue and white checked smock. Once a week they were allowed to see relatives, though visitors were separated from prisoners by three sets of bars. If they wished, they could supplement the unappetizing prison diet with oranges and chocolate from the prison canteen, but there were strict rules against having books or writing materials, with the exception of a few elementary volumes available through the prison library.

This was the prohibition that Victoria found hardest to endure. She could get along with only cold water for washing, uncomfortable beds, bad food, and even the lack of space to move about. But what she missed desperately were her books, especially during the long hours of the night when she couldn't fall asleep. When she asked for a Bible, she was told there were no copies for prisoners; after two weeks, a priest from outside the prison managed to smuggle one to her. The prison chaplain lent her a few books by San Juan de la Cruz and Santa Teresa de Jesus and a copy of the *Confessions* of Saint Augustine that she had requested. This was the full extent of her reading material.

It was a spartan existence unlike anything she had ever experienced. Never before had she been without the comforts of her own room, her servants, her books, and her physical freedom. Although the barrenness of it was a shock, she soon came to feel that the enforced reduction to essentials had a salubrious, cleansing effect. In prison there could be no hiding from the truth and no hypocrisy as there was outside. Ironically, jailed by the dictatorship, she felt freer from its moral contamination than she had before she was arrested.

Perhaps the greatest favor Perón did her by locking her up in Buen Pastor was putting her in a cell with other women, most of whom were totally unlike her in social and economic background. Nearby were prisoners accused of crimes like murder and infanticide, young women whose tragic lives gave their heinous crimes another perspective. Among the political prisoners sharing the same locked room hour after hour, day after day, there were soon no social or economic distinctions. Dressed alike, eating the same food, sleeping next to one another, talking, laughing, and worrying together about what was happening in other parts of the prison, about what unknown destiny awaited them, they became equals, friends, sisters. To pass the long, cold winter hours, they shared stories of their lives, sang songs, and entertained one another as best they could. In the same prison room with Victoria was her old friend Susana Larguía, who arrived a few days after she did. Larguía has remembered how Victoria rose spontaneously to the occasion:

> In the beginning, when she saw almost everyone sewing, embroidering and knitting, Victoria said: "I don't know how to use my hands, but I do know how to use my intelligence. If you want, I can entertain you with stories and poetry." From that moment on, through the magic of her words we were treated to many different expressions of beauty. The *Cántico espiritual* [of San Juan de la Cruz] was dazzling. Recited by Victoria in our common cell, it achieved its true dimension; all else vanishes now before the memory of its beauty.
>
> Each day she would choose something from the bottomless chest of her memory. Almost without gestures she acted out *The Living Room* [by Graham Greene] and *Gigi* [by Colette and Anita Loos] never skipping a scene. She told us an infinite amount of stories and tales, some that she had read dozens of years before. Italian and French films unreeled before our eyes in their original form to the point that I still don't know if I ever saw them or not on the screen.[46]

As the days went by, the interest and concern they felt toward one another grew. When word got around that other prisoners had been tortured with the infamous *picana* or electric needle, there was a special feeling of unity, of solidarity, born of a mixture of sympathy and apprehension that they all shared. For Victoria, the experience of sisterhood on this pure level was unforgettable: "I have said many times already that I never knew before that kind of interior well-being, something like happiness, something that practically blotted out the exterior uneasiness that was taking place on another level."[47] It was a feeling she later expressed in the dialogue of a play called *Entre cuatro paredes* (Between Four Walls), that has never been published.

By her own testimony, the twenty-six days she spent in Buen Pastor were days she never regretted. In fact, she has called them a blessing in disguise, a rare opportunity to know herself in the face of adversity and to feel the manifest power of human understanding and cooperation. Some of Victoria's friends have suggested it was an experience that changed her life; it made her more humble, according to some, more politically aware, according to others. Jorge Luis Borges has said that it made her less domineering; before that, he confessed, she was the only person he knew who could make him feel like a child in her presence.[48] What seems most evident from all that Victoria has said and written about Buen Pastor is that it was a profoundly spiritual experience, perhaps even a religious one. In the prison's austere confines, Victoria felt closer than she ever had before to the reality of the evangelical truth she had been taught in her childhood: faith, hope, and charity—especially to the charity of human beings in mutual need reaching out to comfort one another. She felt as though she had been given the rare opportunity to live directly the philosophy of truth that her most revered teacher, Mahatma Gandhi, had preached. She also believed that she had been privileged to learn first-hand the strength of the anonymous camaraderie that another one of her heroes, T.E. Lawrence, had sought as an antidote to the sin of pride. After leaving prison, Victoria wrote a short essay explaining how she had spent many hours thinking of Gandhi's words: "I must reduce myself to zero. There is no salvation for one who does not place himself last among his fellowmen." And also these words: "I know what an inadequate follower I am of myself for I cannot live up to the convictions I stand for."[49] What Gandhi felt was similar, in another context, to the urge toward monastic asceticism that drove Lawrence of Arabia to join the Arab revolt in the desert, about which Victoria wrote in 1947 in her study on Lawrence, *338171 T. E.*; one must deny the flesh and cultivate the spirit. Buen Pastor had allowed her, in a brief but significant way, to participate in the same kind of spiritual cleansing that she admired so intensely in those heroic men.

Victoria's urge toward asceticism—awakened by her admiration for Gandhi but fueled by a deeper need to shed the burdens of privilege and seek wholeness of spirit—was an urge she had expressed earlier in life. Interestingly, in *Reise durch die Zeit*, Keyserling recalled from their meeting in 1929 that Victoria suffered under the image of the *femme fatale* because she hoped to end her life as a saint.[50] Aside from the personal disillusionment that led him to see her as the embodiment of the "medieval split between spirit and flesh," Keyserling may well have been thinking of that dichotomy when he wrote those words. Another revealing statement is found in a letter Victoria sent to María de Maeztu early in 1944: "You know that I am a person of few friends, even of few relationships, and that if it were up to me, I would live an even more isolated life; Gerald Heard's idea of putting a kind of convent at the disposition of laymen seems wonderful to me." It was a thought she repeated in another letter, apparently stimulated by news from Aldous Huxley about his and his wife's experiences at Heard's "monastery," as Huxley called it, in California.[51] Like Huxley, who was disenchanted with the course of human events and convinced that individual experience must be the test of everything, Victoria found the idea of a spiritual retreat extremely appealing.

To those whose image of Victoria is based on visions of her wealth, her social background, and her peripatetic life as a woman of the world, the notion that she may be an ascetic at heart is improbable. One cannot deny her great *joie de vivre*, nor can one overlook certain weaknesses in her temperament and certain predilections that are far from being saintly or even self-denying. And yet, reading her essays carefully and being in her private company, one comes to understand that she is a deeply religious person with a strong puritanical inclination. Despite having been surrounded by material advantages all her life, she has never been enslaved by possessions. From time to time, she will live like a hermit with her books, seeing no one, going nowhere. Admittedly, her wealth has allowed her this luxury, the means of transporting herself from a material to a spiritual environment where wealth is measured in other terms. However, when she is most reclusive, she is generally bent on sharing the wealth that books have given her, for it is then that she feels the spiritual energy to write.

Gabriela Mistral and Freedom

When news of Victoria's imprisonment reached intellectual communities outside Argentina, friends and admirers were quick to express outrage and alarm. Individually and in groups, they decried Perón's arbitrary jailing of a nonpolitical adversary whose contributions to Argentine culture had been so exceptional. In New York, Louise Crane and Victoria Kent, who had known Victoria for years, formed a Committee for the Liberation of Argentine Intellectuals to appeal to influential politicians on behalf of Victoria and other imprisoned writers and artists. By organizing pressure on Perón, they hoped to force a quick release. The Committee's members included Waldo Frank, Aldous Huxley, Katherine Anne Porter, Marianne Moore, Diana and Lionel Trilling, Blanche Knopf, Anita Loos, Norman Cousins, and many other prominent literary figures, most of whom knew Victoria personally. *The New York Times* reported the activities of anti-Perón protest groups all over the world and published an editorial condemning his "reign of terror" and the jailing of Victoria Ocampo, who was described as an "example of the best type of independent Argentine intellectual." A long letter from Waldo Frank published by the *Times* pointed out that the arrests were the culmination of years of deterioration in Argentina under a dictator's rule:

> Perón's war on democracy in Argentina is an old story. Years ago he began to strip the universities of professors, however nonpolitical, who refused to do him homage. He corrupted the labor unions, replacing their leaders with stooges. His assault on the free press was dramatized by his destruction of *La Prensa*. Despite all this, or because of it, his power grows weaker; inflation mounts; production shrinks (Argentina, one of the great producers of wheat for the world market, has recently had to import wheat) and, of late, bombs have gone off in public places with the periodicity of salutes.
>
> Now he struggles to stem the tide by the arrest of more than two

hundred men and women who constitute a virtual Who's Who of Argentine culture. The work of most is nonpolitical, although they have all expressed their love of liberty and hate of totalitarian regimes, with emphasis on Russia. Here are samples of the two hundred:

Victoria Ocampo, who through her magazine, *Sur*, books and lectures, has perhaps done more than any other single person to interpret for her own people the arts, letters and music of Europe and both Americas. . . .[52]

And he went on to list the names and contributions of other prisoners like Francisco Romero ("one of the outstanding philosophers of our day"), Carlos Alberto Erro ("social philosopher, whose *Medida del criollismo* is a classic interpretation of the Hispano-American mind"), Susana Larguía ("Argentine representative of international agencies for social welfare"), Adolfo Lanus ("jurist and nonpartisan champion of civil rights"), and Roberto Giusti ("veteran literary critic, editor"). He added the name of Jorge Luis Borges; but in fact it was not Borges himself, but his mother doña Leonor, who had been kept under house arrest, and his sister Norah, an artist and wife of Guillermo de Torre, who had been imprisoned.

One of the most concerned and dedicated organizers of worldwide protest was Victoria's old and dear friend, a Chilean author then residing in New York, Gabriela Mistral. Born Lucila Godoy Alcayaga in 1889 (of Basque and Indian descent), she was brought up in rural Chile. From 1904 to 1922, she was a teacher. Then, after winning a poetry prize, she devoted herself more and more to writing, using the pseudonym Gabriela Mistral, and eventually served as a diplomatic representative of her country in many parts of the Americas and Europe. One of her books of poetry, *Tala*, was published by *Sur* in 1938; all of its earnings were pledged by *Sur* and Mistral to aid the refugee children of the Spanish Civil War. In 1945, Mistral became the first Latin American author to be honored with a Nobel Prize for Literature.

She had met Victoria in Madrid in 1930, but they had become truly close friends during her stay with Victoria in Mar del Plata in 1937. In the peaceful setting of Villa Victoria's carefully tended gardens and majestic shade trees—a peace that was joyfully punctuated by the laughter of the housekeeper's young children and their companions — Victoria discovered that she and Mistral had much more in common than the same birthday, April 7. On the surface, Victoria's cosmopolitan refinement contrasted sharply with her Chilean friend's rural simplicity. In the days they spent together, however, they were drawn to one another by their common Basque heritage, their shared admiration of Tagore's poetry, their love of nature, children, the sea, letter-writing, and the enormous concern they both felt for the future of South America as a free continent. At heart, they were both humanists and crusaders for justice, though

Mistral preferred to focus on the problems of racism and the Indians of her native Valley of Elqui, whereas Victoria was more preoccupied with the cause of women's rights.

Mistral was sympathetic to feminism in principle, but she was not, intellectually, a feminist. According to Victoria, "Gabriela Mistral, my well-beloved and faithful friend, was not a feminist until I converted her."[53] One doesn't have to take Victoria's word for it. In 1923, while Mistral was in Mexico as an educational consultant to the Mexican government, she published a book entitled *Lecturas para mujeres* (Readings for Women) intended to be used in a girls' school named in her honor. Basically an anthology of short readings on different subjects which Mistral felt would be appropriate for girls rather than boys, the book opens with a foreword in which she states her belief that a woman's place is in the home: "Whether she is a professional, a worker, a farmer, or simply a lady, her only reason for being on this earth is motherhood, both materially and spiritually, or just spiritually for those of us who don't have children."[54] Today's woman who is involved in work outside the home, she says, may be losing sight of this essential truth which women in earlier ages understood. Sounding like the Fascist leaders she so vehemently hated later on, Mistral adds, "For me, the feminine form of patriotism is perfect motherhood. The most patriotic education one can give to a woman is, therefore, that which accentuates the meaning of the family."[55] The first selection in her anthology is a passage from John Ruskin's "Sesame and Lilies" which describes the different roles of men and women in much the same pattern as one finds in the works of Ortega, Tagore, and Keyserling.

It wouldn't be hard to imagine how Victoria might have taken her friend to task for what her book contained. But it's much more likely that their conversations which touched on feminism had to do primarily with the activities of the Argentine Women's Union with which Victoria was very much involved at the time. As she shared with Mistral her stories of how she and her colleagues had been insulted and abused for their militant stand in favor of women's rights, she no doubt helped raise her friend's feminist consciousness, convincing her of the limitations of her earlier views.

Their letters show enormous affection and mutual respect. They evidently shared a feeling of sisterhood, with Mistral taking the part of the older, more protective sibling. Only a year older than Victoria, she nonetheless treated her with a kind of motherly concern. Her letters, generally undated and often addressed to "dear Votoya," as the children at Villa Victoria used to call Victoria, were full of encouragement and admonitions. In one, she wrote: "No woman and few men in America today write as you do. Don't let your life become infected by what they call *social concerns*—as if social concerns were limited to ladies' tea parties. Keep your precious soul for writing and for the delight of those of us who belong to you. Defend yourself with valiant strength." In another, from Brazil, she said to Victoria: "I can't tell you how glad I am that you are there, like the mother of our freedom; but I need to know that besides that, you are writing vigorous things like that essay on Emily Brontë [a lengthy essay written in 1938] which is the only piece of yours in which you uncover some of those enormous roots, so hidden and deeply buried by foreignism." From Chile, Mistral commented on "the legend of Victoria Ocampo" there which, she said, was "black only on the fringes," adding: "Here there is a strong interest, among young and old, men and women, in Victoria Ocampo." Apparently in response to this, Mistral decided to write an essay on Victoria in the early 1940s (no trace of it has been found), and of this she said:

> I stretched out considerably the aspect of the influence of foreign cultures on you, and successfully, I think; but now I'm thinking of something else. Those foreign cultures are one of your keys, *but they aren't everything, and I know it*. I keep thinking that Racine and Co. had to have removed you *fabulously* from the expression that your body and temperament dictated to you, that you surrendered to them the strongest juices of your being, that, like the Jews, they [Racine and Co.] underwent a kind of holocaust of blood, that you made a kind of vow to put them behind you when you wrote your language, your own personal one, which is better than mine *in its freshness and warmth*, and in its plasticity and *movement*.
>
> By the same token, your literary exigence, like that of a hemp-grinding machine, puts me too much on guard about what I say about you, about what I write. Put roughly: you scare me. You take away the agility and heartiness with which I write about others. You pin me down and make me correct too much. And with that, you dry me out and give me a curious uneasiness born out of discontent with what I've said. But here are the two notebooks, for the time being. I've *not* seen you in vain; I've seen enough to tell at least a side and a half of you. Be patient with me.

More than once, Mistral expressed the concern that Victoria's acquired Europeanism might overshadow her authentic criollismo. "Now listen to me," she wrote in another letter, scrawled as usual in pencil, "what pleases me most in you and what brought me close to you, whether you know it or not, is your miraculous feeling for the earth which I have not seen in anyone else of our race. Not because you talk about this plant or that animal, but because one sees in your face and your attitude that you are feeling the depth of the thing itself." The intensely telluric side of Victoria—the quality of earthbound sensibility in her that Ortega, Tagore, and Keyserling had also noted—found a sympathetic resonance in Mistral, herself a creature attuned to nature's rhythms. She perceived in Victoria what the men who admired her identified as archetypically female; for Mistral, however, it was not an attribute of gender, but rather an intuitive responsiveness, a poetry of the soul. This was what Mistral wanted Victoria to impart more to her writing.

On the morning of their mutual birthday in 1937, Gabriela Mistral wrote this poem and sent it to Victoria in a nearby room:

Message to Victoria Ocampo in Argentina

Victoria, the shore you brought me to
has sweet grasses and a brackish wind,
the Atlantic ocean like a colt's mane and
cattle like the Atlantic ocean.
And your house, Victoria, has lavender,
and — all veridical — iron and wood,
conversation, loyalty, and walls.

Bricklayer, plumber, glazier —
all measured without instruments, measured by looking at you,
measured, measured . .
And the house, which is your scabbard,
is half mother and half daughter to you . . .
Diligently they made it for you of peacefulness and dream;
Doors they gave for your fancy;
A threshold they spread at your feet. . .

I don't know if fruit is better than bread
or the wine better than the milk at your table.
You decided to be "the terrestial one,"
and the Earth serves you willingly,
with corn ears and oven, vine stocks and press.

The children run through the house and garden;
They cleave your eyes coming and going;
Their seven names fill your mouth,
the seven graces make you laugh
and you become entangled with them in the abundant grasses
or you fall down with them going over sandbanks.

Thank you for the sleep your house gave me,
in the fleece of merino wool;
for every blossom of your *ceibo*[56] tree,
for the morning when I heard the wild doves;
for your idea of a bird bath,

for so much green in my wounded eyes,
and the mouthful of salt on my breath:
for your patience with poets
of the forty cardinal points. . .

I love you because you're Basque
and because you're stubborn and ambitious,
aiming at what's coming and hasn't yet arrived;
and because you're like nature's bounty:
like the corn of plentiful America
— plentiful hand, plentiful mouth—
like the winds of the Pampa
and like the soul of almighty God.

I bid you farewell, and here I leave you
as I found you, sitting on the dunes.
To you I entrust the lands of America,
to you, so like a ceibo, so knife-erect,
so Andean, so fluvial
so like a blinding waterfall
and like Pampa lightning!

Keep your Argentina free—
the wind, the sky, the granaries;
free education, free prayer,
free song and free weeping,
the *pericón*[57] and the *milonga*[58]
free, the lariat and the gallop,
the pain and the happiness, free!

For the ancient Law of the Earth;
for what is, for what has been,
for your blood and for mine,
for Martín Fierro and San Martín
and for Our Lord Jesus Christ![59]

Mistral's charge to Victoria to watch over Argentina's freedom was more
prophetic than she could have imagined. As her diplomatic assignments
took Mistral far from Argentina and her native Chile, the freedom she had
entrusted to Victoria became more and more threatened.

When Mistral got word in 1953 that "Votoya" was a victim of Perón's
dictatorship, she was incensed by the injustice that had been committed
and greatly concerned for her friend's well-being. Although it had never
been her habit, she decided to use her influence as a Nobel laureate and
immediately wired fellow writers in many countries, urging them to rally

to Victoria's defense. Among others, she contacted Ernest Hemingway in Cuba, Davis Carver at the London P.E.N. Club, Alfonso Reyes in Mexico, Roger Caillois at UNESCO in Paris, and Radomiro Tomic in Chile. She also wrote various articles alerting readers in Europe and the Americas to the significance of what had taken place. These were her words to South American women reminding them of their debt to Victoria:

> What is Victoria Ocampo, the Argentine woman accustomed to defending culture, freedom, and justice in her country and ours, doing in jail at this moment? What fate have the judges decreed for her now? And what will Argentine women and the women of the twenty-one countries of her language and race do for her?
>
> What indeed will our women do on an occasion of such fearsome responsibility? We all, without recognizing it clearly, owe a great deal to that prisoner who is perhaps still looking at her prison number. Until now, we women have had few opportunities to express conclusive and unwavering solidarity. Victoria Ocampo has worked openly as well as tacitly on our behalf. She belongs to us regardless of national borders; she has benefited us with the creation of a unique review and a publishing house dedicated to the task of expelling the mediocre, lacrymose, and flimsy kind of reading that we have had in almost all areas of Spanish-American language. Everyone knows that publishing is not a lucrative field in our America and that this noble and lucid Argentine woman was willing to lose a great deal of money in order to expurgate slowly but surely the low quality of our reading material. In this difficult undertaking, half literary, half didactic, she finally achieved success.[60]

As a culminating effort, calculated as a means of furnishing Perón with an excuse for liberating Victoria quickly, Mistral sent the dictator a cable on May 27, 1953. It read: "Am profoundly shocked by news of Victoria Ocampo's imprisonment. I beg your excellency to liberate her in consideration of her great contributions to Argentina, Latin America, and Europe. Will be grateful for your intervention. Gabriela Mistral." A copy was sent to the Associated Press in New York for worldwide publication.

It was late in the evening on June 2, 1953 when a nun came into the room where Victoria was already in bed and announced that she was free to leave Buen Pastor "by order of the executive power." The following day, the official press report of her release from prison stated that Gabriela Mistral's plea on her behalf had been the deciding factor. By saying this, Perón was able to save face with the working classes who condemned Victoria as an oligarch but who were sympathetic toward Mistral as one of their own. Those more familiar with the machinery of world politics — including Victoria and Mistral herself — were convinced that the real pressure to which Perón succumbed came through diplomatic channels: Jawaharlal Nehru, Prime Minister of India, had been the one to force Perón's decision. But Gabriela Mistral was the foil Perón needed, and to obtain her friend's release, she was willing to be pragmatic.

Victoria understood, was grateful, but she did not approve. She never said as much to Mistral, but she was less than pleased with the fact that her friend had pleaded with the dictator at all, much less that she had pleaded for his "intervention," as if he himself were not directly responsible for her imprisonment in the first place. It was a matter of moral principle, as she saw it. No more and no less.

A Postscript

For two years after her release, the government continued to harass Victoria by denying her a certificate of good conduct to travel outside Argentina. Other writers, like Borges, did receive one, but she did not. Finally, when Perón was overthrown in 1955, she was free to leave the country, but then there were other problems she had to face. The devaluation of the peso during Perón's regime had so depressed the economy that the future of *Sur*, never financially secure, seemed in jeopardy. From New York, Gabriela Mistral had been coaxing Victoria to come north for a visit. On January 4, 1956 Victoria wrote and explained:

> I'd like nothing so much as to go to New York and for several reasons. To see you, my friends, and that city I ADORE. To eat griddle cakes and doughnuts and cinnamon toast. To go to three movies a day when I want to. To go to the theater (which must now be beyond my means), and to walk along the streets and hear repeated a hundred times a day, "watch your step" or "you're welcome." And many other things like that which must seem insignificant.
>
> The peso isn't worth anything. It's useless to write you that one dollar right now brings 35 pesos, because tomorrow it may change. But that matters little (of course it *does* to those of us who want to travel) in comparison to the supreme happiness of living again, spiritually, like free citizens. It's true that those who had spiritual freedom never lost it, but they paid dearly to keep it [. . .].
>
> *Sur*'s 25th anniversary was just celebrated with a net loss of 85,000 pesos. But of course no one learns about this type of sacrifice, and it really doesn't matter to anyone. Everyone imagines that I have money to give away, which today is absolutely and totally false. Peronism nearly ruined me, as it did with the majority of those who opposed it. Probably (if the situation doesn't improve) I will stop publishing *Sur* next year. I've decided to publish it this year as a last effort; having published it in difficult times during the dictatorship, I now don't have the same moral motives for continuing.

As you know (or maybe you don't) a list of people and institutions was found in the Central Bank of those condemned to "economic death." Naturally, *Sur* was on the list [. . .].

Friday, I'm going to talk on television about my jail experience and about the changes that I believe should be made in the women's prison. All these things concern me and keep me busy, as you can imagine.

Despite the financial burden, she kept on publishing the review. Now and then, the publishing house was able to recoup some of the review's losses with best-selling works by Gide, Graham Greene, and Nabokov, among others. Too many things continued to concern Victoria to allow her to abandon *Sur*, her principal vehicle for communicating with the world. Then too, as she says, she was born stubborn—under the sign of Ares, with Capricorn in the ascendancy.

One of her main concerns, not resolved in 1936 or thereafter, was the status of women's rights in Argentina. Admittedly, some advances in political and civil rights for women had been made under Perón, but Victoria could not forget that everything had been contaminated by his and Evita's fanatical ideology. Some legislation, like the divorce law he instituted, had been rescinded by the new government which returned to a conservative, antifeminist position. One of the things that concerned Victoria most was the perpetuation of *patria potestad*, a legal principle dating back to Roman times that gives the husband rights over his children and household that the wife does not share.[61] So she turned to writing more frequently about the movement for women's liberation abroad, about abuses in women's rights in Argentina, and about her own experiences of growing up and living in a country that was ruled by patriarchal traditions.

In 1970, Victoria decided to devote an entire issue of *Sur* to women and the cause of feminism. As she explained in an introductory essay:

> For years I have wanted to devote an issue of *Sur* to women, their rights and responsibilities. Ever since the review first appeared, this idea has been on my mind. But it wasn't a "literary" theme and it didn't particularly interest the men who shared the review's chores with me. They were in the majority. Though I could have imposed the theme, I didn't do it, perhaps out of laziness. Each time this issue was spoken of seriously, some obstacle appeared, or it was left for "later on."[62]

When it was published in June 1971, it was the first such issue of a Latin American review devoted exclusively to feminism. For Victoria, it was an act of justice; it also gave her a feeling of personal liberation for having said what needed saying.

In *Sur*'s traditional ecumenical spirit, the issue contained articles by contributors from many parts of the world. Approximately a third of its pages reported the results of a poll taken by *Sur* among Argentine women to ascertain current attitudes concerning women's liberation. A final section published excerpts from important international documents calling for an end to sex discrimination. In its spirit and orientation, this special issue of *Sur* anticipated by four years the objectives of International Women's Year, sponsored by the United Nations in 1975. By combining a national and international approach to the problems of feminism, it not only provided a wide focus of information but also conveyed a message of solidarity. It was Victoria's way of reaching out to all women in the spirit of sisterhood.

Although there is still no unified and effective feminist movement in Argentina today, the subject of women's liberation is receiving more and more attention in the media and women are taking part in isolated consciousness-raising groups. More modern and industrialized than many other Latin American countries, Argentina has larger numbers of women employed outside the home who are thus exposed to more sophisticated, international trends. The major feminist event to take place recently in Argentina was a Women's Conference held in conjunction with the celebration of International Women's Year on August 25-26, 1975. Victoria, who is now considered one of the leaders of Argentine feminism —even by those who criticize her—was invited to attend as a guest of honor. Her first inclination, if her health permitted, was to accept and support the aims of the conference. Then she learned that many discussion topics on the proposed agenda were not directed to women's problems but to Marxist political themes. Deciding that she could not attend on principle, she wrote a letter to the organizers of the conference requesting that it be read aloud at the meeting. As it happened, the letter was not read because its message was considered too critical. [63] Later, however, it was published in *La Opinión* (September 10, 1975); it said in part:

> This whole list of [agenda] topics could pertain to a Congress for the International Year of Men and Politics. Frankly, I don't think that this road will lead us forward in the cause we defend. Before helping men to solve the problems that they created, women must try to solve their own problems and, united without boundaries, not leave that terrain for any motive or pressure. To boast about *progressive* legislation when *patria potestad* is still in existence is an absurdity. That one irrefutable fact of flagrant injustice is enough to prove fully our own backwardness.
>
> I have been and am a feminist. For fifty years I have repudiated a state of affairs that couldn't last. In spite of having a female "presidente" (symptomatically, the masculine form of the title has been kept under the

pretext of antiquated juridical procedure — antiquated indeed!), we continue to be what we always were: a country with a backward mentality in matters pertaining to women. But, like it or not, the days of this mentality are numbered.

I fervently wish good luck to young people now joining the struggle for justice; its spirit is falsified and politicized with lamentable ease. But I repeat that, before going to the aid of our beloved adversaries in their political or partisan ideals, we must solve our own problems. Of these problems, one can truly say: if women don't solve them, no one will.

Uncompromisingly direct as always, Victoria is no more willing to make a pact with politicians now than she was thirty years ago. Winds of dissension keep swirling around her, but she remains convinced that her course is the right one.

CHAPTER SIX

CHRONICLES OF AN ADVENTURER

In 1658 a young Mexican girl, a child prodigy just turning seven, pleaded with her mother to dress her as a boy and send her to study at the famous university in Mexico City. So intense was her desire to learn that when her mother denied her request, the child resolved to teach herself from the books in her grandfather's library. By the time she was thirteen, her intelligence and learning confounded the viceroyalty's ablest scholars. Four years later, she took religious vows and entered a convent. As she herself explained: "I became a nun because, even though I knew there were things (accessory, not essential things) about a nun's life that were repugnant to my disposition, all in all, considering I was totally opposed to getting married, it was the least unseemly and the most decent life I could choose in terms of the security and salvation I wanted."[1] A very rational statement describing a very deliberate decision. Her immediate objectives, she said, were "to live alone, not to have any obligatory occupation that might hinder my freedom to study nor the noise of a community that might disturb the peaceful silence of my books." But even inside convent walls, she was confronted with those who envied her knowledge and criticized her for writing verses on profane subjects. Toward the end of her brief life, this unhappy nun, Sor Juana Inés de la Cruz, renounced her secular studies and confessed to the bishop of Puebla that she regretted her "wretched inclination." Still, she added, "I bless God for directing me toward literature and not toward some other vice that I might not have been able to overcome; how well it can be seen that my poor studies have sailed against the current—or rather, have been shipwrecked."

Posterity has proclaimed otherwise. Sor Juana was one of the finest poets of the seventeenth century, equaled in the Spanish language only by the peninsular poets Francisco de Quevedo and Luis de Góngora. She has also been hailed as Latin America's first feminist author, whose verses spoke eloquently but bluntly of the injustice with which men treated women.

Two hundred years later when Victoria Ocampo was born, the attitudes of Latin American society toward women who were intelligent and wanted to devote themselves to learning were much the same. By the time she reached adulthood, customs were changing, but a woman who had the "wretched inclination" to improve her mind still met with hostility and condescension. Like Sor Juana, Victoria felt misunderstood, but it never crossed her mind that to find intellectual freedom she would have to live behind convent walls like those of Las Catalinas on Viamonte Street. Later in life, when Victoria felt the urge to seek a secular form of monastic seclusion and practice a life of ascetic discipline, it was probably for reasons similar to those expressed by Sor Juana when she took her vows. Even then, however, Victoria knew that she would remain actively engaged in literature in the world at large. The time had passed, she believed, when women had to channel their aggressive intellectual energies into acceptably passive lives of frustration. As she said in an interview in 1941, it was high time that Latin American women stopped being the "Cinderellas of culture" and began claiming the right to develop their intelligence openly and freely.[2]

Literature as Testimony

Victoria stands out among Latin American women authors — and maybe among the women authors of our century—as not only a prolific writer but also an accomplished career woman. Outside Argentina she is principally known as the founder and director of *Sur*, not as an author. When she is called *"la señora cultura"* or "the intellectual ambassador of Argentina," her fame rests more on her contributions through the literary review than on her importance as a writer of more than ten volumes of essays and several longer biographical studies and dramas, not to mention dozens of translations and hundreds of published letters.

Victoria herself is partly responsible for her low profile as a writer on the Argentine literary horizon. Ever since *Sur* first appeared in 1931, she has been actively involved in the planning and preparation of many of its issues and has traveled almost yearly in search of new ideas and new contributions while keeping in touch with established authors and artists whose names appeared regularly in its pages. She has also been constantly on the look-out for manuscripts and books for her publishing house. *Sur* enterprises have been her primary vocation, her most important *public* professional commitment.

Writing has been a more private, personal aspect of her life. This is not to say that she doesn't write for publication; most of her essays have appeared first in Argentine newspapers like *La Nación* or *La Prensa*. However, her original reason for writing is to unburden herself, to free herself, as she says, of the ideas and emotions that hold her prisoner. By writing about them, she explains, she comes to understand herself better. Only then does writing become a form of communicating her preference to others: ". . . I believe that born writers, whatever their sex or means of expression, write above all for themselves, to free themselves from themselves, to arrive at a clarification of themselves, to communicate with themselves. The only one who can communicate with others is one who has communicated first with himself."[3] Essentially, it was the private act of self-communication and self-knowledge that led Victoria to the public commitment to found *Sur.* Just as literature had opened new worlds to her understanding, she hoped that the review would transcend national borders and unite the people of South America and other continents on the universal level of intellectual and spiritual brotherhood.

A writer, according to Victoria, an admirer of Jungian psychology, is predominantly either an introvert or an extrovert by nature. In either case, whether one chooses to use the third or the first person, one inevitably writes subjectively: "From the moment we begin to write, we are condemned to not being able to talk about anything but ourselves, about what we have seen with our eyes, felt with our sensitivity, understood with our intelligence."[4] The difference is that "the extrovert reaches himself only through the outside world, while the introvert only reaches the outside world through himself."[5] Individuals of different temperaments tend not to understand one another; thus the abundance of literary squabbling. Because she is an introvert, Victoria explains, she is only comfortable when writing in the first person. As a literary confrère, she points to Montaigne who said, "I am myself the substance of my book," warning his reader that his introspective essays were not meant to edify others, nor to attract attention to himself, but to be a private exercise in self-understanding. Montaigne acknowledged the thorny task he had set for himself and his own limited wisdom and powers of expression; he claimed only an honest intent and a love of truth. By writing about himself, his experiences and feelings about a variety of subjects, he believed he could reach an understanding of the human condition, for "every man carries in himself the complete pattern of human nature."[6]

This was the crux of the humanism of the Renassiance, the age of great individualists who mistrusted authoritarian conformism but who were nonetheless deeply committed to the study of man and ethical self-discipline. As Paul Oscar Kristeller has pointed out, "When the Renaissance humanists called their studies the 'humanities' or *studia humanitatis*, they expressed the claim that these studies contribute to the education of a desirable human being, and hence are of vital concern for man as man."[7]

In literary outlook and spirit, Victoria is a humanist, though in a nonclassical, contemporary sense. Like Montaigne she says: "To try to discover what has taken place in another human being or what has happened in general, I need to begin by explaining what has taken place inside myself. In these cases, personal explanations go beyond the purely personal. Our person is only a starting point, indispensable for arriving at an understanding of what is also true for others."[8] Both as a reader and an author, Victoria is unable to respond to abstract intellectualism or rhetorical displays in which contact with the human spirit is lost. She always prefers the expression of an authentic human drama: "What moves me most in man is his human condition, the condition that he communicates in everything he does, including his books, if he writes them. For me, man is, before all else, a human being, not a writer or a carpenter or a judge or a mechanic; he's that 'besides.' What matters is the human being in him and how this human being shines through in his actions, his work, his creation. *What moves me most in man is the human being who suffers, struggles, and seeks his expression. What interests me is the way in which this being is resolving his human problem, the way in which he is accepting, enduring, and carrying out his human destiny.*"[9] (Emphasis added.)

This confession is fundamental to Victoria's view of life and literature. Carlos Albert Erro has quoted her words as proof of her characteristically feminine — and more explicitly, maternal — approach to literature; he explains that Victoria feels motherly compassion, and that therefore the sentiment that moves her is more characteristic of women than of men.[10] While the quality of compassion—feminine or merely human—clearly figures into her sentiments, as expressed in the above statement, one can also identify a sense of *admiratio*, the wonderment and admiration characteristic of Renaissance humanists who contemplated the grandeur of man in his struggle for existence. It was a reaction inspired not only by the acts of great people, but also by the noble spirit of the common person who confronted his circumstance and lived in dynamic relationship to it.

Victoria may have been influenced—beyond her instinctive response to drama—to view life as a drama through her early readings of Nietzsche, but certainly the stronger influence came from Ortega y Gasset. In him, she recognized a moral philosophy that emphasized each man's responsibility to develop an authentic vocation within his unique historical context. Because this is a solitary undertaking and one in which each person must seek his own truth, Ortega described it as a dynamic dialogue, in other words, a drama: "Each person," he wrote, "exists shipwrecked in his own circumstance. In it, whether he likes it or not, he must swim to stay afloat."[11]

For Victoria staying afloat has necessarily involved writing. As she explains it, the act of writing is not only a form of self-articulation and self-knowledge, but also a means of self-preservation. It offers her relief from intellectual and spiritual anguish, a catharsis that purges and cleanses the mind and spirit and that, in the cleansing process, also enlightens and redeems:

> My imagination reacts in the face of facts, passions, and human cir-
> cumstances. But it almost immediately feels the need to free itself from
> those emotions and images through some sort of clarification. [. . .] When I
> open a book or take up a pen, it is to overcome them, to free myself of them;
> it is so that I may experience that miraculous transubstantiation, that
> redemption through the intelligence and the spirit, which is the only way I
> know of enduring my human condition.[12]

From one who has loved literature religiously, the metaphorical signifi-cance of this confession is not surprising. But it is important to point out that for Victoria, writing has never been a ritualistic act of literary crea-tion, a conscious effort to produce a work of art. Instead she describes it as a vital necessity, an unavoidable urge. When a thought or emotion seizes her, it broods inside her, rises suddenly to the surface, and explodes: "When I want to express myself, I am slow at first; I immediately feel lacking in means and experience, as if the weight of generations and generations of beings who only practiced silence lay upon me. All my thoughts and feelings have the form of a scream, the formless and terrible form of a scream or a lament."[13] Because of this, she has said, her writing has a sprawling quality, like the uncontainable landscape of her country. Indeed, the impatience and intensity of her way of writing resembles the rebellious and expansive nature of a new frontier. For these reasons, Victoria has been known to insist that she is not a true writer but simply "a human being in search of expression."[14]

More than any other literary genre, the unstudied, natural form of the essay — as conceived by Montaigne — suited Victoria's need for maximum expressive capability and minimum formal restraint. Accord-ing to Juan Marichal, the essay's primary appeal is its malleability, its lack of definition, and consequently the "chameleon-like" freedom it affords a writer who can adapt it to his changing moods and circumstances.[15] Because the essay is so flexible and can dramatize in its brevity and intensity the dynamic nature of life itself, it is a more adventurous literary experience both for the author and for the reader. One critic has described the essay as an "epic of the intellect"[16] while another has called it "an errantry in a quest for totality, in a quest for the Self."[17]

For Victoria, the essay was also the natural extension of her passion for writing letters. She has confessed that many of her published essays were really letters in disguise, written impetuously and without literary preoccupations. Like the seventeenth-century letter writer Mme. de Sévigné, or like her own contemporary Miguel de Unamuno, another great individualist and letter-writer, Victoria avoided rhetorical artifice, preferring to let her ideas and feelings flow naturally and subjectively. Marichal has identified this type of prose style in Unamuno and Santa Teresa de Avila as "organic," closely tied to the author's spontaneous rhythms of feeling and thought.[18] Interestingly enough, Victoria has confided that reading Unamuno when she was a young writer had a stifling effect upon her because she felt his thoughts were so identical to her own—and were expressed so much better than hers—that her own urge to write diminished in his presence. They were two plants of the same species, if not growing in the same soil.

Victoria's organic way of writing explains why she and her writing cannot be fully appreciated separately; one must read her essays to know her. To write with organic authenticity involves more than an act of testimony or truth-telling; it requires that the work be a faithful echo of the individual and that it record the melodies and tempos of the author's life. It must complement, not compensate for him or her. Authors who don't have this organic relationship with their work are no less valuable as creative artists; they are simply artists of a different species, a different "psychological type," in Jungian terms.

In choosing the name *Testimonios* for her volumes of essays (the only exception being the fourth volume), Victoria wanted to convey the sense of being called to bear witness to a particular sociohistorical period, to the drama of life as she lived it. She felt that what she had witnessed deserved to be recorded, especially because in her own lifetime, she had seen rapid change and an increased unawareness among the young of what older generations had lived through. She didn't expect, she said, that her testimonies would be read with interest until many years hence; then, no doubt, they would be a kind of historical curiosity. To be a witness to an age that was passing was an awesome responsibility and one that demanded high moral purpose, as Ortega, who saw himself in the same capacity, recognized: "I am a witness, a witness to the great marvel of the world and the beings in the world. And it's no contemptible mission, my friend. . . . If I were a prisoner of my own life, I wouldn't have noticed it.

But I have fulfilled my high mission of witness, and this reality, as amusing as it is fleeting, will forever be saved."[19]

"Am I a good or bad witness?" Victoria once asked, knowing that only posterity could provide the answer. "But," she added, "*that* is what must be determined. [. . .] Each author great or small, brilliant or mediocre, writes only one book throughout his life, even when it changes title and theme."[20] She knew that she, like other witnesses before her, would be held accountable by future generations.

In the literature of Latin America, writing as a form of testimony can be traced back to the era of the Conquest, when the explorers and colonizers of the New World—Renaissance men of the sword and the pen —chronicled their experiences in first-person narratives. Whether it was the proud Hernando Cortés writing for the Emperor Charles V, King of Spain, or the humble Bernal Díaz del Castillo recording in minute detail his adventures as one of Cortés's soldiers for the benefit of his children, the sixteenth-century chroniclers wrote as witnesses to the drama of discovery, aware of the uniqueness of their undertakings and fearful lest they be misrepresented. For them, it was an act of self-justification as well as self-affirmation.

Four centuries later, Victoria expressed a similar awareness. Her writing shows that she, too, felt like an explorer entering a new reality with the clear knowledge of another older reality that had dominated the thinking of all her contemporaries. Being an American and living in an American reality demanded more testimony of its inhabitants because in many ways it was still an unknown, uncharted terrain:

> If I hadn't been American, after all, I probably wouldn't have felt this need to explain, to explain us, to explain myself. In Europe when something happens, one might say that it is explained beforehand. [. . .] Here, on the contrary, each thing, each event, is suspicious and suspect of being something untraceable. We have to look at it from top to bottom to try to identify it, and at times, when we try to apply to it the explanations that analogous cases would receive in Europe, we find that they don't fit.[21]

Being American was another blessing in disguise—or once again, the fecundity of the insufficient, in Goethe's words. As Victoria put it succinctly, "the only advantage of not having a Versailles is that we never had a valid excuse for not visiting the pyramids."[22]

Besides bearing witness as a South American, however, Victoria knew that she could also bear witness to another drama of alienation: that of being a woman in a world mapped out and governed by men. Perhaps this too would be a blessing in disguise, a stimulus for self-explanation and self-discovery. Woman the Muse, no longer content with a vision of the world that was traditionally male-oriented, might become Woman the Artist and Creator in her own right. In this sense too, Victoria felt like an explorer entering new terrain, a terrain that required new tactics for survival, new vision. She was undoubtedly the first woman writer in Latin America to become aware of and respond to this dual challenge.

The open letter she wrote to Virginia Woolf at the head of her first volume of *Testimonios* declared her intention to set new precedents. From now on, she said, women had to express their views more openly. "Whenever the occasion presents itself (and if it doesn't I seek it out), I declare my solidarity with the female sex."[23] This was her earliest pledge as a writer in 1934, and it has continued to be one of the most powerful motives behind her testimony. If she is to be judged by posterity as a witness to her time, she wants to be held morally accountable not just as a writer, but as a woman writer.

Writing "Like a Woman"

Proof that Victoria's importance as a writer is being recognized in Latin America — albeit belatedly — is her recent election to the Argentine Academy of Letters. She is one of the first women in any Spanish-speaking country — the first in Argentina — to have been accorded this honor.

Facing a packed auditorium in Buenos Aires in June 1977, Victoria paused before the opening of the Academy's special ceremony in her honor to allow anxious photographers from Argentina and abroad to take her picture. It was not her nature to be patient with flashbulbs or with the insistent queries of reporters who hoped to coax a few words from her as she waited. Her reluctance was evident as she pulled her fur collar up around her face and refused to take off her ubiquitous white-framed, dark glasses. It was an unusual, even regal occasion, and the public inside and outside the auditorium was eager to catch a glimpse of the woman who had been a queen of letters long before the Academy officially recognized her. Some of those who saw her, still tall and erect at eighty-seven, approach the podium flanked by solicitous male colleagues were long-time admirers, people who had worked with her on *Sur*, friends or members of her large family. Others were more recent admirers, members of a younger generation who saw her as a pioneer of a golden age of Argentine letters, a venerable survivor of pre-Perón feminism, an aged but still legendary beauty. After acknowledging formal introductions and tributes from the men by her side, Victoria faced a battery of microphones and started to read her acceptance speech in a voice that retained the power to move, though it had lost the strength and resonance of former days. She spoke about her election, describing it as a symbolic event that honored all women who had fought for intellectual freedom and dignity. Then, suddenly, an overeager photographer exploded yet another flashbulb, and Victoria stopped speaking. Glaring at the offender with all her queenly indignation, she said, "When it was *your* turn to do *your* work, I respected you; now it's *my* turn, and I deserve the same consideration!" Those in the audience who knew her were not surprised at the rebuke.

The Argentine magazines and newspapers that carried her photo on their cover or in their pages in the months that followed hailed Victoria as a woman writer and compared her to such famous authors as Colette, Virginia Woolf, and Doris Lessing—women who had written about being a woman with artistry and grace. Being singled out as a woman writer rather than just as a writer of universal merit might be interpreted by some feminists as evidence that true equality for women is still a long way off. Yet Victoria herself would not object, provided the term "woman writer" is not used pejoratively, as it so often was in the past, to denote an inferior subspecies of writer. For her, there is affirmative significance in being a woman writer. She is proud to have belonged to a generation of women who were among the first to struggle openly for recognition as writers, for she can remember when it wasn't considered proper for a woman to publish books, when women were rarely treated as intellectual equals by men, and when they certainly didn't win literary awards or get elected to academies.

In addition, Victoria believes that if one is a woman who writes, one is not the same as a man who writes. A woman has a special perception and understanding of reality that, if she is faithful to herself, will be translated into her artistic expression. As she said to Virginia Woolf in 1934, her only ambition was to write "like a woman." Even if she were given the gift of writing like Dante, Goethe, Cervantes, or Dostoevsky, she would not accept it, because "a woman cannot unburden herself of her thoughts and feelings in a man's style, just as she cannot speak with a man's voice."[24] There is, she declared — without defining it any more explicitly than Woolf did—a woman's style of writing that corresponds to her condition as a woman, her perspective, her experiences, her traditions — whether desirable or not, whether induced by cultural conditioning or by biological distinction. In 1976 Victoria repeated this belief: "With regard to feminism, I am a feminist one hundred percent. This doesn't mean that I believe that men and women, in general, are talented in the same areas. Each one of the sexes has its modalities, although at times there are men with feminine talents and women with masculine intelligence. In all of us there is a percentage of both ingredients, just as according to Jung no one is completely extroverted or completely introverted."[25]

Many feminists would be quick to pounce on this statement, accusing Victoria of perpetuating sexual stereotypes by distinguishing between "masculine" and "feminine" talents. To be fair, it should be noted that only recently has there been a broad awareness of the prejudice implicit in the standard practice of identifying qualities as "masculine" and "feminine"; it was simply a cultural truism, a habit that had been taken for granted. Why then, today, do we continue to segregate qualities on the basis of gender, particularly when it is clear that the talents traditionally classified as "masculine" (rationality, objectivity, aggressiveness) and "feminine" (intuitiveness, subjectivity, submissiveness) reflect the one-sided views of a patriarchal society in which men controlled women? Hasn't the history of literary criticism shown us, as Mary Ellmann points out in *Thinking About Women*, that male critics have consistently referred to a "feminine" style of writing with deliberate disparagement, and that when they want to compliment a woman writer they praise her "masculine mind?"[26] Wouldn't it be more accurate to discuss works of literature without reference to the author's sex, only identifying distinguishing qualities for their human, not their "masculine" or "feminine" value?

Theoretically, this would seem to be the ideal. And yet, there are some grounds for retaining the old terminology—*divested of its pejorative implications*—to define a feminine style of writing that can be shown to correspond to a woman's point of view or a "female imagination," as Patricia Meyer Spacks has called it.[27] One could even identify a prose style characteristic of women writers, as Mary Hiatt has done in a recent computer-based study that disproves many of the stereotypical myths about a feminine style while it confirms that women do indeed write differently from men, for reasons that Hiatt suggests are the result of their role in society.[28] As that role changes—if it continues to evolve away from old stereotypes as a result of women's liberation — presumably the feminine style will also change. To be a feminist, one need not cease using the word "feminine."

Victoria herself has been sensitive to being labeled or categorized unjustly as a writer on the basis of her sex when she felt that it implied some form of male prejudice and was not a fair assessment of what she, as a woman writer, intended to express. Witness her first experience with Paul Groussac, who criticized her manuscript on Dante as too pedantic, or her encounter with Ortega over women's creative potential regarding an essay he wrote about Mme. de Noailles. Guillermo de Torre, *Sur*'s first secretary, once described Victoria's way of "preferring passionately" as "very feminine,"[29] and, in his *roman à clef*, *Adan Buenosayres*, Leopoldo Marechal made fun of her feminist intellectualism, calling her "la Ultra, Titania."[30] When yet another man criticized her "acquiescent admiration" for the things she wrote about, calling it a woman's noncritical approach, Victoria answered, "I write for myself, to explain things to myself, and only to get pleasure out of talking about a book that I like."[31] One understands why, in one of her early essays about the life and work of Emily Brontë, Victoria commented sympathetically on the Brontë sisters' decision to use pseudonyms when they wrote: ". . . the repulsive mixture of condescension and praise that is still offered to women writers was much more nauseating in the Victorian era. On the delicate stomach of its victims it must have had the effect of an emetic."[32]

Perhaps her most vehement rejection of sexual stereotyping — aside from her 1951 book in reply to Keyserling's memoirs — can be found in a series of letters to Ernesto Sábato, the Argentine novelist. They were occasioned by an article of Sábato's published by *Sur* in 1952 entitled "Sobre la metafísica del sexo" (On the Metaphysics of Sex), and were published that year in *Sur* along with his answers. (The very fact that Victoria's review printed the article, which she personally found distasteful, is revealing.)

Sábato's article pretended to discuss archetypal differences between sexes within the context of the Jungian psychoanalytic approach (which stipulates the presence of a contrasexual element in both the male and the female). In its generalities and clichés, however, it unmistakably conveys a stereotypical view of women as sexually passive, irrational, altruistic, and oriented toward the concrete and immanent, not the abstract and transcendent. One of the proofs Sábato offers to support his view is that women are not in charge of any big companies (not even in the perfume business, he says!) because they are not as egotistical and hungry for power as men. (It never occurs to him to analyze *why* this is so.) Predictably, he says that the feminist movement is "masculinism," the source of all domestic upheaval, and that what is needed is "a return to the feminine woman" and a "feminization of society" whereby men (not women) would work toward a synthesis of what has heretofore been an antithesis of values between the sexes.[33] Man's world, he evidently believes, is still mainly for men, not women, who should keep their domestic place.

In a low-keyed letter of reply, published in the next issue, Victoria says that there's a great deal she'd like to point out to Sábato, but she limits her objections to contesting his evaluation of Malraux's and T. E. Lawrence's attitudes toward women. After explaining that they were not sexists, Victoria concludes — as she did with Keyserling — saying "let's agree to differ."[34] Sábato's reply, printed in the following issue, is a near-hysterical letter of self-defense in which he accuses Victoria of reacting to his article with the sensitivity of a member of a persecuted minority; he compares her to a "furious priestess of Bacchus, ready to tear me apart alive and eat me raw." [35] Still restrained, but now meeting Sábato head-on, Victoria answers in yet another letter, more ironic and humorously sarcastic than the first, saying she is "neither furious nor a priestess of Bacchus in the slightest," nor at all anxious to eat him "cooked or raw—but stupefied, yes," at reading what he said about her. [36] Women quite naturally tend to react like an oppressed minority, she explains, because in fact they are. Moreover, women are in a better position than men (like Sábato) to talk about what women are like. Thus ends the polemic, though one senses that, were Victoria not the owner of the review and too diplomatic to risk an all-out public confrontation with a colleague who had contributed many worthwhile articles to *Sur*, she would have been more ruthless in her attack.

Perhaps she was also thinking of Virginia Woolf's words of caution against writing out of anger and resentment: "It is fatal for a woman to lay the least stress on any grievance; to plead even with justice any cause; in any way to speak consciously as a woman." [37] Anger distorts and creates distance. The ideal, said Woolf, was to write with an androgynous mind—like Shakespeare or Coleridge—but she herself never managed to do it. Perhaps a special kind of detachment from the world, as it is now, is required before a woman can write that way; perhaps it will be the happier lot of future generations of liberated women. Victoria couldn't help pointing out to Woolf in 1934 that even Dante wrote, in part, out of anger, but she added, ". . . I am as convinced as you that a woman cannot really write like a woman until she has abandoned that concern, until such time as her works, instead of being a disguised response to attacks that may or may not be disguised, tend solely to translate her thoughts, her feelings, her vision." [38] Thus, Victoria clarifies what had remained ambiguous in *A Room of One's Own*: a woman will write most naturally when she is no longer obliged to defend her intellectual freedom and equality. But she is, and always will be, a woman with her own perspective and her own truth to tell.

A Woman's Mission

Several essays Victoria wrote in the mid 1930s, shortly after meeting Virginia Woolf (but before Woolf published *Three Guineas* in 1938), show that they shared the same ideas regarding the civilizing influence that women could exert on society. Patriarchy had produced wars and dictatorships, competitiveness, and materialism, all of which had combined to debase the spirit of modern civilization. Had women not been tyrannized by men, perhaps moral values would be different. Society must seek a harmony of masculine and feminine influences or else face destruction.

In October 1935, a year after she had visited Mussolini in the Palazzo Venezia, Victoria wrote:

The current regressive tendency of some countries that boast of being very civilized, principally Italy and Germany, to reduce the woman to her most elementary expression, to the mere role of prolific female in perpetual gestation, stands out as a threat against culture. The same difference exists between an excellent brood mare and a conscientious mother as between Cro-Magnon man and Shakespeare. And who would dare to sustain that we must go backwards toward the Cro-Magnon age? What state would dare take this type of humanity as a model?

If one looks closely, there is no exaggeration in what I'm saying. He who wants soldiers wants many prolific females in perpetual gestation. Quantity not quality is what matters to him. It all balances out. On the one hand, a mass of men who go out to kill without being allowed to have a thought except that of blind obedience. On the other, a mass of women who give birth with no more conscience than beasts of burden, resigned before hand to seeing their children taken off to the slaughter house.

All this for whose benefit, for what? For the fatherland? For civilization? Come now! [. . .]

If a return to the male of paleolithic civilization is not desirable for man in his current state of evolution, it is not desirable for woman either, in spite of the arguments that supporters of retrograde theories might offer. And a regression for women places in danger, it seems to me, the immediate future of humanity.[39]

A morally responsible woman understands motherhood as a sacred duty which entails the power to influence future generations. "Women," Victoria went on to say in this same essay, "*this* is what matters. The man is in your hands, because he is given to you from your own body. Man is molded by you, and the only slow modification that humanity may undergo depends on you. . . ." This power, not the magical power ascribed to women as muses, is what counts and what women must never abdicate to men.

Naturally, for such power to be wielded responsibly, women must be educated on a par with men and must enjoy all the civil and political rights that have traditionally been denied them. The mission Victoria envisions for women presupposes equality and justice for her own sex.

If, like her, a woman is not a mother in the flesh, she can become one in spirit by creating a better world for women (and men) of future generations:

It is this feeling of maternity toward future feminine humanity that must sustain us today [August 1936]. We must lean on the conviction that the quality of that future humanity depends on our own quality, and that we are responsible for it. What each one of us accomplishes in her small life has immense importance, immense strength when the lives are added together. We mustn't forget this. None of our acts is insignificant, and our attitudes themselves will either add to or subtract from this total sum that we make up and that will tip the scale in one direction or another.[40]

For Victoria, therefore, writing was an act of solidarity with other women who were creating a better world in the same spirit, either as mothers or as caretakers of humanity in some other capacity.

In 1924 when she first read about Gandhi's resistance to British colonialism, Victoria became an admirer of *ahimsa*, an ancient Jain commandment that preached nonviolence to all living things. But ahimsa, as Gandhi taught, was not sufficient in itself; one must also believe in *satyagraha*, or the force of truth and love, a moral and spiritual attitude that gives ahimsa its true meaning. For if one loves truth, one realizes that a love of violence can only beget more violence. Instead of "body-force" the Mahatma called for "soul-force."[41] According to Victoria, all the powers of reason focused on developing scientific knowledge cannot equal the spiritual energy of Gandhi's philosophy, which she has called "the only unsurmountable barrier against barbarism."[42]

With this in mind, Victoria asked women to take a vow, similar to Gandhi's, to oppose the patriarchal tyranny that had denied them their rights in society. Like Gandhi, she conceived of it as an extrapolitical posture that could bolster a political cause by setting an example of moral and spiritual — but not physical — militancy. If Gandhi preached the efficacy of self-purification and self-discipline in the service of truth and love as a way of resisting British colonialism, why couldn't the women's movement adopt similar values—values that women instinctively understood better than men—in its struggle against injustice? Robbed not only of economic independence but also of intellectual freedom and self-respect, women knew from painful and direct experience the evils of colonialism and exploitation. When in 1937 the Spanish author José Bergamín suggested that Victoria was not sympathetic enough to the Communist cause in the Civil War (because she had received Gregorio Marañón, a self-exile, in Argentina), she answered Bergamín saying that she was morally opposed to all forms of slavery and oppression. Then she asked him:

Has it ever occurred to you to think that there has existed and still exists in the world another, more odious exploitation: that of women by men? I refer to the position of absolute inferiority in which women have been obliged to live for centuries and which is today beginning to change. [. . .] This problem, this horrible injustice has been and is, for me, a tremendous and

incandescent reality, just as that of the proletariat is for you. I have suffered
it in the flesh just as you are suffering the revolution in Spain.[43]

The movement for women's "liberation"—a term Victoria purposely
chose in her 1936 essay in support of the Argentine Women's Union—"is
certainly not being made in order that women may invade the territory of
men, but in order that men may finally stop invading the territory of
women, which is a very different matter."[44] Virginia Woolf would have
agreed. Woolf called for a similar crusade in 1929 when she wrote that a
woman must establish the independence of having five hundred dollars
and a room of her own; later, in *Three Guineas* she reminded women that
to "depend upon a profession is a less odious form of slavery than to
depend upon a father."[45] War, both authors agreed, was man's habit, not
woman's; her role as a nurturer of life is inimical to the pursuit of violence
(Victoria sees women members of terrorist groups today as tragic examples of political perversion). Yet nonviolence should not be confused with
submissiveness. Women must learn to be morally aggressive, to fight in
another sense for their rights. In Virginia Woolf's words, a woman must
have the courage to "kill" the Angel in the House—that docile, unselfish,
and conciliatory image of ideal womanhood that inhabits every household
and suffocates the individuality of mothers and daughters.[46] Once rid of
that false creature, a woman—a woman writer in particular—can speak
her truth and civilize an overly masculinized society. As Victoria put it in
1936: "We cannot create anything outside ourselves without first having
created it inside ourselves. I don't doubt that man will end up becoming
what he should, vis-à-vis woman. But what is still more urgent is that
woman become what she should be, vis-à-vis herself. One will be the
consequence of the other."[47]

Forty years later, after decades of war in Europe, the Orient, the
Middle East, not to mention the brutality of guerrilla warfare and terrorism in Argentina and throughout the world, Victoria continues to think
of Virginia Woolf's feminism and Gandhi's pacificism as a single moral
imperative. As she said recently: "For my part—and this is an aside (I
know I'm harping on the same old theme)—I believe that by educating
the child, that is, the man of tomorrow, woman can change the face of the
world. And since up to the present date, 1977, man has failed in his
attempts at peace, each minute becomes more urgent."[48]

The Symmetry of the Spirit

One day, anxious to share some of the beauty of Argentina with her friend
Paul Valéry, Victoria showed him a photograph taken in the area of Jujuy of
an enormous cactus covered with blossoms. "What's that?" asked Valéry,

and when Victoria explained, he remarked, "It must be very ugly." His reaction disconcerted her, to say the least, but it later occurred to her that it was a reply worthy of Monsieur Teste, Valéry's fictional character who hated "extraordinary things," things that didn't relate to his consciousness, his self. In fact, Victoria knew that Valéry himself, one of France's greatest poets, could be very unpoetic, even to the point of claiming once that poetry really mattered very little to him, and that if he had enough money, he wouldn't write at all.[49] Despite her admiration for him as a poet and a friend, Victoria often felt that his intellectual approach to life had a strangulating effect on her: "Yes, I was afraid, for Valéry and for us, afraid of a Valéry hypnotized by the Medusa of the intellect."[50] Next to him, she confessed, she felt "out of place," like an uncultivated South American cactus next to an elegant French rosebush. Her spontaneous but inarticulate enthusiasm seemed awkward and primitive in the presence of his eloquent but unsentimental intellectualism.

In 1939, the last time she was ever to be with him, they went together at Valéry's suggestion to look at the new stained glass windows in Notre Dame. Victoria remembered the occasion some years later:

> I entered the cathedral with him. It astonished me that I was not more overcome, for I was living out a fairy tale. Having dreamt all during my adolescence of approaching these princes that men of letters were for me, here I was, in the heart of Paris, of France, of Europe, of the world—I, from a distant land and having done so little to deserve it — here I was in the company of a king; and that king was serving as my guide. "This morning Paul Valéry is showing me Notre Dame," I said to the far-off adolescent who used to climb up to the gargoyles of the great towers without losing her breath. "Paul Valéry, Notre Dame, do you hear me?" But of course, to him, no word of this was spoken. He would have come out with some remark like the one about the cactus [. . .]. And I wasn't going to allow Paul Valéry to ruin Paul Valéry for me that morning.[51]

In that spiritual place, at that spiritual moment, cold intelligence was out of place; to preserve her reality, Victoria had to avoid his.

A year later, Valéry wrote to her of his desperation over the war. He confided that one "jour de malheur," as he called it, he felt "flashes of spiritual power, brief signals of energy," that gave him the strength he needed to face the future. After that, said Victoria, she no longer felt there was any distance between them: "In spite of the oceans and the climate, from that 'jour de malheur' on, I have been so close to Valéry that I have cried with him rather than cry for him. And this time he knew it."[52]

When he died in 1945, Victoria wrote an essay in tribute to his memory, testifying, as was her custom, to her understanding of his human drama. It was not meant to be an essay in literary criticism but rather a

portrait in prose, an evocation. Through the filter of her lucid memory—
but from an angle that is more spiritual than intellectual—she captures,
not Valéry the writer, but Valéry the human being with his weaknesses
and his strengths. Yet Valéry is not the only one in the picture; there is
Victoria—in the background, perhaps, but there nonetheless, like Veláz-
quez in his portrait of "Las Meninas"—emphasizing the subjectivity of
her perspective and reminding us that she too is a human being with a
drama to enact. The focus is on Valéry, but we cannot help feeling it is *her*
Valéry more than *the* Valéry who is being portrayed. In Victoria's *Testimonios*, the reader is inevitably drawn into the dynamics of a personal
experience, an adventure of the spirit.

She once considered calling her volumes of testimonies "kaleidoscope," but rejected the title on the grounds that it could apply to the
works of any author—Proust, Dante, Shakespeare: "In all of us, small
colored objects are eternally moving around: thoughts, dreams, emotions, memories. In all of us a composite play of mirrors and day-to-day
tumult *regroups* those small objects that don't change, giving us the
illusion of an infinite variety subject to laws of inexorable symmetry."[53]
The colors and shapes of one author's kaleidoscope may vary from those of
another; for each, however, the fundamental components remain the
same and are therefore revealing. In Victoria's ten volumes of testimonies
—each volume contains approximately twenty to thirty essays—the small
colored objects of her life that regroup again and again include memories
of her childhood, equal rights for women, the internationalism of artistic
excellence, nonviolence, her love of music, nature, Argentina, France.
The variety appears infinite, but an inexorable symmetry is nonetheless
there. Whatever she writes has an unmistakable spiritual configuration,
whether it is her early work, such as *De Francesca a Beatrice*, or her later
study of the life of Lawrence of Arabia, *338171 T. E.*

One of her works that few people have read because copies are
difficult to find is a fairy-tale play for children called *La laguna de los
nenúfares* (The Water-Lily Pond). She wrote it in the early 1920s at the
behest of Jacinto Benavente, a Spanish dramatist and Nobel laureate who
admired and encouraged her talents. Another Spanish playwright,
Jacinto Grau, who was visiting Argentina in 1923, read it and sent Victoria
a letter praising it as a "a delight, a fresh gust of optimism and poetry.
Sober, penetrating, uplifting. Like a musical emotion of Debussy, for
example, perfectly modern but with roots in the old themes of the
Orient."[54] Ortega later published it in Spain in 1926.

In eleven short scenes, the play expresses Victoria's philosophy of the
spirit in allegorical fashion. She bases her theme on the legend of the life
of Buddha: the indoctrination of a young innocent into the mysteries of

life. Copo de Nieve, or Snowflake, is a young orphan who has been adopted by a Magician living in a remote castle. The Magician wishes to protect him from the sad truths of life and so, for a few years, Snowflake lives on the grounds of the castle in blissful ignorance accompanied by his two friends, Optimio, the dog, and Atrabilis, the cat; the only discord appears to be in the conflicting temperaments of these two companions. One day some strangers convince Snowflake that he should see what lies beyond his father's kingdom. With the Magician's reluctant approval, the child sets out with Optimio and Atrabilis by his side. On the road he meets the truths of Old Age, Sickness, and Death, and in each case, Atrabilis, the articulate voice of unperturbed reason, assures him that he shouldn't be alarmed: they are merely Laws of Nature. Snowflake, however, cannot accept this explanation. Optimio, more compassionate and intuitive than Atrabilis, senses the boy's bewilderment and urges him to return home, but Snowflake learns of the existence of some Invisible Fairies who can answer his questions about life, and he risks his own life to find them one evening at the Water-Lily Pond. The boy learns, and later shares with his repentant father, that Love gives life its meaning and makes sadness bearable. "It's more beautiful than I imagined, Father," exclaims the child, "the Invisible Fairies live inside men."[55] This is the only natural law that has authentic meaning for Victoria. It is a law that the Atrabilises of the world find hard to accept.

Whether in her portrayal of the antagonistic Atrabilis and Optimio or in her analysis of the *Divina Commedia* from Francesca to Beatrice, Victoria has repeatedly emphasized the dualistic nature of the human condition. It is a concept fundamental to the Oriental philosophies she has admired as well as to the Christian experience; as St. Thomas pointed out, man is a combination of spirit and matter, faith and reason—a hybrid of divine creation that is neither angel nor beast. The struggle of conflicting forces inside each human being has fascinated Victoria as a writer because she has been so aware of fighting a battle within herself that has caused her more anguish than her testimonies reveal. It was the essential drama of her life: an urge to dominate and impose her will constantly at odds with another urge to achieve self-perfection and self-discipline. Her early letters to Delfina Bunge reveal that she was distraught even as an adolescent by this conflict.

What she recognized and tried to control inside herself enabled her to understand the drama of other lives better; it also led her to venture a diagnosis of the ills of her age which she saw as an analogous problem. Writing to Ortega in 1931, she said, "In the Middle Ages, it was the soul that wanted to separate itself from the body and 'live its life': the body is what they tried to deny. But today it is the body that is trying to shed the soul; the soul is what they want to deny."[56] And this she could not accept.

Unlike those who had dehumanized and demystified art in the wake of late nineteenth century materialism and positivism, Victoria believed that art must reflect the essential mystery of life, a mystery that the intellect alone cannot decipher. In the seventeenth century, Pascal wrote: "The eternal silence of these infinite spaces terrifies me."[57] Man's only salvation in the face of such a vast unknown, he said, was to have faith in God. Two centuries later, bothered by the same infinite spaces beyond man's comprehension, Baudelaire looked to nature for symbolic answers:

> Nature is a temple in which living pillars
> Emit at times some garbled words.
> Man passes through these forests of symbols
> That observe him with familiar glances.[58]

For Baudelaire, the imagination was the most scientific of man's faculties because it was the only one capable of comprehending the eternal unities or correspondences between man and nature, the visible and the invisible, the conscious and the unconscious; it was the only one capable of easing man's metaphysical anguish. Art conceived in this manner does not discover but rather rediscovers what has been lost from sight, the artist being a kind of seer or visionary who bridges the gap between two worlds by an act of imagination or intuition.

According to Victoria, there are material and spiritual writers: "The error of material writers—of those who in their eagerness to aim at the heart of life believe they have hit it and always miss the target—is to want to describe the visible world as if its very visibility didn't depend closely upon the invisible world (that is to say, the one that is imperceptible to our senses) around it."[59] A true artist, she says, must convey invisible presences as well as visible ones, the reality of the soul as well as that of the body. Dante, Tagore, Woolf, T. E. Lawrence, and Camus accomplished this. Valéry, she felt, was a plant of another species.

"At times," Victoria once wrote, "I was afraid for Valéry, a silly fear, perhaps, but one I would not have felt for Bergson, who seemed to me to represent the other side of contemporary thought—like twin spires on the same cathedral [of French genius]."[60] Henri Bergson, whose lectures at the Collège de France between 1900 and 1921 attracted throngs of students and admirers, was a professor of metaphysics and an eloquent spokesman for the spiritual and intuitive approach to literature that Victoria preferred. Influenced by Immanuel Kant and Émile Boutroux (who had written a book on Pascal in which he questioned scientific rationalism), Bergson propounded a theory of intuitive knowledge of ultimate reality, or knowledge by direct vision not by intellectual analysis.

Both the intelligence and the intuition must function together, said Bergson, but only the intuition, by expanding consciousness, can bring an understanding of the dynamic "becoming" of all life: the unifying principle beyond matter, or the *élan vital*, as he called it. For the intuition to express itself, he said, it must turn inward and identify organically with the *élan vital* of the object to be described; it must perform a kind of "spiritual auscultation." As he wrote in *Le Rire* (Laughter):

> What is the object of art? Could reality come into direct contact with sense and consciousness, could we enter into immediate communion with things and with ourselves, probably art would be useless, or rather we should all be artists, for then our soul would continually vibrate in perfect accord with nature. Our eyes, aided by memory, would carve out in space and fix in time the most inimitable pictures. Deep in our souls, we should hear the strains of our inner life's unbroken melody, a music that is ofttimes gay, but more frequently plaintive and always original. All this is around us and within us, and yet no whit of it do we perceive distinctly. Between nature and ourselves, between ourselves and our own consciousness a veil is interposed; a veil that is dense and opaque for the common herd,—this, almost transparent, for the artist and the poet. . . .[61]

Bergson also made the distinction between chronological and psychological time, or *la durée*. Psychological time is not measurable on a clock nor does it have any fixed direction, for it is "time in the mind" and thus subject to ceaseless fluctuation between present sensory impressions and past memory, and within the memory itself, between voluntary (or intellectual) and involuntary (or intuitive) memory, as Proust so artfully demonstrated in *A la Recherche du Temps Perdu*. In fact, Bergson's philosophy of intuitive knowledge and his theory of *la durée* corresponds to techniques used in stream-of-consciousness novels by Virginia Woolf, Dorothy Richardson, and James Joyce, although it is doubtful that they were directly influenced by him.[62] As these novelists understood—and as Bergson pointed out—traditional language is often insufficient to express the dynamic nature of the psychic kaleidoscope, the constant creative process of the personality. Linguistic devices such as the frequent use of parentheses, prepositional participles, dots, the imperfect tense, and coordinative conjunctions are often necessary if a writer wants to convey the waves of thought that a character experiences. The conventional arrangement of thoughts and feelings into sentences and paragraphs can be like a straitjacket, an unnatural restraint on the psychic flux that Bergson called "the continuous melody of our interior life."[63]

This psychic kaleidoscope, always moving, always grouping and regrouping thoughts and feelings, was what Victoria tried to convey in many of her testimonies. Music, she often thought, would have translated what she wanted to say much better than words. Her problems were compounded by the mixture of languages in her kaleidoscope of experiences; how could she observe rules of grammar and expression when she wanted to be an authentic and truthful witness? To follow the flow of her ideas and emotions, she would have to use unconventional, sometimes "improper" phrasing and punctuation; at times, she would have to switch to another language to give the precise notion of what she had in mind. Readers used to traditional essays that were more formal and discursive might be put off by her very personal, very unstructured (from without) style. Many of her essays, in fact, resemble prose poems.

For example, just as the phrase of Vinteuil's sonata awakened a surge of memories in Proust's Swann, the news of Virginia Woolf's death brought back to Victoria an abundance of recollections in which Woolf seemed, at times, to merge with her fictional character, Clarissa Dalloway. In her essay, "Virginia Woolf in my Memory," Victoria tried to translate into words the "interior melody" of her memories of the past along with her present feelings. The essay, with its introductory notes echoed at the end, its tripartite structure like three modulations of one composition, and its counterpoint of personal memories and evocations of Woolf's novels, has the lyrical qualities of music itself. The rhythm of her words flows in organic relationship to the rhythm of her thoughts and feelings.

Following the lead of Samuel Johnson and Virginia Woolf, Victoria insisted on calling herself a "common reader," that is, one who reads for the pure enjoyment of it, not as a literary critic. True, Woolf reviewed regularly for the *Times Literary Supplement* on a commission basis whereas Victoria only contributed literary articles to newspapers and magazines when she pleased, but for both of them, reading was a passion they couldn't do without. As Victoria once said in an interview with Ronald Christ:

> What I write is not exactly literary criticism; it is something that mixes life and reading—the two things at the same time: what I read and what I live; and, what I suppose the author lived. It's just the opposite of Borges, who thinks that literature is one thing and the personal life of the author another, and that life ought not to get into it. I can't separate them.[64]

In 1917 Victoria confided to Ortega that she could only respond to books that touched a chord inside her, books that taught her something about herself. To read that way, answered Ortega, citing Goethe as an authority, was the only true way, the rest was erudition. He assured her that literary criticism was also written by readers like herself who let their hearts alight on a page like a bee on a tulip. Besides, he continued, he knew that she was "an intrepid huntress of resonances and affinities — of *sinfronis-mos*."[65] Choosing a book by the Spanish author Azorín to illustrate the nature of sinfronismo, Ortega then pointed out how the author's sensitive temperament sought echoes of his own feelings in other eras and how, while ostensibly writing about them, he was actually writing about himself, thus doubling the intensity of his work. "It's strange but undeniable," wrote Ortega, "that our personality is fortified by finding itself in another. [. . .] We give repercussion to others as others do to us."[66] To be able to understand and feel these affinities, he said, one must be both an active participant and a spectator in life, attentive to other voices as well as to one's own variety of echoes. Ortega's explanation, similar to Bergson's definition of *la durée*, also reflects contemporary psychoanalytic theory: "When we reach maturity, our juvenile self has not expired yet: nothing dies in man until the man himself dies. The past self, the self we felt and thought alive yesterday, persists in a subterranean existence of the spirit. We only need to separate ourselves from the urgent present for all that past of ours to come up to the surface of the soul and begin to resound again."[67] The writer who can express sinfronismos not only fortifies himself by experiencing a resonance inside himself, but he also fortifies his reader who learns, through him, to see history as a vibrant, living continuum. Ortega didn't use Baudelaire's term *"correspondances"* or Bergson's "spiritual ausculation," but he evidently believed, as they did, in the power of intuitive knowledge, and he indicated that Victoria, like Azorín, had the temperament to express this knowledge in her writing.

"Imaginative understanding" is another way of describing this literary gift essential to a successful novelist, dramatist, or biographer. It was this that Victoria relied upon when writing *338171 T. E.*, a brief biography of Lawrence of Arabia, a man who had become a legend in his lifetime, a man who hated war and violence but who fought to secure freedom and justice for the colonized people he loved and then punished himself for his moral guilt. Victoria never knew T. E. Lawrence, but she was fascinated by his life and read every one of his works; she even undertook the considerable challenge of translating *The Mint* into Spanish for publication by *Sur*. When A. W. Lawrence, T. E.'s younger brother, read *338171 T. E.*, he was astonished by Victoria's uncanny understanding of the man so many others had misinterpreted. In an introduction to the 1963 English-language edition, he wrote:

> I started to read it with some reluctance, remembering how derivative and, at the best, superficial I had considered the studies of him written on the European continent, while the more ambitious of them had, in my judgment, wrongly interpreted the character they attempted to portray. This woman, from another end of the world, had presumably been confronted

by far greater barriers to understanding the man she never met, whose problems arose in physical and spiritual environments necessarily unfamiliar to her, and from circumstances which must seem no less strange than the events of remote centuries. I found that she had passed through the barriers as though they formed no obstacle, and that her book gave the most profound and the best-balanced of all portraits of my brother.[68]

Victoria's being a woman or being Argentine did not constitute barriers to her imaginative understanding of T. E. Lawrence because she recognized a spiritual symmetry in his life that touched a chord inside her. In their temperaments and passions they had more in common than A. W. Lawrence could have suspected.

As she strolled through Notre Dame that day with Valéry, it seemed to Victoria that she was living out an adolescent dream. It was an exhilarating experience, yet one touched by sadness because she was no longer the young girl who had climbed the towers of the cathedral in search of gargoyles, nor was Valéry the hero she had once thought all great writers to be. Still the moment was magical precisely because she experienced a flash of awareness—a coming together in her mind of what was, what is, and what might have been; Virginia Woolf would have called it a "moment of being."[69] Even though the moment wasn't what Victoria had once imagined it would be, the drama of it was no less vivid. In fact, she could still take a childlike delight in imagining a reality of her own while, at the same time, she could be conscious of it and savor it with adult awareness. It was "an extraordinary thing" of the sort that Valéry's Monsieur Teste might have disdained; unlike him, Victoria had never "outgrown" her childhood nor her belief in the miraculous substance of life itself. As she once wrote:

> . . . we spend our lives on the edge of miracles, denying their existence on account of their very routineness. Water is turned into wine every day before our eyes and we keep on needing to be told what happened once at the wedding in Cana in order to discover something unusual and unprecedented in it. In a word, we need a saint to point out a miracle before we notice that it exists, as we need a poet, a painter, and even a scientist to add the mystery of the stars to the flavor of the fruit. A child, master in the art of alchemy, lives in a world of transmutations that permit him to do without the good offices of those interpreters, so indispensable for adults.[70]

Why is it that some people have moments of intuitive awareness and others don't? Victoria experienced them and testified to them from time to time. Was she inclined to be more intuitive because she was a woman and therefore instinctively closer to a child's experience, closer also to the intimate emotions than a man? Surely many men have this capacity as well. Is it simply a question of temperament? Does environment play an important part? Victoria herself has suggested this might be so: "The most gifted people I have known on this continent have in common an unusual and almost miraculous quickness of intuition and a no less unusual difficulty in articulating or expressing themselves with words suitable to their intuitions." [71]

The emphasis that Victoria has given to the intuitive and the spiritual in her writing reflects her personal search for wholeness, or what she has called her *"apetito de unidad"* (appetite for unity). Reading Dante as a young woman, she understood that a hunger for what was tangible, visible, and therefore perishable had to be reconciled with another hunger for the intangible and the invisible, the sustenance of the spirit. The Francesca in her realized that life could have not lasting meaning without Beatrice. For Victoria, the boundaries between one hunger and another have never been clearly defined because she was never able to renounce one for the other. One might well say of her what she once wrote about a friend: "You used to love so spiritually what is only matter and so materially what is only spirit! With you, one never knew where spirit began and matter ended. You yourself didn't know." [72]

A faithful portrait of Victoria Ocampo must take this indivisible duality into account. What she has accomplished in her life, in words and in deeds, has been an expression of her appetite for unity, her desire to bring alien worlds together. "I can assure you," she said in 1973 to the Academy of Arts and Letters in New York, "that this eagerness to seek out correspondences, hidden and necessary connections—this eagerness to make the world into which I was born in the flesh coincide with others in which I was reborn—has been my life's undertaking." [73] The bridges she has built—between individuals and between continents, between sexes and between cultures—will undoubtedly last longer than those her father built in the remote provinces of Argentina.

Villa Ocampo

Victoria and her mother, Ramona
Aguirre de Ocampo

iguel Ocampo, Victoria's father

Victoria at age two

*Five-year-old Victoria
with her grandfather,
Manuel Anselmo Ocampo,
at his estancia*

Victoria at about age seven

At about fifteen

At about seventeen

Drypoint etching of Victoria done by Helleu in Paris, 1909

Victoria at about twenty-two

Victoria in Scotland with her uncle, Diógenes Urquiza, 1909

On the steps of Villa Ocampo, ca. 1911: Victoria (reclining with shoes facing camera) and (l. to r.) Alejandro Leloir, Pancha Ocampo, Clara Ocampo, a cousin Saenz Valiente, Rosa Ocampo, and Silvina Ocampo (with arm around a pet goat)

In Rome, 1913

Victoria in Paris, 1913

On the streets of Buenos Aires, 1922

On the beach at Mar del Plata, 1926

Victoria with Rabindranath Tagore in San Isidro, 1924

Victoria with José Ortega y Gasset in Spain, ca. 1930

At the Galerie Pigalle, Paris 1930: the Countess Anna de Noailles, the Minister of Fine Arts, Rabindranath Tagore, Victoria, and Francis de Croisset

Victoria photographed by Man Ray, 1929

Victoria's house in Palermo Chico, ca. 1930

Sur *colleagues, 1931: (standing) Eduardo Bullrich, Jorge Luis Borges, Francisco Romero, Eduardo Mallea, Enrique Bullrich, Victoria Ocampo, Ramón Gómez de la Serna; (seated middle) Pedro Henríquez Ureña, Norah Borges, María Rosa Oliver, Nenina Padilla, Guillermo de Torre; (on Picasso tapestry on floor) Oliverio Girondo, Ernest Ansermet*

Waldo Frank, María Rosa Oliver, and Victoria on the steps of Villa Victoria, Mar del Plata, in 1934

With Igor Stravinsky and his son Soulima in Argentina, 1936

Victoria at about forty-five

Virginia Woolf in 1939 (Copyright Gisèle Freund)

Victoria in 1939 (Copyright Gisèle Freund)

Police record of Victoria's imprisonment

Gabriela Mistral accepting the Nobel Prize for Literature from King Gustav of Sweden in 1945 (Photo courtesy of Doris Dana)

At Villa Ocampo in 1957:
*Angélica Ocampo,
Igor Stravinsky,
Victoria Ocampo,
Vera Stravinsky, and
Robert Craft*

Victoria with André Malraux at Villa Ocampo in 1959

Sur *colleagues in 1961: (standing) Enrique Pezzoni, Eduardo González Lanuza, Silvina Ocampo, Alberto Girri, Adolfo Bioy Casares, Victoria Ocampo, Alicia Jurado, H. A. Murena; (seated) María Luisa Bastos, Guillermo de Torre, Carlos Alberto Erro, Jorge Luis Borges, Eduardo Mallea*

Victoria in her office at Sur, ca. 1970 (Photo by La Prensa)

Victoria Ocampo in 1977: member of the Argentine Academy of Letters
(Photo by Pájaro y Fuego)

PART II

A SELECTION OF ESSAYS
BY VICTORIA OCAMPO

TRANSLATED BY DORIS MEYER

SARMIENTO'S GIFT   *June 1960.*

Many years ago, on the corner of Florida and Viamonte, there stood a very large colonial house with iron grating on the windows, three patios, two cisterns and well-tended plants. Azaleas, camelias, and gardenias leaned against the walls warmed by the summer sun. A small, dark staircase led up to a flat sun-roof covered with pink tiles, but we, the children of the house, were only allowed up there in the company of an older person. What a disappointment! We always wanted to go up to the roof. From those heights you could see the sky all around, and each time it was a marvelous spectacle. From up there you could also get a unique view of the patios, but we weren't permitted to lean over and look because there wasn't any railing. As we never went up to the roof on rainy days, it seemed to us a place that enjoyed perennially good weather.

Attached to some big iron hoops on the sun-roof, like the ones that encircle barrels, were some grayish-colored plants with thick foliage. In summer they produced extremely fragrant and delicate white flowers. My great-aunts, Mercedes, Rosa, Pancha, Carmen, and Victoria, with whom we used to spend each day, would cut them abundantly. Those plants, insignificant-looking when they weren't in bloom, apparently had some special meaning because our great-aunts didn't like us to handle them.

When my great-grandfather's house was torn down — a house in which, along with the green plants, there lived three black servants, intimate friends of us youngsters: the cook Paul (from Martinique), Juan Allende (a faithful member of the family) and Francisca (whose trips to the pastry shop were great events: "What do you have there in that little package?"); when the old house was torn down, the plants — "flores del aire" or flowers of the air, as they're called — were transported in their hoops to the quinta in San Isidro where I'm still living. And then I learned the reason for so many precautions: they had been gifts from Sarmiento to my great-aunt Victoria ("Vitola" to me, since I couldn't pronounce the r in those days).

Years passed and one day, upon returning from a trip to Europe, I was surprised not to see the plants in their usual place. No one could tell me

197

what had happened to them. I don't know if someone took them away thinking they were unimportant, or if one of the workers in the garden threw them out in a general clean-up.

Much later, I found out some more details about those missing plants. After concluding a lecture in which I had spoken about a letter from Sarmiento to my father (when he was a young engineer directing the construction of a railroad bridge in San Luis province), a woman came up to me. She remembered that Sarmiento had been a close friend of Manuel Ocampo, my great-grandfather, and she said that she would send me a copy of a letter from the author of *Facundo*[1] to my great-aunt Victoria (who had been in charge of my education). Sarmiento, so I discovered, used to tell Victoria that she ought to grow flowers and show some affection and concern "at least for a plant" (what Sarmiento asked for a plant, *I* received: I was the plant cultivated by that woman). Victoria responded with jokes. Once she bought an artificial azalea and presented it to him as the fruit of her labor.

Sarmiento died in 1888 (my mother saw my father for the first time as he walked in the rain behind the funeral procession); twenty-two years later, my great-aunt died in Paris. When Sarmiento's documents and papers were being classified for the museum that bears his name, they found this missive on the back of a message he drafted for Congress when he was a minister in 1879:

> Miss Victoria (without combat),
> These flowers come to you without your wanting or deserving them, like your headaches. I searched gardens for flowers that could resign them-selves to being neglected and not die from lack of care. I send you these "from the air" that don't even need to be watched. They live on their own, out of the way. Then one day they appear covered with flowers that redeem their humble origin with a perfume Queen Victoria herself would envy. In Corrientes province there is a Victoria Regia[2] that will not accept the caress of any Victorias who are not queens. "The famous Argentine of the Havana cigars"* cannot get that for you.
> Domingo Faustino Sarmiento.

A long time ago, a little girl used to go down a dark staircase wither-ing with the heat of her tiny hand a white flower that she probably hadn't been allowed to pick by herself. They must have told her: "Don't touch that!" She didn't understand why. Now she does. But the plants are no longer at the quinta in San Isidro, and if they were, there would be no one to tell her not to touch them. Without suspecting it, Sarmiento gave her the gift of "flores del aire" in the summers of her childhood. Without

* There was a family joke about Sarmiento's Havana cigars. (V.O.)

suspecting where those flowers came from, she accepted them. She didn't know who Sarmiento was because he had left the world before she entered it.

How warm and strong the light was when the small door of the sun-roof was opened in those Buenos Aires summers! It was a good spot for the "flores del aire." And a good spot for hearing the bells of Las Catalinas. "Give me a flower," the childish voice would repeat on the pink-tiled sun-roof. They say he brought them from the provinces to the house with three patios, on the corner of Florida and Viamonte.

(From *Testimonios* VI, 24–26)

FANI   *1949.*

> "Sir, I have concerted my wife to let me go with
> your worship wherever you wish to take me."
>   "*Converted* you mean, Sancho," said Don Quijote,
> "not *concerted*."
>   "I've implored your worship once or twice, if I
> remember rightly," answered Sancho, "not to correct
> my words if you understand what I mean by them . . ."
>   Cervantes, *Don Quijote de la Mancha*

She was born in Carrea in the Spanish province of Oviedo. Her father,
who worked as a melter in the cannon factory in Trubia, was left a
widower. He barely had time to contend, all at once, with his job, the
household chores, and his two little children, Estefanía and Filomena.
"But he always wanted us to be very clean, and so that we wouldn't have
disheveled or dirty hair, he would cut it for us himself, just as if we were
boys, and he would wash our heads every morning before going off to the
factory." Estefanía used to explain this to me often, with a certain pride,
even when no one remembered any longer that her name was Estefanía,
since my Aunt Ana, who took her in as a *bonne à tout faire*[1] two years after
she arrived from Spain, would call her "Fani" for short. Estefanía is one of
those names that's difficult to shout repeatedly, and when Fani was in a
house it was inevitable that its occupants would need her continually.

Fani was just a girl then. She was scarcely off the boat when she went
to work in a hospital where she would help the nuns with their tasks. She
quit that job voluntarily, disappointing her uncles who were Scolapian
Brothers and about whom she would always talk with a mixture of admiration and distrust (her uncles were exceptions in a family of semiliterates).
They had gotten the job for her with the hope that she would join a
religious order, but Fani didn't feel comfortable in a place reigned by
monastic discipline and routine. And yet, few human beings can have
imposed upon themselves, as she did, such a rigidly puritan code of
behavior and devotion to duty—a self-imposed duty that almost always
went beyond her obligations.

No one had ever taught her to read. As the years went by she learned to spell out the newspapers aloud with stuttering difficulty. Newspapers appealed to her because she loved to keep up with the latest events and give her opinion about politics or the most recent crimes. Passionate in her opinions, her purely instinctive intelligence didn't lack craftiness. One might almost say she was crafty if that word didn't leave pejorative echoes. Innocently crafty, yes. She learned to sign her name but nothing more. Stubborn and strong (physically strong; she could stand any pain, even the opening of an abscess, without blinking), she harbored bad memories of the priests of her village in Spain to such an extent that the whole clergy inspired her with misgivings. "For me," she would say, "God is the *being of a person*." But she never got around to explaining this somewhat enigmatic, though seemingly philosophical definition to me.

I knew nothing of this in my childhood when I would see Fani go through Aunt Ana's house or garden with a bucket, a broom, or a sprinkling can. But the background of this Spanish woman was such that she was destined to live her life by my side and prove to me irrefutably that selflessness isn't a myth and that a maternal and filial affection can be born without blood ties or educational parity—that it is purely and simply one of the many miracles of the heart.

"Fani, bring me the quinces and the brasier," my aunt used to say. She was going to make quince jam, a complicated ceremony. Then I would see a girl with a round face, prominent cheekbones, a short nose, black, shiny eyes, and a tea-colored complexion appear. Her hair, also very black and abundant (that hair cut so often), was piled up in a neat bun. When she smiled she showed healthy white teeth. But generally she was too absorbed in the jelly ceremony to smile. Solid, like the peasant she was, neither tall nor short, Fani made it a point of honor never to get tired, however rigorous her job might be. I, in a pinafore and braids, would watch her prepare the brasier and bring the fruit, fascinated more by her gestures than by her person, not foreseeing that she would soon enter my daily life never to leave it again until her death.

In 1908 my parents decided to take a trip to Europe. They were concerned about finding a good nursemaid, a completely trustworthy woman for us girls. My Aunt Ana said: "Take Fani along." And so they did. Fani told me later that she had been afraid of me because our former nursemaid Inés, who was staying behind in Buenos Aires (to get married), no doubt jealous of seeing herself replaced, took great pains to predict to her all kinds of catastrophes: "You won't be able to please Miss Victoria. She doesn't like people of your kind. You won't last long in that house, so don't get any ideas." Fani stayed with me for forty-two years. Of course, to me that seemed a short time.

My mother didn't take long to discover her exceptional qualities. If anyone was sick, Fani was the one who watched over and attended to him. She cared like a nurse for all the sick in the family. If there was something valuable to guard, Fani was the one to give it to. And what could be more valuable to my parents than their children?

When I got married (I was the oldest child), it was decided that I would receive a special gift: my parents deprived themselves of Fani so that she could follow me. They entrusted me completely to her—as she herself told me on various occasions—and she took their bidding so to heart that throughout her life she continued to treat me as if my age and judgment hadn't changed. For her I never stopped being an adolescent. I never succeeded in getting her to think of me and treat me like an adult.

More than a maid or a housekeeper, she became the gray eminence of the house. She managed everything, and since she didn't like waste, she would find a way to hide money from me if, according to her criterion, I was spending extravagantly. She even decided what underwear I was to use on such-and-such a day, having established God-knows-what system of rotation that would prevent wastefulness. Without beating around the bush, she would express the sympathy or distrust that my friends inspired in her as well as her approval or disapproval of my conduct (what she knew of it). Everything that I was or did was sifted through her censorship. Naturally this unusual attitude provoked reactions in me that were proportionate to such extreme limitations. We used to fight frequently and violently. These arguments, which generally took place when I was dressing in the morning or undressing at night, were followed by periods of silence during which neither one of us would say a word to the other. Fani had adopted a system — she applied different systems to an infinite number of things — that consisted of commenting aloud about my behavior, but without naming me or addressing herself to me, as if she were talking to herself. And I'd be standing there. Of course, this system only worked for criticism. She would invariably begin with: "It seems unbelievable . . ." or "What a scandal. . . ," according to the gravity of the situation as she judged it. After two or three minutes at most, the accused (indirectly) would burst out: "Enough! This is the limit! Don't talk about what you don't know!" Fani would then take advantage of the occasion to show me that nothing escaped her notice. Her puritan Spanish rigidity, her candid eagerness to protect me from imaginary evils, made her as arbitrary and unjust as parents can be. She would transform my house, for a few moments, into that of Bernarda Alba. I abhorred this very Spanish mania and was too young to take it lightly: "Enough! Leave me in peace, woman!" I would shout exasperated, and would send her out of the room venting my rage with a slam of the door. What a penchant she has for butting into everything, I thought. She, unperturbed, would continue her monologue in the adjoining room. How many times must I have left my own house slamming three or four successive doors in her honor! To avenge myself, and knowing that it would be an unbearable punishment for her, I would make her feel, for the next few days, that I could do without her attentions. "Thanks, I don't need anything. I didn't call you. Don't wait up for me tonight. Don't come to my room if I don't call you tomorrow." When peace was spontaneously restored, she would resort to the kind of *chantage*[2] typical of mothers: "When I'm dead and gone . . ." I wouldn't let her finish the familiar phrase: "But you're not going to die, my good woman. I'm going to kill you any moment now." Secretly delighted to prove to what extremes she could provoke me, she would answer, "Bah! bah!"

In certain ways, Fani resembled Proust's Françoise and Vita Sackville-West's Genou (*All Passion Spent*); but she distinguished herself from them by her exceptional, unbridled, and very Spanish generosity which the two French women lacked. The nobility of her heart was as congenital as the blackness of her eyes.

Recently I questioned Vita about Genou. She answered: "Genou really existed, just as I painted her. One day I asked her permission to put her in one of my novels. She told me that she would be thrilled, and not to change her name." I don't think Fani would have minded my describing her either. I even believe she would have felt flattered and happy, not out of vanity — if she had any, she had transferred it to my person — but because, as she grew older, she only thought about pleasing and spoiling me, doubtless because she had given up trying to perfect me according to her canons.

For my part, I gave up trying to change her in the slightest. What was the use? Fani's manias or habits imposed themselves in a way parallel to my own; they were granted *droit de cité*.[3] I couldn't even influence her in matters of pronunciation. She continued to say things the way she liked [. . . .][4] If I corrected her, she would answer the way her compatriot Sancho Panza did: "I have never seen it written," and she would keep on pronouncing it as she pleased under the pretext that she was too old to learn new things.

She had a prodigious memory and recalled details that had been erased from my mind for some time: "It happened the day that the 'Israelists' came to lunch, when one of them bumped his head against the door and we had to put ice on it." At first I didn't understand. "What 'Israelists,' Fani?" "How could you have forgotten? Those 'Israelists' that used to come over when we lived on Avenue Malakoff." After racking my brain for a while, I figured out that the "Israelists" were the "surrealists," and the one with the bump was Eluard.

It amused her to look at books with engravings, and the ones by

Gustave Doré of the *Divina Commedia* intrigued her. "What awful adventures this married couple had!" "It's not a married couple, Fani." "Well then, what is it? You tell me." The explanation wasn't easy. "I like the story of *Quo Vadis* better," Fani said.

When Count Keyserling sat down at the piano one night to improvise, Fani began to worry: "That man is capable of breaking the piano. Be careful, señora." She called Jacques Maritain and his wife "the slaves of God," and she added, "but they're good people." The "but" was not inspired by God but by the possible relationship of Maritain with the clergy.

From conversations overheard in passing, here and there, Fani became informed about politics and the police calendar. While I ate breakfast, she, sitting beside my bed, would comment on the latest news. "Do you know what happened in the grocery on Viamonte Street? Do you know what they say such-and-such a Minister did?" I generally answered: "No." Then, with a surprised and reproving tone, she would ask: "But what do you read when you read the newspapers?" And she brought me up to date on what had happened.

— Who told you that? I asked.
— A person.
— So I gather, but who?
— I can't tell you.
— Did you hear it on the train?
— No.
— On the streetcar?
— Oh no.
— In the French Academy?
— If I were in the Academy, I wouldn't be here.
— Well, I'd like the academicians to have to deal with you.

She would often lament: "Oh, if I knew how to write, the things I would write! . . . (about one thing or another)." So she would tell me, because with me, she wouldn't watch what she said. For others, she modified the phrase: "The story I could write *with* the señora!" I imagine she feared that to express herself otherwise in front of other people could be interpreted as a lack of admiration for me, which she would never allow.

Our most serious fight had to do with a ring that was stolen from my sister Angélica. Fani suspected a certain person, and I forbade her to interrogate the person in question as she planned to do. There was no reason for her to get involved in the matter. I even warned her that to ignore my orders on this occasion would mean her leaving my house (a threat that I naturally didn't intend to carry out). Of course she didn't pay the slightest attention to me. She decided that her intervention was indispensable in the name of justice. So she spoke with the suspect. The latter came to see me bathed in tears — I don't know if they were the crocodile variety or not—to complain about the insult. As soon as I was alone again, I called Fani and, really annoyed, I reminded her of my ultimatum. We were in my country house; Fani packed her bags and left for . . . my house in Buenos Aires. She stayed there about two weeks in seclusion. Communications were cut. One morning she appeared again, but without giving the least indication of contrition, affirming that, in accord with her conscience, she could not have kept silent. In her view, a robbery of that magnitude (the ring was valuable) dishonored the old (and young) servants of the house. If the guilty one were not discovered, a suspicion would weigh forever on the household help. I explained to her a thousand and one times that no one was placing their honorability in judgment, which was true. No use. Fani's stubbornness was almost always impervious to reasoning.

To those who arrived from Spain looking for a job, she would lend her aid (powerful aid, since a recommendation from her was worth more than one from any of us) and find work for them. On occasion, she asked my permission to bring the people she would "speak for" to the house for a meal. Her dedication in this sense never faltered.

My smallest debts worried her, and so she would offer to pay them for me out of her savings: "What do you want me to do with that money?" she would say. "I have everything I need and I'll never leave this house. If I get sick, there will always be a hospital. I don't want to be a bother. You know that." And I said to her: "Do you think you're going to end up in a hospital? Are you dreaming? Have you forgotten that I'm going to kill you one of these days!"

When Tagore, convalescing in Buenos Aires, spent three months as my guest, I delegated Fani to take care of him. They had immense affection for one another, often greeting each other with a kiss. She could jabber unintelligibly in broken French, perhaps fifty words that she had picked up from hearing me say them. In English, she knew the necessary words to ask for breakfast, soap, an iron. Tagore spoke hardly any French. Nonetheless, they would carry on a dialogue. Tagore used to tell me, smiling: "She's as strong as a horse." And she was. Years after his stay in San Isidro, I met him again in Paris. Fani would go daily to the hotel where he was staying, examine his clothes and darn his tunic. At that time, a photograph was taken of Tagore with Madame de Noailles and the minister of fine arts. The immaculately white tunic that he's wearing in the picture was washed by Fani the night before. "Dear Fani," Tagore used to call her. And in the letters he wrote me from India, he would ask about her.

On another occasion, I went with Fani to spend a few days in the home of Aldous and Maria Huxley in Sanary. When I received the invitation, I answered that I would also bring my *femme de chambre*,[5] and I asked them to reserve a room for her in the hotel nearest to their villa. Maria confessed to me later that the term "femme de chambre" had worried her, as the Huxleys lived in a very simple manner; she thought I would appear with one of those haughty, demanding, disdainful, and stylish *soubrettes*[6] who were more snobbish than their mistresses. How surprised she must have been, then, the next day, to find Fani in her big apron helping the cook peel vegetables for lunch! I might add that Fani never tired of helping others, and her kindness never had any ulterior motive.

In Rome, when we were the guests of an Italian minister, the same thing happened. Fani discovered that the gentleman's suits were not as well pressed as they might be, and she offered to help Nina, the minister's maid. His shirts didn't pass her inspection either, I imagine; the fact is that she got involved in washing them herself. On occasion, I would search the house without finding her. She would do these secret chores in hiding: "Where are you? What are you up to now? Do me the favor of concerning yourself with my things, your things, and then go out and enjoy yourself. Do you hear me? Otherwise they'll say you're my slave!" She would shake her head: "Bah! bah!"

On board ship (we traveled a lot together), after the second day afloat, she had carte blanche to do as she wished, to bring to my stateroom whatever snacks I desired. She'd go herself at any hour, as if in her own home, to the steward's pantry in search of the cookies I liked and she would obtain for my personal use the finest strainer on board (no one knew better than she my allergy to the scaldings of hot milk). She knew how to say "strainer" in four languages, and when I forgot how to say it in English—I always forget that useful word—she would remind me with a triumphant smile: "strainer." She would become friendly with families with numerous offspring in order to have the pleasure of taking care of the children. It was not unusual to see her strolling about on board holding one in her arms or by the hand.

I would always take a cabin for her next to mine (it never even occurred to me to travel without Fani). She took to locking my door when she left my stateroom at night, after I was in bed, explaining that this way I would not have to get up and take off the chain lock when they brought me breakfast. Her system, which I didn't rebel against out of laziness, caused me a good scare. Early one morning when the ship was in quarantine, motionless on the waters of the River Plate, I found myself locked in my room in the company of an enormous rat, as shocked by my presence as I was by his. My shrieks were of such a magnitude—"FANI, FANI"—that I alarmed the crew. From that day on she refused to lock me in my cabin.

On occasion I used to ask her, "Why haven't you ever married, Fani?" She would answer: "Bah, bah, what an idea! Stop joking. But I assure you it's not for lack of opportunities." Once, I believe, she almost took one of those opportunities seriously, but she discovered in time that the suitor (a butler that the Princess Isabel de Borbón brought with her when she came to Buenos Aires) was "bah, bah, a fag." Although it's true that Fani readily believed whatever she heard in passing on trains, streetcars, and in stores, she was extremely skeptical in regard to the faithfulness of men. I suppose she preferred not to experience it first-hand. But this was not the principal impediment. The principal one was her vocation of forgetting about herself.

My fear of thunder was no secret to her. On stormy nights, she would enter my room silently with the pretext of seeing whether the windows and curtains were tightly closed. After inspecting them, she would sit down on the sofa opposite my bed, and finally she would end up bringing her pillow and blanket there. We spent many a night that way, hearing the violent wind shake the trees and the thunder which seemed to explode in the sky and then roll along the barrancas of San Isidro.

—Fani, are you asleep?

—I'd have to be deaf to sleep tonight.

—Fani, what did you say? I have my ears covered.

—Ave Maria! So much shouting when you get angry and now you're afraid of the thunder. I'm going to unplug the phone. With a storm like this, nothing can stay in one piece.

—Don't turn off the light. With the light on you see less lightning.

—Bah, bah. What can lightning do to you? Who as brave as you would be afraid of lightning?

—And what about your fear of mice?

When she fell mortally ill (up to that moment she had been a woman of excellent health), her great worry was the money I was spending on doctors and medicine. I would go and sit in the corridor across from the door of her room in the clinic. I didn't stay beside her bed long, because seeing me there upset her. "Go away! You're wasting your time. I'm fine and I don't need anything. Here they do everything in a big way. Too much luxury." I pretended to leave, but the fact is that I lacked the courage to go anywhere else. To whom could I adequately explain what Fani meant to me? Not even to her. To whom could I explain what was happening at that moment—what I felt? Who could understand that to go home, for me, was to return to Fani? And that without Fani there would be no home to return to? That I was, at that moment, a tightrope walker whose safety net is taken away.

The morning she left San Isidro to undergo treatment in Buenos Aires, she came to my room very early to say goodbye. I didn't want to accompany her for fear that my solicitude might alarm her, and I tried not to vary the routine of our customs so that she wouldn't suspect my concern. But she didn't let herself be fooled: "I've come to say goodbye. Goodbye to this house." She looked at me; she looked at the room. I could barely endure it. I said to her: "Are you crazy? When you go to Mar del Plata, do you say goodbye to the house? Go on, go on, I'll come to see you as soon as I get up." She had more courage than I: she was crying. She dared to live the truth, she dared to face the goodbyes (although I had hidden her true illness from her). This was her last farewell, as she never mentioned again that she felt she was dying. She embraced me crying. I waited for her to leave the room before I cried.

The night she died there was rain and thunder. The doctor warned me: "She will last only until daybreak." It's the hour that the dying rarely survive. She was under an oxygen tent that seemed to isolate her even more. When they put her in it, she said to the nurse: "It must cost a great deal." Those details still worried her because they concerned me materially. She didn't say so to me. She didn't complain, but in her this didn't mean anything. She was unbelievably long-suffering. In spite of the doctors' assurances, one never can be certain that the dying are beyond the zone of pain. I thought: "And with her it's even more impossible to know. What if she's suffering? Let her die, let her die."

Seated in the corridor, across from the door of her room, I saw the lightning through a large, wide window. The corridor smelled of sad disinfectant, not of the blessed aroma that the water brings when it mixes with the earth in the countryside and filters in through every crack. She was no longer hearing the thunder, nor would she come into my room again to protect me with her presence from the storms of San Isidro. I felt a great indifference to what had previously caused me fear—an irrational and infantile fear.

As the doctor had foreseen, she passed from the coma to death at daybreak, when the storm turned into a gentle rain, at the hour when she would have left my room with her pillow and blanket saying to me: "The thunder has stopped. Turn off the light and go to sleep."

Of the "give and take" there was between us, I thought that night, the *give* was hers and mine the *take*. I know of no "island" with which I could have shown her all that the "simplicity of her condition and the faithfulness of her service" meant to me, and what it deserved, unless it be this island of my heart.

(From *Testimonios* V, pp. 108–118)

A KING PASSES BY   June 1972.

Among the letters I've kept from Ernest Ansermet, I found some old clippings of the London *Evening Standard* and the *Daily Express* referring to concerts he had conducted in Albert Hall. One of the headlines reads: "The Conductor who Accompanied the Prince's Ukelele." The article tells how Ansermet met the then Prince of Wales in Buenos Aires at the home of a friend and how the prince, accompanied by the maestro on the piano, played "Bright Eyes" and three English ballads on his Hawaiian guitar. The prince's enthusiasm, it said, and the atmosphere, devoid of protocol, "made the experience a delightful one."

Since I was the owner of the apartment where the heir to the throne and the conductor, king among conductors, gave that improvised concert, I can confirm that no etiquette was observed at the get-together. The prince, according to Ansermet, played well. Coming from him, this was great praise. It all happened by chance.

I was living in a small apartment on Montevideo Street in 1926, the year of the boyish prince's first visit (he looked quite like a boy with his blond hair, turned-up nose and good looks, though he intimidated some by dint of his shyness). My books were piled up everywhere in a disorder that was increased by the space needed for a grand piano. One evening at the British Embassy, I was introduced to the future Edward VIII. We spoke about jazz, which both of us liked. We danced and talked about jazz some more. At that time, I had a very complete collection of records that I used to listen to with Ansermet, who sometimes took one with him to Europe for Stravinsky, who shared our passion. When the Prince of Wales, no less a devoté, learned of this, he asked if we could go that night to my apartment to listen to them. I thought uncomfortably about my living room and the piles of books on the chairs and how I should make some temporary order out of it before he came to visit. So I asked him to put it off until the next day and he agreed. I explained why: "I must tell you that my apartment, because of its size, suffers from chronic confusion. If I don't watch out, there are books on the chairs, the floor, and the dining table. It's not Buckingham Palace." Laughing, he answered, "Thank God."

209

The next day I anxiously called the embassy: "What should I do? Should I invite some friends? I have no idea what might interest him besides jazz, nor am I accustomed to receiving this kind of visitor. I live among writers and musicians." The ambassador's wife encouraged me and assured me that she was certain the prince would have a good time with a few friends of my own choosing. I shouldn't worry. So I gathered together Ricardo Güiraldes and his guitar, Ansermet and his baton, and six or seven other people.

The prince arrived punctually at the appointed hour after having called personally by phone to know if I was expecting him. How could I *not* be expecting him considering who he was? The question surprised me. When he entered and I introduced him to my friends (in my now-decent living room, the books having disappeared), there was a moment when we couldn't come up with anything to say (nor could he). But I grabbed the lifesaver of my record collection and we didn't drown in silence; everything loosened up. We played the phonograph (the prince himself wound it up, it was one of those), we danced, and Ricardo played the guitar. The enchanted (by the music) prince then decided to send for his own Hawaiian guitar so he could play too. When they brought it to him, Ansermet sat down at the piano and accompanied him. The prince's secretary had brought along some sheets of music that were left behind. Later, when I moved, they were lost.

That was an unexpectedly pleasant afternoon for my friends, for me and, I hope, for the principal, princely guest. As I said, there was no tension. Nonetheless I had a few worrisome moments when the prince stopped before a photograph of Gandhi. In India in those years, they hadn't received the prince with too much sympathy (even though the Mahatma had forbidden any hostile demonstrations). Looking with curiosity at the photo, he asked me, "Is he a friend of yours?" And I answered, "No, because I haven't met him, but I admire him." The boyish, blond prince smiled and changed the subject. I liked his reaction. His smile wasn't forced, nor did he show any displeasure. Either he had been well-trained for his position or he himself had an instinct that allowed him to navigate gracefully the shoals of his far-from-easy job as future king.

After those two encounters and a kind telegram he sent from the *Reprise* upon leaving, and apart from the telegrams we exchanged when his father died, I only saw him once again from a distance on Park Avenue. He and the Duchess were coming out of Mary Chess where they were (I suppose) buying perfume. At that time, he lived in the Towers of the Waldorf Astoria. I was in the democratic and cheaper (relatively) lower portion of that immense *caravansérail*.[1]

But even if I lost sight of him, I did converse with him again indirectly. After dinner, I frequently walked along Lexington Avenue because I liked that avenue and its shops. On several occasions I passed a black man who was taking four identical pugs—lovely specimens of a kind of dog I do not prefer—for their evening walk. But I'm a dog-lover who doesn't really discriminate among breeds, and one day I couldn't contain my curiosity and my desire to strike up a friendship with the pugs, so I stopped and spoke to the man who cared for them. The pugs were indifferent, though courteous, to my caresses. How could they not be? They belonged, their "nanny" proudly told me, to the Duke of Windsor. They were well-mannered dogs. Did I know who the Duke was? "I've heard about him," I answered. The pugs' keeper looked at me as if to say, "What a dumb one she is!" and he walked away with his four charges. That was the last I heard of that blond, unsuspectingly timid boy who spent a whole afternoon in my home in Buenos Aires between an Argentine and a Hawaiian guitar. After his departure that day, my old butler commented with surprise, "Señora, you should have seen how worn the gloves and hat he left on the rack were!" And I warned him, "That's the elegance of princes. Don't be guided by gloves and hats that are very new. They aren't titles of nobility."

I didn't know that king (who only sat on the throne as if passing by) well enough to judge him. But I do keep a memory of a man who wanted to put protocol aside and to feel happy at being among others who forgot it as well. I don't know if it's prudent for a monarch to do so. But don't we perhaps live in times when prudence is becoming practically impossible?

(From *Testimonios* IX, pp. 115–118)

MARIA DE MAEZTU   1948.

It was in the old hall of the Friends of Art in Buenos Aires in 1926. I had just given a lecture when a woman I didn't know, tiny, lost in a coat of light gray fur, came up to me and shook my hand effusively. Her very blue eyes followed and intimidated me. She began to speak rapidly and eloquently, and I listened, impressed by that verbal dexterity so foreign to my nature. This situation was destined to repeat itself for years.

Not only in the lectures she gave during her first stay with us in Argentina, but also in my home, where she became accustomed to visiting me daily, María de Maeztu would speak and I would listen. I would lead her toward themes that interested me (the education of women, for example) and then I would listen tirelessly. She would relate to me her experiences as the founder and director of the College for Women in Madrid; her struggles at the start, her deceptions, and her final success—the College was, at that moment, a flourishing enterprise. Our favorite theme—the one we would return to constantly—was the emancipation of women. For me, emancipation was synonymous with education, and María had a great deal to teach me in this regard. As we were of the same opinion on the subject, there was no possible argument between us. And since María was eloquent—a talent that I completely lack—she spoke and I drank in her words. Thus the weeks passed and the bonds of our friendship were established.

I tried in clumsy terms to explain to María what Emmanuel Mounier would point out so magnificently in one of his essays years later: "Public opinion seems to concern itself solely with men's problems, problems in which only men have the right to speak out. Many hundreds of workers disrupt history in every country because they have realized they are the oppressed. A spiritual proletariat a hundred times more numerous—that of women—continues to exist outside history without causing surprise. Its moral situation is not, however, any more enviable in spite of more favorable appearances. The impossibility for a person to develop his own life—which in our opinion defines the proletariat more essentially than material poverty—is the destiny of practically all women, rich and poor, middle class, workers and farmers." I remember having read these lines to María when they appeared.[1] It was such a miracle that a Catholic and Latin man could have written them.

Despite appearances, the emancipation of women is a fact that this century will see, we would say to one another. For the time being, there are only a few liberated women in our Latin countries. Nonetheless, the emancipation of all women will come as did that of all slaves. It has been in the air for some time now; it will do no good for its adversaries to try to prevent it. But if education and instruction don't accompany emancipation, it will be of no use. Ignorance will void or pervert its effects. It is therefore primordial and urgent, terribly urgent, that women receive an education, an instruction as careful as that of men. Not tomorrow but today; and not just today but this very instant. Otherwise, beware the consequences! And let no man act surprised later!

These interminable conversations bound me closer and closer to María. I not only liked her for herself, but I admired her for the very arduous work that she was accomplishing against the wind and the tide, thanks to the torrent of energy and the exceptional will to work that kept her going. In Spain, to run—and to run well — an institution like the College for Women was not a task for the lazy or the cowardly when María undertook it.

"The education of women, the education of women, there's no problem more urgent!" we used to repeat like maniacs, walking up and down through the little rooms of the apartment on Montevideo Street where I lived then and which of course was not adequate for our frenetic peripatetics. "*You* say it—you're the one who knows how to speak. Say it right and left, north and south. For goodness sake, say it!" I would plead with her. And María, lost in her coat of light gray fur, would enter and leave my home at all hours, carried by the tide of her own eloquence, with her tiny steps, her blue eyes, her large enthusiasm and her even larger indignations.

I saw her in action in her College some years later in Madrid. On two occasions I was her guest. María would call at my door very early when I had just finished breakfast and was lounging in bed: "Come in! Already dressed to kill? Ready to attack?" I would say to her yawning, laughing and stretching myself. "Working, Victorita, working," she would answer with a tone of comic desperation. But did she ever do anything else from morning til night? María enjoyed her work, she relished it. There was always something like the hum of a beehive around her. I never found her inactive. Always in movement like a flame or the sea. And nevertheless— a rarity in a temperamental person — she was essentially ordered and persevering. In her house on Fortuny Street in Madrid, where she had gathered books and furniture to her taste, each thing had its place and kept it. Nothing thrown on the tables, chairs, or beds. María was horrified by bohemia in any of its manifestations. The same scrupulous order prevailed in all the rooms and all the apartments she occupied.

From the most distant corners of Spain, the human material, the female youth to whom she had dedicated her life, would arrive at the College. The project was well worth it. María couldn't complain about her luck, although the work might be hard and the struggle continuous and subterraneous. She *didn't* complain. I have observed her at length in one of those compensating moments that repay one for an accumulation of disgust. It was a twenty-fourth of December in the College. With unabashed pride, María asked me to attend their dinner. Students and professors had seated themselves around the large tables filled with dishes especially prepared for the occasion. Of course, not all the students, María explained to me, but only those who for some reason weren't able to go home to celebrate Christmas. Nonetheless, there were quite a few, and from all the provinces of Spain. Surrounded by these happy young people, brought together by her under the same roof, María enjoyed the occasion. She was happy. I would have guessed it by only watching her look at the well-served plates and the smiling and satisfied faces.

The Spanish Civil War was to put an end to that happiness with abrupt violence. Its shadow extended over the house on Fortuny Street. When it broke out, María was in France, but she wanted to go back and occupy her post at the College with all haste. She wouldn't resign herself to abandoning the fray without defending her rights. How could she not fight to the last instant in order to try to save what she had built with her own hands and with so much forebearance?

María's situation in Spain was not only delicate and complicated but anguishing for ideological and sentimental reasons. Warning her of the extent to which this situation could aggravate itself, I begged her by phone and cable to come to my home in Buenos Aires. At first, she would not accept this all-too-comfortable solution. But soon she had no choice but to give in to the evidence: the College was no longer hers. The horrible bitterness of this realization, along with her grief over the shooting of her favorite brother, Ramiro, were terrible blows for her. They didn't leave hidden scars; they marked her with irremissibly visible wounds whose existence couldn't be ignored either by the one who bore them or by the one who looked at them.

Thanks to the intervention of Julio Alvarez del Vayo, then Minister of Foreign Relations, who demonstrated as much efficiency as good will — for which I will always be grateful — it was arranged for María to leave

Madrid under painfully difficult circumstances. Ricardo Baeza was also a great support for her in those moments of affliction, a fact María never ceased remembering and pointing out.

Safe and sound but undone and tearful, she finally arrived to give some lectures in Buenos Aires under the auspices of *Sur*. That job had the merit, at least, of keeping her busy right away and entertaining her. She told me about her odyssey, mixing tragic episodes with comic anecdotes; María could be extremely witty and brilliant when she told her adventures and invented dialogues, lending her interlocutors an eloquence and fluidity of expression they probably lacked.

One day, describing to me a conversation with a volunteer soldier, she told me that he had called her a "fallen tree." These words had deeply offended and angered her. She used to recall them frequently. Two or three years later, she still repeated the story about the "fallen tree" in a joking tone, but with a trace of irritation.

The fact is that no one deserved that epithet less than María. After having lost what mattered to her most, materially and spiritually, she kept her power to work intact with a surprising vitality. The "fallen tree," upright again after the gale, with new roots. Within a few months I saw her start her life again, become interested in things and people and plan projects. During her period of moral convalescence, she lived in my home and rarely a day passed without our spending some hours talking, even arguing, because having her around, I ended up learning to speak out, and our opinions sometimes clashed.

I saw María for the last time one September afternoon at *Sur* in that office where she came so often to offer me her help. I was leaving that night for New York. We really didn't have a chance to talk. Other people were coming in and going out, the proofs of the English issue were piled on my desk, and in my head were problems of translators and translation. I think I remember that she even offered to help correct proofs. María was always ready, in spite of her being busy, to lend a hand to us unfortunate ones, unaccustomed to disciplined work, who lose our heads at the slightest difficulty and drown in a glass of water. A generous mania caused her to be grateful to others for the favors they owed her; she exaggerated the importance of the smallest things her friends did for her and never gave any importance at all to those she did for them. Carried by this current, María often went overboard in the praise of those she loved. The excess of fervor in her nature was hastily interpreted as adulation by some malevolent critics.

I didn't know her in death,[2] and it's impossible for me to imagine her face silenced by absence—absence of what kept it in reach of our voice. In my memory, María is still wearing her coat of light gray fur and raising her blue eyes toward me. I visualize her the time she stuck her head in the crack of my door very early in Madrid and caused me remorse for prolonging my sleep while she was beginning her tasks; I will also have to be thankful to her for that. In the image I keep of her, that great worker never ceases to work.

I suspect that she never knew laziness. But she certainly did know the most justified depression, and she overcame it. I treasure the memory of this hidden virtue. María had many others, but none of the others inspired me with such profound and tender respect.

(From *Soledad Sonora* IV, pp. 270–276)

LIVING HISTORY*   March 1935.

"Pyramids on the one hand; personal liberty on the other. We have
an ever increasing number of pyramids or their modern equivalents;
an ever diminishing amount of personal liberty. Is this merely a
historical accident? Or are these two goods essentially incompatible?
If they turn out to be essentially incompatible, then, one day, we
shall have to ask ourselves very seriously which is better worth having —
pyramids and a perfectly efficient, perfectly stable community; or
personal liberty with instability, but the possibility, at least of
a progress, measurable in terms of spiritual values."

Aldous Huxley, *Beyond the Mexique Bay*

I think there's something miraculous about *présence d'esprit*.[1] In one of
the most beautiful places in the world (facing three open windows overlooking the tip of the Quai Bourbon) I met a woman in whom this miracle
had occurred. It seems that, having granted her an audience, Mussolini
asked her point-blank why she had wanted to see him. "Because I like
living history," she replied.

No such question was put to me the day of my conversation with "il
Duce," for which I thank heaven, since who knows what inept answer I
would have stammered. But with enough time — and with the help of
esprit d'escalier[2] — no doubt I would have finally found the answer that
Princess Murat managed to fire off with such opportune rapidity. Only *I*
would have found it too late.

It was thus because I, too, like living history that one clear autumn
afternoon, I climbed the steps of the Palazzo Venezia — so severely
magnificent, built with stones from the Coliseum—whose perfect beauty
is insulted day and night by the proximity of the Victor Emmanuel
monument. Counting myself among those who, not believing in ordinary
divinities, have transferred to writers of genius their share of credulity, I
found myself for the first time about to encounter a genius of another
kind: that of Caesar, the perpetual dictator.

Amid greetings in the Roman style and noiseless guards, and after a
brief wait during which my eagerness to meet the Duce had time to

* This essay was the result of an interview with Benito Mussolini that took place in Rome on September
  24, 1934; it was written before Italy invaded Abyssinia in October 1935.

dissolve in apprehension as a toothache vanishes in the dentist's office (however much one may repeat the "me ne frego"[3] popular among Fascists, at times it's of no avail), I was abandoned once and for all on the threshold of an immense hall. The austerity of its furnishings, which need not be described now, says *no* to the superfluous, the plural, with a violence that stuns even the least discerning visitor. In order to write, proclaims this austerity, one only needs a table; to sit down, a chair; for light, a lamp; to think and decide, a head. . . . It would be hard for me to remember the table, the chair, or the lamp. But the head would be hard *not* to remember. It's a monument to Resistance. One sinks into that face beyond the point of recovery, or so it seems. How can one be submerged in such a hard material? There's nothing in that proud (in the full sense of the word) face that doesn't offer terrible resistance: the eyes, the forehead, the nose, the mouth, the unexpected strength of the jaw—all resist. The gaze attracts just as the flame in a fireplace attracts one's eyes in a room.

The first words we exchanged aren't any easier for me to remember than the table, the chair, or the lamp. They matter very little. What matters is "that presence" which the visitor must swallow as the boa constrictor swallows his prey: whole. (Digestion comes later.) What one "hears" is that presence: it is massive, compact. One endures it like a shock. It takes up so much room that it alone seems to fill the immense hall of the Palazzo Venezia.

Some days earlier when 23,000 youngsters paraded before Mussolini, I had watched from a reviewing stand opposite his on the Via dell'Impero, and I had photographed something that made an extraordinary change in the expression of his face: his smile. Imagine a stone mask broken by a smile in which all hardness seems to melt instantly.

His smile seems to me as characteristic of him as his gaze, a gaze so sustained, so direct with his round eyes wide open, that one wonders if the fixed, immobile eyelids ever manage to close. This power of not blinking (in the strict and the figurative sense) is reinforced by something analogous in his elocution: not the slightest vacillation of any kind. I asked the Duce several questions about the role of women in the Fascist State and his opinion of their aptitudes. His answers were hurled at me as from a catapult. The precise sentences, interrupted by short silences, left no room for any doubt or misunderstanding. His tone was sharp; there was no Gordian knot it couldn't cut. Yet, in his lack of circumlocutions there was something appealing, even when the answer contradicted my most intimate convictions. Why?

"Fascist Italy," I said to the Duce, "thinks that the first duty of women is to give children to the State. But don't you believe that women can also collaborate with men in another way?" The Duce answered: "No." A definitive no. "Do you believe," he added, "that Julius Caesar, Napoleon, or Bismarck had any need of such collaboration?" And then, in reply to my silence which he interpreted perfectly: "Do you think that Dante wrote the *Commedia* because of Beatrice? No. What inspired Dante was his hatred of Florence."

Certainly a measure of hatred entered into the *Commedia*, but one has to be short-sighted not to see something else in that poem too. And even if we admit the hypothesis that it might have been that way for Dante, there are other poets. . . . And history also includes, if I'm not mistaken, Cleopatra's nose. That nose which, if it had been any shorter, would have changed the face of the world.

Mussolini's opinion of women doesn't lend itself to equivocation. They shouldn't get involved in politics because they don't understand it. Nor in philosophy, music, or architecture, for the same reason. Of course there are exceptions, but they only confirm the rule.

In parenthesis, and apropos of architecture, all praise would be insufficient to commend the Duce's support of young architects and modern architecture. These young people are beginning to demonstrate their talent in the most convincing manner. Both Le Corbusier and Gropius have spoken to me about them with the greatest esteem and the most sincere admiration. Whereas in Germany and Russia the modern architect has entered the ranks of the unemployed, seeing all his proposals rejected and rescinded, in Italy he finds the effective and intelligent approval of the Duce.

Going back to the opinions of Mussolini concerning women (the principal topic of my conversation with him), in his judgment, a woman can be useful in medicine as long as she's not in surgery. He finds her excellent as a nurse and irreplaceable in early childhood education.

In his opinion, women cannot move in abstract spheres. Instinct is their element. Mussolini concedes the right to have a child, no matter what the circumstances, with the State's support. And, as in Spain or Russia, all children are equal before the law. This is simple justice.

Nonetheless it's evident that his categorical manner of limiting women by the north and the south, the east and the west of their humanity is very debatable from many points of view. Why pretend to be concerned with certain women's problems when one believes in the ideal that everything should be sacrificed to the State, with a capital S, so that the State may be great and strong?

Just as London is a city where the pedestrian's glance is most captivated by articles for men: pipes, ties, vests, tweeds, canes, shirts, scarves, in sumptuous stores (whose luxury is expressed only by quality);

similarly Fascist Italy appears to the ingenuous traveler to be a country for men, a country in which the accent falls on unmitigated masculinity. Italy seems to apply to everything the grammatical rule of agreement which requires that after enumerating names of both genders, the only gender that should be taken into account is the masculine. Since "State" belongs to the masculine gender (so it seems) and since everything must agree with "State," the consequences are clear. But in the long run, couldn't this provoke an imbalance—that is to say, progress in one sense and simultaneous retrogression in another?

The fact is that when one dreams of a better world, the place conceded to women by Fascism is not enough.

There are two countries in Europe that are undergoing a thrilling moment in their history—and that of the world: Italy and Russia. At the Convegno Volta where I witnessed the magnificent and generous hospitality (a hospitality I shared in response to a very special invitation for which I am sincerely grateful) offered by Rome to outstanding individuals who had come from all over Europe to expound their ideas about the theater, there were two Russians among the invited guests. One of them, known to the public in Buenos Aires, was Tairoff. I had occasion to converse with him and to question him about the USSR. But even more interesting than what he told me and what I heard him declare in his report to the Convegno Volta was what André Malraux told me about his own trip to Russia. This French writer (author of *La Condition Humaine*, one of the best novels to appear in recent years) had just spent several months there, and one of the things that impressed him most was the mentality and attitude of the young women. As I don't want to run the risk of altering someone else's ideas and as I know that Malraux himself will write about the subject, it is to him, to his next books, that I refer the reader who is curious about observations of this sort. For my part, throughout the conversations I had with him, I was able to infer that today's Russian woman is offered all the possibilities for development. This time—and it is perhaps the first in contemporary history—what tomorrow brings her depends solely on her abilities, her conscience, and her aptitudes. It's too early to judge the outcome of this experience, but the future will not fail to do so.

What is being born in Russia as well as in Italy is a new youth, a youth molded in exaltation. I'm not acquainted with and haven't seen that of Russia, but one day I hope to. I *have* seen that of Italy.

Beautiful, well-formed children who played gravely at being soldiers; adolescents full of impulse and grace who marched one warm September afternoon along the Via dell'Impero with a rhythmic step. Happy in their own rhythm, they left me with an unerasable memory:

that of their joyous faces turned toward the Duce. That human material was beautiful, beautiful like the Latin sky, more so than all the beautiful dead stones that Rome is so filled with and justifiably proud of. I have seen the Duce smile at the young with a smile that changed even the hard material of his face.

My memory continues to focus on those enchanting new faces stamped with ecstasy—*balillas, avanguardisti, piccole italiane, giovane italiane*[4]—more than it focuses on Rome, renewed by a thorough cleaning that makes the value of each ruin stand out; more than the *autostrade* that unfold in clear ribbons around the peninsula; more than the drained Pontine marshes; more than the organization of the *dopolavoro;*[5] more than the aviation exposition in Milan that is a work of art of its own kind; more than all that has been accomplished successfully in Italy thanks to the Duce. I focus on that memory and on the irrepressible smile that it provoked on his lips—that smile that changes even the hard material of his face. Whoever has not seen Mussolini in the shadow of his blossoming country has not seen him. Those ecstatic faces on one side, that smile of irresistible paternal pride on the other: what will emerge from this love? Because there is love between those children and that man.

In my capacity as a woman, what may come of that reciprocal love strikes me as more important than everything else; more important than what may come of all the hatreds. Hatreds don't interest me. In my capacity as a woman, I cannot subscribe to the idea of the game of destruction of young bodies, for example. If men—even the greatest ones —call the violent repugnance which that game inspires in me foolishness, I won't feel mortified or humiliated. If they explain to me with compassion that that game has existed as long as the existence of man and that it will only disappear from the earth with him, they won't change me or convince me. Cannibalism exists too, and in certain tribes human sacrifices. Why then be shocked by them and try to repress them? They are forgotten customs to which we could return, and nothing more.

Is it possible that women, destined to build the bodies of men with their own bodies, may have the supreme inferiority not to oppose the destruction or systematic mutilation of their creation?

Men and women — I repeat, and women — have never achieved anything great without heroism. That I know. But heroism is applicable to so many things that don't have to do with war (the word has finally come out), to so many things that don't deal with what Marinetti calls "the aesthetic of war in all its splendor of individuals, masses, terrestrial and aerial machines, in all its stimulation of the most luminous human virtues." One can, one must be ready to die—and even to live—for certain ideas such as the fatherland. Those ideas *are* the fatherland. No woman worthy of the name disputes that. But no woman worthy of the name can resign herself to believing that the masculine game of systematic destruction of young bodies is an indispensable sport for wicked children (who are sometimes grown men) solely for the reason that they have always enjoyed that game. She hopes that wicked children will learn to conduct themselves otherwise, just as she hopes for the discovery of an anticancer serum (hasn't the vaccination against smallpox been discovered?). Is it perhaps hoping for the impossible? And how can one not feel despair for humanity if one doesn't have that hope?

More beautiful than all the beautiful dead stones of which Rome is so proud, as beautiful as the Latin sky, are the young Italians who turned their faces toward the Duce. What will become of this human material? Just as in Russia, only the future can be the judge of this.* Whatever happens will depend on the Head of State. I have seen Italy in blossom turn its face toward him. And in my heart there is only one fervent desire: that the smile of the Duce — that smile that changes even the hard material of his face—may protect and guide that youth to a safe harbor for the greater glory of a country which, by its nature, its traditions, and the art treasures it possesses, is unique in the world.

(From *Domingos en Hyde Park,* pp.9–25)

---

* The future has already judged: the Italo-Abyssinian war. There is where a part of this beautiful Italian youth has ended up. I wish to declare here publicly my adhesion to the two manifestos published in France and motivated by this war: that of the liberal and democratic intellectuals and that of the Catholic intellectuals answering the manifesto of the Fascist intellectuals. Both manifestos condemn this war of aggression which is the most odious form of war.

And today (in August 1936) at a time when Argentine Catholics are protesting en masse against the anticlerical excesses provoked in Spain (against the leftists) by the civil war that is destroying the country, it is opportune to recall to these same Catholics the extreme indifference or the open Fascism that they showed during the Italo-Abyssinian war. Meanwhile, the true Catholics, the only ones deserving the title, declared in France: "Christianity makes us understand and realize this truth of natural order—that justice is for all men with no exception for persons, races or nations, and that the soul and life of a negro are as sacred as the soul and life of a white." (V.O.)

ADRIENNE MONNIER   *Mar del Plata*
February 1956.

"Moitié ferme et moitié couvent
J'ai fait ainsi ma librairie."[1]
Adrienne Monnier

Adrienne dressed in dark gray, a long billowy skirt like those nuns wear, an austere, fitted bodice with no adornment and something white near her face. Adrienne arriving at my hotel (Paris, winter) in a full woolen cape of the same color as her dress, always the same one, either followed or preceded by Sylvia Beach. Adrienne, the one with the clear skin, clear eyes (the eyes of a seer), clear handwriting, and clear thoughts. Adrienne Monnier, 7 rue de l'Odéon: her bookstore run by her personally. The Adrienne of great friends: French writers, known or still unknown, old, middle-aged, young, adolescent.

Ricardo Güiraldes was the one who first told me about her. "When you go to Paris," he said, "you'll see." And in 1929 I did. If someone wanted to find out what was happening in the literary world of that European capital, "the latest fashion of the West," he only had to stop by that small bookshop on the Left Bank. Adrienne started her business there in 1915 when she couldn't have been more than twenty. "La Maison des Amis des Livres," as she decided to call her place, also became very quickly the House of the Friends of Writers and particularly of *the Friend* of Writers: Adrienne.

Ever since my first visit I've thought of the rue de l'Odéon as *her* street. The atmosphere, the personality of the owner of the small shop (so easily missed by passersby who didn't know her) fascinated me. But it wasn't until after a dinner given at my flat that I felt I really knew that woman—so discreet and sure of herself, that is to say, of her *selections* (her bookstore became an institution due to the perceptive and infallible taste of that woman, capable of swimming against the current and keeping afloat), so intuitive and generous, so spiritually earthbound. The other two guests were Sylvia Beach and Ricardo Baeza. I was living at that time

(1939) in a small apartment on the rue Raynouard, the street where Balzac's house still stands. The panorama of the Seine and the Eiffel Tower made my living room seem immense. From the balcony we looked at that other face of Paris, so different from the rue de l'Odéon. Then we sat down to dinner.

Here, a parenthesis: to eat in Adrienne's company, either as your guest or hers, was always a double banquet. Being a food-lover, she not only knew how to enjoy the dishes served to her, or which she herself served, but she knew how to describe them in a very peculiar, very French manner. She was well acquainted with what her compatriot Montaigne called "l'art de la guele."[2] Although she didn't learn the joy of eating vegetables until the Nazi occupation ("Moi j'apprends à aimer les légumes que je désdaignais"[3]), I don't believe she needed complicated dishes — those dishes prepared, according to Brillat-Savarin, "pour émouvoir des estomacs de papier mâché, pour faire aller des éfflanqués chez qui l'appétit n'est qu'une velléité toujours prête a s'éteindre."[4] In culinary matters the exquisite isn't necessarily complicated. I can boast of having listened to Adrienne talk about these subjects with more interest and enjoyment than most people would have, except possibly Colette. (The kingdom of tastes has more deaf and blind people than one might think; even water has markedly distinct flavors to one with a keen palate.) Adrienne was a woman with a delicate palate for literature as well as for cooking. You had only to hear her say: "Come have a *good* roast chicken and some golden fried potatoes with me," to have your mouth begin to water. There was no doubt that the chicken would be *good*. When Adrienne spoke of earthly foods, she wasn't broaching a common, material subject. "Je savais que c'était aussi de l'esprit,"[5] she once wrote. By her own confession, Adrienne "honnorait les saveurs autant que des génies."[6] She spoke of all this in a letter addressed in 1942 to her friends in the free zone. When rationing came, when pastry, bread, and sweets became totally unavailable (in Paris, no less!), Adrienne the gourmande endured all sorts of privations admirably.

This reminds me of a charming anecdote that María de Maeztu used to tell about Santa Teresa de Avila. One day the saint, who was very fond of partridges, was eating one of those little birds, innocent victims of our greed, with visible relish, when she noted a look of surprise, perhaps even of reprobation in the eyes of a young nun who was watching her savor her meal. Whereupon the great Teresa, answering the unspoken but discernible thoughts she noticed, said: "When penance, penance; when partridges, partridges!"

I don't know how true the anecdote is, but I do know that Adrienne proved to us that she felt the same way. When her turn came for penance, she put partridges aside and didn't sell herself for a plate of lentils (like our ancestor Esau).

So great was Adrienne's reputation as a food-lover that, on the day they tried to assassinate deGaulle, Hemingway went to the rue de l'Odéon to see if she needed his help. As she tells it, he wondered if her gluttony might have driven her, in a weak moment, to collaborate. "Evidemment, devait-il penser, cette grosse gourmande n'a pas pu endurer les restrictions; elle a dû faiblir à un moment ou à un autre."[7] But no. Adrienne didn't have that sin on her conscience. Still the worried Hemingway insisted, "Are you sure, Sylvia, that Adrienne hasn't collaborated and needs a helping hand?" "Of course not," Sylvia replied. "If she collaborated, it was with us Americans!"

When penance, penance! And her penance wasn't only limited to meager and insipid food. The cold was also a torment for her. "My apartment is freezing. I can't read or write." It's quite probable that Adrienne's premature illness and death were due in part to what she suffered during the occupation. Certain forms of passive resistance are paid for with one's life.

But let's close the parenthesis and return to that night when we succumbed in thought, word, and deed to our major sin (ce vice tant puni,[8] I might say). "I love fattening things and I'm not afraid of gaining weight," Adrienne said. And I answered, "Even if you were, what difference would it make? I am afraid, and that spoils everything but prevents nothing. Attrition is not contrition." The conversation during the meal must have centered on "to eat or not to eat" which is so intimately linked with "to be or not to be" and can precipitate the "not to be" as much by excess as by want. Over coffee afterward (there is always someone who doesn't have it because if he does he won't sleep, but if he doesn't have it he complains bitterly that he can't and then the talk turns to insomnia and from insomnia to some other unrelated subject), one way or another we got around to talking about the subject of graphology. I had been told that Adrienne was an expert at this and I wanted to put her to the test, so I gave her various samples of handwriting: envelopes, paragraphs of letters from people she didn't know. The results of the session—for which a less able graphologist would have charged who knows how much—were disconcertingly accurate. She read the character of each one just as if she had known the person intimately. Either she was particularly gifted as a medium for thought transmission or she possessed a profound knowledge of a science that deserves to be classified among the exact sciences. Adrienne described to us with uncanny accuracy people she had never heard of. And with such delicacy in the analysis and such precision in the details! This demanded penetration, intelligence, and an uncommon level of intuition. Baeza and I were amazed.

In Adrienne's *Gazettes*, I have found certain pages that remind me of her accomplishments that evening with the Seine and the Eiffel Tower in the background. Why didn't she write more?, I asked myself as I read them. Perhaps because she had to devote herself to something at which no one could replace her: living Adrienne Monnier instead of writing her. And I say it as one says: "So-and-so lived the War of 14."

I'll never forget the welcome she gave me when I returned to Paris after six years absence during the last war. She took such trouble to give me pleasure! So much time that she should have devoted to other things!

How can I write anything about the image I keep of her without referring to the *Navire d'Argent*, the review she founded, directed, and paid for while she had the means to do so? Commenting on the sad end of that publication, she wrote: "Here we are at the end of our first year. What effort and expense to be able to assure the regular publication of those twelve issues! Only those who have put out a review can conceive of it!"

The little money Adrienne had of her own and that which Sylvia Beach gave her was used up in no time. To pay the outstanding debts, she sold her most precious treasure—the only one she had—the books given and dedicated to her by the most celebrated authors of France and the world. This forced sale tormented her and seemed to her a sacrilege. A few weeks later, she received a book from Rilke with a dedication and a poem in manuscript. That day she wrote: "Dedicated to me, unworthy as I am, having just sold the precious books that poets have dedicated to me. I fell to my knees crying."*

This was the way Adrienne loved poets, books, and literary reviews. Just the name of James Joyce is enough to prove what she and her friend Sylvia Beach (the North American whom I remember and love so well, the one who had, across from Adrienne's, another small bookstore, "Shakespeare and Company") were capable of doing out of love for a great and "difficult" writer who was definitely not on the list of potential best-sellers then.

In her *Letter to a Young Poet* (1926) Adrienne explains: ". . . no doubt on account of being a woman, that is, being of a passive nature, accustomed as we are to taking little notice of our *chétives productions*,[9] . . . I have been endowed with more disinterest than most of my brothers. . . ."

I never left Adrienne's bookstore without feeling myself comforted and enriched. And surely I was not the only one. There are people who absorb our reserve of optimism, vitality or faith like voracious sponges,

---

* I felt like doing the same after selling the manuscript of *Perséphone* given to me by Stravinsky. I was afraid for political reasons of being without money in a foreign country. (V.O., 1976).

leaving us submerged in a kind of discontent and uneasiness with an overwhelming sense of internal poverty. They take what we have, and yet what we give seems of no use to them. I never had that experience on the rue de l'Odéon. I've never known a bookstore like "Les Amis des Livres." Nor have I ever known another Adrienne capable of selling what she loved most to pay the debts of her review and later capable of feeling guilty about it and unworthy of receiving a manuscript from Rilke without crying.

"To write," she used to exclaim, "when there's so much to do to help those who take the risk of doing it!"

In winter she would arrive at my place in her full woolen cape—as full as those of Piero della Francesca's virgins—and I would understand perfectly why Leo Ferro saw in her a woman *that he would have liked to call symbolic*. That would have suited her. Adrienne has probably done, in honor of those who take the risk of writing, what others have done for the destitute. One shouldn't forget that a writer can be destitute too. Poets, great adventurers of the spirit, expose themselves to dangers that the public — enamored of bullfighters, mountain climbers, experts in racing, soccer, politics, or parachuting — doesn't see. Adrienne could have said to her poets:

> I'm not like that saint
> Who gave half his cloak to a poor man.
> Take from me my whole cape,
> And if it's more than you need, so be it.

She could have said this symbolically to the literature of France which she loved above all else, to the point of sacrifice.

The January issue of the *Mercure de France*, dedicated to her, proves that she didn't live among ungrateful friends. That homage to Adrienne Monnier, 7 rue de l'Odéon, makes clear what this woman meant to the European intellectual community. The Argentines who knew and visited her will miss her when they return to the Left Bank. For the Argentine woman writing this, Adrienne's death will mark the fourth Parisian street she is unable to walk along without feeling deep melancholy.

(From *Testimonios* V, pp. 99–105)

WOMAN, HER RIGHTS AND HER
RESPONSIBILITIES   June 1936.

"Je n'ai pas besoin d'ordre et me rend de plein gré
Où non point tant la loi que mon amour me mène. . . ."[1]
André Gide, *Perséphone*

The revolution signifying the emancipation of women is an event destined
to have more repercussions in the future than the world war or the advent
of the machine age. Millions of men and women don't yet know that it has
occurred, or they attribute this phenomenon to a passing fad, or they
imagine that it can only bring humanity a shameful increase in licentious-
ness, or they smile with superiority at the mention of something so
inadmissible. In no way does this alter the accomplished fact. The revolution has taken place since it has already slipped into the consciousness of
certain people.

I only wonder whether the word "emancipation" is correct. Wouldn't
it be more appropriate to say "liberation?" It seems to me that this term,
applied to serfs and slaves, better encompasses what I want to say. Let's
not forget that the intolerably coercive methods that men use with women
so naturally, and that women accept with surprising meekness, are still
legal in many parts of the world. The story of the wife who gets indignant
because a compassionate onlooker wants to stop her husband from beating her is perpetuated and reproduced in a thousand ways. The English
thinker who affirmed that the masculine sex is sadistic by constitution and
that the feminine sex is masochistic has found, as I see it, part of the
explanation of the problem — but only if you take away the words "by
constitution" and substitute "by force of habit."

In other words, it is true that women have learned to enjoy letting
men mistreat them, as it is also true that men, for their part, have learned
to enjoy allowing themselves to mistreat women. Of course this mis-
treatment is generally not physical but moral, and occasionally it takes
very refined forms. One cannot expect men to renounce immediately the
voluptuousness in which they have immersed themselves daily for cen-

turies. Women themselves will have to take the initiative and "deprive" themselves of the delightful narcotic to which they have become no less addicted.

It is incredible, and I speak now without irony, that millions of human beings have not yet understood that current demands made by women are simply limited to requiring that a man stop thinking of a woman as a colony for him to exploit and that she become instead "the country in which he lives."

In a book on racial problems recently published by three English men of science, Julian Huxley, A. C. Haddon, and A. M. Carr-Saunders, I have found pages on the subject of heredity that seem extremely important to me if considered from the viewpoint of the current problems of women.

In the chapter to which I refer, the subject dealt with is the physical stature of the English. Being emulators of St. Thomas's dictum "seeing is believing," the authors of *We Europeans* — the book in question — are guided solely by facts and statistics. Their religion is scientific investigation and precision. These gentlemen assure us:

1. That the average stature of the English has increased during the second half of the last century (as is the case in some other nations), and

2. That the average stature of the different social classes in England (and in other nations) varies — that of the upper classes being larger.

With regard to the first topic, these gentlemen believe that the average stature has increased because of better food and better conditions of life, not because there has been an intrinsic change in constitution. In other words, racially, the Englishman has not undergone appreciable alteration, and if he were to be returned to his former state of existence, he would be what he had been before.

The second topic is more difficult to resolve. Of course, say these gentlemen, the greater part of the difference in stature between one social class and another is due to the fact that the children of the privileged classes enjoy many more advantages. But it can also be said that there is an average genetic difference between the different classes: that is, that there could be a lineage of large genetic stature in the upper classes, descendants of the Norman invaders, and a lineage of low genetic stature in the lower classes, descendants of a Mediterranean type that inhabited Great Britain before the Norman invasion. One could also say that selection might have favored the type of large genetic stature in the upper classes (through the preference for tall women) and the type of low stature among the proletariat (this type being better able to adapt itself to life in the cities and conditions prevalent in factories). Both causes, probably, the genetic and the environmental, have functioned at the same time.

At this point in their logical deductions, these gentlemen are led to consider the question from a new angle, which is the one that interests us with respect to women because it touches us directly and places arguments at our disposal that are difficult to refute:

What is applicable to stature can be applied equally—and with how much greater force, affirm these gentlemen—to psychological character, that is, to intelligence, to special aptitudes, to temperaments. In the first place, this character suffers much more from changes in environment than does the physical character. In the second place, the social environment manifests a larger scale of differences than the physical environment does.

For instance, an extraordinary mathematical talent would not be capable of expressing itself in paleolithic society or among contemporary savages. The most perfect artistic gift would have little meaning on a desert island. The temperament that allows its owner easily to put himself into a state of trance or to have visions would, in an industrial country like Great Britain, expose him to the danger of being locked up in a mental institution or classified as a pathological case. By contrast, in various American countries and in certain Asiatic tribes, it would favor his rise to power and would bring him great prestige as a magician, medicine man, or shaman. A warrior's temperament, which would have found adequate means of expression at the start of Jewish history, would have remained sterile in the era of captivity.

In sum, the same capacities of invention or initiative that can assert themselves powerfully in favorable circumstances can be reduced to nothingness in equally unfavorable circumstances.

Generally, the expression of a particular temperament seems almost always to be determined in childhood—a fact that accounts for the idea that any change in the atmosphere of the home and in prevailing theories and educational methods profoundly affects the child. Thus also, and I continue to transcribe the opinions of these gentlemen, the peremptory affirmation, repeated to satiety, is that differences in aptitude and character between men and women are related in most instances to the difference between the education that males and females receive and to the difference between the economic and social situation of the two sexes. An amusing illustration of this is the indignant exclamation of a Greek of third-century Athens: "Who ever heard of a female cook!"

It is evident, they continue, that individuals endowed with an exceptional combination of genes will probably conquer the obstacles that confront them. But it is also evident that the quantity of innate talent that a person possesses depends for its realization and expression upon the outlets it encounters for its development, and these in turn depend upon such factors relative to environment as economic resources, social climate, and existing educational systems. An apparent reason why the children of the upper classes have proportionately better results in their studies than the children of the lower classes is that they have had more opportunity to receive a better education, whether or not they are gifted by heredity.

Now let's leave these gentlemen.

For my part, I believe that all we have just said about children can be said equally about women. As compared to men, they have always had the same handicap that the children of the proletariat have had as compared to children of the privileged classes. And they have had it for centuries. Although there may once have been a reason for this state of affairs, nothing justifies it today. Neither in one case or the other.

What men, apart from a minority that I bless, do not seem to understand is that we are not at all interested in taking *their* place (this is an error that our extreme reaction to their attitudes may have contributed to creating), but in taking *our own* completely—something that has not happened as yet.

The revolution that is being brought about in our world today—that of women, the most important one—is in no way an *ôte-toi que je m'y mette*[2] like the majority of revolutions. It is certainly not being made in order that women may invade the territory of men, but in order that men may finally stop invading the territory of women, which is a very different matter. Just as in the case of the other revolution (the one that was born in Russia and that, because of the extreme situation that caused it to erupt also created error, brutal attitudes, and terrible misunderstandings), it should not be undertaken, at least the way I understand it, in order that the proletariat may abuse the privileged classes in the same way as the privileged classes have abused it (which would create a vicious circle); it should be undertaken so that every child, having received the same wealth of care in what pertains to his physical and moral health and his education, may ultimately develop his innate talents as well as possible (thereafter inequality of distribution will be based only on this factor), and so that once he is an adult, he may reach the level that corresponds to his true vocation and his authentic worth.

I believe that the great role of the woman in history, played up to now in a rather subterranean way, is beginning to crop out at the surface. It is *she* today who can contribute powerfully to creating a new state of things since all her physical and spiritual being is concentrated on the very fountain of life—the child. She lives, therefore, closer to the future man, since the child over whom she exercises her power, consciously or unconsciously, is that man.

Therefore, I believe that if today's world, which is turned toward chaos, is going to recover an order, a lost equilibrium, it will be the woman who will find herself—whether you admit it or not, take it seriously or not, whether the masses ignore it or not—in the first line of the trenches. Without her collaboration, without awakening her consciousness to the share of work, responsibility, and struggle that is incumbent upon her, I do not see a possibility of salvation. Most grown men do not change, they only wear disguises. When they have reached a certain age, men are as unchangeable, physically, as a child just out of his mother's womb. One can dye his hair but not alter the color of his eyes.

I believe then that everything that leads to awakening the consciousness of the woman so that she will be given an exact notion of her responsibilities, everything that leads to raising her spiritual level and carrying out her education under the best possible conditions analogous to those of man, granting her the means to develop all her faculties whatever they may be, *that* is what interests us essentially. The rest will come with it.

For this reason, I also believe that every person who wishes to take up this cause should put the elevation of the spiritual and cultural level of women first on the agenda, and I believe that by working for this cause, one works for peace among nations and within nations.

War is an abomination that awakens a woman's rebelliousness much more than a man's because it is the woman who builds with her own body the body of man. And when man mutilates and reduces to formless shreds the very body that, with all her female instinct, she feels the need to protect and conserve, man kills woman as well—and in the cruelest way: obliging her to survive that death.

Woman is capable of heroism and of understanding the heroism of man. She knows very well that, to live life fully and with dignity, it is necessary at times to sacrifice it. But war, today's war, has become so monstrous, so stupid, threatening in such a way the whole human species, that one cannot now see heroism in it — only the most dangerous and contagious insanity that the planet has ever suffered.

What can be done to counteract it? As long as the consciousness of man is not transformed—and in this transformation one of the principal factors must be the woman, mother not only by flesh and in flesh, but also mother by spirit and in spirit — all the great pacifist declarations, the abstract plans of action, the societies of nations will, in a word, fail. Peace among nations cannot become a material reality until it acquires a spiritual reality in individuals pure enough to create it. The present League of Nations has not had sufficient strength because it has not had sufficient purity. Dominated by nations that pretend to forget that their current prestige is due to past violence, it can therefore hardly exert any moral power over nations which, by their current violence, try to achieve a future prestige.

Let's try to shed light on these errors. As Aldous Huxley has just said magnificently in a pamphlet on "Constructive Peace," what is needed are men and women who think, feel, and wish—that is to say, with mind, heart, and will; and all must gather together around this cause with a spirit of sacrifice and with absolute fervor. Because this ideal of peace either must be taken as a new religion (what Christ said seems new, so forgotten has it been in practice) or it is better not to mention it, so useless will it be.

In order that the consciousness of the male-child may change or become clearer through the woman, it is necessary that the woman herself rise to the occasion of that task, a task that is hers. We cannot create anything outside ourselves without first having created it inside ourselves. I don't doubt that man will end up becoming what he should vis-à-vis woman. But what is still more urgent is that woman become what she should be vis-à-vis herself. One will be the consequence of the other. From this new attitude will be born a much truer, stronger, and more worthwhile union between man and woman. The magnificent union of two equal beings who mutually enrich each other since they possess different wealths. A union that can only exist among those who accept, *with knowledge of cause*, their independence.

In order for man and woman to cooperate with each other it is necessary that, on man's part, his coercive and patriarchal morality disappear ("patriarchal" used in the same sense as the word "matriarchal," that is, the imposition and absolute predominance of one sex over the other). On the woman's part, the false point of view that has been able to create in her the antagonism of her sex, the rebellion against the oppressor, must also disappear.

The emancipation of woman, as we understand it, is not made to separate her from man but, to the contrary, to bring her closer to him in the most complete, most pure, and most conscious way. In the struggle for life—so rough in our day and prone to pitting individuals against each other in distrust, competition, brutal defense of interests, or opposing doctrines—man and woman have only one natural means of escape from their intolerable isolation: mutual love. In that refuge, at least, they will have to lay down their weapons.

I know that this is not easy or simple. The union of man and woman is a human feat with something of a miracle, and even under the best conditions it is not accomplished without tenacity and patience—I would almost say the combined heroism of two beings—just as a work of art is born of the tenacity, patience, and heroism of a single being possessed of a great love.

But in order to achieve the conditions in which this more perfect union can be accomplished—that is, in order, as women, to find ourselves and occupy the place that belongs to us—we must not wait for the help of men. It cannot occur to them to recover for us the rights of which they do not feel deprived. It is never the oppressors who rebel against the oppressed. Before the rebellion of the oppressed, the attitude of the oppressors is always the same: a small minority gives in to the evidence, understands, accepts, and is ready to do justice; a greater majority feels dispossessed, outraged, and lets forth howls of indignation and anger.

In these cases, only the minorities count. In these cases and, in my judgment, in all cases. The minorities will always be, willingly or not, the world leaders.

Not only can we not logically expect for the moment the help of men, or rather their initiative in these questions, but we must also be prepared to find resistance or indifference (which is even more disheartening) on the part of a large number of women. They will invoke a thousand reasons, some in order to block our progress, others in order to preserve neutrality. There may even be the case, which I think will be common, of their being with us but, nevertheless, abstaining from taking a definite and active role.

Many women, supported by many men, will say that they have enough to do nursing children, feeding them, and changing their diapers. We know all too well that the ones who are working (except of course those who have made a profession of caring for children) have only a limited time to give to these chores, whereas the ones who are idle, dedicated in general to other pursuits, will find excuses for limiting it.

A friend of Madame Curie told me that it was when she was warming milk for her babies' bottles that she also began working seriously with her husband, thereafter becoming the admirable woman that the world has just lost. Is it not desirable that this type of woman be stimulated and cultivated?

The emancipation of women, as I conceive it, attacks the very roots of the evils that afflict female humanity and, on the rebound, male humanity since one is inseparable from the other. And through an inherent justice, the miseries suffered by one produce instantaneous repercussions on the other in different ways.

It is my firm and ardent wish that a group of Argentine women, however small, may acquire a consciousness of their duties which are rights, and of their rights which are responsibilities. If the women of this group can answer for themselves, they will be able to answer shortly for innumerable women.

(From *Testimonios II*, pp. 251–267)

VIRGINIA WOOLF IN MY MEMORY
April 1941.

"Against you I will fling myself,
unvanquished and unyielding,
O Death."
Virginia Woolf

"To Vanessa Bell—
But looking for a phrase
I found none to stand
Beside your name."

With these words of dedication to her sister, Virginia Woolf prefaces one of her first novels, *Night and Day.* I find no others that express better the difficulty I feel in writing at this moment, and I only wish I could limit myself to them.

Virginia would understand me better than anyone else. One of her heroines says to a young novelist (as Virginia probably once said to herself): "Why do you write novels? You should write music. . . . Music goes directly to things. Everything that must be said, it says right away. This business of writing seems a lot like scratching on a matchbox."

One after another, I keep discarding the matches that don't want to light. Does telling about the noise they make when I scratch them against the box lead anywhere?

Yes. Music goes directly to things. Which is to say that there are states of anguish or delight that only music succeeds in translating. Music, when we submerge ourselves in it, as in our element, frees us of the weight of our loneliness; in a like manner, the sea relieves the swimmer of the weight of his limbs. In it, our movements become easy and we become fluid. And when we leave these oceans we enter again the opaque heaviness of our feelings and our arms.

Years ago it was customary among our families to close and lock the piano for several days when a relative or a friend of the household died. That prohibition made no sense to me, because music never seemed as natural a refuge as in those moments. I knew that there I would be able to disembark with all my baggage. And I would say to myself: "When I grow up, I'll never allow the piano to be closed and locked when someone dies." I understood perfectly that music spoke our pain best; that through music one could express it better than through those people, who mournful-by-courtesy, would come to give their condolences and whose very presence seemed to me an inadmissible intrusion. I had already discovered that, in grief or in joy, one is only "in tune" with music.

Since then I haven't known how to lock a piano or make a funeral speech. The dead whom we love dwell in us. The love we have for them makes them live in us, with their attributes and defects (yes, their defects: that part in every being that it's essential to know well, since it's the price one pays for the right to enjoy a possession completely). But since they only live in our life because we have lived in theirs, there is a moment, more difficult to endure than any other, in which we must abandon their dwelling and return with them, forever, to our own, already so inhabited. . . . And we say to one person, "That gesture that you would use to call me when I was a child, you keep on making it, I see it." And to another, "Your steps behind the door when you used to come early on my birthday to kiss me! Your steps, I hear them, although you don't open the door." This, in us, is eternity.

The dead are not dead except when their slightest gestures or steps are not perpetuated in anyone. Those gestures, those steps, can't mean anything to those who didn't love them. But it is precisely such details that echo in us, amplified, in a jarring way. The thought that one who has died loved us to the point of sacrifice can stay cold like an abstraction. But the memory of a little phrase ("Put the napkin here. Let her sit by my side; she has arrived today from Europe.") or the sight of a walking stick, is enough, if it takes us without warning, to make us start weeping.

These details acquire a value for us that the profane in no way recognize in them. "The profane" are all those who don't feel as intensely as we do the passionate preference that concentrates our attention on a given person. To speak of that person in the terms that our feelings dictate to us, isn't that, more exactly, to profane him? Or profane the feelings that he awakens in us since they are incommunicable? But is there any other way of speaking about that person without affectation? Can we pronounce empty, conventional phrases at the very moment when everything that is not a faithful expression of our emotions revolts us? And wouldn't silence for its part be a sin of omission?

Those to whom the memory of a gesture of a hand we have loved says nothing by itself carry with them, perhaps, the memory of other hands whose gestures move them with equal tenderness . . . Perhaps they may read their memories in ours. When Narcissus looks at himself in the river, the river looks at itself in the eyes of Narcissus. We're all made of the same substance. So close to one another without knowing it, without on occasion accepting it. United by our common human condition.

Speak today about the work of Virginia Woolf? But there it is, intact. It's not her work that has ceased to be. It's not her work that is departing from this world. When they told me this morning by telephone, "Virginia Woolf has died," I didn't think of that work.

Later when I read the papers with their reference to a river near Lewes (Sussex), I remembered that Virginia had a little house in that area, and I seemed to hear her: "Come! I'll show you my garden. I do the cooking myself. Does that matter to you?" I didn't have time to go, precisely because I thought I would have time. I didn't see that river that the papers talk about. I said to myself, "The next time. . ." And now there'll be no next time. Ever.

The telegrams are vague. Nothing precise is known yet. Not even whether she chose the day or the night for that last trip, for that *voyage out*.

Maybe it was while I was saying to the gardener that the red dahlias weren't as big this year as the yellow ones, or while I was scolding him for not fighting the ants more actively; or while I was playing in the casino, foolishly, my chips on number 11; or while I worried as I read the newspapers; or while I was laughing with the children at the beach. It was while I was thinking about something else.

Twice in these last days, I saw the Spanish translation of *The Waves* in the window of a bookstore and I stopped to look at it. The cover seemed to me to be in bad taste (green, with waves and rocks, to emphasize the title and attract the reader). I said to myself, "I'm going to write her. But right now she must have other things to think about." And, my God, what things!

Maybe it was while I was looking at that horribly common cover, saying to myself: "It's so unlike the contents of the book" (". . . maints diamants d'imperceptible écume"[1])! While examining that cover, I imagined her ironic smile if she were to see it. Many times I had thought, "She's probably as pretty as ever." But I didn't foresee that the austere and charming face that I had kissed the night of my departure twenty-one months ago ("The next time you come to London you'll have to stay long enough so that we can really talk, without haste"); that the face whose image I had wanted to preserve at all costs ("You know that I detest being photographed. What for?"); that the face, modeled by intelligence and reverie, whose charm didn't diminish even with the years and the weariness ("You're making fun of me! How can you say such foolish things?"); that that face was soon to be the face of a stranger whom we now don't dare to kiss goodbye for fear that it may take the place in us, for always, of the familiar person who responded with looks to our looks, with smiles to our smiles, and whom we'll never meet again, from now on, outside ourselves.

Mrs. Dalloway, Orlando, To the Lighthouse, A Room of One's Own, Flush, Roger Fry ("They've asked me to write this biography; it's so difficult to speak of a dead friend without running the risk of displeasing or hurting those who loved him") are there, on the shelves of my library, and in other libraries, in bookstores, translated into various languages. But her face?

What Virginia thought about the interior monologue or Kew Gardens, about Jane Austen or the sound of bells, about Elizabeth Browning's dog or the streets of London—that we haven't lost. One can buy it for three dollars. It's a veritable treasure that is still and always will be in reach of everyone ("When they have, dear Victoria, three dollars in their pockets," she would have added maliciously, "and when they don't prefer to spend it on something else, which would be more natural!"). In any case, we don't have to ask ourselves, like Clarissa Dalloway, moved by the suicide of that Septimus whom she didn't even know: "But this young man who killed himself—had he plunged holding his treasure?" We know that she has left us, of her own, the part she considered most important. But the other part? The part that Virginia was so stingy with? Her person? Herself? Where shall we find her again? ("But what do readers have to do with that? And don't try to make me believe they're interested in me in South America!")

But herself, coming down the stairs of her house at Tavistock Square ("Look! I've hung your butterflies there. Each time I go by I look at them"); herself, sitting at her table at teatime ("The maid has a sick child: measles. I'm alone. You'll have to excuse me if I give you a very meager tea," and everything was delicious); herself, showing me the walls of her room ("They're paintings by Vanessa"); herself, smoking at my side while the noises of London reach us muted ("They've been in that vase for three days, and look at them: still fresh. But I'm against your throwing your money away like that. You must keep the money for your magazine and your books. Do you know that we live off the Hogarth Press? Of course I like to look at these roses, to have them in my room; that's evident to you. But I'm going to get angry if you keep sending them").

Luckily, I never promised you, Virginia, to stop sending them. Because when I picked the flowers from a garden that you never knew and that was waiting for your visit, it is you to whom I'm sending them today, although they may stay in my vases, on my tables in America.

"Mrs. Dalloway, coming to the window with her arms full of sweet peas, looked out with her little pink face pursed in enquiry. . . ." Thus you would observe me if, from the place you're hiding, you could still look at things as from your door at Tavistock Square, with that passionate and impersonal curiosity, with that questioning that burned like ice and disconcerted those who approached you for the first time. Your door at Tavistock Square (number 52) where we would stop for a few final words; where in June of 1939 we said goodbye forever, without suspecting it. And you reproached me that day for having brought along Gisèle Freund so she could photograph you. You wrote me immediately afterwards: you didn't want to see anyone or have anyone photograph you. And I inflicted that displeasure on you. Those last hours that we were to spend together I wasted in argument. In spite of my joy at having obtained the perfect images of you, I wonder if I didn't pay too dearly for them. But I didn't know. It seemed so likely that I would see you again after six months to renew our conversation. And here I am, alone with your books. Alone and far — who knows until when — from that sky of Westminster in which Clarissa Dalloway thought she found something of herself; a sky so agitated these days that you wrote me: "*For the moment*, the house is still here." Maybe it's still there, intact; but destroyed for me. You must have already had your fill of those capricious houses that one can't count on. That disappear overnight. Those houses that, suddenly, no longer have beams or rafters, "poutres ni chevrons," like that of Cadet Roussel. Life itself doesn't offer more solid guarantees; it, too, is a house of Cadet Roussel.

Here I am, alone with your books.

Here I am facing Clarissa Dalloway. Once she had thrown a shilling into the Serpentine; Septimus Warren Smith, the young stranger, had thrown himself from a window. Clarissa felt a certain envy. The suicide of Septimus was, for her, an anguish. It was a penance to see a man or a woman disappear in the unexplored darkness and to remain there herself, standing in an evening dress.

Clarissa was horrified too by persons like Sir William Bradshaw, capable of what she called an *indescribable outrage*: forcing our conscience, forcing our soul. This kind of man was enough to make life intolerable.

What would have become of Mrs. Dalloway in a moment like this when the William Bradshaws try to impose their law on the world? Would she have known how to keep her *sang-froid*?

And besides, there was, for Clarissa, the terror, the unbearable inability to march serenely to the end with the life that our parents have given us so that we may carry it like a bundle, at times too heavy for our strength. Clarissa often said to herself that if she hadn't seen her husband, Richard, reading the *Times*, and if she hadn't been able to snuggle up in the warmth of that presence, she wouldn't have saved herself. Because "death was an attempt to communicate; people feeling the impossibility of reaching the center which, mystically, evaded them; closeness drew apart, rapture faded, one was *alone*. There was an embrace in death."

Clarissa felt that temptation to communicate through death. When Lady Bradshaw explains to her why she and her husband are arriving late at the dance (a client of Bradshaw, the poor crazy Septimus, has just committed suicide), Clarissa is upset: "Oh, in the middle of my party, here's death!" And that obsession pursues her. When she hears Big Ben strike, the sound repeats that a young man has killed himself: "But she did not pity him; with the clock striking the hour, one two, three, she did not pity him, with all this going on."

"With all this going on" I left Virginia one summer day in London. Virginia, very thin, in black, without powder, without rouge, without jewelry: infinitely lovely, the stamp of all her dreams printed on her face ("The next time we meet . . . But you come for too short a time to London . . ."). I left her at the moment when she was working on her *Roger Fry* ("It's so difficult to write about a dead friend . . .")

So difficult! One feels so much fear of displeasing, of betraying their most intimate wishes!

That's why I would have liked to have been able to limit myself to writing:

To Virginia Woolf —

Because I, too, looking for a phrase, found none to stand beside your name.

(From *Testimonios II*, pp. 415–428)

THE FOREST   1965 (and 1943).

"We can live a thousand centuries in
a moment, or spin out a moment across
unending years."
                              Adrien le Corbeau

One of the things I wanted to see most in the United States was the big
trees, the redwoods. The two varieties of sequoias, *gigantea* and *sempervirens*, are the only survivors of the glacial period. Some of these trees are
up to 4,000 years old and have an average diameter of from four to six
meters.

Due to unforeseen circumstances that shortened my stay, I had to
forego a visit that I had planned to Yosemite and Sequoia National Parks
and settled instead for Muir Woods, the forest named for the naturalist
and explorer of the region, John Muir. There I found trees 2,000 years old.
The afternoon spent in their shade—in 1943 during the war—remains
vivid in my memory.

I had lunched in San Francisco with Waldo Frank and his wife. It was
a luminous day like those of Mar del Plata in the month of March when
there is no wind to disturb the calm of that radiance. The trip from
California's loveliest city to the forest took an hour. We had to drive across
the Golden Gate, a prospect that delighted me since my appetite for
colossal bridges has never been satiated.

Approaching Muir Woods, I began to look more closely at the trees
that lined the highway. I thought I recognized two redwoods announcing
the proximity of the forest. When I told this to Waldo, he answered: "I
believe they're just some common pines or spruces." Thinking that a
North American would be better informed about these things than I, I
didn't insist, especially since that afternoon would be the first time I ever
entered a temple of sequoias. But I kept thinking as we went by that I
recognized that stiff and sharp-pointed foliage, so very deep and intensely
green, and that hard, reddish trunk.

In fact, on our way back, I asked if we could stop near the trees that had caught my eye on the way out. We then determined that they really were redwoods. Of the two Americans, one from the North and the other from the South, the South American had been the one to identify the species and variety. (Do you remember, Waldo?)

The truth is that it was not because I knew botany but because I knew a familiar face when I saw it. How could I not recognize a tree that had grown up with me at the quinta in San Isidro? Only as an adult did I learn that it was a sequoia *sempervirens*. For many years I had known by heart a tree whose name was unknown to me. It had been planted between two ombu trees whose inviting trunks were good for all kinds of childhood games and antics. One might even suspect that ombus not only lend themselves to these games but that they also join in them. For a child, the trunk of an ombu is very much like a gigantic animal that one tends to pat on its patient back as it docilely stretches out across the ground with a life of its own. In contrast, the other tree with an inexorably vertical trunk and needles that prick the tender flesh of the fingers, that other sullen tree was hard, distant, and indifferent. Small hands weren't able to extract any secrets from it—no gifts: no cones as from the pines, no little gold balls as from the *paraíso*,[1] no "black's ears" as from the *pacará*,[2] no fiber canoes as from certain palms, nor lots of small yellow or violet flowers (delightful confetti) as one collects at the foot of *tipas*[3] or *jacarandás*,[4] nor tiny pips like the ones from an oak when you take the cap from the acorn. The redwood didn't give anything apart from its austere trunk that would get red with rage if you scratched it and never seemed to be in a mood for fun. You couldn't take long strips of bark from it as from a tame eucalyptus. In a word, it had not been created for children—so given to touching whatever they see. Nevertheless, we dared to hang a Paraguayan hammock between one of its branches and a branch of the ombu. It took our boldness calmly, and we became friends.

On the way from San Francisco to Muir Woods, how could I not have recognized that towering, mute sentinel keeping close watch over his native soil just as he does in the garden by the barrancas of the River Plate? How could I not have recognized his taciturn and erect beauty? He used to offer such a contrast to the other soft and lazy friend who gathered together his roots above ground so that we could climb around them.

Poets have sung the praises of trees, but not enough in my opinion. I've never read anything that resembled the voices of the trunks, branches, and leaves that kept me company in my childhood with such unforgettable persistence.

I was six or seven when I entered a forest for the first time. It was in France. Which forest? I don't know. Probably the one in Fontainebleau or

Chantilly. A civilized forest, to be sure. It must have been autumn according to the smell that my memory retains (without being able to recreate it) and the soft sound of withered leaves that I still hear under my footsteps. My happiness and wonderment, my eagerness before this thing I had never imagined, filled my eyes and my nostrils. The crunching sound beneath my feet as they sank into it is still with me today.

I wasn't familiar with that kind of countryside. The flat plains of the earth, river, and sea, yes. But this was different. It was a little as if nature itself, after meeting me in its vastest scenery, suddenly locked me, key and all, in its bedroom. It became so intimate and palpable, so concentrated around my smallness, so close to me that its breath passed rhythmically over my joyful face. There, nature pressed itself against me, no longer leaving that space, that emptiness that had taught me to think of it as another version of the sky. The sea, the River Plate, the pampas with flax, alfalfa or wheat, created blue, green or golden oceans. . . . didn't they look like the sky to a child's eyes?

My first impression upon finding a forest, then, was one of wonderment. If it had been near me since birth, I wouldn't have noticed it; I would have had to rediscover it later as I rediscovered the River Plate and the Sunday Missal, too familiar not to become invisible; re-encounter it, rediscover it, as I re-encountered and rediscovered that mass of faceless water or those empty words. Suddenly they began to reverberate under the sun of surprise or sorrow. In my barrancas of San Isidro, the river was no more than a prolongation of something else: of the grass, of the willows, of the *tosca*,[5] of the mud; a prolongation of my eyes, of myself, no more important than my braids that brushed against my San Martín copybook when it was lesson time.

On Sundays — before the great disorientation or *dépaysement*[6] of sorrow made me see it differently — the Missal was merely a lifeless catechism that was pounded into me weekly: words and more words.

One day I was taken to a quinta in Martínez and through the trees, known to me as species if not as individuals, the river caught my eye. Not as a mass of water, but as "water," a thing of beauty. Its beauty emerged from the shadows in which custom had enveloped it. *Dépaysement* returned it to me. Had the river hidden from me until that moment in order to reveal better the power of its enchantment? Between other branches and other tree trunks, when it didn't seem to belong to me, it suddenly invaded my being as if I had never seen it before: "You looked at me every day without seeing me," it said. "I wanted to talk to you but you wouldn't listen. I would spy on you from behind every tree on the shore, but you didn't understand my game of hide-and-seek. And now the game will continue. Don't think it's over. Now and always, for centuries on end. I'm here before you and you hardly know who I am." That's how the river spoke the day I was startled by its unknown beauty.

And that's how, in the midst of youthful desperation, words that until that moment had had no meaning for me came out from the shadows into the implacable light of a complete *dépaysement*:

> Quare tristis es, anima mea, et quare conturbas me?
> Judica me, Deus, et discerne causam meam de gente non sancta;
> ab homine iniquo et doloso erue me.
> Emite lucem tuam et veritatem tuam . . .[7]

No longer were they just words. It was the Word. That light, that truth, that God—what game of hide-and-seek had they subjected me to? Was the test of that horrible *dépaysement*, the jolt of sharp suffering, necessary perhaps to make me see them and to make those dead words come to life and accost me with their brightness?

For two hours we walked through the redwoods. Not a ray of sun or even a bird penetrated the inside of the temple. Silence accompanied us. The dense silence of all those trees that had grown there, it seemed, for millennia without a bird's coo or warble.

Not just because of the atmosphere conveyed by the music, but also because it reminds me of my first forest, the first words of Golaud in *Pelléas et Melisande* ("Je ne pourrais plus sortir de cette forêt"[8]) has always made me shudder. I'll never be able to leave my first forest either. I've lost it outside of myself, like something separate from me, because it is part of me.

The shape of a leaf, the color of a bud, miraculously swollen with life on the bare wood of a branch, the talons of new-born ivy, delicate and ferocious—all the inexplicable wonders that nature sets before our eyes and that our glances slide over—explode at times like fire from a rocket. At that moment we think we have the key to the mystery, that we have captured it in the shout of forms and colors. But the premonition that we are on the edge of a discovery more important than the astronauts' trip to any galaxy fades away as if we didn't have sufficient strength to keep it lit.

Every single plant has its own attitude. Form and color are the expressions of this attitude which they translate. The spherical chestnut trees, the poplars as sharp as cypresses, the pyramidal spruces, the uneven ginkgos, the weeping willows and *aguaribay*[9] (each with its own lament), the palms like temple columns (with the happy sound of silk petticoats made by their fronds), the melancholy *casuarinas*[10] that sing like the sea (to exhale their sadness)—each of them speaks, in spite of their similar destinies, in a language of its own. Each one in its own way is a prisoner of the soul it is born in, happy or sad, and each one clamors with its branches toward heaven. They seem inhabited by characters that pronounce the same words in different ways. Surely the Arabs were thinking of this vegetal peculiarity when they insisted that trees were haunted by angels. There are different kinds of angels; Saint Augustine points out differences of morning and evening knowledge among them. In plants, there is also a morning and evening behavior (rather than knowledge), and some carry these vivid ways of being to an extreme. Some flowers open and others give their perfume only at certain hours. Like the mysteries of angels.

There are moments — very rare ones — when one sees, hears, and understands on a level that does not correspond to everyday life, on a level that surpasses in intensity that with which our senses have acquainted us. Almost as if the vibrations — either too slow or too quick — that escape our perception suddenly became noticeable. On these occasions we are left dumb, immobile, almost breathless even though we are not short of air. We enter a kind of interior silence like that of a blank page, ready to receive a word that cannot be foreseen.

That's how the forest struck me that first time in France. The use of my senses seemed to flow from it. I never had an experience of that sort again, not even among the *coihues*[11] of Nahuel Huapi or the redwoods of California. But that never-repeated experience continues within me. From that day, or rather that moment, I feel that I am always falling without finding solid land to block my fall. It is a fall into eternity. I'm falling, leaving only a trace of smoke (this stammering) that takes shape and then vanishes behind me, a perishable witness to an imperishable fire — to an unutterable ecstasy.

(From *Testimonios* VII, pp. 31–36)

GABRIELA MISTRAL AND THE NOBEL PRIZE
1945

So much sad news has come over this telephone in Mar del Plata since the beginning of the war (suicides, deaths) that it's a surprise to hear anything good. When someone calls long-distance and asks, "Have you heard the news?" the first impulse is to reply, "No! I prefer not to!" The world is emptying itself of friends. The distance and the difficulty of communicating physically—even when there are no ideological differences of opinion—is like a general rehearsal for that final absence.

This time, at last, it has to do with an event that we celebrate with joy. I doubt that those who haven't had the privilege of long talks with Gabriela Mistral will understand how delighted one can feel at the good news. Prizes tend to have poor aim, and they often miss the target. This time, the choice was a happy one. And although we can be justifiably no less proud of certain other American writers in the Spanish language, ones whose merits are known the world over, I see no one more worthy, all things considered, of receiving such a distinction.

I believe that certain prizes, like the Nobel Prize for Literature, should not be awarded—save in exceptional cases—to a writer solely for what he has put into his work. What a writer stands for, not only as a writer but as a particular specimen of humanity, should also be taken into consideration. Gabriela fills these conditions. Tagore filled them as well. Thus I feel that this choice has been a particularly happy one.

Gabriela's three great loves are, without a doubt, poetry, children, and the American continent. To be more exact: one zone of the continent. Especially that part where there's an abundance of Indian blood.

"I began to teach as a rural school mistress at the age of fifteen," she tells us. But teaching, for Gabriela, was not a trade, an ordinary means of earning a living. It was a vocation which fortunately could be harmonized with her perpetual concern for the destiny of Hispanic American people as well as with her literary talent. I shall not venture to say which one of these three passions seems strongest to me. At that level of intensity, it's too easy to be mistaken. And moreover, isn't poetry the necessary form that her other two loves assume?

246

I met Gabriela Mistral in Madrid in 1930. We had already crossed paths in other capitals. One of us would arrive when the other had just left. Finding oneself face to face for the first time with a person as unique as Gabriela who has such a captivating personality is an event that keeps echoing in one's life. I remember very particularly the first moments of that encounter. Seated beside her, examined by those strange green eyes, so unexpected in that beautiful face that seemed severe and immobile, I began right away to feel like a school girl caught making a mistake. What mistake? Gabriela hadn't opened her mouth and I already knew that she was accusing me of a crime whose unknown nature intrigued me. She didn't delay the revelation (because it was one): 1) Why was I born in the most cosmopolitan city of South America? 2) Why was I so "Frenchified?" and 3) Why had I ignored Alfonsina Storni (a writer with whom I had occasion to converse just once, by chance)? Disconcerted by these reproaches made in such quick succession, I didn't know where to turn. How could I defend myself when I didn't choose the place of my birth? As to my being "Frenchified," it, too, was the result of involuntary circumstances: my parents lived in Paris during my childhood and my education was entrusted to a French governess. In the matter of Alfonsina Storni, we had never had the chance to develop a friendship, nor did it occur to me to consider it indispensable.

These reproaches, which Gabriela fired at me seriously in spite of her sweet smile, could have easily irritated or shocked me since they were, at first glance, arbitrary and absurd. But such was not the case. I listened to the sermon meekly, with my mouth open. While she was talking, I decided: "It's incredible that anyone can be so magnificently unjust. This woman is generous even in her injustice." And I thanked Gabriela for having thought to make me the gift of her reproaches, for having judged me worthy of them. For not having waited to know me to talk to me so frankly. For having foreseen that the only thing that counted between us was the intention, not the possible error.

Gabriela had firmly made up her mind to make me a present of America. She had fantasies like that. In return she required that I give myself without reservation to America, a meager repayment. I suspect there already existed an understanding between America and me and that we had already anticipated her desires somewhat. Otherwise, would I have understood her so quickly? I doubt it. Gabriela cannot be deciphered or explained without the key that is this continent: hers and mine.

> . . . the shore you brought me to
> has sweet grasses and a brackish wind,

>the Atlantic ocean like a colt's mane
>and cattle like the Atlantic ocean,

she said in a poem that she wrote right here in my country home in Mar del Plata, whose trees she liked so much and where she came to spend a few weeks in 1937. April was arriving with its tranquil, transparent, and cool days, as often happens on this coast where marvelous and solitary autumns remain in the keeping of a small group of enthusiasts and of the regular inhabitants of the resort (who, having seen it too much, are perhaps less sensitive to it). Gabriela discovered the delights of this new landscape (we would drag her off to surrounding estancias; she didn't much like "going out"), and I discovered the ones inside her. It so happened that we also discovered, a few days before the seventh of April, that we had been born on the same day, if not the same year. To commemorate the date and the coincidence, she dedicated to me the poem I have just quoted, the original of which, scribbled in pencil, I kept so well that I've now lost it.

Gabriela quickly recognized that, in spite of my love for France, I was as fatally and irresistibly American as the most humble plant or the most common bird of the region, so she forgave me the place of my birth and the unerasable effect of my first years of training. She gave me her poem as if she were knighting me. Besides the pleasure, what a relief it was!

The fact is that, in Gabriela, the concern for her land and her race is intense and urgent. But this near-obsession has a very different meaning for Gabriela than for the nationalists of some countries in which this kind of self-worship en masse has wreaked havoc. Gabriela is proud of the Indian blood that mixes with Spanish blood in her veins; she is proud because she loves the Indians she is descended from and because she sees in this race today the disinherited of the earth. Children and the deprived will always be her true country.

>In the fields of Mitla, one day
>of cicadas, of sun and of travel,
>I bent over a well and an Indian came
>to hold me over the water,
>and my head, like a fruit,
>was in his palms.
>I drank what he drank,
>my face together with his,
>and in a flash I knew
>that the race of Mitla was mine as well.

Gabriela is still almost drunk with this recollection of her youth, drunk with those two faces she saw together in the limpid water. That gesture, that thirst, that sun, that coolness still survive.

I am beginning not to doubt this form of eternity. Gabriela is still in this room that was hers. She is eating blue and red figs from a plate that has a turquoise border. She speaks to me about the Valley of Elqui, about Mexico, the Midi of France. She gazes with me at the linden trees and the lambertianas whose shades of green contrast so happily. We are still in Cannes, facing a balcony through which the Mediterranean enters a room of the Hotel Miramar. We are in Nice next to a garden where one hears the wind among the phoenix palms.

> I am where I am not,
> in the silvery Anáhuac . . .

Don't we spend the greater part of our time this way? Being where we aren't, isn't it one of our principal ways of life? It seems to me that I have never stopped conversing with Gabriela and that her presence in me is more real than what I'm looking at or touching this very instant. I complain to her, the same as ever, about how thorny it is for us Hispanic Americans to handle Spanish. I tell her that, when we speak with Spaniards, they seem to think that we abuse their language and their patience as soon as we open our mouths, that we're an intolerable race of intruders, of grammatical truants and all that. She answers me: "A Spaniard always has the right to speak about matters of the language which he yielded to us and whose tail-end he continues to retain in his right hand, that is, in the most experienced one. But what do they want us to do? Much of what is Spanish doesn't apply to our people, places, birds, and plants compared with those of the peninsula. We're still their clients in matters of language, but now many of them want to take possession of the surface of the New World. Any attempt to invent will be grotesque; that of repeating from a to z what came over in the caravelles, equally so. Some day I must answer my colleagues on the subject of the tremendous conflict between being faithful and being unfaithful in verbal colonization."

I don't know how Gabriela has managed it, but it seems to me that she has already found, for her own use, a solution to the problem. To hear her speak, for example, is a miracle. Through her, one hears America. Words have a new flavor when she chooses and pronounces them. Gabriela "prend son bien où elle le trouve,"[1] with no hesitation and with no apparent effort. The most formal or pompous terms look like our everyday fare when Gabriela helps herself to them and changes them into part of her own language.

Gabriela believes that we Hispanic Americans were born in a monstrous fashion, with no infancy—in full puberty—and that the jump from Indian to European is capable of breaking our bones. Nevertheless, when we listen to Gabriela, that's no longer true. We forget that it might have been so. We forget everything except the pleasure of hearing the America she translates with such richness, serene rapture, and grace. And when she isn't with us, we continue to hear her if we think of her or read her work. She has left a rhythm in our ear which recreates itself in us when we evoke her. Gabriela can even use the most peninsular terms without their seeming that way. From the most traditional words come warblings that only emerge from the throats of American birds, or a foliage that can only extend its shade over American soil: the peninsula has become our continent.

Gabriela Mistral goes back to the problem of language in one of her recent pages (from *Ternura*): "Once more I take up here, knowingly, the original sin of verbal 'mestizaje' . . . I belong to the group of unfortunates who were born without a patriarchal age or a Middle Ages; I am one of those who find their insides, their face and expression disturbed and irregular because of the graft; I count myself among the children of that twisted thing that is called a racial experience, better yet, racial violence."

In different degrees, we all share the same adventure. But to hear Gabriela speak of her continent is to hear a branch blossom — if that entertainment were destined for the ear—when the sun leans on it with all its strength. The sun of America which is the same as Europe's, to be sure, but whose rays extract from each land the various things that are hidden, jealously, from any other master.

> I bid you farewell, and here I leave you,
> as I found you, sitting on the dunes.

The news that the Nobel Prize has been given to the author of *Tala*, published by *Sur* in 1938, finds me, after so many cataclysms, sitting in the same place. For an instant, I have the impression that nothing has changed since the day when Gabriela was walking across this lawn. But the children of her "Message" are no longer children. She wouldn't recognize them.

We can't pin down or hold back anything. That we know; philosophers and poets have been repeating it to us for centuries. Why do we always find it hard to accept?

The almond trees whose aroma you talk about, Gabriela—an aroma that each spring brings back to us ("The almond trees have arrived," says the voice of the breeze)—only bloom once for each of us, but their aroma floats eternally in our memory:

> An aroma comes, broken into gusts;
> I'm very fortunate if I feel it;
> it's so faint that it's not an aroma,
> but rather the smell of the almond trees.

> My senses become children again;
> I look for a name for it and can't find it,
> and I smell the air and the places around
> looking for almond trees I cannot find . . .

Gabriela, the "aubépines" inhaled by Proust that immersed him in a happiness he didn't know how to name or what to do with are the neighbors of the almond trees you describe. Believe me, it's not so far from Combray to the Valley of Elqui. My heart has measured the distance.

(From *Testimonios* III, pp. 171–181)

THE MAN WITH THE WHIP* 1955.

The very earliest memories that we have of our childhood have never seemed to me the result of chance, but rather of a choice dictated by our character, the nature of each person. They may even be a clue to our destiny.

No two people have the same fingerprints, and that difference is used by the police to identify us. Childhood recollections are, for me, the fingerprints that our character leaves on our memory; they have been closely observed by psychoanalysts to help them in understanding their patients. Siblings of the same approximate age, having lived through identical events in an identical environment and under identical circumstances, will remember different small details of the same events. And the small details are the true remembrances.

In the days when there were still many empty lots along Alvear Avenue, we would always go that way for our daily promenade because, as I later learned, my mother believed that even babies should be taken outdoors in all seasons. One day, returning from that systematic ventilation to which we were subjected, I saw something in one of those lots that suffocated me with shock and horror. A man had tied a poor, lame horse to a tree and was beating it violently with a whip. The animal struggled, reared up, and tugged in vain at the rope that held it prisoner. The man whipped it relentlessly. Slowly, our carriage left behind what seemed to me a spectacle of inconceivable cruelty. The incident was to stay imprinted on my memory; it was still vivid when the carriage stopped in front of the door of our house on the corner of Florida and Viamonte. Trembling, I insisted that my nursemaid let me go report the atrocity to the policeman on duty. Nothing else could calm my indignation. I had to say to the policeman, that uniformed man whom I knew punished the wicked: "They're beating a defenseless animal. Save him!"

The lot, the tree, the house, the house on the corner of Florida and Viamonte have all disappeared. The man with the whip, the nursemaid,

---

* A speech delivered to the Women's Council in Buenos Aires on November 9, 1955, under the auspices of The Commission to Abolish Torture. (V.O.)

the policeman have died. So has my mother, to whom I must have told the story. But that incident has not paled in my memory. It was my first major encounter, the first confrontation of my childhood, with the abuse of force. The repugnant idea of torture had reached me through the door of my eyes before I knew what to call it. I thought I had discovered it, and imagining that I was the only one to be horrified by it, I wanted to reveal that monstrosity to someone with sufficient power to prevent its existence.

Childhood, adolescence, and youth went by. The specter of the man with the whip and the beaten horse that was trying to break away reappeared under different forms, almost always artfully disguised. One fine day, brutally and unmistakably, the totalitarianisms of the left and the right appeared, culminating in the swastika outlined on the horizon. A storm of persecution and terrorism blew across the world. Of course, nothing is new under the sun, not even the atrocities of Hitlerism, from which, years later, we Argentines were to appropriate certain methods; without going as far as mass extermination, some of the same infamies were adapted on a small scale to the needs and tastes of those who tyrannized us. Nevertheless, each one of us has to discover what is new for him, though well-known by others, just as I discovered the existence of torture through childhood eyes. Therefore, it can also be said: everything is new under the sun as long as mankind is reborn in each of us. One after the other, we discover the same old things as if they never existed. And whoever does not discover them for himself cannot boast of knowing them. For such a person, nothing will be new under the sun.

We know that, since the world began, man has practiced cruelty, and, what's worse, he has enjoyed it. There have even been men of the caliber of Demosthenes and Aristotle who believed that torture was an efficient way of obtaining confessions. It was practiced by Greece, Rome, China, the world of the Inquisition (Torquemada alone had two thousand heretics burned), to mention only a few of the examples of brilliant civilizations that have preceded us. The most uneducated people are aware that, at a certain time in history, the custom of offering succulent feasts of human flesh to wild animals did not appall or infuriate anyone (except perhaps the ones being served as food). Nor was crucifixion a privilege exclusive to Christ. But since the end of the eighteenth century, the suppression of torture has passed from the status of a wish to that of an imminent possibility or even a reality. In 1789 it was abolished in France; in 1786 in Tuscany; in 1805 in Prussia; in 1816 a papal bull decreed its prohibition. In Argentina it was abolished in 1813, but that didn't prevent Rosas[1] from feeling exempt from the prohibition. I remember having questioned my great-aunts, who lived in the era of don Juan Manuel, about it. (We are related to the tyrant on my mother's side—a disquieting fact and nothing to be proud of.) I used to ask my great-aunts: "Were you very afraid? Did you wear red ribbons?[2] Did you see heads cut off? What were the *mazorqueros*[3] like? What did the watchmen shout in the streets?" The answers were never minute enough to satisfy me. That era seemed so remote! Another world! Such was the extent to which we felt we had left it all behind. A return to *that* seemed as impossible to us as meeting Cromagnon man on the street. That stage, we believed, was over in civilized countries. And suddenly, we were thoroughly disabused of the notion by the totalitarianisms of the hammer and the sickle, of the fasces, and the sinister swastika gleaming in a threatening sky. We had a presentiment, through clairvoyance or intuition, that under those stars, whoever was not on the side of the man with the whip would be fatally on the side of the animal tied to the tree. The technique of organized lies, the system of dominating the masses by playing to their lowest instincts, achieved, little by little, its most devastating perfection.

Hitler, at least, did not hide from attentive readers of *Mein Kampf* his satanic proposal, his strategic necessity to demean the human being. In that profession of faith, he tells that he had to laugh loudly when he read criticisms by the German intelligentsia of the speeches of Lloyd George, that great English demagogue, as he called him. The intelligentsia considered them intellectually and scientifically inferior, plagued with clichés, dull. But when Hitler read them, he declared them to be "psychological masterpieces." Through them, he said, Lloyd George had tried to exercise the greatest possible influence over the masses: "Looked at from this viewpoint, the speeches of this Englishman were the most wonderful achievements, as they gave proof of an astounding knowledge of the soul of the greatest layers of the people."[4] What disdain for the masses is contained in this observation! A disdain characteristic of all dictators. That disdain was matched by an equal measure of coldness in the face of suffering and human lives. And surely that coldness was worse in a man with imagination who had the passions of an ambitious and perverted maniac.

Even though the swastika cross, replacing the Latin cross, was rising over the old continent, not over ours, we already felt its psychological effects. Concentration camps began to operate over there and to make their innocent victims disappear. Five friends of mine were tortured in them and finally went to the gas chambers. The five were Jews. Two of them, writers, had visited our country: Crémieux and Fondane. Many people here refused to believe in such abominations and attributed them to anti-Nazi propaganda. In 1946 I was invited by the English to attend the Nuremberg trials. There I saw the shades made of human skin, the shrunken heads, the soaps made from what they could conserve of the fat of those exhausted human bodies. I saw films taken by the Nazis in their concentration camps. They were such that one only looked at them with one's stomach. The stomach received the impact; the brain was no longer recording. The only reaction was nausea.

The end of the war brought us the illusion that the world was going to change. But that happiness was dampened among us Argentines by the way in which we were prohibited from expressing it. Mounted police dispersed the most inoffensive demonstrations of joy with their galloping horses.

The mark of dictatorship, which we have all endured to a greater or lesser degree, is still too fresh in our memory to require a list of concrete details.

How many years had passed since the day I ran to tell the policeman —with unswerving faith in his protection and in his mission to aid the helpless victim—that someone was beating a horse to death in an empty lot on Alvear Avenue!

Nevertheless, those years must have slipped over me like the drops of dew over the leaves of the nasturtiums, without leaving traces, because one night, I was struck again by the same suffocation, the same rebelliousness, the same need to turn to an authority capable of imposing justice. The only difference was that now I knew there was no justice available, that when justice collapsed, so did freedom and individual security. I knew that now we couldn't count on anything but our own reserve of internal strength, our own spiritual energy.

Yes. One night I knew again the trembling I once felt before an empty lot on Alvear Avenue where physical punishment was being inflicted on a defenseless animal.

It was in Buen Pastor prison. We had just finished our not very appetizing meal and were washing the dishes. A nun warned us that two new political prisoners were going to join us that night. The news only pleased us partially; from the point of view of our small egoisms, we would have less space in our room. Moreover, we would have to accustom ourselves to sharing everything with two new fellow prisoners when we had just begun to adapt to a routine, to feel more at home, and to know each other better. But to compensate for those inconveniences there was the curiosity of talking to women who were coming from the outside world and would perhaps bring us news. Then too, we sympathized beforehand with any political prisoner. If I recall correctly, a nun told us that the "new ones" would probably be tired and hungry. I remember that we brought out clean plates and helped make the two as yet unoccupied beds. One of them gave us a lot of trouble because, try as we would to flatten the mattress, it had a big lump in the center, like a small mountain, and you rolled off to the right or the left when lying on it.

The two prisoners—one very young and worn-out with emotion, the other sixtyish and with an air of security that, whether feigned or authentic, was admirable — wore the same faded blue and white checked uniforms we all wore. It's hard, with this type of Buen Pastor "fashion," not to inspire a certain wariness in people when you first meet. Clothes tend to make the person. I know that one of the women, the younger, was frightened by me and wondered—not knowing what people she had fallen in with—what kind of villain this one was, so tall, wearing braids, and asking right away: "What's your name?" I wanted to cry and embrace her. That this could convey an unfriendly attitude proves to what extent the inhibitions of timidity make us, at times, translate our sentiments poorly.

One of the new prisoners invited us to share some sandwiches she had, asking us about our habits and customs. We welcomed each new arrival with fraternal solicitude, and our curiosity to hear what she might tell us about the course of events outside the prison was always intense. The day of my arrival, one of the nuns had warned me that it would be prudent not to talk too much with my future companions. (I only counted four at first.) But of course that kind of advice wasn't followed by any of us. How could it have been? Talking was the only activity permitted. We suspected that they could hear our conversations, especially at certain hours, but that didn't keep us from commenting abundantly on the misfortunes of our country in general and of ourselves in particular without taking very special precautions. Nonetheless, when we wanted to be sure of not being heard, we waited until the recreation hour to talk to each other in the patio where they hung the prison wash.

This time the arrival of the two new victims of the dictatorship brought us more atrocious certainties than we had foreseen or desired. The two of them had been tortured with the famous electric needle. We only dared speak of that in whispers. A mixture of rebelliousness and terror, of pity for the victims and horror for the perpetrators, electrified the room they kept us locked in, both day and night. As for me, it seemed that I trembled on my narrow iron bed with the same trembling as in my childhood when I had felt the brutality of the man with the whip as if he were beating me. Only now, I couldn't run to any guard or police chief, minister of justice or president of the nation. Now there existed no justice for those who thought freely and refused to adopt the dictator's doctrine. What's more, someone had declared it openly in a speech, which must be recorded in newspaper archives: for our friends, everything, she had affirmed; for our enemies, not even justice. This time, at least, the unsuppressible truth had erupted from the mouth of a woman who, by her own confession, believed fanaticism was a virtue.[5]

What could the nine prisoners who had been classified as enemies of the triumphant regime, expect? It mattered little that they only had the defense of free thought and free speech on their conscience. Such a crime demanded expiation. Three of the Socialists (for the first time, we told them kiddingly, *they* were in the majority: five out of eleven women — among whom two were Peronists, the rest were divided among Radicals and Democrats, and myself, who didn't belong to any party and was content to learn gentleness and passive resistance meditating on the message of Gandhi), three of the Socialists, I repeat, had been thrown into the Black Maria because they were crying as they watched the House of the People (the Socialist Party headquarters) go up in flames—that was forbidden. True, one of them was the sister of Pan (secretary to the Socialist representative Americo Ghioldi, in exile in Montevideo).

I don't know if those who haven't been prisoners can imagine what it means to find oneself lying at night in a bed, in the same prison, in the same room and very close to two women who have just been tortured. No great effort of the imagination is needed to understand the impossibility of thinking about anything else. One meditates on the fate of those victims with the kind of trembling from pity and indignation to which I have already referred, and one winds up asking: "Why wasn't it *I*?" This meditation does not induce sleep. From then on, whenever they called one of us for interrogation, the others anxiously awaited her return. The day they called me, the person who interrogated me began in these terms: "I've been charged with a disagreeable mission. . . ." I thought to myself: "This must be it." I confess that, at one point, I had the feeling that my legs were weakening, but the interrogation was no more or less bearable than the interrogations to which I had been subjected for hours when I had asked for my passport. The only difference was that now I lived day and night in contact with two women who knew with their flesh the electric needle of the Special Section. This was hard to forget.

Such things are perturbing in proportion to one's powers of imagination. Montaigne, well-versed in this, wrote in his *Essais*: "Je suis de ceulx qui sentent très grand effort de l'imagination: chascun en est heurté, mais alcuns en sont renversés. . . . La veue des angoisses d'aultry m'angoisse matériellement. . . . Un tousseur continuel irrite mon poulmon et mon gosier. . . . Je saisis le mal que j'estudie et le couche en moy."[6]

I think that being locked up in prison stirs even the most indolent imagination. Ours was collectively shaken two times in a most vivid way. One gray afternoon we were all sitting there on the benches or on our beds trying to kill time. After much insisting, the political prisoners, condemned to idleness, had been allowed to knit or embroider. I have no aptitude for any such work. Playing cards was forbidden. A game of dominoes was brought to us only shortly before my departure. Two or three books I had asked for were equally slow in arriving. Even the Bible, which I had requested the first day of my detention, took fifteen days to reach my hands, and I owe that to a good samaritan who felt sorry for me and smuggled it in.

Writing? We couldn't dream of it. They gave us very little paper, one pencil, and everything was subject to censorship.

One gray afternoon, then, we were killing time as best we could. I amused myself by watching the knitters and by thinking up variations to that well-known advertisement:

> The diligent grandmother knits
> With "la Religiosa" wool . . .

Naturally, I no longer recall whether or not it was a "grandmother" who did the knitting. But I do remember that we laughed over the silliest variations like:

> The diligent sheep knits
> With "misguided" wool . . .
>
> There's no "Religiosa" wool
> For a diligent convict . . .

Suddenly, we began to hear the sharp cries of a woman. They gradually became louder, louder and more horrifying. Those who were embroidering raised their heads from their work (Velia Robles, you were embroidering flowers on a tablecloth), those who were knitting stopped moving their hands as if the clicking of the needles might keep them from hearing clearly the screaming that was coming from somewhere in the prison. We looked anxiously at one another. Instinctively, we began to huddle together like a flock of frightened animals. What was going on? Why those cries? Where? Who? How? "Do you think they're beating her?" we asked each other. The cries went on for quite a while. Then, little by little, they became weaker and stopped. We stayed as we were, listening to the ominous silence. Those screams, whose cause was unknown to us, gave us chills. When the nun—flanked by two regular prisoners (one convicted of homicide, the other of infanticide, both of whom inspired our compassion) who helped her do her chores—when, as I said, the nun came in bringing us something to eat, we surrounded her immediately. What were those cries, we asked? She explained that some woman had had an attack of hysteria. No doubt that was true, but the commotion caused among us by the screaming took some time to die down.

We were thinking: "That's how they must scream when they're tortured." When one is in prison, each thing acquires unusual proportions and special meaning.

Another time, around four in the morning, those who were sleeping were awakened by a kind of religious chant. The voices of the nuns seemed to come closer and then fade away as if they were walking in procession through the corridors of Buen Pastor. It was oppressive and mysterious to listen in the darkness to that urgent invocation, that insistent call, in which the same inflections of voice and the same notes were repeated. In Latin, of course.

I breathed in that sonorous incense which transported me—as does all music—to another place. No longer did I feel myself a part of the dreary prison of Buen Pastor or of the prison of time and space to which our bodies condemn us. Fleeing from time and space, I entered the cathedral of voices that rose around me with its vaulted arches, its columns, rosettes, and saints of stone. I was shaken from this rapture by the noise of a conversation. Usually after eight in the evening, one only talked in whispers. A shout or a laugh ran the risk of provoking an immediate scolding. This time, one of my companions was speaking in a hysterical tone. It was one of the Peronists. Upon hearing the nuns' voices that night, she sat up in bed and, showing openly her agitation, she began to insist that the Church only sang those litanies to implore heaven when some public calamity occurred. It was a tradition. Therefore, something dreadful had happened in the city or was about to happen at that moment. Perhaps the burning of Buenos Aires. The woman in question had a daughter whom she adored, and she began to moan and cry thinking about that child and what could happen to her. We tried in vain to calm her down; her agitation only increased. If they set fire to the prisons, no one would think of opening the doors for us, she said. We would be burned alive, just like that. Gradually, the atmosphere of alarm spread as we continued to hear the litanies of the procession come closer and fade away. Our Peronist fellow-prisoner kept on prophesying that a great catastrophe was hanging over our heads, and we began to ask ourselves if she might have some valid reason for believing it. In prisons, anxiety easily becomes contagious. Finally, after hearing catastrophe predicted for the tenth time, another prisoner, a Socialist and a nurse by profession who had good sense and a quick mind, said: "And what's more of a catastrophe than the one we have now? Does it seem small to you?" It was a way of dissipating with one blow the state of collective apprehension into which we were beginning to sink. But I must confess that, at a given moment, imagining a city and a convent (ours) in flames made me break out in a cold sweat. Subsequent facts proved that my apprehensions were not so unfounded. When Sister Mercedes arrived at seven followed by the regular prisoner who always carried the enormous kettle of boiling *mate*, we asked her if something had happened and what the unusual, early-morning litanies meant. She replied that nothing had happened but, in fact, the custom of singing litanies three days before the Lord's Ascension had arisen centuries ago as a prayer for God's help during a public calamity. This ritual has existed, I believe, since the time of St. Gregory.

Afterwards, I have had in my hands a historical-liturgical study of the Roman Missal in which I found the litanies whose words I could hardly understand that night in Buen Pastor. And, at the end of a long invocation to the saints and martyrs—those who have suffered death, torture, exile, and prison rather than deny their faith—I found the words that, deformed by distance, had moved me by their accent, as if the accent were enough to reveal their meaning.

I read Psalm 69 [sic, 70], which was added to the litanies of the Middle Ages: "Let them be ashamed and confounded that seek after my soul. . . . Thou art my helper and my redeemer: O Lord, make no long tarrying."

And I read the supplication: "From anger, hatred, and all evil intent, deliver us, Good Lord." Always the same supplication transmitted from century to century: "Ab ira et odio et omni mala voluntate. . . ."

And today, outside the walls of that prison—an experience impossible to forget—I repeat: "From anger, hatred, and all evil intent, deliver us, Good Lord." And not only from anger, hatred, and the evil intent of which we may be the victims, but also from the rancor that we ourselves are inclined to feel toward our enemies.

Today, no reasonably decent person needs to be tortured in order to believe, to understand, that torture must be abolished, regardless of the crime that is being punished or the confession that is being sought or the criminal against whom this repugnant and inhuman weapon is directed. We are united here to proclaim that we do not admit torture of anyone under any pretext, not even for the torturers themselves. That would be to accept their methods, obey their satanic codes. But even though it's true that one need not experience torture oneself in order to want to eliminate it from the list of more or less secret customs, it is perhaps necessary to have seen a prison up close or to have been a "guest" in one in order to want passionately to reform, improve, and humanize the lot of prisoners. I don't know how things are in men's prisons, but in women's, it seems to me—and I could even say, it seems to *us*—that there is a great deal to reform. And it is a reform that we ex-prisoners must ask for and support, since we can speak of it with first-hand knowledge. We have rubbed elbows daily with women punished even for homicide. We were forbidden to talk to them, but we still exchanged some words and we observed them. We were all impressed more by their misfortune than by their perversity. I'm not saying that there aren't cases where perversity dominates: there are, perhaps, congenitally abnormal criminals, just as there are occasional ones. But those serious cases deserve special handling if it's true that we are real Christians and not simply pharisees. And if it's true that scientific advances can be put to use.

One afternoon I was sitting alone and not very happily in the prison patio. Three companions whom I liked very much had just been set free. Those departures were always emotional, full of shared happiness and poorly disguised tears. I didn't know that I was going to be freed a few hours later. My other companions were in the room where we lived; I, alone outside on a bench. A girl, one of the regular prisoners or an ex-prisoner who worked in Buen Pastor for the nuns and always cleaned the patio, passed by my side and whispered to me: "Don't be sad; you're going to leave soon." I answered softly: "Thank you, thank you." Then she went off in her faded uniform, wearing no stockings and scuffing along in her worn-out slippers. We used to give her (secretly because it wasn't permitted) some chocolates we would buy in the prison canteen. I was one of her principal providers. And yet she was happy about my departure. I don't remember her name, nor probably did she know mine, but I owe her one of the greatest gifts I received in prison. And I received many like that. There is one—the only one that took material shape—that I am wearing today. It is a piece of cotton with my name embroidered on it in green thread. The nuns had asked us to put a tag on our uniforms in order to identify them, so we decided to embroider our whole names and sew them on the uniforms where one generally puts the Legion of Honor. María Teresa González embroidered mine, and I have kept that little slip of cloth as a reminder of our marvelous sisterhood. We never suspected, before being in prison, how much that feeling could mean. Thus, we are always indebted for something to others, even to our enemies. Because it is to our enemies that we owe the possession of a treasure that they cannot take away from us: we have known one of the purest forms of human solidarity. And may I be allowed here to pronounce some names as in the litanies, the names of those who have lived this very rich experience with me: Susana, Nelly, Delia, Elena, Nélida, Ana Rosa, Isabel, María Teresa. And even the names of those who were not in prison for the same cause: María and Angelita, with whom we shared our confinement and our daily bread, which wasn't especially tasty.

We all know now what it's like to find oneself reduced to something similar to my horse on Alvear Avenue. Because there are and there will be in the world for a long time still to come—let's not fool ourselves—men with whips and tied-up animals, animals that rear up and wait, trembling, to be beaten. And also children who will read prophesies in empty lots without understanding that they tremble before an annunciation.

But let's not ever stain our hands with the whip or the rope. The whip and rope which have been for me, since my childhood, the symbols of torture and infamy.

(From *Testimonios* V, pp. 237–249)

ALBERT CAMUS   *May 1960.*

The veranda that surrounds my house is like the deck of a ship, a ship that sails amid all the greenness of the earth. It was summer. I was walking up and down that deck dictating. José Bianco was typing. I had just read — just discovered with enthusiasm — *Caligula*, the work of an unknown author. But I already felt I knew him. That was how I met Albert Camus in Mar del Plata, a place that he would never have time to visit—physically.

Caligula, his first play, written when he was twenty-five, appeared in *Sur* in March 1946.

In a copy of *L'Etranger* with twenty-nine etchings that Camus gave me in Paris in November of that same year, I reread this dedication:

Ce livre que n'explique rien—avec l'amitié qui resoud tout: celle du coeur. [1]
   1. *L'Etranger*
   2. New York
   3. Paris
   4. ?Buenos Aires, Août 1949
   5. ?

Number 4 referred to a trip that he planned to make to Buenos Aires. Number 5—a solitary question mark—is now, more than ever, a question: where? Is it possible that there exists an absurdity so perfect as for there to be no "where?" That road lined with plane trees and that twisted wreckage — can *they* be the only answer? It was raining.

The same year that *Caligula* appeared in *Sur* I was in New York where I saw the announcement of a lecture to be given by Camus. We had arrived in that city almost at the same time. Naturally I went to the lecture, but with mental reservations. Would the author be like his work, I wondered? The lecture and the tone in which it was delivered pleased me as much as what I had read by him up to that moment. And fortune decreed that my wishes were fulfilled: the author and his work turned out to be one and the same. Greeting the lecturer that afternoon ("I am your translator. *Sur*. Buenos Aires. *Caligula*."), I had the feeling this would be the case. In this sense, Camus is like T. E. Lawrence. Neither one went farther with words than he did with deeds.

We saw New York together, he for the first and I for the third time. He liked what he saw, though he used to get irritated. He would complain in a mockingly mournful tone that he always went around crying on the wide avenues and narrow streets of New York because of the "escarbilles" (tiny pieces of soot) that, according to him, bombarded the defenseless pedestrian and lodged in his eyes. As soon as he managed to free himself of one by rubbing his eye or taking the upper lid between his fingers and pulling it over the lower, he had to begin the operation all over again with the other eye. It was unbearable. I would laugh at his exaggeration, at his caricature of what sometimes happens in New York just as in any large city. Who hasn't blinked from soot at one time or another in the streets of Paris, I would ask him. The word "escarbille" became for us the symbol of our discussions and of the disadvantages of New York, which he felt more than I. "How are your escarbilles?" I would ask whenever we met, as one might say "How's your health?" But I never observed in Camus the allergy attacks that the massive accumulation of New York skyscrapers unfailingly brought on in some European writers and which became, at times, a chronic sickness. I recall having said to Camus during one of our first conversations — quoting Drieu la Rochelle's phrase, "le Français qui se refuse a la géographie."[2] "You're much more open to the world than most of your compatriots." To which he replied, "Don't forget that I'm also African."

Along Fifth Avenue, Broadway, Lexington Avenue, in the unpretentious *Child's* where we used to go for fried eggs and bacon (Camus avoided luxurious restaurants), in theaters and movies, we used to talk about everything around us, but we didn't always agree. One night I took him, practically dragging him, to see the play *Born Yesterday*, which had amused me so much and in which the irresistible Judy Holliday played the lead. Camus was so spectacularly bored by it that after the first act I decided, in annoyance, to walk out: "If you aren't amused by North American humor, I'm not amused by your long face." This type of bad upbringing, I thought, was characteristic of our best Argentine writers. It must also be common to Africans, more closely related to us, no doubt, than the French. I don't remember if I told him that when I got over my bad mood.

But it bothered Camus to think that he might have hurt me, however light the scratch. Later, he dedicated one of his articles to me, *Pluies à New York*: "En souvenir d'une ville que nous avons aimé ensemble."[3] The article ended like this: ". . . but yes, of course, I loved the mornings and the evenings of New York. I loved New York, with that powerful love that sometimes leaves you full of uncertainties and hatred: sometimes one needs exile. And then the very smell of New York rain tracks you down in the heart of the most harmonious and familiar towns, to remind you there is at least one place of deliverance in the world, where you, together with a whole people and for as long as you want, can finally lose yourself forever."[4]

That same year we saw each other again in Paris, barely recovered from the war. I met Francine, his wife, of whom I have thought so often these last months. I see her looking happy in that photograph taken at the reception in December 1957 for the Nobel Prize, alongside the Gallimards, smiling as she had ten years earlier when she and Camus witnessed with amusement my hasty and disorganized packing as I was about to leave the Hotel Crillon.

In a letter dated April 19, 1947 (I was still in Paris then), written from a country house in the Loire Inférieure, Camus said to me: "Je vis dans la peste."[5] He was also living among trees and admirable light, having found just the place to finish his book. The book was, of course, *La Peste*.

On June 13, 1949 Camus sent me good news: he was getting ready for his trip to South America. "Tout arrive," he added in parentheses. But he complained that "this unfortunate trip is ill-fated." He had just found out that they had prohibited the performance of *Malentendu* in Buenos Aires. This put him in a very difficult position, he explained: "I don't know if you will approve of my decision. It simply consists of refusing to go in any official capacity to Argentina and refusing to give advertised lectures there. Perhaps you will think me too sensitive, but it's not that. It just happens that I rarely go to eat in houses where one cannot talk freely. I hope to see you, as I think I will go to Buenos Aires on my own and in my own right to meet my friends." He added that he would come by boat since he had a "healthy horror" of airplanes. He hoped that I might be able to meet him in Rio, "neutral terrain." I couldn't. But when Camus arrived in Buenos Aires, he came to live in my home in San Isidro. One might say he almost never left it. There, on that less than neutral terrain, he saw old and new friends who wanted to talk with him. He didn't accept any kind of official invitations. Naturally he gave no lectures.*

How could this attitude seem exaggerated to me! It was an act of solidarity toward all Argentine writers opposed to the dictatorship, not just a protest against the censorship applied to his work. This was, after all, the man who had taken part in the underground struggle in France

---

* In an issue of the *Nouvelle Revue Française* (March 1960) dedicated to Camus, I read these lines in an article by Etiemble: "But who, besides you, would have refused to enter Argentina when Perón, aided by Evita, ruled there?" Camus came to Buenos Aires during Perón's regime. He came to see his friends, as I said, but he had no contact with the government. (V.O.)

against the Nazi invaders, the one who had been the author of the famous editorials in *Combat*. Camus knew perfectly to whom he was lending his support and why—here as in other parts of the world. And his support was always clear and open. He made no deals. Moreover, he understood very well that we were ripe for the symbolism of *La Peste* and that we were a country paralyzed by a growing plague, a plague that undermined our moral organism. And he understood that it would be difficult for us to straighten up and cure ourselves, recover our dignity, march without any more immediate hope than that of continuing to march, relearning the lost cadences. Camus realized all this as soon as he breathed the atmosphere of our country for a few days (I don't say "of our land" because that air doesn't change). This man who, as one of his friends said, "had taken upon himself the struggle against injustice as a personal matter," was not mistaken about these things.

After those days in San Isidro—imperfect days, but days of happy friendship—I saw Camus again in Paris. The last time it was raining. We ate in *Roma*, a little restaurant around the corner from my hotel on the rue de la Trémouille. I can still see his dripping raincoat, but I can't remember what we talked about. I thought that we would have time to go on talking.

That was at the end of 1956. Then, just this past January, I was planning to hop from New York to Paris to see friends. Camus had written me: "I am working for myself and trying to write the book of my maturity (don't worry, I feel younger than ever). It's a novel or something like that. But since now I don't impose limits on my nature, it is already very long and I'll have to spend a lot of time on it. I'm leaving Paris to go to work in the Midi or outside the country. If Argentina weren't so far away, I would have gone to visit you. I haven't forgotten San Isidro nor the peace I found there."

He was happy that I had finished translating *Les Possédées*, and he regretted that I hadn't been able to attend the performance in Paris: "The show was better than average, I think. Actually it was the realization of an old dream of my youth. The night of the opening I was very moved and alone with my emotion." He also told me that, if I had "l'humeur Sévigné," I should write him telling him what I was doing and what was going on here. What with the plans for my trip to the States, I didn't have the slightest epistolary itch. Besides, I thought that soon we'd be able to talk. I owe Camus a letter.

On January 4 I was alone reading in my hotel room in New York. It was already quite late. The telephone rang and an Argentine voice said: "I can imagine how upset you must be." I asked why. "Haven't you heard on the radio? Camus. . . ." The name and the tone of voice was enough. How? Where? After I heard the answers, we hung up.

It *would* have to have been there that the news reached me *pour boucler la boucle*.[6] They say it was drizzling that day on the other side of the Atlantic, there in France along a road lined with plane trees. "Et l'odeur elle-même des pluies de New York vous poursuit alors. . . ."[7] Was the smell of rain there with him? What must he have thought at that last instant? (In automobile accidents there must almost always be a last instant when one sees the catastrophe coming without being able to avoid it. That was my experience in an accident that could have cost me my life.) What must he have felt? Did he feel his possible death as a loss or a deliverance? Or as a losing himself that was itself a deliverance?

His absence leaves us all silent. So many times he was our voice, the one who said what we could not say as well as he.

That night in New York loneliness resounded:

> Homme infesté de songe, homme gagné par l'infection divine,
> Non point de ceux qui cherchent l'ébriété dans les vapeurs
> du chanvre comme un Scythe . . .
> Mais attentif à sa lucidité . . . et tenant clair au vent le
> plein midi de sa vision. . . .[8]

This is the way I have seen Albert Camus. This is how he will live inside me.

(From *Testimonios* VI, pp. 180–188)

HEROES WITH AND WITHOUT
SPACE SUITS   1965.

Thomas Mann's secretary, Konrad Kellen, has told how the great German writer particularly enjoyed listening to music by Wagner. Surprised by this, Kellen once asked Mann how it was possible that he, an anti-Nazi, and Hitler could have the same preferences. The author of *The Magic Mountain* answered: "There's nothing mysterious about that. Hitler is attracted by the nationalist element in Wagner, and I by the international element."

This can happen with books as well. Very different people are sometimes attracted by the same writer and interpret him in accordance with their own temperament.

There has been considerable argument about the personality of the soldier-author who carried out the campaign in Arabia during the War of 1914 and later secluded himself in the Royal Air Force, as if in a cloister, under the names of Ross and Shaw.

The argument continues. An article entitled "The Tragic and the Epic in T. E. Lawrence" just appeared in the *Yale Review* (Spring 1965). Its author, James A. Notopoulos, thinks that the epic and the tragic are Homeric qualities and that the most perfect example of this form of obsolete literature is *The Iliad*. The epic and the tragic, says Notopoulos, are not characteristic of our age. And yet, he affirms, our modern society has a unique representative of these qualities (since his work is unique) in T. E. Lawrence.

Lawrence has lately become the battling ground for psychological and literary analyses, an enigma that psychoanalysts or amateur followers of those methods try to explain in their own way. Notopoulos compares *Seven Pillars of Wisdom* to Xenophon's *Anabasis* and Caesar's *Commentaries*. He sees Lawrence as a Greek hero, and he assures us that whoever takes Lawrence out of that framework (especially if he takes him to Freudian terrain) has not known how to understand him.

The heroic world was the center of the interior and exterior life of T. E. Lawrence. Who can doubt that? Nevertheless, I don't believe it was the only thing that mattered to him. In this, my opinion differs com-

pletely with that of Mr. Notopoulos. Lawrence was an incredibly complicated human machine.

Notopoulos says that "no one more than Lawrence was conscious of
the absurdity and anachronism of the heroic act in the world of the
twentieth century." And he adds that we live in an "unheroic age," that
destiny launched T. E. on a "heroic way of life" in an age in which such an
attitude lacked meaning.

This I don't understand, or else the words mean something different
to me. One could say that the form in which heroism manifests itself in
man has changed, but that's all.

Citing Gilbert Murray, Notopoulos says: ". . . [the Heroic Age]
provided a combination of rare dangers and rich chances, of indescribable
terrors and bewildering hopes, in which, amid the crumbling of external
protections, a man had to stand or fall by what he was really worth, by his
fighting power, his courage, his strength of will, and the degree to which
he could either make his fellow men follow him and his friends love him
and die for him, or, if need were, himself follow and love and die." I don't
see why one can't say the same thing today. We live in the midst of rare
dangers and unexpected chances. Many external protections have crum-
bled. Man must stand or fall according to who he really is and what he is
really worth. It might seem to a superficial observer that in our century of
transition things don't happen that way: false values triumph, and no one
cares a bit about those Lawrencian virtues appreciated in remote times.
But Mr. Notopoulos ably points out that even if the epico-tragic is the
quality that constitutes the greatness of Homer (in the past), wherever it
reappears again in literature thereafter (as an anachronism), it captivates
human hearts.

In spite of how much the motion picture (in which Lawrence is
portrayed by Peter O'Toole) disfigures and betrays the character of the
protagonist, it has awakened a very special interest—at least in Europe
and the United States. People who have never read Lawrence's books
want to know them. Responding to this demand, Professor A. W. Lawrence, T. E.'s younger brother, authorized a pocket edition of *Seven
Pillars*; a similar edition was published in French translation.

If we are living in such an "unheroic" century, to what can we
attribute this curiosity? A 338.171 would not be necessary when an 007 is
within reach. Why the interest in Lawrence of Arabia—so complex and
difficult to interpret—when James Bond (Bang! Bang! Kiss! Kiss!) is there
with his sex appeal and violence in the person of that magnificent animal
Sean Connery (no slight to his talent intended; I refer to his physique)?

Violence is fashionable. If it's spiced up with sex appeal, then there's
no more appetizing dish. This mixture was repugnant to Lawrence. In

spite of the fact that we live in a century that no longer understands the epico-tragic and heroism (according to Mr. Notopoulos), and in spite of the fact that Lawrence lacked those attractions that bring in hundreds of millions of dollars to the Bang! Bang! Kiss! Kiss! of Ian Fleming in complicity with that irresistible Scotsman (I enjoy those pictures and was one of the first to point them out), Lawrence captivates hearts.

A few days ago, I received a letter from the Peruvian author Mario Vargas Llosa. I had written him with regard to his book *La ciudad y los perros*, which surprised and truly interested me. The backdrop of this novel is the Leoncio Prado Military Academy in Lima. In my letter, I told Vargas Llosa that his book had reminded me of the time when I was translating *The Mint* and that my familiarity with that work by Lawrence helped me a great deal to enter into contact with his. In summary, without there being any describable similarity to speak of, there was a bond between the English youths and those of the Peruvian military academy. The countries were very different and so were the eyes that observed them, however. . . . Mario Vargas Llosa answered me in a letter I have kept, telling me he was proud that *La ciudad y los perros* had reminded me of *The Mint*, a book he had read and admired five years earlier. It made me very happy to know that young and talented South Americans appreciate Lawrence.

In a letter to Mrs. Bernard Shaw, Lawrence writes that his years in the barracks have taught him that mankind is heading toward the supremacy of the flesh. The sensual and the sexual prevail, he says, and since he lives apart from those things, he will undoubtedly be looked upon as weird. True and not true. The influence Lawrence exercised over his companions (those in the barracks didn't know his true name) was remarkable. Both in the RAF and in the Arabian campaign, the men who lived near him felt, after a short time, that he was the leader, that he dominated them, even though he did nothing to place himself above them.

What made him—the unknown called Ross or Shaw—take charge of the RAF recruits or the African tribes of the desert is the radiation of something that Bergson called "spiritual energy."

In the latest issue of *Correo* published by UNESCO, Alexei Leonov tells us of his first steps in space. On the cover of the review we see his two legs and feet supported by nothingness. The picture of the Soviet cosmonaut suspended in space, "dénoué de l'humain,"[1] and only tied to Voshkod II by the umbilical cord of a cable that allows him to communicate with his companion and with the earth, is a moving sight—to me, a nightmare. There's that man floating, liable to "tomber pendant l'éternité"[2] if one single calculation is incorrect. He tells us that he had so much faith in his space suit and in the instruments installed in the space craft that *he was not afraid*. That was all I was missing for my admiration to be complete: a bit of fear.

"Le silence éternel de ces espaces infinis m'effraie . . ."[3] said Pascal, without imagining that someone would someday plunge into that silence. When the cosmonaut, the first traveler in those infinite spaces, recognizes the Black Sea or the Caucasus beneath him, he doesn't feel frightened of the incommensurable silence that surrounds him. For the cosmonauts of the Soviet school, he explains to us, their equipment holds no secret. They know exactly how it's going to function in every given situation. Why be afraid in such circumstances?

Perhaps those who are subject to such a technically delicate and complicated test have no time to be afraid. But faced with all that wonder, it would have seemed completely normal to me to have felt a bit of common, ordinary fear as well as a great deal of amazement. (I suppose that the American astronaut wasn't afraid either.)

A well-known French professor (who is no cosmonaut), referring to the advances of astronomy and the space flights preparatory to a landing on the moon, said to me: "Pascal would no longer be able to write his famous words about the eternal silence of the infinite spaces he feared." I looked at him disconcerted and disappointed (he's an intelligent man). For me, these words have never had more validity.

Victor Hugo says the same thing in another way:

> Nous ne voyons jamais qu'un seul côté des choses,
> L'autre plonge en la nuit d'un mystère effrayant.
> L'homme subit le joug sans connaître les causes. . . .[4]

Do we know the causes? It has just been announced that Mariner IV, a space laboratory, will travel a distance of 520 million kilometers to approach and get a glimpse of Mars. Then it will transmit the data it gathers to earth. Not only is it admirable; it's incredible. These miracles of science—that is to say, of man—fill us with pride and respect. But what are the earth, Mars, the moon, Venus, and the sun? Very little compared to what lies beyond.

The silence of the stars in the desert made Lawrence feel ashamed of his smallness. I cannot help wondering what he would have felt faced with that other silence, the one that Leonov and White, prisoners of their space suits, have known.

I don't believe that more courage is needed to go out and meet the most powerful army than is needed to go out of a space craft into weightless space. One can only call those who have risked their lives to do it heroes (heroes in this age without heroism). Yet we are so hungry to know what they have felt and seen that we can't resign ourselves to the fact that they aren't writers too. If they had been, they would have fulfilled a double mission: that of using a photographic camera to film their *exterior* movements as cosmonauts, and that of being themselves a photographic camera that records the *interior* movements of man launched into the unknown. The man with his human and conscious frailty who goes, nonetheless, where the hero in him commands.

I know it's asking for the impossible. That's why Lawrence's case has almost no parallel. Cosmonaut of the rebellion in the desert, he was also the photographic camera that filmed the battle and recorded the beats of his own heart.

For reasons of this kind, *Seven Pillars of Wisdom* is a unique book.

(From *Testimonios* VII, pp. 113–118)

THE LAST YEAR OF PACHACUTEC
July 1975.

"All the leftist parties of the world are concerned with the proletariat, with the sub-proletariat, with decolonization. And women? There is no reason, it would seem, to be concerned *specifically* about them."

"My adversaries often used against me the fact that I was a woman. Too often, for our masculine colleagues, lawyers of the female sex are before all else women practicing men's games. And I did not want to be *a woman who litigates*; I wanted to be *a lawyer*. Just as a man is called *a lawyer* and not *a man who litigates*. It took a lot to get them to admit it. . . ."

Gisèle Halimi, The Cause of Women

One frequently hears of women who, because they happen not to be men, live on the border of the territory that would otherwise be theirs. I was the guest of one of those women a short time ago in Madrid. On the last of our happy days together, we went to a bookstore (don't we always?) on a street that, if I remember correctly, bears the name of her father: Ortega y Gasset. I was looking for something I didn't find. Instead I was attracted by a tempting work by Ferdinand Anton, published in Leipzig, *La femme dans L'Amérique ancienne.* Copiously illustrated, the book interested Soledad as much as it did me. Its beginning didn't disappoint us: "The art of ancient America begins with a portrait of an unknown woman; and it was with the help of another woman whose name history has preserved, Malinche, later called doña Marina, that Cortés succeeded in conquering a large part of Central America." It seems that an Indian chieftain made a gift to the Spaniards of twenty women, among whom was Malinche. With a clinical eye, the conquistador selected her as his mistress and interpreter. So says Bernal Díaz del Castillo.[1] Men are not slow to take advantage of such good opportunities. At a glance, Cortés was aware that this girl had abilities, intriguing possibilities, which his companions in adventure evidently lacked.

The fact that she had been offered to the invaders as an object by those of her own blood released Malinche, in our judgment, of all obligation to them. But I doubt that she had any notion of how degrading the treatment she received was. It was simply *a custom*. Few people insist on examining the reasons behind a custom, good or bad. They accept it just as a shopper puts on a ready-to-wear dress. For Malinche, it wasn't, surely, a problem of conscience to leave the inhabitants of the south of the Gulf of Mexico and go off with the invaders, just as it probably didn't surprise her too much that the lover "to whom," says Bernal Díaz del Castillo, "she devoted herself" should give her the kind of treatment that, in developed countries, is generally reserved for a domestic animal. The fact is that one day Cortés passed her on to another Spanish gentleman without blinking an eye.

We already know that customs are implacable as long as they prevail, and if one disdains or ignores them, one must pay a price that may well range from scandal to the death penalty. Malinche seems to have struggled against the customs only obliquely, in a discreet way, by showing herself to be more efficient than the majority of those proud, white Spaniards.

This question of customs has its good as well as its tragic or ridiculous side. To give a trivial, contemporary example, the first women in Argentina to drive automobiles were met by a deluge of street insults. This didn't discourage them. Nowadays, no one stares at women drivers, and even the few nuns that one sees around these days drive. I hope for no greater tribute to our cause than that no one will take notice of us when we come to occupy positions reserved until now for men (except where now inconceivable laws govern: those of hereditary kingdoms); it should be a natural phenomenon, like getting behind the wheel of a car.

Upon taking home and leafing through the book that attracted me that Madrid day, I thought about the fact that in this "Women's Year," * Malinche's name had not even been mentioned—at least as far as I knew. By making a very brief commentary on *La femme dans l'Amérique ancienne*, I shall try to correct this grievous omission.

Malinche was born in a little village near Coazacualco where they spoke both the Aztec and the Mayan languages. She considerably facilitated the victory of her helmeted lover. "Without her," according to Bernal Díaz, "we would never have been able to understand the natives of

---

* Heinrich Finke, one of the most eminent medievalists of this century, begins his work, *Die Frau im Mittelalter* (The Woman in the Middle Ages) (1913), affirming: "Nothing reveals better the singular position of the woman in history than the fact that one can speak of the history of women. If we used the term "The History of Men . . . in the Middle Ages" we would note without hesitation the surprising nature of this expression. Universal history is the history of men and their evolution. Only as an accident does the woman and the history of her evolution appear." This is exactly the impression one receives upon hearing talk of the Women's Year decreed by the United Nations. It simply confirms the state of inequality in which women have been kept. (V.O.)

New Spain." Malinche went out of her way to understand the Spaniards. The *godos*[2] didn't take the same trouble with the natives; what's more, they have always been hostile, I suspect, to any living language that wasn't their own. I am, of course, referring to the majority of them.

In love — or whatever Pre-Columbian Americans called sentiments or instincts that began with the rib and the apple — with Hernando Cortés, Malinche preferred above all else to serve that powerful foreigner, sparing no effort (I cite Bernal, changing his vocabulary). And her love was important since, from it, was born her collaboration. Ferdinand Anton notes, somewhat ashamedly, that today only an extinct volcano carries the name of that American woman.

He shouldn't worry. The idea of the volcano seems an excellent one to me. Extinct though it may be, it has a countenance that is lacking in bad statues of bronze or marble, surrounded by plants and devoured by municipal insects, in South American plazas. Right now I would sign a petition to see that, in the year 3000, monuments destined to commemorate outstanding women would be forests, lakes, islands, tended gardens, valleys. What better name for the Valley of Elqui in Chile than that of Gabriela Mistral? But I suspect that, for the moment, only undesirable atmospheric turbulences will be baptized as women.

The author of the work I refer to makes a discerning observation: "If, in the most ancient sources, women were already apparently reduced to a secondary role, the reason is that the principal authors of these works were priests. Nevertheless, it is possible to reconstruct the jobs and customs of women in everyday life thanks to the Florentine Codex of Sahagún and the chronicles of the Peruvian Indian, Poma de Ayala."

No doubt, doña Marina found a way to learn Spanish and serve as a translator with as much efficiency and more important results than the women who fulfill the same function today in the United Nations. At the beginning of the conquest of America, interpreters were a commodity of prime necessity. They were scarce. Malinche was a bargain for her Hernando Cortés and, through this concubinage, for the crown of Spain.

The Aztecs evinced a notion of values which our western civilization has not shared, as exemplified by the following: a woman who gave birth was, by that fact, equal to a warrior. Custom dictated that the midwife let out a war cry to celebrate a child's arrival into the world. The same honors were accorded to a woman who died in childbirth as to a warrior killed on the battlefield. But let's compare the deed of one with that of the other: to give life, to take away lives. This is not an attack on the virtues of the army. God forbid! It is simply a *weighing*.

As still happens in our civilized countries, the Aztec woman, upon marrying, passed from one dependency to another: first the father, then the husband. In one of my articles, I have commented on the poet Countess de Noailles's cult of Napoleon, and I pointed out that her association with this cult was enough to classify her as an antifeminist. I'll clarify for those who don't know the following details; the compilers of the Napoleonic code stipulated in their preparatory works: "Woman is handed over to man so that she may bear his children. She is, then, his property, as the fruit tree is the property of the gardener." The spirit of this code — insofar as it concerns questions categorized today as sexist, just as one might say racist—could not be closer to that of the Mussolinis and the Hitlers.

Engels said: "In the family, the man is the bourgeoisie, woman the proletariat." That remains a self-evident truth. Whoever has the money generally has the right to dictate, since economic power creates a hierarchy *sui generis*. A known fact. An independent woman, thanks to her work, can have a type of relationship with a man that is infinitely more valuable: love based on equality of rights and responsibilities. I don't believe that a fruit tree-gardener relationship is healthy for any couple.

In Pre-Columbian America, according to the chroniclers, virginity was either highly prized or else it didn't matter, depending on different superstitions (customs). Among Aztecs and Mayas, the discovery that an engaged girl wasn't a virgin was sufficient motive for annulment. The same grounds for annulment were suggested in the year 1935 in our Argentine legislature by the gentlemen entrusted with a regressive reform of the civil code. Needless to say, they did so with a Pre-Columbian mentality. Since, of course, men are of a superior essence, they wouldn't be subject to the same requirements. Or so I was told by one of the legislators, although he didn't use those words. "It would be legitimate for the man to protest," I remarked, "if there were deceit involved. Deceit always warrants annulment. However," I added, "slaves almost always deceive. Only free beings learn to despise a lie."

Let's go back to Ferdinand Anton. The Chorotegas and the Nicaraos had a system of laws that was quite advanced in matters of rape. Whoever raped a girl was condemned to work for the family of the victim for the rest of his life. They were a utilitarian people. These Indians, sensitive to weaknesses (or ferocities), did not, of course, resort to capital punishment. In my view, the crime of rape deserves a cage in a zoo. But those people probably didn't have either one or the other.

According to Angela Davis, the leniency that men show toward rape, if it doesn't happen to their daughter or their wife, comes from being tied to the social and political function that grants supremacy to the man. Davis writes: "In the past as much as at present, cultural sexism defines rape not as a crime against the woman but as an offense that affects whoever dominates her, father or husband. . . . The woman is doubly a victim. First by being raped; second, because this crime is not considered a serious one unless it is endorsed by men of power. Rape, then, is an assault against the man as proprietor of such-and-such a woman, not against the woman herself." Considering that Angela Davis is black, she must have seen or heard about a great deal of abuse. I believe what she says is right.

Since through paternal descent I am from Cuzco, I was pleased to read that in the Empire of the Incas, the woman was duly appreciated as a member of the work force and a guarantor of the reproduction of the species. She owed duties to the state and she received, in turn, protection equal to the man's. I wonder if as much could be said for our Christian and democratic republics.

Nevertheless, there's no doubt that the men were victorious after death. The Chibcha princes left for the other world accompanied by their wives and servants who used to be immolated in their honor. Only men were accorded such pomp on the American continent. One single and more modest exception is known, however. A Jesuit chronicler testifies that in a town in Mississippi in 1704 a woman of high rank died leaving behind a husband who didn't belong, as she did, to the nobility. He then was strangled so that he might have the privilege of sharing his wife's destiny. For the Natchez of the Mississippi Valley, there was no doubt that this was an enviable lot. Customs.

Ferdinand Anton assures us that, in the age of the Spanish conquest, people remembered that, after one of the most violent earth tremors known in Arequipa, the sister-wife (as in Egypt) of the Inca Pachacutec successfully directed, in the absence of her husband, the rescue and support of the region. But when the Inca himself was present and there was some disagreement between them, she prostrated herself at his feet and stayed in that position until, his rage passed, he ordered her to rise.

Will it forever be necessary that there be a state of emergency or that the master be absent for her to be able to demonstrate her ability? I rather think that we have arrived at a point at which the signal to rise will only be tolerated by the canine race. Therefore, in spite of my skepticism about the practical results of this Women's Year, I think that it's not far from being the last year of Pachacutec. Except, of course, in such fastidiously patriarchal countries as Uganda.

(From *Testimonios* X, pp. 39–46)

WOMEN IN THE ACADEMY* 1977.

I congratulate us — first you members of the Argentine Academy of Letters, then us women — for the decision you have taken to include a woman among your members. I congratulate you first because *motu propio* you have conquered a prejudice, and that always requires effort. I say *motu propio* because, although we women have campaigned for the vote and for other rights we have not shared with you men, I have not heard of any campaign to gain entry to the Academy. So you haven't yielded to pressure. This is a historic fact within the context of what the Academy means to the culture of our country. It shows that this institution has a sense of justice that others like it have not shown. The French Academy could have had the good fortune to open its doors to Colette, whose handling of the language was masterful, but it did not do so. Thus it is *you* who have taken a step that even the nation that symbolizes refinement in the arts and letters has not taken.

I suspect that the honor I receive today has fallen to my lot indirectly. An accumulation of years is often confused with venerability. It's a superstition that tends to disappear in a world dominated by youth; in time, a new one will replace it. In my case, the old one was still functioning.

Perhaps my appointment was also influenced by the longevity of the review *Sur*, founded a few months before the Academy itself. Forty-six years is a long time for a review and a short time for an academy. (The one Richelieu founded dates from 1635.) The abnormal survival of a purely literary review testifies to a massive dose of stubbornness. I don't know if it's a virtue or a vice, but *I* am responsible for that part. Let's also point out something that I know better than anyone. As much as to me, the review belongs to all those who have worked on it and made its survival possible. Therefore, the compensation I receive today is exaggerated as far as I am concerned.

Another explanation must be added to the above: whatever I have

* V. O.'s speech upon being received on June 23, 1977, as a member of the Argentine Academy of Letters where she occupies the chair named for Juan Bautista Alberdi, Argentine statesman and author, and contemporary of Sarmiento.

done for the review and the publishing house I have done for pleasure, not out of what my philosopher friends would call a categorical imperative.

Please don't think that this introduction is meant to be a show of false modesty. I have never resorted to that cheap tactic. I'm as aware of my faults as I am of my talents.

Let's come back to what is most important on this occasion: the possibility of qualified women participating in the Academy. Some of my present colleagues will recall that I was invited to join this institution several years ago. I refused. I refused because I considered myself little suited to its activities, just as I refused an ambassadorship that was offered to me by Bonifacio del Carril. I don't have the disposition of an academician or a diplomat. I'm a self-taught woman and a *franc-tireur*[1] in the land of literature. These characteristics come from having been born at the end of the Victorian era; it was a tremendous handicap for a woman.

Why, then, you will say, have I accepted now what I didn't accept a few years ago. Because I became convinced that my refusal might momentarily block the entrance into the Academy of other women who I feel are more qualified for the position. Why, you will insist, do I think I might have blocked their entrance? As I said earlier — superstitions.

The next to the last time I saw Malraux, I went to his home in Verrières-le-Buisson with a mission I knew would fail. Three academicians had entrusted me with the task of trying to convince my friend to enter the French Academy. I knew the author of *La Condition Humaine* and his honorable manias, so I had no illusions. When I had exhausted all my arguments, he looked at me ironically and said, "I'm amazed that you should waste so much eloquence trying to persuade me to accept something that you in your own country didn't accept." I answered that I had changed my mind for the reasons I have just given you. He replied, "*Those* are valid reasons. But I don't have even one." I did not insist. Thus ended my diplomatic mission in Verrières-le-Buisson.

I hope I have clarified my reasons for entering this Academy. Let's put an end to this part of my short speech.

When I was young, a friend placed a work of Alberdi's in my hands urging me to read the works of my talented compatriots. I was reluctant to read Spanish and I remained so until I met Ortega y Gasset. In those days I was engrossed in French and English literature, which were almost our Greek and Latin. I'm not ashamed to say that I still live with them today.

The friend I mention was not a writer, but he was an intelligent and sensitive reader. He tried to create an atmosphere in which the inclination of what he called my vocation might develop. He tried and he succeeded. Without his enthusiasm and encouragement, I would have lost more time than I did in an environment that was adverse, or at best, indifferent to my interests. The growth of plants depends not just on the plants themselves but also on the soil that nourishes them. Everyone knows this law. And I shall take advantage of the opportunity to warn you that my writings abound with truths of this caliber. Courteline used to call them, in jest, "des vérites premières."[2] I never set out to surprise, only to explain, because it's the best way to analyze things for oneself. And I am an eternal student.

In reference to this (the mania I have for explaining), I will take as an example one of my first adventures in the world of letters—an anecdote I've told before. The six hundredth anniversary of Dante's death was approaching. I had begun my contributions to *La Nación* with an article about Canto XV of the "Purgatorio," and they had asked me for another. But I had embarked on something more ambitious than a brief newspaper essay, and I dared to climb the steep staircase of the National Library to take some pages of my manuscript to the gifted Cerberus who guarded that fortress. An imprudent idea. Groussac proved to be mistaken, not in his skill and judgment as a critic, but with regard to my aims and desires. He wrote me a letter that I have kept along with another, later, and more rewarding one that was written after he heard me recite "Le Roi David." *That* pleased him. In his first letter, he said that too much had already been written about the *Divina Commedia* and that unless I had some unpublished information or an original interpretation, it would be better to let it be. He then applied a mustard plaster to me, thinking that it was a necessary evil: he used the word "pédantesque" in French, with all its satiric resonances, and he advised me to write about something more within my grasp, something more personal.

At that moment, his harsh criticism of Auguste Rodin's "Sarmiento"[3] didn't occur to me; except for obvious distances, it would have comforted me. But I was an unskilled apprentice and didn't have the right to reply in the way the French sculptor did: "That's how I see him." And I was crushed. Something personal? This man didn't realize that nothing was more personal for me at that time than the *Divina Commedia*. It was part of my self-education.

I almost decided to throw the notes I had accumulated over months of reading into the wastebasket. Luckily, my friend who was not a writer succeeded in calming me down when he learned the contents of the letter. I remember his words: "Since when are you intimidated because a gentleman, who may know a lot but doesn't know *you*, dictates that you shouldn't write about a poet who appeals to you? Do you answer by giving up right away? You'll never get anywhere that way. I don't recognize you! Why should you care if he says it's pedantry if it's not?"

Actually I was certain that my commentary of the *Commedia*, good or bad, didn't bear the slightest relationship to pedantry. Groussac's diagnosis was incorrect in that sense. I had peered fervently into a world that a *temperament* (I underline temperament) similar to mine had discovered in the depths of his being. I, too, was lost in the woods. In Dante, I had found what my equilibrium craved: a poet concerned about the laws and the meaning of life. In other words, a philosopher poet.

Groussac was a great prose writer, but he lacked the clear-sightedness needed for a case like mine, situated, strictly speaking, beyond the frontiers of literature—in a spiritual zone that is linked with poetic genius. W. H. Hudson observed that "Darwin . . . apparently did not possess the ability to 'read' men with the same miraculous intelligence that he applied to his investigations" of another kind. Groussac's case was similar, and it gave his intellectual honesty a sharp cutting-edge.

La Divina Commedia, according to T. S. Eliot, provides a complete scale of the peaks and abysses of human emotions. I understood this intuitively and headed straight for it. What could that have to do with pedantry?

Dante's encounter with Cacciaguida in the circle of Mars and what he says there about "il coraggio della verità" is a passage of the poem that can remain engraved on a young reader who discovers it at an opportune moment:

> . . . Tutta tua vision fa'manifesta;
> E lascia pur grattar dov'è la rogna!
> Chè, se la voce tua sarà molesta
> Nel primo gusto, vital nutrimento
> Lascerà poi, quando sarà digesta.[4]

Without prolonging the list of my memories, you will understand that my reaching the Academy under Alberdi's protection is like following a road that was laid out from the beginning just for my footsteps. It's not strange that I should keep very much in mind those who had faith in me—those like my great-aunt who was a friend as well as the daughter of a friend of Sarmiento's. In my childhood and adolescence, she prevailed upon me to study languages, thinking that along with my love of reading, they would give me the key to marvelous secrets. She put those keys into my hands.

In a speech upon being received into the French Academy, Roger Caillois said, ". . . you know that I arrive from farther than usual and have had to travel an abnormally long distance. . . ." I could say the same, and with greater reason.

To address you as custom requires on occasions like this allow me to follow Groussac's advice: "Speak about your life." I shall also follow the example of an author to whom Saénz Hayes, a distinguished member of this Academy, has devoted an extensive study: Montaigne. For certainly, within myself, I know no subject other than the one that essayist used: "Je suis moy mesme la matière de mon livre."[5] I thus depart from what is supposed to be a classic speech of acceptance into the Academy. But you, by receiving me, by receiving a woman, have also departed from the norm.

Virginia Woolf has written that until a short time ago women students could not tread the lawns of the great English universities, reserved for men. This will give an idea of the distance that a woman a little younger than Virginia had to travel to arrive at Alberdi's chair in 1977. In 1934, I dedicated the first volume of my *Testimonios*, published by the Revista de Occidente, to Virginia. She had encouraged me to write even without knowing exactly to whom she was charging such a delicate task. She didn't read Spanish. But she wanted women to express themselves in any language, in any country, and about any subject, however trivial or vast it might seem. In my dedication, I said to her: "You say it is important for women to express themselves *in writing*. You encourage them to write *all kinds of books, hesitating at no subject*. . . . You find that men's books inform us rather imperfectly about them. In the back of our heads, you say, there is a spot the size of a shilling that we cannot see with our own eyes. Each sex must assume the responsibility of describing that spot for the benefit of the other. We women, therefore, should not show ourselves ungrateful. We should repay men in kind."

Not to hesitate at any subject, however trivial or vast it may seem, was exactly my thought. In 1924, Ortega y Gasset published my first endeavor, my commentary on the *Commedia*. I shall never forget the way he extended his hand to me.

To return to Virginia—she and I agreed perfectly about the place that women should occupy in literature. She achieved that place. And today, when her work is so often studied, no one questions her feat. Her triumph comforts me, as does that of Emily Brontë, lost in the moors of Yorkshire, who never knew the fate that awaited her books. She was not one of those who enjoyed public recognition during her lifetime. But it was not essential. When human beings are truly individual, recognition or lack thereof doesn't change them.

The Nobel Prize didn't change Gabriela Mistral, who was half Indian and was born in the Valley of Elqui. This Chilean woman, a schoolteacher in her youth, was one of the most mysterious, attractive, stubborn, and noble figures I have ever known. I mention her today because she represented America in a very special way that few have been able to match. In 1937, she spent her entire visit to Argentina in my home in Mar del Plata. After a few days, she wrote me (we would write from room to room): "You have done me a great deal of good. I needed to know, *to know*, that an entirely white person could be genuinely American. You cannot fully understand what this means to me." And later she added: "I was enormously surprised to find you as criolla as I." I took Gabriela to several estancias near Mar del Plata during that autumn, and together we looked at plants, stones, and pastures. In Balcarce I showed her some *curros*, spiney bushes covered, in March, with little white flowers that smell of vanilla. The curro is considered a national plague. Nonetheless I like it so much that when it blooms, I always pay it a visit. After her departure, Gabriela wrote me: "I still see you with the stones, pastures and little animals of our America. Even if you weren't so noble or superior, I would see you that way; . . . Do you remember that magnificent bush that was at the estancia you took me to and from which you had some branches cut? I see that geometry of thorns, that look-at-me-but-don't-touch, that machine-gun of silence. . . . That could be *you* (and *I* was that way too at times), at least that's the way I think of you. Because that plant, also disconcerting, is truthful, and what ties me to you most is your truthfulness. Your culture and so on, I can get from others in Europe. Your truth and your vital violence, only *you* can give me. It's the most open-air American style there is." I know Gabriela believed that. It's the only letter of recommendation I want to offer you.

After Gabriela died, I found out something that would have given her even more of a surprise. I used to accuse her, half-jokingly, half-seriously, of being a racist. She had a passion for the *inditos* (dear little Indians, as she called them), and she felt herself a part of them. What I discovered was that, on my mother's side, I am descended from Domingo Martínez de Irala, a companion of don Pedro de Mendoza, and a Guaraní Indian woman, Agueda. This Spanish man and this American woman had a daughter whom her father legally recognized as his. Given my feminist "prejudices," I sympathize more with Agueda than with the one who spoke to the founder of Buenos Aires on equal terms. This is not a demagogic stance. I am as incapable of demagogy as I am of pedantry. But in my capacity as a woman, it is both an act of justice and an honor to invite my Guaraní ancestor to this reception at the Academy and to seat her between the English woman and the Chilean. Not because she deserves, as the others do, to enter an Academy of Letters, but because I, for my part, *recognize* Agueda.

This has nothing to do with literature, you will probably say. No.

Though perhaps it has something to do with inherent justice and with poetry. Or so Virginia's fantasy would have imagined. And so would Gabriela's passion, as when she wrote in her "Saudades":

> On earth we shall be queens
> and of a truthful kingdom . . .

For this "truthful kingdom" to exist, we need some ideas and attitudes that Agueda was not aware of, nor, most certainly, was the Spanish conquistador. The "truthful kingdom" will be born out of great patience. And my most fervent wish is that a woman never accept a position for which she is not qualified or one which does not coincide with her authentic personal aptitudes. That's why I insist on pointing out that my presence here is the result of my eagerness to remove barriers, nothing more. That is also why I repeat these explanations. If one is to be queen, one must reign truthfully.

And so I have made my confession to you. It's the only thing that I think appropriate under the circumstances. I bring with me today three women because I owe to them something that has mattered in my life. To one, a portion of my existence. To the others, in part, my not having been content just to exist. The one who would be most astonished if he could see us here today would be Domingo Martínez de Irala.

In a letter of petition sent to the conquistador in 1556 by a navigator, a certain Bartolomé García, from Asunción, García said: "Worthy sir: this is to bring to your attention how much I have worked and served in these lands." I, too, have worked and served as a navigator of other voyages in these not always peaceful lands. Four and a half centuries had to go by after Irala lived before I was allowed—before we women were allowed—to tread the lawns of universities.

You, my dear colleagues, know this. And you know that changes are taking place everywhere. The world is adapting to a new reality, one that can no longer be denied, one that will benefit you as much as it will us women.

(From *Testimonios* X, pp. 13–23)

CHAPTER NOTES

Notes pertaining to the ten volumes of *Testimonios* (including the fourth volume, *Soledad Sonora*) will be cited by essay title, volume number in roman numerals, and page. References to other works by Victoria Ocampo will indicate title and page only. For a complete citation, see the Bibliography following these notes. Any translations in the following quotations are mine, unless otherwise indicated. Ellipses within brackets indicate omissions made by me; other dots are part of the text cited.

Preface

1. *Le Nouvel Observateur* (November 29, 1976), p. 85.
2. From a letter of Camus to V. O. dated January 22, 1953. (Unless otherwise noted, personal letters are cited from original copies.)

Chapter One

1. In *The Lost City of the Incas* (New York: Duell, Sloan and Pearce, 1948), p. 59, Hiram Bingham, the discoverer of Machu Picchu, mentions "Captain Baltasar de Ocampo, a contemporary Spanish soldier who went to the Vilcabamba Valley after gold a few years later and prepared an account of the province." Captain de Ocampo apparently lived in Cuzco in the sixteenth century and wrote a chronicle that has since been translated into English: *The Execution of the Inca Tupac Amaru*, ed. Sir Clements Markham (London: Hakluyt Society, 1907). Although the genealogy on the Ocampo side of V.O.'s family has not been traced back farther than the eighteenth century, it is more than likely that this soldier-turned-scribe was one of her ancestors.
2. R. B. Cunninghame Graham, *The Conquest of the River Plate* (London: Wm. Heinemann Ltd., 1924), p. 84.
3. *Habla el algarrobo*, p. 52. The Sound and Light performances at the chacra were widely acclaimed, but when Perón returned to power in 1973, he ordered them stopped.
4. "La trastienda de la historia," *Sur* (Sept.–June, 1970–1971), p. 9.
5. "Prilidiano en San Isidro," IX, p. 87.
6. Domingo Faustino Sarmiento, *Facundo* (Mexico: UNAM, 1957), pp. 258–259.
7. John J. Johnson, *Political Change in Latin America: The Emergence of the Middle Sectors* (Stanford: Stanford University Press, 1958), p. 98.
8. James R. Scobie, *Argentina, A City and a Nation* (New York: Oxford University Press, 1964), p. 173.
9. "Racine et Mademoiselle," II, p. 172.
10. "And So Shall I Have Mine," II, p. 507.
11. *Ibid.*, pp. 504–505.
12. From a personal note to the author (January 1977).
13. "Lecturas de infancia," III, p. 13.
14. "Historia de mi amistad con los libros ingleses," II, p. 200.

15. "Carta a un joven poeta norteamericano," VII, p. 169. Victoria recently took issue with something Virginia Woolf wrote in a short essay titled "A Sketch of the Past." According to Woolf:

> These then are some of my first memories. But of course as an account of my life they are misleading, because the things one does not remember are as important; perhaps they are more important. If I could remember one whole day I should be able to describe, superficially at least, what life was like as a child. Unfortunately, one only remembers what is exceptional." (*Moments of Being*, ed., intro. and notes, Jeanne Schulkind. New York: Harcourt, Brace, Jovanovich, 1976, p. 69.)

In Victoria's opinion, the moments we remember, whether exceptional or not, are the ones that tell us most about ourselves.
16. "El reinado de las institutrices," VI, p. 50.
17. *Ibid.*, pp. 46–50.

Chapter Two

1. "Al margen de Gide," *Domingos en Hyde Park*, p. 51.
2. Norman Kiell, *The Universal Experience of Adolescence* (Boston: Beacon Press, 1964), p. 490.
3. "Emily Brontë (Tierra incógnita)," II, pp. 115–116.
4. Katharine Rogers, *The Troublesome Helpmate: A History of Misogyny in Literature* (Seattle: University of Washington Press, 1966), p. 189. See Chapter VI of Rogers' book for a detailed discussion of the nineteenth century literary heroine.
5. "Racine et Mademoiselle," II, pp. 182–184. English translation from *Phaedra* (Act IV), trans. Bernard Grebanier (N.Y.: Barron's Educational Series, Inc., 1958), p. 65:

> "So black a lie might justly make me hot
> to tell the truth, my lord; but I suppress
> the secret touching close your honor. If
> my lips are sealed, commend my reverence.
> I do not seek you should augment your woes —
> but think you what my life has been, and what
> I am. Great crimes are wont to follow on
> the heels of lesser crimes. Who breaks the law
> will end by violating sacred ties,
> for crime, like virtue, has its own degrees.
> There is no man has ever yet beheld
> shy innocence become extremest vice
> in one quick move. One day will not suffice
> to turn a virtuous man to murderer,
> or traitor cowardly incestuous.
> A breast heroic, chaste, it was, which gave
> me suck. I never yet belied my blood.
> I do not wish to paint myself in boastful
> portrayal, but allow some share to me
> of virtue, father, and concede I've shown
> most notably abhorrence of those crimes
> imputed now to me."

6. "Las memorias de Victoria Ocampo" (selecciones), *Life en español*, (September 17, 1962), p. 68.
7. *Idem.*

8. "Una visita a Victoria Ocampo," (An interview by Fryda Schultz de Mantovani), VIII, p. 298.

9. Waldo Frank, *Memoirs of Waldo Frank*, ed. Alan Trachtenberg, intro. Lewis Mumford (Amherst: University of Massachusetts Press, 1973), p. 165.

10. Adelina del Carril de Güiraldes in *Testimonios sobre Victoria Ocampo*, ed. Hector Basaldúa (Buenos Aires: 1962), p. 141.

11. "Las memorias de V.O." (selecciones), p. 68.

12. Her earliest poems date from 1906. From then until approximately 1909 she wrote sometimes two or three a month. Titles include "L'Idéal," "Fleur étrange," "Chopin," and "A Musset." Many are included in her letters to Delfina.

13. On this subject, see José Luis Romero, *El desarrollo de las ideas en la sociedad argentina del siglo XX* (México: Fondo de Cultura Económica, 1965), especially Chapter II, "El espíritu del centenario." Also see James R. Scobie, *Buenos Aires, Del centro al barrio, 1870–1910* (Buenos Aires: Solar, 1977), pp. 274–275.

14. There is evidence to support this in a novel called *Xamaica* by Ricardo Güiraldes in which a character named Clara Ordóñez, based in part on Victoria, confesses to her lover, Marcos Galván, that she married blindly and left her husband because of "the tragedy of brutality." Güiraldes began writing the novel in 1917 when he and Victoria were close friends. She gave him permission to use one of her letters to him in the novel; it is not in this letter, however, but in another section where the reference to brutality is made. See Güiraldes, *Obras completas* (Buenos Aires: Editorial Emecé, 1962), pp. 290–291 and p. 300.

15. From a typescript, in French and signed "R. Levillier," in V.O.'s possession.

16. "Una visita a Victoria Ocampo," VIII, p. 297.

17. "Pasado y presente de la mujer," VII, p. 238.

18. "Malandanzas de una autodidacta," V, pp. 19–20.

19. David Viñas, *Literatura argentina y realidad política* (Buenos Aires: Editorial Jorge Alvarez, 1964), p. 277.

20. "Al margen de Ruskin (Algunas reflexiones sobre la lectura)," I, p. 60.

21. *De Francesca a Beatrice*, p. 27.

22. "Babel," I, p. 52.

Chapter Three

1. *El viajero y una de sus sombras: Keyserling en mis memorias*, p. 68.

2. "Algunas cartas de Ortega y Gasset," *Sur* (Sept.–Oct. 1965), p. 1.

3. *Idem.*

4. For a detailed discussion of this trend in Latin American intellectual history and the reaction against it, see Martin S. Stabb, *In Quest of Identity* (Chapel Hill: University of North Carolina Press, 1967).

5. "Malandanzas de una autodidacta," V, p. 21.

6. "Palabras francesas," I, p. 33.

7. "Algunas cartas de Ortega y Gasset," p. 2.

8. "Azorín o primores de lo vulgar," *Obras completas de José Ortega y Gasset* II, 5th ed. (Madrid: Revista de Occidente, 1961), p. 168.

9. *Idem.*

10. Julián Marías, an eminent Spanish philosopher and a disciple of Ortega's, makes note of this in *Acerca de Ortega* (Madrid: Revista de Occidente, 1971), p. 118, as does Barbara B. Aponte in *Alfonso Reyes and Spain* (Austin: University of Texas Press, 1972), p. 113.

11. Ortega, "Epílogo" to *De Francesca a Beatrice*, pp. 125–126. The epilogue was later given the title "Influjo de la mujer en la historia" (The Influence of Woman in History) in

an amplified second edition of Ortega's *Sobre el amor* (Madrid: Editorial Plenitud, 1963), pp. 13–41.

12. Ortega, "Epílogo" to *De Francesca a Beatrice*, p. 128.
13. *Ibid.*, p. 141.
14. For a discussion of Weininger's theories in the historical context of changing approaches to the female character, see Viola Klein, *The Female Character: History of an Ideology*, intro by J. Z. Giele, 2nd. ed. (Urbana: University of Illinois Press, 1972), pp. 53–70. In V.O.'s personal English edition of *Sex and Character*, one finds her comments "False! horribly false!" written in French with a red pencil all over several pages.
15. Ortega, "Epílogo" to *De Francesca a Beatrice*, p. 153.
16. Ortega, "Esquema de Salomé," *Obras completas* II, p. 361.
17. Ortega, "Epílogo" to *De Francesca a Beatrice*, p. 156.
18. Ortega, "Vitalidad, alma, espíritu," *Obras completas* II, p. 473.
19. Ortega, "Epílogo" to *De Francesca a Beatrice*, p. 147.
20. *Ibid.*, p. 161.
21. *Ibid.*, p. 169.
22. *Ibid.*, p. 163.
23. "Contestación a un epílogo de Ortega y Gasset," I, p. 202.
24. Ortega, "La poesía de Ana de Noailles," *Obras completas* IV, p. 433.
25. "Ana de Noailles y su poesía," *Sur* (July 1934), p. 32. The lecture was published in its entirety in this issue.
26. Virginia Woolf, *A Room of One's Own* (1929) (New York: Harcourt, Brace and World, 1957), p. 36.
27. From a letter by V.O. to María de Maeztu, January 21, 1934.
28. Stabb, *In Quest of Identity*, p. 69. Stabb discusses Ortega's visit and the Argentine writers influenced by him; those writers included Martínez Estrada, Carlos Alberto Erro, Eduardo Mallea, Canal Feijóo and H.A. Murena. An interesting collection of essays on the subject of Argentina's search for identity is *Argentina, análisis y autoanálisis*, ed. H. Ernest Lewald (Buenos Aires: Editorial Sudamericana, 1969).
29. Ortega, "Epílogo" to *De Francesca a Beatrice*, p. 165. Ortega also expressed his view of the Argentine people in a 1924 essay titled "Carta a un joven argentino que estudia filosofía," *Obras completas* II, pp. 347–351.
30. Ortega, "El hombre a la defensiva," *Obras completas* II, p. 648.
31. Ortega, "Por qué he escrito 'El hombre a la defensiva,'" *Obras completas* IV, p. 73.
32. Ortega, "Pidiendo un Goethe desde dentro," *Obras completas* IV, p. 406.
33. "Quiromancia de la pampa," I, p. 147.
34. *Ibid.*, p. 153.
35. *Ibid.*, p. 154.
36. "Aporte de Victoria Ocampo," *La Nación* (Buenos Aires), November 5, 1976.
37. From a letter written in Madrid on February 19, 1930, reproduced in V.O., "Algunas cartas de Ortega y Gasset," p. 7.
38. From an undated letter of Ortega's, in *Ibid.*, p. 3.
39. From a letter by Ortega written in Paris on March 23, 1937, in *Ibid.*, p. 11.
40. From *Gitanjali* (LXXXVII) in *Collected Poems and Plays of Rabindranath Tagore* (New York: Macmillan, 1962), p. 32.
41. *Tagore on the Banks of the River Plate* (translated into English by V.O.) in *Rabindranath Tagore: A Centenary Volume* (New Delhi: Sahitya Akademi, 1961), pp. 28–29. (Also published in Spanish with slight modifications as *Tagore en las barrancas de San Isidro.*)
42. Henri Bergson, "Life and Consciousness" (a lecture delivered in England on May 24, 1911) in *Mind-Energy Lectures and Essays*, trans. H. Wildon Carr (New York: Henry Holt and Co., 1920), p. 32.

43. "Prefacio y confesión" (for the special issue devoted to Gandhi), *Sur* (Jan.–Dec. 1975), p. 6.
44. "Testimonio sobre Gandhi," VIII, p. 25.
45. *Tagore on the Banks of the River Plate*, pp. 33–34.
46. Krishna Kripalani, *Tagore, A Biography* (New York: Grove Press, 1962), p. 135.
47. *Tagore en las barrancas de San Isidro*, p. 47, ("una dulzura avasalladora").
48. Kripalani, *Tagore, A Biography*, p. 316.
49. *Tagore on the Banks of the River Plate*, p. 43.
50. Rabindranath Tagore, "The Indian Ideal of Marriage," in *The Book of Marriage*, ed. Hermann Keyserling (New York: Harcourt, Brace and Co., 1926), p. 119.
51. *Ibid.*, p. 121. An earlier lecture by Tagore, entitled "Woman," written during the First World War, shows that he felt the war was the result of a too-masculine civilization and that women as "guardians of individuals" should assert their "divine vocation," not through feminism but through "putting the full weight of the woman into the creation of the human world," in other words, by "feminizing" the world, exerting women's values. See Tagore, *Personality: Lectures Delivered in America* (London: Macmillan, 1917), p. 169–181.
52. Kripalani, *Tagore, A Biography*, p. 316. Most of the poems of *Puravi* were inaccessible to Victoria because of the language barrier until many years later when Kshitis Roy translated some of them into English, at her request, so that *Sur* could issue a Spanish translation by Alberto Girri, called *Canto del sol poniente* (1961), to commemorate the centenary of Tagore's birth.
53. Reprinted in Apéndice I of *Canto del sol poniente* (Buenos Aires: *Sur*, 1961), p. 53. Another version in English by Kshitis Roy, totally unlike this one by Tagore, is also reproduced in the volume to illustrate the difficulties of translating from the original Bengali.
54. Kripalani, *Tagore, A Biography*, p. 138.
55. Quoted in *Ibid.*, p. 318.
56. Quoted in *Ibid.*, p. 319.
57. A prose translation from the Bengali quoted in *Ibid.*, p. 317.
58. *Tagore on the Banks of the River Plate*, p. 40.
59. Quoted in Kripalani, *Tagore, A Biography*, p. 345.
60. (V. O.), "Antimemorias," VII, p. 283.
61. "Prefacio," to *Jawaharlal Nehru: Antología* (Buenos Aires: *Sur*, 1966), p. 18.
62. "Mi deuda con Ortega," V, p. 44.
63. Virginia Woolf, *Orlando* (New York: Harcourt, Brace, Jovanovich, Inc., 1956), pp. 197–198.
64. *Ibid.*, p. 214.
65. Hermann Keyserling, "My Life and Work as I See Them," in *The World in the Making* (New York: Harcourt and Co., 1927), pp. 7–8.
66. *Ibid.*, p. 11.
67. Hermann Keyserling, *The Travel Diary of a Philosopher*, Vol. I, trans. J. Holroyd Reece (London: Jonathan Cape, 1925), p. 26.
68. "Quiromancia de la pampa," I, p. 148.
69. Keyserling, *The Travel Diary of a Philosopher*, p. 43.
70. *Ibid.*, p. 32.
71. *Ibid.*, p. 49.
72. *El viajero y una de sus sombras*, p. 28.
73. *Ibid.*, pp. 32–35.
74. *Ibid.*, p. 30.
75. *Ibid.*, pp. 36–37.

76. Hermann Keyserling, *America Set Free* (New York: Harper and Brothers, 1929), pp. 540–541.
77. *El viajero y una de sus sombras*, p. 53.
78. *Ibid.*, p. 72.
79. Hermann Keyserling, *South American Meditations*, trans. Theresa Duerr (New York: Harper and Brothers, 1932), pp. 7–8.
80. *Ibid.*, p. 21.
81. *Ibid.*, p. 41.
82. *Ibid.*, pp. 30–31.
83. *Ibid.*, p. 296.
84. *Ibid.*, p. 44.
85. *Ibid.*, p. 316.
86. *Ibid.*, p. 9.
87. A recent French edition of Keyserling's *Méditations sud-américaines*, trans. A. Beguin (Paris: Stock, 1976), contains an epilogue by Victoria and a final section quoting those who praised Keyserling's book, including Freud, Mann, Guy de Pourtalès and even Tagore; see pp. 391–397.
88. Eduardo Mallea, *Historia de una pasión argentina*, 4th ed. (Buenos Aires: Espasa-Calpe, 1945), p. 122.
89. According to Jung, on the subject of man's anima:
    "Woman, with her very dissimilar psychology, is and always has been a source of information about things for which a man has no eyes. She can be his inspiration; her intuitive capacity, often superior to man's, can give him timely warning, and her feeling, always directed towards the personal, can show him ways which his own less personally accented feeling would never have discovered." From "The Relation between the Ego and the Unconscious," in *Two Essays on Analytical Psychology*, trans. R.F.C. Hull, 2nd. ed. (Princeton: Princeton University Press, 1966), p. 188.
90. *Ibid.*, p. 189.
91. C.G. Jung, *Letters*, Vol. I(1906–1950), eds. Gerhard Adler and Aniela Jaffe, trans. R.F.C. Hull (Princeton: Bollingen Series XCV, Princeton University Press, 1973), pp. 72–73.
92. The dualistic structure of Jungian theory that perpetuates the masculine-feminine division of human qualities has been criticized as stereotypical and sexist, i.e., Naomi R. Goldenberg, "A Feminist Critique of Jung," *Signs* II (Winter 1976), pp. 443–449. It is true that Jung retains this standard division, as it is also true that he explains the animus with far less clarity and detail than he does the anima; however, by recognizing socio-cultural factors as responsible for the repression of so-called contrasexual archetypes, he is far more progressive than many thinkers of his time. Female disciples of Jung, including his wife, Emma Jung, M. L. von Franz, M. Esther Harding, Irene Claremont de Castillejo and Ann Belford Ulanov, have defined the animus more fully from a woman's viewpoint. According to Ulanov:
    "As a pattern of behavior, the animus archetype represents instinctive drive behavior related to the masculine as symbolizing an elemental dynamism of life. It is not to be confused with 'masculinity' as it may be ascribed to specific men or women. The masculine symbolizes those drive elements related to active initiative, to aggressive assertiveness, to the search for meaning, to creativity, and to one's capacity for discrimination, separation and judgment." From *The Feminine in Jungian Psychology and in Christian Theology*. (Evanston: Northwestern University Press, 1971), p. 41.

93. C. G. Jung, *Letters*, Vol. I, p. 84.
94. Keyserling, *South American Meditations*, p. 310.
95. *Reise durch die Zeit* in Graf Hermann Keyserling, *Die gesammelten Werke* II (Darmstadt: Holle Verlag, 1958), p. 384.
96. *Ibid.*, pp. 389–390.
97. *Ibid.*, p. 391. For Keyserling, life is art ("Leben als Kunst"), and thus the origin of the term "fictionalize."
98. *Ibid.*, p. 392. Victoria would not have been sympathetic to this characterization of Dante's love for Beatrice.
99. *Ibid.*, p. 385.
100. *Ibid.*, p. 407.
101. From "Carta del Conde Keyserling sobre el coloquio," in Marcos Victoria, *Coloquio sobre Victoria Ocampo*, 2nd. ed. (Buenos Aires: Talleres Gráficas Incograf, 1963), pp. 7–8, a book which shows V.O.'s controversial position in Argentine society in the 1930s though it is of flimsy content otherwise.
102. Virginia Woolf, *A Room of One's Own*, p. 94.
103. *El viajero y una de sus sombras*, p. 135.
104. *Ibid.*, p. 116.
105. *Ibid.*, p. 55–58.
106. *Ibid.*, pp. 110–111.
107. *Ibid.*, pp. 40–41.
108. Simone de Beauvoir, *The Second Sex* (1949), trans. H. M. Parshley (New York: Vintage Books, 1968), p. 144. Victoria had read de Beauvoir when she wrote her book.
109. C. G. Jung, *Letters*, Vol. I, p. 52. It should be remembered that Jung uses symbolic language to describe the "feminine" as a type of behavior identifiable in both sexes. Jung accepted Freud's theories regarding Oedipal complexes and repressions, but not his views of "biology as destiny."
110. *El viajero y una de sus sombras*, pp. 68–69.
111. Quoted by Eric Bentley, *A Century of Hero-Worship*, 2nd. ed. (Boston: Beacon Press, 1957), pp. 9–10.
112. In fact, Guillermo de Torre, an early colleague of Victoria's at *Sur*, even took a private survey concerning the V.O.-Keyserling encounter and reported that there was little sympathy for Victoria among the Argentines he had consulted; most of them agreed with him that the nature of any dialogue between "the intellectualized woman and the imaginative intellectual [man, that is]" must take into account the woman's primary role as "intellectual inciter." See "Victoria Ocampo, memorialista," in *Tres conceptos de la literatura hispanoamericana* (Buenos Aires: Editorial Losada, 1963), p. 108.
113. Ulanov, *The Feminine in Jungian Psychology and in Christian Theology*, p. 44.
114. *El viajero y una de sus sombras*, p. 46.
115. *Ibid.*, pp. 102–103.
116. *Ibid.*, p. 93.
117. "Pasado y presente de la mujer," VII, pp. 239–240.

Chapter Four

1. "Las memorias de Victoria Ocampo" (selecciones), *Life en español* (September 17, 1962), p. 74.
2. Articles on Teresa de la Parra and other female authors of Latin America can be found in *Latin American Women Writers: Yesterday and Today*, eds. Yvette E. Miller and Charles M. Tatum (Pittsburgh: Latin American Literary Review, 1977).
3. "Supremacía del alma y de la sangre," II, pp. 319–320.

292

4. "Carta a Ricardo Güiraldes," V, p. 61.
5. Quoted by V.O. in "Ansermet en mis memorias," VIII, pp. 211–212.
6. "El poeta de la arquitectura," VII, p. 140.
7. "Hommage à Victoria Ocampo" in *Testimonios sobre Victoria Ocampo*, ed. Hector Basaldúa (Buenos Aires: 1962) p. 177.
8. Enrique Andersonú Imbert, "María de Maeztu," *Sur* (Sept. 1937), p. 86.
9. "Lo único que pedimos," in *Antología del feminismo*, ed. Amalia Martín-Gamero (Madrid: Alianza Editorial, 1975), p. 169.
10. Quoted in *The Very Rich Hours of Adrienne Monnier*, trans. with intro. and commentaries by Richard McDougall (New York: Charles Scribner's Sons, 1976), p. 51.
11. "El caso de Drieu la Rochelle," IV, pp. 13–14.
12. *The Very Rich Hours of Adrienne Monnier*, p. 167.
13. "Palabras pronunciadas por André Gide en un homenaje a V.O.," *Sur* (August 1946), p. 88.
14. "Pasado y presente de la mujer," VII, p. 236.
15. *Waldo Frank in America Hispana*, ed. M. Benardete (New York: Instituto de las Españas, 1930), pp. 30–31. Also see Frank, *The Rediscovery of America* (New York: Charles Scribner's Sons, 1929).
16. "Quiromancia de la pampa," I, p. 147.
17. *Tagore on the Banks of the River Plate*, p. 44.
18. "Quiromancia de la pampa," I, pp. 147–148.
19. "Vida de la revista *Sur* (35 años de una labor)," *Sur* (Indice), (Nov. 1966–April 1967), pp. 6–7.
20. "En Harlem," I, pp. 180–181.
21. "Testimonio," I, pp. 391–393.
22. In 1931 there were four issues, starting with Summer followed by Autumn, Winter and Spring; in 1932 only two issues were published, Summer and Autumn; three more issues followed in 1933 and 1934. Between July 1934 and July 1935 no issues were published. Beginning thereafter, *Sur* was published on a monthly basis until the end of 1953, then bi-monthly from 1953 until 1972 when regular publication was suspended. Since then special issues have appeared at irregular intervals, the most recent being one devoted to Sarmiento (July–Dec. 1977); two more are planned in 1978. In addition to an index published by *Sur* in the Nov.–April 1966–1967 issue, there is another index covering the years 1931–1954 put out by the Panamerican Union in 1955.
23. "Carta a Waldo Frank," *Sur* (Summer 1931), pp. 16–17.
24. María Luisa Bastos, *Borges ante la crítica argentina, 1923–1960* (Buenos Aires: Ediciones Hispamérica, 1974), p. 132.
25. Some of the books and articles critical of *Sur* and V.O. include: H. R. Lafleur, S. Provenzano, F. P. Alonso, *Las revistas literarias, 1893–1967* (Buenos Aires: Centro Editor de America Latina, 1968); A. Jauretche, *Filo, contrafilo y punta* (Buenos Aires: A. Peña Lillo, 1964); B. Verbitsky, "Proposiciones para un mejor planteo de nuestra literatura," *Ficciones* (March–April 1958), pp. 3–20; and a particularly virulent attack, J. Hernández Arregui, *Imperialismo y cultura* (Buenos Aires: Plus Ultra, 1973), which is full of inaccuracies and inflammatory rhetoric.
26. The first chapter of Bastos' book, *Borges ante la crítica argentina*, is an excellent introduction to the history of literary reviews in Argentina in the 1920s, the era of the controversy between the Florida and the Boedo groups that preceded the founding of *Sur*. Also see Nélida Salvador, *Revistas argentinas de vanguardia (1920–1930)* (Buenos Aires: Universidad de Buenos Aires, Facultad de Filosofía y Letras, 1962).
27. "Después de 40 años," IX, pp. 206–207.

28. "Vida de la revista *Sur* (35 años de una labor)", *Sur* (Nov. 1966–April 1967), p. 11.

29. On this subject, see Bastos, *Borges ante la critica argentina*, pp. 136–150. Also regarding V.O.'s friendship with Borges, see Emir Rodriguez Monegal, *Jorge Luis Borges, A Literary Biography* (New York: E.P. Dutton, 1978), pp. 233-238.

30. Quoted in Danubio Torres Fierro, "Entrevista a Victoria Ocampo," *Plural* (December 1975), p. 19.

31. "Nuestra actitud," *Sur* (Sept. 1939), p. 7.

32. See "Pablo Neruda y *Sur*," *Sur* (March–April 1953), pp. 121–125, for an account of Neruda's accusations and *Sur's* replies.

33. Translation from Pablo Neruda, *Las uvas y el viento* (Santiago: Editorial Nascimiento, 1954), pp. 359–362.

34. Bianco resigned his position after a controversy with Victoria over his trip to Castro's Cuba in 1961. Bianco refused to state publicly that he was not going as an official representative of *Sur*, and so Victoria published a letter clarifying *Sur's* viewpoint. They have since reconciled their differences, and in a 1970 interview, Bianco said: "*Sur* has been a very open review. Open to young people who wrote with some grace what they felt. . . . *Sur* was not pro-Franco, pro-Fascist, pro-Nazi, pro-Nationalist or pro-Peronist." *Primera Plana* (Dec. 29, 1970).

35. In *Testimonios sobre Victoria Ocampo*, pp. 279–280.

36. Sylvia Molloy, *La diffusion de la littérature hispano-américaine en France au XXe siècle* (Paris: Presses Universitaires de France, 1972), p. 183.

37. From a typescript in English of Victoria's acceptance speech on the occasion of the award.

38. Boyd Carter, *Las revistas literarias de Hispanoamérica* (Mexico: Ediciones de Andrea, 1959), p. 169.

39. From an article published on August 14, 1935, in an unidentified newspaper; cut out and in V.O.'s possession.

40. From the *Gazzetta di Venezia*, September 1934.

41. "Maneras de ser: una visita a Jung," *Domingos en Hyde Park*, p. 183.

42. Virginia Woolf, "Am I a Snob?" in *Moments of Being*, ed., intro and notes, Jeanne Schulkind, (New York: Harcourt, Brace, Jovanovich, Inc., 1976), p. 188.

43. Quentin Bell, *Virginia Woolf: A Biography* (New York: Harcourt Brace, 1972), p. 148.

44. "Virginia Woolf, Orlando y Cía.," II, pp. 82–83.

45. Woolf, "Am I a Snob?" in *Moments of Being*, p. 182.

46. From an undated letter, probably written by V.O. in early 1935. With the help of Nigel Nicholson, I was able to locate three letters from Victoria to Virginia Woolf in the library of the University of Sussex. To my knowledge, no others survive.

47. From an undated letter, also probably written by V.O. early in 1935, originally in French. This letter and the one previously cited are written on stationery from the New Clarges Hotel on Picadilly.

48. "Carta a Virginia Woolf," I, pp. 11–12.

49. *Virginia Woolf en su diario*, pp. 98–99.

Chapter Five

1. Cited by V.O. in "Sarmiento," II, pp. 346–347. See also Frances G. Crowley, *Domingo Faustino Sarmiento* (New York: Twayne, 1927), pp. 134–136.

2. Nancy Hollander, "Women: The Forgotten Half of Argentine History," in *Female and Male in Latin America*, ed. Ann Pescatello (Pittsburgh: University of Pittsburgh Press, 1973), p. 142. One of the few books to record the history of women in Argentina is Fryda

Schultz de Mantovani's *La mujer en la Argentina, 1810–1928* (Buenos Aires: Plaza and James, n.d.).

3. Hollander, "Women: The Forgotten Half of Argentine History," pp. 142–143 and 147.

4. *Ibid.*, pp. 143–144.

5. From an interview of the author with Sra. Alicia Moreau de Justo in Buenos Aires, August 12, 1976.

6. Hobart A. Spalding, Jr., *Organized Labor in Latin America: Historical Case Studies of Workers in Dependent Societies* (New York: Harper and Row, 1977), p. 52.

7. Hollander, "Women: The Forgotten Half of Argentine History," p. 145.

8. Hollander, "Women Workers and the Class Struggle: The Case of Argentina," *Latin American Perspectives* IV (Winter–Spring 1977), p. 184.

9. Hollander, "Si Evita Viviera," *Latin American Perspectives* I (Fall 1974), p. 44.

10. Marysa Navarro, in "The Case of Eva Perón," *Signs* III (Autumn 1977), pp. 229–230, points out (ftn.2) that there are no reliable biographies of Eva Perón: "The various works that have been written about her are diatribes or eulogies based on gossip, rumors, or ideological prejudices." Navarro intends to publish a biography of her own in the near future. The most recent biography in English is John Barnes' *Evita, First Lady* (New York: Grove Press, 1978). It is a much more objective portrait than most that have preceded it; however, I cannot subscribe to Barnes' theory that Evita, not Perón, was the manipulating power behind the scenes.

11. Barnes, *Evita, First Lady*, p. 22.

12. Hollander, "Women: The Forgotten Half of Argentine History," p. 148.

13. For a description of this organization and its political influence, see Alberto Ciria, *Partidos y poder en la Argentina moderna, 1930–1946*, 2nd. ed. (Buenos Aires: Editorial Jorge Alvarez, 1968), pp. 207–210. Ironically, Victoria's girlhood friend and correspondent, Delfina Bunge de Gálvez, was one of those who spoke out as a Catholic against working women.

14. Hollander, "Women Workers and the Class Struggle: The Case of Argentina," p. 185.

15. "Al margen de Gide," *Domingos en Hyde Park*, p. 66.

16. Torres Fierro, "Entrevista a Victoria Ocampo," *Plural* (December 1975), p. 24.

17. María Rosa Oliver, *La vida cotidiana* (Buenos Aires: Editorial Sudamericana, 1969), p. 350.

18. *Ibid.*, p. 354.

19. From notes in the possession of V.O.

20. "La mujer y su expresión," II, pp. 282–283.

21. *Ibid.*, p. 286.

22. Thomas F. McGann, *Argentina: The Land Divided* (Princeton: Van Nostrand, 1966), pp. 41–42.

23. Dexter Perkins, *A History of the Monroe Doctrine* (Boston: Little Brown and Co., 1955), p. 349.

24. *Ibid.*, p. 362.

25. "La mujer y la guerra en los Estados Unidos," III, p. 269.

26. "Impresiones de Nuremberg," IV, pp. 53–54.

27. Navarro. "The Case of Eva Perón," p. 231.

28. *Idem.*

29. Marvin Goldwert, *Democracy, Militarism, and Nationalism in Argentina, 1930–1966* (Austin: University of Texas Press, 1972), p. 96.

30. John J. Johnson, *Political Change in Latin America: The Emergence of the Middle Sectors* (Stanford: Stanford University Press, 1958), p. 113.

31. Barnes, *Evita, First Lady*, p. 76.

32. Hollander, "Women: The Forgotten Half of Argentine History," p. 151.
33. *Ibid.*, p. 150.
34. From a pamphlet of V.O.'s speech titled "La mujer y el voto."
35. Hollander, "Women: The Forgotten Half of Argentine History," p. 153.
36. Hollander, "Si Evita Viviera," p. 47.
37. Navarro, "The Case of Eva Perón," p. 240.
38. Hollander, "Si Evita Viviera," p. 47.
39. Quoted in *Idem*.
40. Eva Perón, *My Mission in Life* (1951), trans. Ethel Cherry (New York: Vantage Press, 1953), pp. 182–183.
41. *Ibid.*, pp. 185–186.
42. *Ibid.*, p. 190.
43. *Ibid.*, p. 213.
44. Statement published in *Panorama* (April 21, 1970) and quoted in Carlos Abeijón and Jorge Santos Lafauci, *La mujer argentina antes y después de Eva Perón* (Buenos Aires: Editorial Cuarto Mundo, 1975), p. 194.
45. "La hora de la verdad," V, pp. 232–233.
46. Susana Larguía, "In the Women's Prison," in *Testimonios sobre Victoria Ocampo*, ed. Hector Basaldúa (Buenos Aires: 1962), p. 170.
47. "Aries y Capricornio," VII, p. 241.
48. From an interview of the author with Borges on August 14, 1962.
49. "A propósito de una cita suprimida y de un aforismo de los Upanishads," V, pp. 11–12.
50. ["Damals hofte sie dereinst als Heilige zu enden, und aus dieser Stimmung heraus litt sie unter ihrer Macht als *femme fatale*."] *Reise durch die Zeit* in Keyserling, *Die gesammelten Werke* II (Darmstadt: Holle Verlag, 1958), p. 388.
51. Huxley mentions this in a letter to Victoria in September 1943; see *Letters of Aldous Huxley*, ed. Grover Smith (London: Chatto and Windus, 1969), p. 495. The last letter written by Huxley before he died in 1964 was addressed to V.O.
52. *The New York Times*, June 14, 1953.
53. Torres Fierro, "Entrevista a V.O.," p. 22.
54. Gabriela Mistral, *Lecturas para mujeres*, 3rd ed. (San Salvador: Ministerio de Educación, 1961), p. 13.
55. *Ibid.*, p. 16.
56. A native Argentine tree whose flower is considered the national flower.
57. An Argentine dance.
58. An Argentine tango melody.
59. "Recado a Victoria Ocampo en la Argentina," *Tala* (Buenos Aires: Sur, 1938), pp. 265–268.
60. From a typescript of an article in the possession of Doris Dana.
61. The Argentine Civil Code (Book I, Section II, Title III, Article 264) stipulates that *patria potestad* is still the law of the land in 1978. It should be noted that a bill passed by Congress to reform this law in 1975 was vetoed by the chief executive, Isabel Martínez de Perón.
62. "La trastiendo de la historia," *Sur* (Sept. 1970–June 1971), p. 5.
63. Maria Angélica Bosco, one of the co-presidents of the conference, told me that, to her regret, the proceedings were disrupted by political factionalism and even moments of near-violence.

Chapter Six

1. Sor Juana Inés de la Cruz, "Respuesta de la poetisa a la muy ilustre Sor Filotea de la

Cruz," in *Obras escogidas*, 10th ed. (Mexico: Austral, 1959), pp. 144–145. Following quotes also come from this edition, pp. 145, 150–151 and 68–69, respectively.

2. V. Sánchez-Ocaña, "Entrevista con V. O.," *La Nación* (Jan. 12, 1941).
3. "Anna de Noailles y su poesía," I, p. 321.
4. "Palabras francesas," I, p. 26.
5. "Huxley en Centroamérica," I, p. 362.
6. Montaigne, "On Repentance," in *Essays*, trans. J. M. Cohen (Middlesex, England: Penguin, 1958), p. 236.
7. Paul Oscar Kristeller, *Renaissance Thought: The Classic, Scholastic and Humanist Strains* (New York: Harper and Row, 1955), pp. 124–125.
8. "Palabras francesas," I, pp. 24–25.
9. "Huxley en Centroamérica," I, p. 375.
10. "Sobre Victoria Ocampo," in *Testimonios sobre Victoria Ocampo*, ed. Hector Basaldúa (Buenos Aires: 1962), p. 96.
11. Ortega y Gasset, "Prólogo para alemanes," *Obras completas* VIII, 5th ed. (Madrid: Revista de Occidente, 1961), pp. 433–43.
12. "Al margen de Gide," *Domingos en Hyde Park*, pp. 57–58.
13. *El viajero y una de sus sombras*, pp. 44–45.
14. "Palabras francesas," I, p. 28.
15. Juan Marichal, *La voluntad de estilo* (Barcelona: Seix Barral, 1957), pp. 12–13.
16. Jaime Giordano, "Feijóo y el genero ensayístico," *Grial* (Nov.–Dec. 1970), p. 410, cited in Thomas Mermall, *The Rhetoric of Humanism: Spanish Culture after Ortega y Gasset* (New York: The Bilingual Press, 1976), p. 2. For a history of the essay in Latin America see Robert G. Mead, Jr., *Breve historia del ensayo hispanoamericano* (Mexico: Ediciones de Andrea, 1956).
17. Fernand Ovelette, "Divagations sur l'essai," *Etudes Littéraires* (April 1972), p. 13.
18. Marichal, *La voluntad de estilo*, p. 110.
19. Ortega, "Conversación en el 'golf' o la idea del 'dharma,'" *Obras completas* II, p. 405.
20. "Carta al lector a propósito del título," II, p. 8.
21. "Palabras francesas," I, p. 40.
22. "Argentinidad de los extranjerizantes," VI, p. 244.
23. "Carta a Virginia Woolf," I, p. 15.
24. *Ibid.*, p. 12.
25. From a typescript of a TELAM Radio Network (Argentine) interview with Victoria broadcast in 1976, entitled "V. O. contesta." On this subject, Victoria has praised a book by a Dutch author, F.J.T. Buytendijk, called *Woman*, a Spanish translation of which, published by the Revista de Occidente in 1955, is in her library, heavily marked and annotated.
26. Mary Ellmann, *Thinking About Women* (New York: Harcourt, Brace and World, Inc., 1968), p. 42.
27. Patricia Meyer Spacks, *The Female Imagination* (1972) (New York: Avon, 1976), pp. 3–6. "Surely the mind has a sex," writes Spacks (p. 6), "minds *learn* their sex—and it is no derogation of the female variety to say so."
28. Mary Hiatt, *The Way Women Write* (New York: Columbia University, Teachers College Press, 1977); see Chapter 9, "The Feminine Style," pp. 121–138.
29. Guillermo de la Torre, "Victoria Ocampo, memorialista," in *Tres conceptos de la literatura hispanoamericana* (Buenos Aires: Editorial Losada, 1963), p. 101.
30. Leopoldo Marechal, *Adán Buenosayres* (Buenos Aires: Editorial Sudamericana, 1948), p. 517.
31. "Jacques Rivière, *A la trace de Dieu*," I, p. 79.
32. "Emily Brontë (Tierra incógnita)," II, p. 127.

33. *Sur* (March–April 1952), p. 45.
34. "Carta a Ernesto Sábato," *Sur* (May–June 1952), p. 169.
35. See "Ernesto Sábato y Victoria Ocampo: Sobre la metafísica del sexo," *Sur* (July–August 1952), p. 159.
36. *Ibid.*, p. 161.
37. Virginia Woolf, *A Room of One's Own* (New York: Harcourt Brace and World, 1957), p. 108.
38. "Carta a Virginia Woolf," I, p. 15.
39. "El despuntar de una vida," II, pp. 247–248.
40. "La mujer y su expresión," II, p. 284.
41. Ved Mehta, "Mahatma Gandhi and his Apostles," *The New Yorker* (May 17, 1976), p. 72. Also see Heinrich Zimmer, *Philosophies of India* (1951) (Cleveland: Meridian Books, 1961), p. 171 and passim.
42. "La energía espiritual," X, p. 269.
43. "De Victoria Ocampo a José Bergamín," *Sur* (May 1937), p. 73.
44. "La mujer, sus derechos y sus responsabilidades," II, p. 259.
45. Virginia Woolf, *Three Guineas* (New York: Harcourt, Brace and World, 1966), p. 16.
46. Virginia Woolf, *The Pargiters* (The Novel-Essay Portion of *The Years*), ed. and intro. Mitchell A. Leaska (New York: Harcourt, Brace, Jovanovich, Inc., 1977), pp. xxix–xxxi.
47. "La mujer, sus derechos y sus responsabilidades," II, p. 263.
48. "Malraux: Las dos parejas de *la Condition Humaine*," X, p. 203.
49. "Paul Valéry," III, pp. 126–127.
50. *Ibid.*, p. 130.
51. *Ibid.*, pp. 135–136.
52. *Ibid.*, p. 138.
53. "Carta al lector a propósito del título," III, p. 8.
54. From a letter by Jacinto Grau to V.O. written in Buenos Aires on July 17, 1923.
55. From a typescript of the play, act eleven.
56. "Contestación a un epílogo de Ortega y Gasset," I, p. 206.
57. From "Nécessité et excellence de la réligion chrétienne," in Pascal's *Pensées* (1670).
58. From the poem "Correspondances," in *Les Fleurs du mal* (1857).
59. "Virginia Woolf, Orlando y Cía.," II, p. 63.
60. "Paul Valéry," III, p. 130.
61. Quoted by Enid Starkie, "Bergson and Literature," in *The Bergsonian Heritage*, ed. Thomas Hanna (New York: Columbia University Press, 1962), p. 88.
62. See Shiv K. Kumar, *Bergson and the Stream of Consciousness Novel* (New York: New York University Press, 1963), p. 35 and passim.
63. Quoted in *Ibid.*, p. 101.
64. Ronald Christ, "Figuring Literarily: An Interview with Victoria Ocampo," *Review* (Winter 1972), p. 11.
65. "Azorín o primores de lo vulgar," *Obras completas* II, p. 168.
66. *Ibid.*, p. 167.
67. *Ibid.*, p. 161.
68. "Introduction" to *338171 T. E. (Lawrence of Arabia)*, p. 13.
69. See "A Sketch of the Past," in *Moments of Being*, ed., intro. And notes Jeanne Schulkind (New York: Harcourt, Brace, Jovanovich, Inc., 1976), p. 73.
70. "Lecturas de infancia," III, P. 16.
71. "A Eugenia," IV, p. 283.
72. *Ibid.*, p. 284.
73. "Las noches de Itaca," IX, p. 194.

ESSAY NOTES

Sarmiento's Gift

1. A book published by Sarmiento in 1845 condemning the "barbaric" ways of the caudillos of the pampas, like Juan Facundo Quiroga and Juan Manuel de Rosas, and advocating a "civilized" program of national reconstruction based on public education, European immigration, and social and economic progress.
2. An aquatic plant.

Fani

1. "general servant"
2. "blackmail"
3. "freedom"
4. Omitted here is a short, untranslatable passage dealing with Fani's mispronunciations (much like Sancho Panza's).
5. "lady's maid"
6. A saucy, coquettish lady's maid.

A King Passes By

1. Originally, in the East, an inn built around a large court to accommodate caravans; a large hotel.

María de Maeztu

1. Mounier published "La femme aussi est une personne" (Woman Is Also a Person) in June 1936 in *Esprit*, a review he edited.
2. Maeztu died of a heart attack in Buenos Aires in 1948.

Living History

1. "keeping one's wits about one"
2. "after-wit or afterthought"
3. "I don't give a damn"
4. Fascist youth groups
5. A Fascist organization that provided after-work-hours activities.

Adrienne Monnier

1. "Half farm, half convent / That's how I made my bookstore."
2. "the art of fine eating"
3. "I'm even learning to like vegetables that I used to disdain."
4. "in order to rouse stomachs made of *papier mâché* and whet the appetites of skinny people, appetites that are nothing but a whim and always on the verge of extinction"
5. "I knew that it also belonged to the realm of the spirit."
6. "paid as much homage to flavor as to genius"
7. "Evidently he must have thought this big gourmande hasn't been able to endure the rationings; she must have weakened at one moment or another."
8. "that oft-punished vice"
9. "paltry productions"

Woman, Her Rights and Her Responsibilities

1. "I do not need order and I deliver myself willingly / Not so much to where the law, but to where my love leads me." These lines are from the final portion of Gide's poem, set to music by Stravinsky and recited by V.O. in several performances directed by the composer.
2. "get out and let me in"

Virginia Woolf in my Memory

1. ". . . myriad diamonds of imperceptible foam."

The Forest

1. A tree from India that grows in Argentina; "almost my favorite tree," says V.O. who admits to being unable to single out one in preference to all the others.
2. Native Argentine tree.
3. Native Argentine tree.
4. Native Argentine tree.
5. A porous stone common to Argentine riverbeds.
6. A change of country or, figuratively, of atmosphere.
7. "Why art thou afflicted my soul and why dost thou disquiet me?/ Judge me, O God, and separate my cause from the unholy;/ From the iniquitous and deceitful deliver me./Send forth thy light and thy truth."
8. "I will never again be able to leave this forest"
9. A native Argentine tree, sometimes called a pepper-tree.
10. A large, long-needled Argentine pine tree.
11. Native Argentine tree, similar to the redwood, that grows in the mountainside forests of the Andes.

Gabriela Mistral and the Nobel Prize

1. "takes what she wants where she finds it"

The Man with the Whip

1. Juan Manuel de Rosas, governor and virtual dictator of the province of Buenos Aires from 1829 to 1852.
2. Red was the color of Rosas's Federalist Party as opposed to the blue of the Unitarian Party.
3. Rosas's secret police force.
4. From Adolf Hitler, *Mein Kampf* (New York: Reynal and Hitchcock, 1939), p. 712.
5. Eva Perón had so declared in a public speech to Perón's followers.
6. "I am one of those who are very much affected by the imagination. Everyone feels its impact, but some are knocked over by it. . . . the sight of another's anguish gives me real pain . . . A perpetual cougher irritates my lungs and my throat . . . As I observe a disease, so I catch it and give it lodging in myself." From "On the Power of the Imagination," in *Essays*, trans. J. M. Cohen (Middlesex, England: Penguin Books, 1958), pp. 36–37.

Albert Camus

1. "This book that nothing explains—with the friendship that resolves everything: that of the heart."
2. "The Frenchman who denies geography"
3. "The Rains of New York": "In remembrance of a city we loved together."
4. From "The Rains of New York," in *Lyrical and Critical Essays*, trans., Ellen Conroy Kennedy (New York: Knopf, 1969), p. 186.
5. "I'm living amid the plague."
6. "to loop the loop or, figuratively, to add insult to injury"
7. "And then the very smell of the New York rain tracks you down . . ."
8. "Man ravaged by dream, man possessed by the obsession with the divine / Not in the

manner of those who seek intoxication in the smoke of hemp like a Sythian / But jealous of his awareness . . . sustaining the brightness of his vision in the face of the wind."

Heroes with and without Space Suits

1. "detached from the human"
2. "fall throughout eternity"
3. "The eternal silence of these infinite spaces terrifies me."
4. "We only see one side of things, / the other plunges into the night of a terrifying mystery. / Man submits to the yoke without knowing the causes. . . ."

The Last Year of Pachacutec

1. A soldier under Cortés's command during the conquest of Mexico (1517–1521) who wrote a lengthy chronicle of his adventures: *Historia verdadera de la conquista de la Nueva España* (True History of the Conquest of New Spain).
2. An Argentine colloquialism meaning "Spaniards."

Women in the Academy

1. "free-lancer or sniper"
2. "the first truths"
3. A statue in a plaza in Palermo Park in Buenos Aires.
4. ". . . make plain all thy vision, and then let them scratch where is the itch. For if thy voice is grievous at first taste, it will afterwards leave vital nourishment when it is digested." From Canto XVII of the *Paradiso*, trans. John D. Sinclair (New York: Oxford University Press, 1972), p. 249.
5. "I am myself the subject of my book."

SELECTED BIBLIOGRAPHY

I. The following is a list in chronological order of selected books by Victoria Ocampo. Additional works (including articles, lectures and translations) by her that were published separately can be found in the indices of *Sur* (put out by the review in 1966–67 and by the Panamerican Union in 1955) and in these independent bibliographical studies: Beatriz Tuninetti, *Contribución a la bibliografía de Victoria Ocampo* (Buenos Aires: Universidad de Buenos Aires, Facultad de Filosofía y Letras, 1962) and, soon to be published in Argentina, Carlos Adam, *Aproximaciones a la obra de Victoria Ocampo*, a major compendium of all her works.

De Francesca a Beatrice. Madrid: Revista de Occidente, 1924.
La laguna de los nenúfares. Madrid: Revista de Occidente, 1926.
Testimonios I. Madrid: Revista de Occidente, 1935.
Domingos en Hyde Park. Buenos Aires: Sur, 1936.
Testimonios II. Buenos Aires: Sur, 1941.
San Isidro, con un poema de Silvina Ocampo. Buenos Aires: Sur, 1941.
338171 T. E. (Lawrence de Arabia). Buenos Aires: Sur, 1942.
Testimonios III. Buenos Aires: Editorial Sudamericana, 1946.
Soledad sonora IV. Buenos Aires: Editorial Sudamericana, 1950.
El viajero y una de sus sombras: Keyserling en mis memorias. Buenos Aires: Editorial Sudamericana, 1951.
Virginia Woolf en su diario. Buenos Aires: Sur, 1954.
Testimonios V. Buenos Aires: Sur, 1957.
Habla el algarrobo. Buenos Aires: Sur, 1959.
Tagore en las barrancas de San Isidro. Buenos Aires: Sur, 1961.
Testimonios VI. Buenos Aires: Sur, 1963.
Juan Sebastián Bach, el hombre. Buenos Aires: Sur, 1964.
Testimonios VII. Buenos Aires: Sur, 1967.
Diálogo con Borges. Buenos Aires: Sur, 1969.
Diálogo con Mallea. Buenos Aires: Sur, 1969.
Testimonios VIII. Buenos Aires: Sur, 1971.
Testimonios IX. Buenos Aires: Sur, 1975.
Testimonios X. Buenos Aires: Sur, 1977.

II. This is a short selection of works in chronological order written in English and Spanish *about* Victoria Ocampo. They have been chosen on the basis of their content and their availability. Listed first are the three books that have been written about her in Spanish, one an imaginary dialogue written in 1934, another a volume of tributes, and the third a short biographical study in Spanish introducing portions of her essays.

Books:

Marcos, Victoria, *Un coloquio sobre Victoria Ocampo*. 2nd ed. Buenos Aires: L. Fariña, 1963.
Testimonios sobre Victoria Ocampo. Ed. Hector Basaldúa. Buenos Aires: 1962.
Fryda Schultz de Mantovani, *Victoria Ocampo*. Buenos Aires: Ediciones Culturales Argentinas, 1963.

Articles:

Leopoldo Marechal, "Victoria Ocampo y la literatura femenina," *Sur* (January 1939), pp. 66–70.
Eduardo González Lanuza, "Keyserling y Victoria Ocampo," *Sur* (July 1951), pp. 99–106.
"Las memorias de Victoria Ocampo," (selecciones), *Life en español* (September 17 and October 1, 1962); these are actually selections from V.O.'s memoirs, written by her.
Guillermo de Torre, "Victoria Ocampo, memorialista," in *Tres conceptos de la literatura hispanoamericana*. Buenos Aires: Editorial Losada, 1963.
Mildred Adams, "First Lady," *The New York Times* (October 2, 1966).
Emiliu Estiú, "El problema estético en la obra de Victoria Ocampo," *Cuadernos del idioma* II (Buenos Aires), (August 1967), pp. 27–49.
Ronald Christ, "Figuring Literarily: An Interview with Victoria Ocampo," *Review* (New York), (Winter 1972), pp. 5–13.
Carlos Adam, "Bio-bibliografía de Victoria Ocampo," *Boletín Capilla Alfonsina* 29 (Mexico), (1974), pp. 38–67.
Eleanor Munro, "Viva Victoria!" *MS* (New York), (January 1975), pp. 76–101.
Danubio Torres Fierro, "Entrevista a Victoria Ocampo," *Plural* (Mexico), (December 1975), pp. 18–25.
Lisa Sergio, "A Word with Victoria Ocampo," *Americas* (Washington, D.C.), (May 1976), pp. 2–4.
Ronald Christ, "To Build Bridges: Victoria Ocampo, Grand Lady of *Sur*," *Nimrod* (Tulsa, Oklahoma), (Spring–Summer 1976) pp. 135–141.
"Victoria es académica," *Gente* (Buenos Aires), (July 7, 1977).
Ernesto Shóo, "Victoria Ocampo: la viajera y una de sus sombras," *Pájaro de fuego* (Buenos Aires), (September 1977), pp. 13–17. Includes other short articles.
Luis Mazas, "La señora cultura," *Somos* (Buenos Aires), (December 9, 1977).
Celia Correas de Zapata, "Victoria Ocampo y Virginia Woolf: La rebeldía en el ensayo," *Ensayos hispanoamericanos* (Buenos Aires: Ediciones Corregidor, 1978), pp. 165–181.

III. Works by Victoria Ocampo published in English:

Books:

338171 T. E. (Lawrence of Arabia). Trans. David Garnett. Intro. A. W. Lawrence. New York: E. P. Dutton, 1963. (Out of print.)
Tagore on the Banks of the River Plate. Trans. Victoria Ocampo. In *Rabindranath Tagore: A Centenary Volume*. New Delhi: Sahitya Akademi, 1961.

Essays:

"The Lakes of the South." Trans. Harriet de Onís. *The Green Continent*. Ed. Germán Arciniegas. New York: Alfred A. Knopf, 1944, pp. 116–122.
"Aldous Huxley." Trans. Victoria Ocampo. *Aldous Huxley (1894–1963), A Memorial Volume*. Ed. Julian Huxley. London: Chatto and Windus, 1965, pp. 73–85.

"Letter to Waldo Frank." Trans. Victoria Ocampo. *Review* (Spring 1974), pp. 51–52.

"The Untranslatable Isadora." Trans. Victoria Ocampo. *Review* (Spring 1976), pp. 39–41.

"Virginia Woolf in My Memory." Trans. Doris Meyer. *Nimrod* (Spring–Summer 1976), pp. 142–150.

"Yesterday, Today, Tomorrow." Trans. Renata Treitel with Maralee Waidner. *Nimrod* (Spring–Summer 1976), pp. 151–156.

"Malraux's World and Ours." *Malraux: Life and Work*. Ed. Martine de Courcel. London: Weidenfeld and Nicolson, 1976, pp. 212–221.

'Victoria Ocampo Pays Jung a Visit." Trans. Martin Nozick. *C. J. Jung Speaking: Interviews and Encounters*. Eds. William McGuire and R. F.C. Hull. Princeton: Bollingen Series XCVII, Princeton University Press, 1977, pp. 82–84.

INDEX